# Praise for *Square Pegs*

There is an old African saying: 'Until the lions have their own historians, the tales of glory will always be written by the hunters.' Fran Morgan has assembled here some lions and while they don't write too many tales of glory – although there are some – they do make us all realise why so many square pegs unnecessarily gain so little from our schooling system. Twelve years ago, Michael Gove sent a King James bible to every school. The next secretary of state for education should send a copy of this book to every new head teacher and put it on the reading list for all initial teacher training courses.

Tim Brighouse, former Commissioner for London Schools

This is one of the most riveting books on education I have read in a long while. Its aim – to provide practical solutions for schools and families struggling with the increasing number of children who don't thrive in our current system – could not be more timely. The array of richly qualified writers places compassion, purpose and student autonomy at the heart of best practice. Their approach would surely work not just for those who avoid school, but for those stuck within it. *Square Pegs* is a must-read for parents, governors, staff and students who're up for a quiet classroom revolution.

Madeleine Holt, filmmaker and education campaigner

This is a book that is firmly on the side of children as they try to come to terms with a school system that is designed to encourage conformity. It highlights the way some schools manage to set the child at the heart of what they do in every sense of the term. There are case studies that shine a light on the child's perspective and solutions offered for other schools to try. Reading it is both heart-wrenching and uplifting ... but uplifting wins.

Mick Waters, Professor of Education, University of Wolverhampton

This book is steeped in the experience and expertise of families, teachers and leaders. It tells the story of a system that is fraught with unintended consequences, brings the lived experiences of young people alive and challenges the notion of one-size-fits-all strategies. The voice of school leaders and teachers, ambitious to see the young people in their care thrive, roar at us across the page. It's a book of confidence for professionals and parents alike to rise above the distracting noise about attendance, exclusion and 'what works' narratives. A much-needed book ensuring the voice and experience of young people is heard and helping to inform what happens next.

It's a must-read for everyone with a vision of an education system that can be 'fixed' through collaboration and brave actions.

Margaret Mulholland, Inclusion Specialist, Association of School and College Leaders

Our high-stakes, test- and exam-focused system is failing too many children. It literally fails those who struggle to attend school or are marked as failures in exams. It metaphorically fails those who attend and get their grades, but at a personal cost to themselves, their love of learning and their families. This will continue to be the case for as long as schools are judged in the main on test and exam results, placing the burden of whole-school success or failure on children's shoulders.

For the good of every child and, indeed, of educators themselves (most of whom want to provide the best possible learning experiences and strive to do so in spite of our one-size-fits-all model for education), it's time to listen to the canaries in the cages – the children who simply cannot cope, let alone thrive, within our restrictive, reductive system. Change made for those who suffer most will benefit the whole school community.

Alison Ali, More Than A Score campaigner and strategic communications expert

In recent years, many schools in England have started to implement strict policies around behaviour, curriculum and attendance. As the screws tighten, more and more square pegs (read 'deeply distressed young people') have started voting with their feet. When you stop going to school, it creates all kinds of problems: home visits, financial penalties and, incredibly, the threat of custodial sentences for the parents and carers of persistent 'offenders'. The fact that so many young people should choose such strife over attending school should tell us something very important about their lived experience of our one-size-fits-all education system. It seems likely that increasing numbers of square pegs will continue voting with their feet until we reach crisis point. But this crisis can be averted if we listen to the voices of those affected now. This brilliantly curated book is an absolute must-read for anyone interested in creating a more diverse, empathic, responsive educational ecosystem that works for *all* young people.

Dr James Mannion, Director, Rethinking Education and co-author of<br>*Fear is the Mind Killer* with Kate McAllister

No child should miss out on a good education and the chance of opportunities in life just because their school doesn't give them the support they need to succeed. Most schools cherish and value the children who have special educational needs; there are also some who do not place inclusion high on their list of priorities, and exclude or marginalise children rather than provide the mental health and therapeutic support they need.

Recently, a 13-year-old girl with autism gave me a list of what a good school for her would look like: well organised, supportive, calm, focused on learning, there to help. These are all things we would want to see for every child in every school. After spending two years out of the classroom because a succession of schools was unable to meet her needs, she went on to find a school which understood her and provided the springboard she needed to do well. She went on to achieve great things in her GCSEs and is now in sixth form. Like Square Peg, I want all schools to see the potential in all children and provide the support they need.

We should all be grateful to Square Peg for all they do to advocate for children who need most help, and for showing how schools and parents can work together with children to provide a positive environment to learn. Every child deserves the best start in life, and positive outcomes for all children must be at the heart of a successful education system.

Anne Longfield, CBE, Chair of The Commission on Young Lives

In order for a society to become healthy, whole and progressive, it must be willing to listen to the square pegs that it has created within itself. It is when square pegs choose to be silent and when they choose to communicate that we must pay careful attention to, for the sake of all of us. Everyone who was gifted with a square peg in their life will tell you so. Square pegs are our compass and our orienteers: they are the first to notice when we lose our way, the first to see that we have crossed our own boundaries, and the first to feel when we single-mindedly keep digging one-shaped holes. This is why this book had to be written, and this is why it must be read by anyone who cares about the education system of this country.

I have been following Fran, Ellie and their many supporters, diligently collecting piece by piece of evidence for several years, to assemble the overly complicated puzzle of square pegs, to improve our society. The result is brutally honest, yet optimistic. It is visionary yet chooses a pragmatic approach and offers many quick wins. It offers a sensitive choice of a diverse set of writers, through which one thread of pearls is coming out very clearly: it is about compassion, consent, community and relationships. It is about holding our societal compass close to our hearts and struggling to keep it safe. This is the struggle of all of us – or at least it should be.

Dr Carmel Kent, lecturer at the Open University, educational researcher, author of *AI for Learning*
and a parent with lived experience

Making schools more inclusive is essential to ensuring the wellbeing and ability to thrive of every young person. Creating a sense of belonging and using trauma-informed strategies to help the system welcome the square pegs, rather than continuing to force them into round holes, is clearly the way forward. The current government one-size-fits-all approach, particularly to SEND and behaviour, needs a rethink.

This book offers a wealth of practical examples of how collaboration between schools and families, alongside the will to make a culture shift, can lead to successful inclusion practices. It is very readable and contains practical advice and solutions, framed within the current educational context, that leaders, teachers and support staff can use to create the right systems and support to ensure that every child and young person really is more than just 'fine in school'.

Judy Ellerby, Lead Policy Manager, SEND, Disabled Members, Behaviour, Exclusions,
National Education Union

'It's not that she wouldn't, she couldn't.' These words, written in the introduction of the book, struck a chord with me. The educational system we work in has, in my opinion, been created for the round pegs who fit perfectly into the round holes and yet the young people in our schools are all unique and are not carbon copies of each other. This book is utterly refreshing in that it addresses the biggest of misconceptions – that we should treat all children the same. Not all young people are the same and the sooner we learn how to teach and support them in the way they each need, the better it will be for all. This book explains what the issues are and how as a profession we can begin to address this. I cannot recommend this book enough. Thank you, Fran, Ellie and all the contributors for helping us to better understand and support our square pegs.

Toria Bono, primary teacher, coach, host of 'Tiny Voice Talks' podcast and author of *Tiny Voices Talk*

# SQUARE
## PEGS

### Inclusivity, compassion and fitting in
### A guide for schools

Fran Morgan with **Ellie Costello**
Edited by **Ian Gilbert**

independent
thinking **press**

First published by

Independent Thinking Press
Crown Buildings, Bancyfelin, Carmarthen, Wales, SA33 5ND, UK
www.independentthinkingpress.com

and

Independent Thinking Press
PO Box 2223, Williston, VT 05495, USA
www.crownhousepublishing.com

Independent Thinking Press is an imprint of Crown House Publishing Ltd.

Edited by Ian Gilbert.

British Library Cataloguing-in-Publication Data
A catalogue entry for this book is available from the British Library.

Print ISBN 978-178135410-0
Mobi ISBN 978-178135418-6
ePub ISBN 978-178135419-3
ePDF ISBN 978-178135420-9

LCCN 2022937125

Printed and bound in the UK by
CPi, Antony Rowe, Chippenham, Wiltshire

square peg *or* square peg in a round hole

*informal*: a person or thing that is a **misfit**, such as an
employee in a job for which he or she is **unsuited**[1]

The trouble with square pegs is that by forcing them to fit the system's round holes,
you end up damaging the peg, not the hole.

1   See https://www.collinsdictionary.com/dictionary/english/square-peg.

# FOREWORD BY SIR NORMAN LAMB

I have long been a supporter of Square Peg. I first became aware of their work in my time in Parliament and have been keenly following them ever since. The support they provide families facing challenges in education is of immense value, and they have given a voice to those children and young people who are experiencing persistent absenteeism, many of whom have mental health problems and unmet needs. Square Peg has also played a significant part in promoting the importance of an inclusive and supportive education system that works for all children and young people.

Education is a key pillar in children and young people's lives as they grow and develop, and in particular, plays an important role in their mental health and wellbeing. It's crucial in improving life chances, maintaining social connections, providing access to support and helping children learn how to look after their mental health.

Education should be inclusive of everyone no matter what a child's needs and experiences may be, and this is a principle I have strongly endorsed throughout my career. However, the reality lies far away from this, and sadly the education system currently operates to celebrate uniformity rather than embracing diversity.

We have seen this most recently in the behaviour agenda, where the use of punitive approaches has become commonplace in responding to children and young people's behaviour. I have been particularly horrified by the rise of school exclusions as a form of punishment, with data showing a steady increase in the use of both suspensions and permanent exclusions before the COVID-19 pandemic hit.

Often, the children who face exclusion are the ones with the greatest need. Children communicate their distress through their behaviour, and challenging behaviour can often be the result of underlying conditions, unmet emotional needs, difficulties at home, at school or in the community, and exposure to trauma. We also know that the use of punitive approaches to behaviour can be harmful to children and young people's mental health and actually has the potential to re-traumatise. The cost of exclusion both to the individual but also to society is incalculable. The loss of human potential is tragic.

We need to urgently move away from a system where we punish and exclude children and young people for their life experiences and needs, and instead move to a place of compassion and understanding. This means creating supportive and inclusive school environments for all children and young people to thrive and offering help to those who are struggling most.

It's my strong belief that by seeking to understand children and young people and their needs in a more sophisticated and compassionate way, then learning can be facilitated. After all, happy, healthy children are better able to learn. At the heart of this should be prioritising whole-education and trauma-informed approaches to mental health and wellbeing in every setting across England. Such approaches are vital in helping to create a culture where every student is recognised and valued.

I am sure this book will be of great practical value to many school leaders, educators, practitioners and professionals, and I would like to thank Square Peg for all they do to advocate for those who need it most, including our education workforce.

# THE CANARIES IN THE MINE
# BY JO SYMES

What if our 'square pegs' aren't the problem? What if they are actually the canaries in the mine, alerting us to the mounting problems in our education system?

In her book, *Troublemakers: Lessons in Freedom from Young Children at School*, Carla Shalaby (2017) discusses 'animal sentinels', animals which are purposefully used to provide advanced warning of disease, toxins and other environmental threats to humans. She explains that these species are selected based on their heightened susceptibility to particular hazards. They are often sacrificed to save us.

The most famous example is the canary, used in coal mines in the early 20th century to give advanced warning of deadly gases, such as carbon monoxide. Because these birds were small and had particularly sensitive respiratory systems, the poison killed them quickly, leaving the miners with enough time to get out and save themselves. What if, suggests the author, we saw our square pegs as such canaries?

> The child who deviates, who refuses to behave like everybody else, may be telling us – loudly, visibly, and memorably – that the arrangements of our schools are harmful to human beings. Something toxic is in the air, and these children refuse to inhale it. It is dangerous to exclude these children and silence their warnings. (Shalaby, 2017: xxxiii)

Shalaby learned the canary metaphor from Thomas, a father of a 5-year-old boy who could not – and would not – comply with the behavioural expectations of his kindergarten teacher:

> Though the child suffered a mood disorder, Thomas challenged the assumption that the disease made his son inherently broken or bad. Much like the canary's fragile lungs, this child's brain leaves him more susceptible to the harms of poison. He's more sensitive to harm than the average child. Still, the problem is the poison – not the living thing struggling to survive despite breathing it. After all, in clean air, canaries breathe easily. (Shalaby, 2017: xxii–xxiii)

Look at our square pegs. Look at the list of children refusing to attend your school, with or without the knowledge/agreement/complicity/other of their parents.[1] Look at those who are constantly in trouble when they do attend. Look at those who have been excluded, shamed, moved on. Look at those in your bottom sets, in your nurture rooms, in your 'special classes', in your conscience. What are they saying? What warning are they giving you? What will you do now you hear them?

## References

Shalaby, C. (2017) *Troublemakers: Lessons in Freedom from Young Children at School*. New York: New Press.

---

1   This is discussed further in the Introduction. Am I complicit if I prioritise my child's mental health and knowingly agree not to force her into school? The law says I am. What do you say?

# ACKNOWLEDGEMENTS

Square Peg wouldn't exist had it not been for my own square peg, my daughter, and Peter Kyle's support which gave me the momentum I needed at the beginning. It wouldn't exist now had it not been for Square Peg's director, Ellie Costello, her two children and their journey through the special educational needs and disabilities, health, social care, children and adolescent mental health services, and education systems.

It also wouldn't exist without Ian who proposed the idea of a book in the first place, and who supported us in pitching the concept to our publisher, Crown House. His wisdom and experience in the editing process – and with a growing number of contributors that was a mammoth task – allowed us to piece together a diverse range of views and writing styles. He has been an advocate of change in the education system for many years, and continues to support schools in this regard, alongside his many Independent Thinking associates.

In compiling this book, we ploughed our own Square Peg network and that of Ian's Independent Thinking network. Several others submitted contributions which didn't quite make it into this book, so our grateful thanks go to: Dr John D'Auria, Dick Bryant, Sophie Christophy, Ritam Ghandi, Ros Gowers, Sarah Harrison, Dr Rebecca Johnson, Dot Lepkowska and the team at Educate Ventures, Dr James Mannion, Andrew Morrish, Stephen Steinhaus, Lucy Stephens, Niamh Sweeney, Adele Tobias, Tom Varley and Aliyah York.

Our thanks also go to Eliza Fricker-Baines, another square peg parent, for her insightful illustrations which mark the start of each of the five parts of the book. You can see more of Eliza in her blog, Missing the Mark, and in her illustrated book, *The Family Experience of PDA: An Illustrated Guide to Pathological Demand Avoidance* (2021).

A final and most important word of thanks goes to the small but perfectly formed team at Crown House Publishing, who were not only prepared to invest in us, but who have been an amazing source of encouragement and support throughout.

This book represents the work and passions of so many wonderful people, and our heartfelt thanks go out to all of you.

# CONTENTS

# LIST OF ABBREVIATIONS

| | |
|---|---|
| ACE | adverse childhood experience |
| ADHD | attention deficit hyperactivity disorder |
| AP | alternative provision |
| ASD | autistic spectrum disorder |
| CAMHS | children and adolescent mental health services |
| CPD | continuing professional development |
| DBS | Disclosure and Barring Service |
| EbE | expert by experience |
| EHCNA | education, health and care needs assessment |
| EHCP | education, health and care plan; all references to statements of educational need now refer to EHCPs |
| EP | educational psychologist |
| EQL | Equalities Literacy |
| FII | fabricated or induced illness |
| FPE | fixed-period exclusion |
| FSM | free school meals |
| HCPC | Health and Care Professions Council |
| INSET | in-service training day |
| MAT | multi-academy trust |
| PGCE | Postgraduate Certificate in Education |
| PRU | pupil referral unit |
| PSED | personal, social and emotional development |
| PSHE | personal, social, health and economic (education) |
| SAPB | school attendance problems and barriers |
| SATs | Standard Assessment Tests |
| SEMH | social, emotional and/or mental health |

| | |
|---|---|
| SEN | special educational needs |
| SENCO | special educational needs coordinator |
| SEND | special educational needs and disabilities |
| SLT | senior leadership team |
| TA | teaching assistant |
| TAC | team around the child |
| TOPS | Taking Outdoor Play Seriously |

# LIST OF CONTRIBUTORS

## Dr Helen Andrews

Helen runs Family Matters in Warwickshire (www.familymattersinwarwickshire.co.uk), offering child clinical psychology services to children and their families in and around Warwickshire. Prior to this, she worked in child and adolescent mental health services for 15 years and convened on and taught the child and adolescent module on the University of Warwick's master's course in clinical applications of psychology.

## Dr Chris Bagley

Chris is a psychologist working in Bristol and was formerly based in a youth offending team. He is director of research at the social enterprise States of Mind, co-director at Square Peg and a tutor at UCL's Institute of Education. He has a keen interest in educational transformation and systems change. His academic work, media publications and other writing can be found at www.chrisbagley.co.uk.

## Adele Bates

Adele has been a teacher for nearly 20 years, empowering educators to support pupils with behavioural needs and social, emotional and mental health needs. She is an international keynote speaker, a BBC Radio 4 expert on teenagers and behaviour, the author of 'Miss, I don't give a sh*t': Engaging with Challenging Behaviour in Schools (2021), and an international researcher on behaviour and inclusion. For her tips and resources, check out www.adelebateseducation.co.uk.

## Andrew 'Bernie' Bernard

Bernie started Innovative Enterprise (www.innovativeenterprise.co.uk) in 2006 to help those within organisations (including schools) to perform better. He has delivered more than 1,800 workshops and international talks to more than 165,000 young people, and is a TEDx speaker and entrepreneur. His book, *The Ladder: Supporting Students Towards Successful Futures and Confident Career Choices*, was published in February 2021.

## Adrian Bethune

Adrian runs Teachappy (www.teachappy.co.uk), which puts happiness and wellbeing at the heart of education. He is also an instrumental figure across several wellbeing organisations and initiatives, including as deputy chair of the strategic board of the Well Schools Movement.

## Dr Beth Bodycote

Beth is the founder of Not Fine in School (www.notfineinschool.co.uk), which had a membership of nearly 30,000 in its closed Facebook group for parents by the end of July 2022. She is a parent with lived experience, and has recently completed a PhD on the parental journey when a child faces barriers to attendance.

## Ginny Bootman

Ginny is an educator with over 25 years in education as a classroom practitioner, special educational needs coordinator and head teacher. She is passionate about all things SEND, has been published multiple times in the *TES* and is an associate of Undiscovered Country. She speaks nationally about promoting home–school links through an empathy-based approach. Find her at www.ginnybootman.com and @sencogirl on Twitter.

## William Carter

William is a PhD student at the University of California, Berkeley and a Fulbright scholar with a first-class degree in politics from the University of Bristol. On top of studying for his doctorate in political geography, specialising in Atlantic history, William is a neurodiversity campaigner and spends much of his time engaged in high-level meetings, policy development and advocacy with university leaders. He has featured in profiles in *The Times*, *i* newspaper, on ITV's *This Morning* and on Ian Wright's *Everyday People* podcast.

## Mike Charles

Mike is a senior director and chief executive officer at Sinclairslaw (www.sinclairslaw.co.uk), specialising in education law and human rights. He frequently appears on BBC *Breakfast News* and national radio, commenting on high-profile stories involving education and disability law.

## Professor Luke Clements

Luke is the Cerebra professor of law and social justice at the School of Law, University of Leeds (www.lukeclements.co.uk). As a practising solicitor, he has conducted a number of cases before the European Commission and Court of Human Rights. His academic research, litigation experience and input to parliamentary bills focuses on the rights of people who experience social exclusion.

## Dr Wendy Coetzee

With over 25 years in clinical practice, Wendy has developed a specialism for supporting children with attachment and developmental trauma, using dyadic developmental practice (DDP) and trauma-informed practice. She is an accredited DDP trainer, helping schools to develop trauma-informed practice using playfulness, acceptance, curiosity and empathy (PACE) to support vulnerable learners. Find her at www.the-foundationsconsultancy.co.uk.

## Andrew Cowley

Andrew was formerly a primary school deputy head teacher and is now a wellbeing writer and speaker, co-founder of the Healthy Toolkit, and author of *The Wellbeing Toolkit* (2019) and *The Wellbeing Curriculum* (2021).

## Dr Ian Cunningham

Ian chairs the governing body of Self Managed Learning College. He created Self Managed Learning in the late 1970s and is widely published on learning and education. His latest book is *Developing Leaders for Real* (2022). He has been a visiting professor in Hungary, India, the UK and the USA. Find SML College at www.sml-college.org.uk.

## Dr Andrew Curran

Andrew is a practising paediatric neurologist and neurobiologist who brings this knowledge to the education space. He has authored several books, including *The Little Book of Big Stuff about the Brain* (2008). He has presented on the BBC3 series *Make My Body Younger* and is an associate of Independent Thinking.

## Natasha Devon, MBE

Natasha is a writer, broadcaster and activist, founder of the Mental Health Media Charter and involved in several other mental health organisations. She hosts a weekly radio show on LBC and writes regularly for national newspapers. She is a published author. Find her at www.natashadevon.com.

## Professor Helen Dodd

Helen is a professor of child psychology at the University of Exeter Medical School. She has over 10 years of published research to her name, specialising in children's play and mental health. She is funded by a UK Research and Innovation Future Leaders Fellowship.

## Dr Simon Edwards

Simon is a founding member and CEO of Beyond the School Gates (www.beyondthe-schoolgates.co.uk). He has been involved in youth and community work for over 34 years and lectures in youth studies at the University of Portsmouth. Beyond the School Gates emerged through his work at Portsmouth, and he now leads their mentor team and supports excluded young people and their parents as a mentor.

## Richard Evea

Richard is chair and trustee of Beyond the School Gates (www.beyondtheschoolgates.co.uk). He spent 40 years in secondary education, with the final 20 years as a head teacher in two secondary schools in South East England.

## Dr Naomi Fisher

Naomi is an independent clinical psychologist living in Hove and working as a therapist, speaker, trainer and author. Her book about self-directed education, *Changing Our Minds*, was published in February 2021. Find Naomi at www.naomifisher.co.uk, naomicfisher.substack.com and @naomicfisher on Twitter.

## Karine George

Karine is an author, keynote speaker, education consultant and chief education advisor for Educate Ventures. She was a primary school head teacher for 25 years and speaks nationally and internationally on parental engagement, leadership and learning. She also co-founded Leadership Lemonade (www.leadership-lemonade.co.uk).

## Rhia Gibbs

Rhia is the founding director and CEO of Black Teachers Connect (www.blackteach-ersconnect.co.uk) and a sixth-form sociology and criminology teacher. The organisation seeks to build a community for Black teachers by supporting and promoting the recruitment and retention of Black teachers in the UK and worldwide.

## Dr James Gillum

James is the principal education psychologist at Coventry City Council. He works with Square Peg to chair a research group of education psychologists from around the country, aiming to identify the most appropriate screening and interventions for extended non-attendance.

## Dr Peter Gray

Peter is a research professor at Boston College, Massachusetts and a widely published author. His books include *Free to Learn* (2015) and *Psychology* (2010). He is a founding member of the non-profit organisations Alliance for Self-Directed Education and Let Grow. Read Peter's posts in *Psychology Today* at https://www.psychologytoday.com/gb/contributors/peter-gray-phd.

## Stuart Guest

Stuart is the head teacher at Colebourne Primary School in Birmingham (www.colebourne.bham.sch.uk), a therapeutic parent and a trainer in attachment, adverse childhood experiences and trauma-responsive schools. With more than 15 years of experience as a head teacher, he writes and talks regularly on becoming a trauma-informed, attachment-aware school.

## Dave Harris

Dave is an educational author with five books to his name, including *Brave Heads* (2013). He is also a speaker, consultant, Independent Thinking associate and part of the leadership team at Stone Soup Academy. He has 30 years of experience in all phases of education, including 12 in the role of head teacher.

## Kerrie Henton

Kerrie is principal at Stone Soup Academy in Nottingham. She has worked in education since 1997 and in senior leadership since 2005. Find Stone Soup at www.stonesoupacademy.org.uk.

## Martin Illingworth

Martin has over 30 years of teaching experience and is currently a senior lecturer in education, leading the English and drama PGCE courses at Sheffield Hallam University. His book *Forget School* (2020) is the result of interviewing self-employed 20–30-year-olds about their experiences of school.

## Nina Jackson

Nina is an author, Independent Thinking associate, mental health ambassador and creator of the Mind Medicine approach. She is also an award-winning motivational speaker. Her work as a mainstream and special educational needs and disabilities pedagogical and pastoral champion has bestowed her with the well-deserved title 'Ninja' Nina.

## Sarah Johnson

Sarah has worked in pupil referral units and alternative provision for around 20 years, and is the president of the national organisation PRUsAP. She is a published author and regular speaker, and has been the Department for Education's project manager for an alternative provision innovation fund project. Sarah is also a member of the Department for Education's Alternative Provision Stakeholder group. Find her consultancy at www.phoenixgrouphq.com.

## Dr Debra Kidd

Debra published her first book, *Teaching: Notes from the Frontline* in 2014. Since then there have been three more: *Becoming Möbius* (2015), *Uncharted Territories* (2018), co-authored with Hywel Roberts, and the latest, *Curriculum of Hope* (2019), which explores how a curriculum can be as rich in humanity as it is in knowledge. Debra is an Independent Thinking associate.

## Lucie Lakin

Lucie is principal at Carr Manor Community School in Leeds (www.carrmanor.org.uk). She works closely with the executive principal, Simon Flowers.

## Rt Hon. Sir Norman Lamb

Sir Norman Lamb served as the MP for North Norfolk and in various ministerial health roles between 2001 and 2019. He was awarded a knighthood in 2019 for his mental health campaigning. He is currently chair of three organisations working in this field: Kooth (chair of the advisory board), the South London and Maudsley NHS Foundation Trust and the Children and Young People's Mental Health Coalition. In 2019, he also established a mental health and wellbeing fund in Norfolk.

## Gina McCabe

Gina was a youth worker for many years and now runs Place Innovation, a specialist consultancy for a more socially just and environmentally sustainable world. Place Innovation has led Gina to start planning the Place Schools Trust, a free school concept in the making, which puts wellbeing at the heart of the curriculum and with a framework developed in partnership with the Innovation Unit.

## Alasdair McCarrick

Alasdair has a background in youth and social work and currently lectures on the undergraduate youth studies and youth justice courses at Nottingham Trent University. He began teaching on the new BA in youthwork and MA in youth leadership courses in 2021/2022.

## Dave McPartlin

Dave is the head teacher of Flakefleet Primary in Lancashire (www.flakefleet.lancs. sch.uk), which won Happiest Primary School and Primary School of the Year Runner Up at the National Happiness Awards in 2019. Its real claim to fame, though, was as a recipient of David Walliams' golden buzzer at *Britain's Got Talent* in 2019. Dave also presents on BBC Bitesize and Live Lessons.

## Mary Meredith

Mary is assistant director of learning and skills at Hull City Council. She was a teacher, special educational needs coordinator and senior leader for 20 years prior to moving into a local authority role, initially at Lincolnshire County Council as a special educational needs and disabilities and inclusion lead. She advocates for trauma-informed approaches in schools. Find her at www.marymered.com.

## Marijke Miles

Marijke is head teacher at Baycroft School (www.baycroftschool.com), a special school in Hampshire, and chair of the SEND sector council at the National Association of Head Teachers. She has more than 15 years of experience as a head teacher and has written for the *TES* and *Huffington Post*. She has a wealth of experience supporting children with special educational needs and disabilities, particularly those in local authority care.

## Professor Georgina Newton

Georgina is an associate professor of education at the University of Warwick. Her research focuses on teacher wellbeing and agency.

## Edward Pearson

Edward has been a paramedic on the front line for 23 years. His experience in dealing with 999 calls involving children and young people has taught him the importance of putting parent voice front and centre.

## Lorraine Petersen, OBE

Lorraine is an education consultant and special educational needs and disabilities specialist based in Worcestershire. She has 25 years of experience in the mainstream school environment as a teacher and head teacher, and was CEO of the National Association for Special Educational Needs for nine years. Find her at www.lpec. org.uk.

## Dr Jane Pickthall, MBE

Jane is a virtual school head who promotes the education of looked-after children in North Tyneside. She is a trauma and attachment expert, and was awarded an MBE in the New Year Honours list in 2021.

## Dr Maddi Popoola

Maddi works for Nottingham City Council and is keen to collaborate with other services to ensure that educational psychologists are key contributors to national government policy through quality evaluation and research. She co-authored a report in 2021 with Dr Sarah Sivers and the Pupil Views Collaborative Group on young people's experience of education in the context of the COVID-19 pandemic.

## Tom Quilter

Tom is senior development officer for the Information, Advice and Support Services Network at the Council for Disabled Children (CDC – www.councilfordisabledchildren.org.uk). He studied social policy and held a variety of roles within both local authorities and the charity sector prior to joining the CDC.

## Professor Kathryn Riley

Kathryn is professor of urban education at the Institute of Education, UCL's Faculty of Education and Society and co-founder of the Art of Possibilities (www.theartof-possibilities.org.uk). She is an international scholar whose work bridges policy and practice. International work includes two years heading the World Bank's Effective Schools and Teachers Group. She has taught in inner-city schools, held political office in London as an elected member of the Inner London Education Authority and been a local authority chief officer. Her work on belonging is widely published.

## Dan Rosenberg

Dan is a partner at Simpson Millar (www.simpsonmillar.co.uk), specialising in education and public law. Qualified since 2004, he works across a wide range of areas in education law and community care, with a particular interest in children and young people.

## Alison Sauer

Alison is the chair for the Centre for Personalised Education (www.personalisededu-cationnow.org.uk), runs the Sauer Consultancy and is a regular contributor to government consultations on elective home education. She is widely regarded as an expert on flexischooling.

## Nick Shackleton-Jones

Nick is the founder and CEO of Shackleton Consulting (www.shackleton-consulting.com), following on from more than 10 years as director of learning at BP, PA Consulting and, more recently, Deloitte. He is the author of *How People Learn: Designing Education and Training that Works to Improve Performance* (2019) and a regular public speaker.

## Dr Sarah Sivers

Sarah is a child, community and educational psychologist. Along with Dr Maddi Popoola, she co-authored a report in 2021 on young people's experience of education in the context of COVID-19. She also set up the Education Psychology (EP) Reach-Out webinar series during the pandemic to support education psychologists. Find EP Reach-Out at https://www.youtube.com/c/EducationalPsychologyReachOut/featured.

## Andy Sprakes

Andy is co-founder and chief academic officer of XP School in Doncaster, which was set up following the principles of High Tech High and Expeditionary Learning schools in the United States. He was previously head teacher of Campsmount Academy for eight years and deputy head for four years prior to that. Find XP Trust at www.xptrust.org.

## Dr Bo Stjerne Thomsen

Bo is vice president and chair of Learning Through Play at the LEGO Foundation (www.learningthroughplay.com) and a visiting scholar at Harvard University. He spent nine years building the research agenda, network and organisational expertise on children's development, play and learning in order for the LEGO Foundation to become a leading authority on learning through play.

## Trevor Sutcliffe

Trevor is a co-founder of Challenging Education (www.challengingeducation.co.uk), providing education consultancy, training and monitoring to maintained and academy schools across all phases. The main body of Trevor's work is in supporting schools and organisations to improve the life chances of children who are 'disadvantaged' or in receipt of free school meals.

## Jo Symes

Jo created www.progressiveeducation.org as a resource for those exploring alternatives to conventional methods in education. This inspiration hub showcases innovations both inside and outside of the mainstream. Mainstream schooling was unsuitable for her children and she deregistered them in 2018. You can join the conversation and connect with thousands of others on a similar journey in the Progressive Education Group on Facebook.

## Dave Whitaker

As a former executive principal of a number of special schools, alternative provisions and pupil referral units, Dave is now director of learning for Wellspring Academy Trust (www.wellspringacademytrust.co.uk), with its 28 schools across Yorkshire and Lincolnshire. He is an Independent Thinking associate. His first book, *The Kindness Principle*, was published in 2021.

# MY DAUGHTER IS A SQUARE PEG

I founded Square Peg to try to effect change in a system which is failing an increasing number of children. They are not just the special educational needs and disabilities (SEND) children. And they are not just the 'challenging' ones who end up in isolation or excluded. Many young people have developed excellent coping mechanisms to get through each day, and with budgets stretched and an ever more dictatorial curriculum, they often pass unnoticed by teaching staff who are just trying to survive.

This book is for those in education who want to do the right thing by their square pegs, but are constrained by (often counterproductive) government and local authority directives. We know it is possible to forge a different path within the current system, and we have contributions from schools which are doing just that. This book was compiled to provide creative, inspirational and pragmatic advice, so that those in the mainstream sector are better able to support their square pegs; supporting the supporters, if you like.

My story – the beginning of this book's journey – is one of many; all unique but with common elements and similar, often catastrophic, end results.

It was after a particularly traumatic summer that my 8-year-old daughter missed nearly a year of primary school. Later on, she missed most of secondary school. Why? That's simple: she couldn't do it.

Let me repeat that: she simply couldn't do it. Not *wouldn't*, but *couldn't*.

You may know this as 'school refusal', but I would like you to erase that phrase and reframe it in terms of barriers to attendance instead. She was not refusing to go to school. She just couldn't. Initially, her particular barrier was not trusting that I was safe when she was at school. Later, on moving to secondary school, she didn't trust the adults who were tasked with keeping her safe. She also couldn't see the point of a lot of what she was being taught or the way in which it was being taught. She is a great judge of character and, to be fair, she was often on the money. The secondary school prioritised its position in the league tables above all else, and made it clear that children should be seen and not heard. Her strength of character was her undoing in a system that allows – even encourages – such an approach from schools. Ironically, that same strength of character which meant that she didn't fit the system will most likely be her springboard to an extremely successful future.

Many children 'mask' in school by pretending they are fine. I know my daughter did. They desperately want to be there and fit in along with everyone else, but attending is a daily struggle – one that eventually breaks them. Persistent absentees (a Department for Education label for those whose attendance drops to 90% or less) are a real problem for schools because they lower attendance figures, with the threat of a potential downgrading by Ofsted if average attendance is deemed inadequate. I have heard of head teachers whose performance reviews include an attendance key performance indicator, with personal consequences for missing the target. For parents, absenteeism brings with it the threat of fines and prosecution if a child's attendance falls below a magic threshold (increasingly upwards of 95%). Yet 'chronic' or 'persistent' absence is a global problem, widely recognised to be multifaceted and complex, and only made worse by threats and sanctions. It's a problem with no quick fix in an education system where one-size-fits-all is sadly both convenient and cost-effective (in the short term).

Like many parents in the same position, our journey was a roller coaster. At times it was horrendous; at others we were lifted up by wonderful individuals – 'champions' who changed our trajectory. And that is really the message of this book: that, despite a system which frequently causes damage and exacerbates problems, it is within the gift of governors, school leaders, senior leadership teams and individual teaching staff to rewrite that narrative and make a huge difference to the lives of square pegs and their families. And all the children who struggle in different ways and for many and varied reasons are just that – square pegs in a system of round holes. They are often made to fit the system rather than the system being made flexible enough to meet their needs.

The first step to addressing a problem such as this is recognising that it's a problem and not just a few wayward children with lenient parents. I'm sharing our story here, but we are far from alone. Before we go any further, I want to share with you the messages we have received from just a few other square pegs – their pleas to schools and expressions of what it has felt like for them to be forced to do something they simply cannot do. Please read these and remember them; these children and their families are the driving force behind this book.

To many people
Scary
work is to hard
no ~~friens~~ friends
Cant cope
Pains in my Stomach
Worry for the next day when I come home
Cant eat in School because I feel Sick with worry
hard to find lessons
to loud

C, age 11

Please can I go to a sthool where I ~~dont~~ feel safe
and accepted for being different. I dont want to keep
going to Schools where I get bullied, hurt and
covered in bruises 😠
I want to wake up excited to go to school
and do my work and also enjoy my time there.
I want to go to a school where I am listened to.
I dont want to be awake all night worrying about
going to school.
I want to spend time with my mum and dad and not
watching them doing work 24/7 on calls and filling out
forms. They look tired and they sometimes get upset.

WHY dont you help me and children like me more?

I will be a grown-up soon and it will be too late!

Z, age 13

3

I feel like I don't fit in at school because I am different and it's really confuseing because there has been loads of assemblys about evryone being equal and how to treat evryone right but I feel like I'm not being treated properly by the people who Said it. I feel like nobody understands me and so I feel like I cant show my real feelings. I also feel like I don't fit in because I'm not normal What's it like to be normal. I just feel so alone at school I wish there were more people like me. Assemblys and break times are to busy I feel like I'm being surrounded by a big mob of people.

M, age 9

I feel werse than other children and i cant do things that they can my teacher doesent understand

H, age 8

It is almost like everything from 9:00 to 3:20 is CONSTANTLY on my back, I could go on and on and on and on forever

I come in and there is telltales messing about in the cloakroom
I go in and we have a full R.E afternoon and my least favorite subjects because it is, from my perspective, complete and utter bullcrap.
I can't hear the teacher
I lose my pen and get in trouble from the annoying teaching assistant, like unbridge but not obsessed with kittens and pink.
I can't see the board
I go for a drink and trip over
I am not allowed to go to the toilet when I am desperate
The teacher gets angry for litterally the smallest thing
She punishes the WHOLE class for the telltales actions
I could go on forever and I have had to go through
1050 days (approximately) of it
I have just had enough and can't do it anymore, wanting to just die and get it over with, not needing to have responsibilities and having to get up and go to a school I'm not happy in with git teachers and git telltales and bloody fictional subjects that will help me in no way, shape or form get a decent job
How do I pay taxes?
I DONT KNOW.
But atleast I know the lord's prayer off by heart!

S, age 10

I don't understand why I cannot go to school. Primary said I couldn't even go in for class photos or my last day because they didn't have anyone to look after my diabetes but people who have been trained were all still there. My friends asked me why the Head hates me so much and that made me really sad. I really wanted to start secondary in September and get back to learning but I still don't have a school to go to. I don't think it is fair that I don't have a school just because I need someone to help me with things. It would help me if people at school would understand that I have autism and dyslexia. I wish they helped me with stuff when it is difficult instead of just making me feel stupid and telling me I need to try harder. Don't keep telling me I am rude when I can't make eye contact and don't keep telling me off when I can't answer questions or tell you how I am feeling because that is really difficult for me. It makes me really unhappy that I have diabetes when people at school say I can't do things or even be at school because I need some help to stay safe. The nurses always say having diabetes doesn't stop you doing anything but that wasn't true at my school. I just want to feel normal and not hate myself for all the things I have. Even when I have told people at school how I feel they have ignored me or told me it isn't true. I feel safe and happy at home and football because people there help me and listen to me and make me feel normal and I just want it to be like that at school.
O, age 12 (asd, type 1 diabetes, hypermobility, dyslexia)

O, age 12

Every lesson yesterday felt so long I felt trapped. I couldn't escape, the whole of my body hurts and yesterday I got a head ache and tummy ache. Sometimes my leg twitches and that's when its really bad.

If I feel like there wasn't an exit that day then the next day I cant go in because it feel like there will be no exit again.

Sometimes I've been to the hub and its no help at all. Sometimes I've used the card and everyone has been in a meeting. Or I've used it and I've said that I cant do the lesson because I'm so stressed and I'm told that not being in lessons is not an option, refusing is not an option. So I feel that I can't do anything to save it and it makes me more stressed.

If I go into school and have a rubbish day like I usually do then the next day there is more of a chance that I wont go in.

People say if I go in, it makes it easier for me the next day, but it doesn't work like that for me, it makes it worse. Basically 60% of the time, if I've gone in that day its been so bad that I've not gone in for the next 2 days because going in didn't help me in any way.

In school I have thought about committing suicide many times, more than anywhere else. I've thought about hanging myself . I've planned how to do it. It relieves me.

F, age 12

To the school

I would like to inform you how I feel at school and at home.

AT HOME:

At home I feel very stressed and most of the time at least 30minutes to 1 hr I cry or feel sad and can't do the normal day to day based things like getting dressed, simple things like that and this affects me at school to be independent. To be honest I feel like I'm a clumsy person that no one wants to listen to because I feel like I can't be heard, and no one wants to listen.

AT SCHOOL:

At school I might not show it but I feel uncomfortable and very stressed as people say they promised to do something and it never happened for example on the start of term 1 I asked to work alone or in a smaller group they said " I promise you this will happen in 1-2 weeks " and this was 1 of the 5 things that they/you have promised me that never happened. The canopy door drop off isn't working either as I was told I can wait there as long as I want until I go into class  this never happened and I felt overwhelmed and I ran out back to my mum and dad crying unable to go in and what dint help was how they dealt with it by getting me quickly away from my mum  and dad which increased the impact of stress and most of those reasons are a few of about 23  of why I feel unable to go into school and this is sometimes why I don't go into school

p.s I need this to change quickly as its getting worse and I cant be happy at the weekend and I am getting nightmares and I break things and not paying attention and to be honest I don't feel like I should be living as I am not being listened to which I have a right to and I'm always stressed which I shouldn't be.

Looking Happy

feeling sad

F, age 12

13.9.2020

To anyone reading this

I wanted to write how I am feeling, because apparantly you didn't have the heart to believe my mum when she told you. You have - theres no other way of putting this- ruined my life. You have put my life on hold for the last two years and I am so sick of it. Every day I dream, hope for a better life but all you have done is shut my life down. How dare you. You are supposed to be there for the youth, to help them grow up into better people. All you have done to me, and many others, is disgrace and ruin us. I don't understand how any of you sleep at night. We are children, kannot stress this enough, CHILDREN and you are making us wish we were dead. I wish I were dead because of your actions. Not a day goes by where I don't consider it. I live in isolation, NOT because of the pandemic, but because you can't show 1 bit of empathy to me. You are evil people. I just want to be happy, is that so much to ask for? Why is it that you and your families can be happy but I have to sit in my bed all day doing nothing but wishing for a better life. It is honestly so morally wrong and unacceptable. You have took my life from me and I hope karma meets you one day. You have had 12 years to help me but you delayed it every day of those years. I hope you won't decide to stay this way. I hope you have atleast 1 ounce of humanity left in your money-hungry soulless bodies. I hope you realise that I have dreams too.

the 14 year old whose life you ruined.

I, age 14

8

## A Square Peg's 10 Commandments

Dear Teacher

I wanted to write to tell you my 10 top tips for children like me.

1. Be more respectful to children, listen to their feelings and do not ever doubt them. Otherwise I just give up telling them to you at all.

2. Don't tell me to stop crying when I'm upset. Don't tell me to turn my frown into a smile because the other children are staring at me.

3. Don't put me on the Buddy Bench. They don't work, they make me feel rubbish and hot inside. That's not how friendships work. When you felt lonely and no one was noticing, did sitting on the Buddy Bench help you?

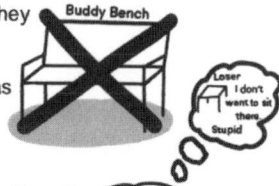

4. Don't put me in the same room or same table as my bullies. It gives them more chances to kick or push or threaten to stab my hand with their pencil. And children who are a friend stop being a friend once the bullies are on the same table.

5. Don't change where I sit every time it's a new term. Making work friends in new topics takes ages. It's like someone has died when you change the seats around.

L, age 13

6. Don't do tests on the first day of term. Or the second or the third. It makes my brain fizz and my mouth goes dry and the clock ticking is so loud and I can't remember anything especially from before the Christmas holiday. Just because I can't remember right then, it doesn't mean I can't tell you about it. When it's a new term, please can we focus on having fun together first?

7. Understand that bullies don't give up. Just because you've made them apologise, and you say 'it's done,' it isn't. And if I pluck up my strength to tell you they're doing the same things again, don't sigh or make your mouth small. Making a bully say sorry doesn't change what they're doing every day.

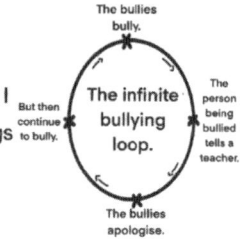

The bullies bully.

The infinite bullying loop.

But then continue to bully.

The person being bullied tells a teacher.

The bullies apologise.

8. Don't take my playtime away if I haven't done all the work in time. I can't think of an acrostic poem on the spot sometimes, especially when you said yesterday my writing wasn't good enough. If my brain has frozen, I'm not naughty. A run around and fresh air might be a good time to make a new friend instead especially if you have bullies.

**ALONE**

9. Don't move me down the learning board for not remembering something or asking for help. It's not my fault if I don't understand something. I don't care if everyone else in the class understands and I don't, it doesn't make me bad. You're the teacher.

10. When you are kind and gentle, I feel so much better. If you tell me I haven't got something right YET, I can try to do it again. When I make you laugh, I feel brilliant. I like it when you are happy.

L, age 13

This school is ruining my life. I am angry all the time and it's really frustrating. When I'm in the school I am trapped. If I ask to get out of class they just tell me to do deep breathing and that makes me have a panic attack. Because I mask, they ~~don't~~ think I am fine in the school. THEY ARE DOING NOTHING. If I go in all the time, I just come out.

B, age 11

## How School Made Me Feel

Through years 8 to year10 (age 12 to 15) i felt genuinely scared to go to school. The idea of walking through the school gates made me scared and made me feel sick. The school were not supportive of me, and i felt that no one beyond the school gates cared about my wellbeing. It felt as if the only thing they cared about was my attendance and they had no empathy or understanding of my situation.

I felt embarassed to tell the support people at school how i felt because i knew that they wouldn't do anything different. I used to cry every morning and it would be a physical battle to get me into school. Inside school i felt trapped and felt like i couldnt be myself. I wanted to leave and never go back.

I didnt enjoy anything anymore and i was always sad. I was constantly upset, stressed and worried.

School made me lose myself.

- Becky 17

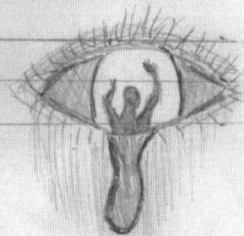

B, age 17

#C (in my head)   fMLB

OMFG. I keep | Good Lord
hearing | Every time
these people | I walk in to
speaking | #nd the school gates
negative thing | it is like a bounty
#tts to me | hunter chasing me

School Sucks! | KILL ME!

Every body tells me it's ok
but really I feel like I am
on my own and every body
is against me And I have
had soi many bad / traumat-
izing excperience in my
life that I honestly dont
belive ANYONE anymore
And Lets be honest with
our selves here I am going
through this alone no matter
what any body says or
does I am still going to
be that one AUTISTIC kid

A B C D E F G H I hate myself and you no I always
will want to kill myself.

A, age 11

13

There are common threads in these words – of not fitting in, being understood, or valued. Of a lack of flexibility, 'solutions' chosen by adults that don't work for the children they are designed to support, of children trying to be heard and their words falling on deaf ears. And of parental concerns being disregarded (see Chapter 8: 'Lessons from a 999 call'). No child should feel like this on a daily basis, with no way out. And for those who may still think it's just a few wayward children, let's see what the data has to say. Since exclusion receives a lot of attention, we will start with the most recent pre-pandemic data on suspensions and exclusions (on the basis that the pandemic skewed much of this data).[1]

In 2019/2020, there were 5,057 permanently excluded pupils in England, with 154,524 receiving a suspension or fixed-period exclusion (FPE). However, only 61,608 received more than one FPE and only 156 were 'repeat offenders' with 20 or more FPEs.[2] We know that there is a well-trodden path from exclusion to youth justice (Arnez and Condry, 2021), and that the numbers have been growing steadily. Of course, behaviour that puts the safety of the child, their peers or staff at risk needs to be addressed, and behaviour that disrupts the class must be managed. All of this has led to exclusion being in the spotlight, with commensurate attention, investment and resources. The controversial debate in education is how this sort of behaviour should be managed, with advocates of zero tolerance focusing on disciplinarian behavioural approaches and advocates of trauma-informed, attachment-aware neuroscience seeing behaviour as a means of communication and focusing on relationships and compassion.

Now let's look at persistent absence. For the 2018/2019 academic year, there were 771,863 persistent absentees, rising to 921,927 in the autumn term of 2019. That is more than nine times as many pupils as those who have received more than one suspension, yet absence receives little attention bar the standard 'attendance equals attainment/bums on seats' narrative. In the autumn term of 2019, 60,247 pupils missed 50% or more of the academic year, up from 39,250 three years previously.[3] These are huge numbers compared to exclusions, yet until COVID-19 arrived they sat completely under the radar. More recent numbers probably disguised a continuing growth in persistent absence within discounted COVID absences, and we may not be able to accurately separate the impact of the pandemic for some time.

What is also astonishing is that for approximately 40% of 'persistent' absences,[4] there is no formally recorded reason (usually coded O for 'other' unauthorised absence, C for

---

1   We have consciously used pre-pandemic data throughout this book, for the reason cited above.
2   For data on permanent exclusions and suspensions in England for the academic year 2019/2020 see https://explore-education-statistics.service.gov.uk/find-statistics/permanent-and-fixed-period-exclusions-in-england.
3   For data on pupil absence in schools in England for the academic year 2018/2019 see https://www.gov.uk/government/statistics/pupil-absence-in-schools-in-england-2018-to-2019.
4   For average data on pupil absence in schools in England across recent years see https://www.gov.uk/government/collections/statistics-pupil-absence.

'other' authorised absence, N for no reason yet or I for illness).[5] In contrast, for exclusions, there are no less than 11 reasons, ranging from theft to physical assault against an adult (Department for Education, 2017: 17) and only 17–18% are classified as 'other'[6] (with a proposal that the 'other' category now be removed). 'Attendance equals attainment.' 'It's vital for safeguarding.' 'One day missed is one grade dropped.' We hear these messages constantly, but how can we know what support to put in place or what interventions might help if we don't understand the underlying problem?

The really dangerous consequence of a lack of accurate data is the assumptions that are made. To illustrate this point, let me share two conversations about the total number of persistent absentees. One was with an ex-deputy head teacher who simply *believed* that 90% of these pupils were disengaged from education. In other words, they were just truanting. The other was a psychiatrist who stated that, in her professional opinion (and she sees non-attenders on a daily basis), 80% of these pupils had an anxiety-related issue which impacted directly or indirectly on their ability to attend school. That is a discrepancy of hundreds of thousands of children. We cannot simply make assumptions about the truth, when the only truth is that we don't know why these children are absent. There is also a conflated argument, reinforced through teacher training, that because excluded children often have a history of persistent absence, persistent absentees are therefore more likely to exhibit antisocial behaviour or end up in prison. That is just another unfounded and dangerous assumption.

Despite claims to the contrary, we have an education system that has been starved of cash, that is coerced into valuing academic attainment above all else, that has a process for identifying and supporting children with SEND which is great on paper but failing miserably in practice (House of Commons Education Committee, 2019), and it's generally accepted that our child and adolescent mental health services are hugely overstretched and failing to meet need (Crenna-Jennings and Hutchinson, 2020). On top of that, the UK has some of the least happy children in the world (Children's Society, 2021), who are arguably under more pressure than any prior generation and facing a future that doesn't look too appealing (think climate change, the economy, Brexit-related issues, COVID-19 and its ongoing fallout, a cost of living crisis). Of course, the square pegs have always been there, and in increasing numbers in recent years, but the pandemic has shone a stark light on the disadvantages that many children and young people face.

If the data doesn't tell us what is behind issues like non-attendance (and, remember, this is just one aspect of what makes a square peg), what do we know? Although anxiety can so often be the trigger that leads to persistent absence, as was the case with my daughter, underlying causes are many and varied.

---

5   See https://www.gov.uk/government/statistics/pupil-absence-in-schools-in-england-2018-to-2019.
6   See https://explore-education-statistics.service.gov.uk/find-statistics/permanent-and-fixed-period-exclusions-in-england.

We do know that in terms of pupil characteristics, the square pegs (or at least those who appear in the official absence and exclusions statistics) are all the usual suspects: pupils on free school meals, who account for 32% of all persistent absentees, and those with SEND (25%) – mainly children on SEN support, but also 25% of all children with an education health and care plan (EHCP).[7] Those from ethnic minorities and with English as an alternative language feature too, but to a lesser extent. Many square pegs will have social, emotional or mental health (SEMH) issues, which covers a vast array of need and could apply to any of us at some point in our lives. Yet even with – or despite – these acronyms, we are still missing the nuances involved.

Take SEND. There are children with undiagnosed SEND and there are those who have been diagnosed but remain unsupported. Indeed, the term SEND covers a massive range of need, from complex physical disabilities to underlying health conditions (including SEMH), which create secondary needs with debilitating anxiety and mental health issues. It spans those with EHCPs and the much larger numbers on SEN support, not to mention the intersectionality issues that arise when we cross-reference these challenges with factors such as gender, sexuality, social background and ethnicity. Put simply, for many children and for many reasons, the mainstream school environment is just too much.

Some square pegs – whether they go to school or not – will have experienced bullying. Some, perhaps many, will have experienced trauma, and we touch on this in more detail later, particularly in Part IV. Some will have chronic health conditions which constitute a SEND issue or simply require some ongoing process of adjustment to the norm. Then there are those children whose needs are fuelled by circumstances at home or in their local community, which not only make school a low priority but create behaviours deemed unacceptable by the system (from being there and causing problems to causing problems by not being there). Some will struggle to fit temporarily; for others it's a more permanent state of affairs.

So, what can we do when faced with such a vast and diverse range of underlying needs? My experience suggests that the only way school leaders can respond effectively is to build trust, invest in relationships and collaborate with families in order to help create the right culture and environment which allows them to meet each child's needs. It starts with ensuring that those needs are accurately and comprehensively identified, in order to agree the support (in its widest sense) that is necessary for the child to utilise the education system and carve out their own best path. Securing that support can be another mountain to climb, but if the trust and relationships are strong there will be things that can be done to help along the way.

---

7    See https://www.gov.uk/government/statistics/pupil-absence-in-schools-in-england-2018-to-2019 and https://www.gov.uk/government/statistics/permanent-exclusions-and-suspensions-in-england-2019-to-2020.

All of this starts with genuine, empathetic listening (often referred to as 'active listening'). That means listening (and really hearing) the square pegs and their advocates – in most cases, their parents. Square pegs are the canaries in the mine, telling us that there is a palpable tension between an education system driven by efficiencies of scale, top-down control, data and results, and trying to educate children who are, like the rest of us, confoundingly and beautifully unique. If we do not show ourselves as willing to listen, we leave children, especially younger children, with two main routes for expressing their emotions: they act out or they shut down. Those who act out and exhibit 'challenging' behaviour often find themselves sanctioned and even excluded. Those who shut down and withdraw may remain under the radar, going unnoticed behind masked struggles for the entirety of their school career. Others may survive in that mode until their coping strategy fails, their attendance plummets and they become one of those pesky 'school refusers'.

My daughter was a case in point. We never really got to the bottom of her unmet needs (too often the system is just looking for a diagnosis box to tick). In primary school, things improved, although not through the children and adolescent mental health services support we received, which was potentially counterproductive, but through a member of the school's senior leadership asking a simple question in a staff meeting: was there a teaching assistant prepared to work with us? That led to our first 'champion' (and square pegs and their families need all the champions they can find). Mrs B earned our trust and gave both me and my daughter the supportive relationship we so badly needed. It took many months, and was only possible because she was committed to helping us and really believed that she was 'the one' who could help my daughter to return to school. She *was* the right person; it wouldn't have worked with Mrs C who had spare capacity, or Mrs D whose job it was to support all the square pegs. Genuine relationships are the only ones that genuinely count. They allow support to be tailored to specific needs and delivered under an umbrella of trust.

It's also worth noting that blanket interventions don't work. Many of the standard strategies (arriving a little late or leaving a little early, a 'get-out-of-class' card, building up a part-time timetable and so on) work some of the time for some square pegs but their effectiveness is limited (Not Fine in School, 2020). Just as adults don't 'mend' or perform after a standard offer of therapy, so the speed with which a square peg can heal, and the support they need at any point in time, will vary hugely.

We were lucky in other ways too. We were never actually fined or prosecuted, although my daughter was told on several occasions that we would go to prison if she didn't go to school (please note: this doesn't work). One of the huge frustrations with persistent absence (or school 'refusal' as it remains stubbornly known across much of academia) is the judgement of whether parents are knowingly allowing their child to be absent, as this then makes them complicit. *Knowledge, agreement* and *complicity* all (obviously) have different meanings and their use will be extremely sensitive, loaded and triggering to those whose children have struggled to attend. It's tied up in the legal stuff too – parental responsibility and the lack of recognition that it's not refusal.

It's also tied up in some of the research in which academics have pigeonholed school 'refusers' according to whether the absence is with their parents' knowledge and/or complicity. If my daughter had been 'acting out' and received a FPE instead, the same argument would apply, except that it wouldn't be a criminal offence. If she was 'truanting' (another word we don't use), I may have known or not known, understood or been complicit. But if it was a result of her needs not being met at school, then we would still have remained unsupported and potentially been fined or prosecuted. I would probably have had little agency over any of these scenarios other than trying to advocate on her behalf. Of course, I could have not cared, but this may have been because the system also failed me, so why would I expect anything different for my own children?

Back to our champions. Later, in secondary school (our second), we were gifted a deputy head teacher who believed that his school was there to serve his local community, whatever that looked like. Mr A took my daughter on roll, and she 'did' secondary school without ever setting foot on site. A Statement of Educational Needs meant that we could pay for a tutor (other-worldly and with buckets of wisdom, but that's another story), and we had a fortnightly exchange of work with the school. He registered our home as an exam centre, even sending invigilators so she could take her GCSEs. That gave my daughter the results she needed to go to a mainstream sixth-form college, and, combined with her jaw-dropping strength of character, she never looked back. Without Mr A that wouldn't have been possible. His school and the first secondary school in my daughter's story are less than two miles apart, but a whole cosmos separates their ethos and culture.

All of this requires time, flexibility and resources, but, even before that, it needs senior leaders to step in and protect families from the rigidity and inflexibility of the system. They must create a culture and environment that can scaffold each child and collaborate beyond the school walls to find innovative and creative solutions. They must bend the rules where necessary and use all the resources they have within their school and community networks (and some) to make it work. That is what this book is about.

By the way, my daughter has now completed a degree in criminology. She never fitted in and went through hell as a result; we weren't far behind. She will be a success despite the system, and I am all the more proud of her because of it. So, here's to all the square pegs out there. Because those that don't fit the system teach us the really important stuff in life – and we need to listen.

# References

Arnez, J. and Condry, R. (2021) Criminological Perspectives on School Exclusion and Youth Offending, *Emotional and Behavioural Difficulties*, 26(1): 87–100.

Children's Society (2021) *The Good Childhood Report 2021*. Available at: https://www.childrenssociety.org.uk/information/professionals/resources/good-childhood-report-2021.

Crenna-Jennings, W. and Hutchinson, J. (2020) *Access to Child and Adolescent Mental Health Services in 2019*. London: Education Policy Institute. Available at: https://epi.org.uk/wp-content/uploads/2020/01/Access-to-CAMHS-in-2019_EPI.pdf.

Department for Education (2017) *A Guide to Exclusion Statistics* (September). Available at: https://assets.publishing.service.gov.uk/government/uploads/system/uploads/attachment_data/file/642577/Guide-to-exclusion-statistics-05092017.pdf.

Department for Education (2020) Pupil Absence in Schools in England: 2018 to 2019 (26 March). Available at: https://www.gov.uk/government/statistics/pupil-absence-in-schools-in-england-2018-to-2019.

House of Commons Education Committee (2019) *Special Educational Needs and Disabilities. First Report of Session 2019*. HC 20. Available at: https://publications.parliament.uk/pa/cm201919/cmselect/cmeduc/20/20.pdf.

Not Fine in School (2020) *School Attendance Difficulties: Parent Survey Results* (March). Available at: https://img1.wsimg.com/blobby/go/a41082e1-5561-438b-a6a2-16176f7570e9/NFIS_Parent_Survey_Results_March_2020.pdf.

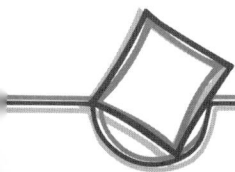

# Part 1

# SQUARE PEGS AND ROUND HOLES

# Introduction

What happens when you try to force a square peg into a round hole? We start here because it's highly probable that many in education would be abhorred to fully understand what life is like for square pegs and their families.

Individuals go into education to inspire children, to reap the rewards of working with young, curious minds, and to see the young people they teach flourish and fulfil their potential. Yet, we have a system where increasingly education, and unwittingly those who work within it, are causing untold damage to the very children they are there to nurture. It's crucial that the scale of this problem is properly understood, and that the level of distress and long-term, catastrophic damage to whole families is recognised. And so we begin here.

Highlighting the experience of families also provides important background on those parents who appear to enter new school relationships all guns blazing, hauling behind them a removal van's worth of baggage. It requires those on the receiving end to remain calm, participate in active listening and meet those parents where they are at, with oodles of empathy and a desire to build a very different, wholly positive experience. It requires those on the receiving end to be professionals, not to take it personally and not to attribute a 'difficult' label to parents who have simply been exposed to too many system failings already.

One common response is that parents like me are just the unlucky few. We are keen to evidence the scale and severity of the problem, not just through the official statistics but also through the experiences of literally thousands of parents. Not Fine in School, a support group for the families of non-attenders, launched its closed Facebook group for parents in 2018 with under 100 members. By July 2022 it had almost 30,000. In Part I, we reference some of the survey findings from this group and explore the many commonalities of experience, despite each child's needs being unique. The good news is that it doesn't have to be like this; as Ginny Bootman says, there is big power in little things (see Chapter 4).

# Chapter 1

# WHEN IDEAS MEET REAL CHILDREN

## Naomi Fisher

Hayley was finding school difficult. She had managed to cope in reception and Year 1, but as Year 2 rolled by and expectations were changing, Hayley was falling behind. She just didn't seem to be able to remember things and spent more time looking out the window than focusing on the lesson. Her teacher was concerned and told her parents. Her parents started going over her work with her each evening and rewarded her with a sticker once she had read four pages of her book. Her teacher would write her name on the board when she didn't complete her work. If her name was there three times, she lost some of her Friday Golden Time.

Soon Hayley was refusing to go to school. She was waking up at night saying how worried she was about her name appearing on the board. At the same time, she was even more easily distracted in lessons. She was less and less keen to practise her reading at home and, in fact, started refusing to let her parents read stories to her, something she had loved before.

Hayley is a square peg.[1]

There is much written on how children learn. Then there is more about what they *should* learn – what needs to be in the curriculum, what knowledge they must know and by what age. Each country does this slightly differently, of course, but they all assume that the way to 'do' education well is to get the curriculum right and deliver it effectively.

Then these ideas meet real children.

Like the 'we're all working remotely now' idea during the COVID-19 pandemic (as parents soon found out), persuading a child to comply with the requirements of school is hard work. There is so much time, energy and money focused on *how* children learn, with the underlying assumption that if we could just get the techniques

---

1   These examples are composites rather than individual children, but the scenarios are based on real events I have encountered during my research and clinical work. Any resemblance to an individual is accidental.

right, learning will flow. Yet, this focus on the mechanics of learning – whether that is neural connections, cognitive science, phonics or whatever is the flavour of the month – misses something that is fundamental to any child's educational experience and success: the child themselves.

# Learning as interaction

A child's motivation, their interests and their personality are an integral part of whatever education they are receiving. Nothing is objective in education because everything is an interaction between the learner and the environment. There can be no such thing as an interesting and comprehensible lesson for everyone, since what is fascinating to one person may bore another to tears. Diversity and individual differences are, beautifully, the norm, not the exception.

This may be something that teachers know by experience, but in recent years it has been backed up by a body of research which at first may seem counterintuitive. For example, over the last 30 years, there has been an increasing amount of research interest in behavioural genetics – studying the genes that influence our day-to-day behaviour. Researchers have looked at the genetic influences on matters like how well children do at school and many other aspects of behaviour. Studies have found that the variation in just about everything has a genetic component, including things that seem to be clearly environmental (Plomin, 2018) – for example, how much TV children watch each day (van de Vegte et al., 2020) or whether a person gets married or divorced (McGue and Lykken, 1992).

This might seem odd: how can the amount of TV a child watches be influenced by their genes? Isn't that due to their home environment and whether a parent makes TV available or not? Well, yes, of course it is, but that isn't the whole story. After all, even within these constraints some children will choose to watch as much TV as they can, while others will be uninterested and may prefer to spend their time building with LEGO or reading a book.

No environment has the same effect on everyone, and the research shows this again and again. Children shape their environment through the influence of their personal characteristics (Dick, 2011), and this then affects their learning experiences (Coll et al., 2004). A child's teacher is also part of the environment that a child is shaping. Teachers speak to girls differently than to boys, and adults speak differently to tiny babies depending on whether they think the baby is male or female (Eliot, 2010). We are also becoming increasingly aware of how factors such as ethnicity and social class affect how teachers interact with a child (Tenenbaum and Ruck, 2007). And, right from the start, children who have placid temperaments get different reactions from those who are more reactive. In other words, interactions between adults and children are bidirectional (Paschall and Mastergeorge, 2015). Children's behaviour and characteristics affect adult behaviour, and then adult behaviour affects how children behave. This makes the relationship between genes – yours and theirs – and the environment a fascinatingly complex adaptive system.

Interactions between a child and the world around them also happen in an active way, as the child acts intentionally on their environment. Think of your average nursery class full of diverse children. In that environment, children often have choices about how they spend their time. Some of those children will seek out the book corner, whether they can read or not. Others will spend their whole time playing outside. Some may move from activity to activity, while others play in groups. Some prefer solitary play, while others play with a single friend. The experience of each child each day can be entirely different, and yet they are all still learning. A child in nursery creates a personalised learning environment for themselves, based on their interests at the time. This makes their learning efficient and fun.

## Not everyone finds the same things interesting

As children go through the school system, the choices available in their environment narrows. By the time they are 8 or 9, they have many fewer choices than when they were at nursery. Now, there is no option to play outside all day or to spend time with a favourite book. The process of schooling is inherently one of expecting greater compliance while providing fewer options for children to make interest-based choices. Even at age 14, when they choose GCSE options, the choices are far more limited than in a good nursery classroom. There are no options to throw yourself into a passion wholeheartedly, for example, by spending weeks of intense focus on something that interests you. There is certainly no option to spend your whole day outside, engaged in open exploration and construction. Ultimately, choices are reduced to and guided by which exam you will take at the end.

For some, school works as intended. They progress academically, enjoy it and do well. For others, the process is miserable. They just don't seem to be able to learn in the same way that everyone else does, and so are often labelled as having learning difficulties. Others refuse to go to school or protest loudly through their behaviour when they are there, resulting in sanctions and exclusion from the classroom or from the school itself. At times, despite best intentions, everything the school does seems to make things worse, especially for the children who become less motivated, not more, as they move through the system. And, when it comes to academic achievement, motivation matters (Alivernini and Lucidi, 2011).

# Motivation starts with meaning

In the world beyond formal education, we usually learn things either because we need to or want to. We know that learning works best when the learner wants to learn (e.g. Tokan and Imakulata, 2019), something psychologists call 'intrinsic motivation'. The small child who is fascinated by dinosaurs will acquire specialist knowledge very quickly if their parents provide them with opportunities to do so. The child doesn't need to be incentivised with a sticker (or a threat). Learning is its own reward. In older children, we can see this at work as they become expert in playing video games, learning an instrument or playing football. This is equally the case for children who are labelled as 'learning disabled' or who have significant problems with attention and concentration at school. They will often have areas in which they are learning effectively. It's just that these areas are not valued by the system.

Having to learn what the system deems they should know at a certain age means the child does not necessarily learn because they need to know something right now or because they are fascinated. This poses an immediate motivation problem.

Meet Harminder:

---

Harminder is 5. She came into nursery with very little English and has done well in learning to talk and interact with other children and the teachers. She is now fluent. She was highly motivated to learn English as she could not make herself understood without it, and she wanted to be able to play with the other children. She has several friends with whom she plays regularly. Harminder particularly enjoys playing outside and will often construct things with wood and sand. She did not receive extra help or tuition in English as her nursery has a policy of immersion and, because this worked well for her, there was no need for extra support.

As Harminder goes into Year 1, expectations change. She is now expected to learn to read, and her parents are given a list of key words to work on with her at home. Harminder is not interested. Her interests are social and imaginary play for which she does not need to read, and outdoor play for which she does not need to read. She cannot see the point in phonics and finds it boring, wanting to be off and running about with her friends. Her teacher tells her that reading is very important but Harminder isn't convinced. It certainly doesn't seem to be something she needs in her life right now. By the end of Year 1, Harminder is still unable to read the list of key words. She just doesn't seem to be able to remember that 't-h-e' represents 'the'. It isn't the case that Harminder has not been learning, though. She has learned how to tell the time, both analogue and digital, so that she can hide whenever the time for her phonics group is coming up and re-emerge when the 30 minutes are up. She learned this herself, without instruction, simply through asking people what time it was and noticing what it said on the clocks.

Harminder is becoming a square peg.

---

She is also now at risk of several things. She may be identified as being less capable, something we know could influence her later academic achievement (Susperreguy et al., 2017). She may be identified as having difficulties in attention and concentration, since she refuses to sit still and prefers to run around. She is also at risk of becoming disengaged from school and of becoming unhappy there, if she starts to associate school with feelings of failure. Yet we know that Harminder is capable of learning – she is bilingual at age 5 and she learned how to tell the time entirely by herself – when she is motivated and when she finds a purpose in learning a topic that is *meaningful to her*.

Once the real-world reasons for learning have been removed, schools are left with the puzzle of how to motivate children to learn the curriculum. For many, this means using behavioural approaches which can, unfortunately, create problems of their own.

## Rewards and consequences

Most schools that I know of run along behavioural lines and are encouraged to do so (e.g. Rhodes and Long, 2019). Children are rewarded and praised if they do well and are sanctioned if they do not comply. Behavioural strategies include Golden Time, putting children 'on report', giving marks and detentions and, Hayley's nemesis, writing names on the board. They also include traffic light systems, end-of-term outings for classes with full attendance, and summer reading schemes where children get prizes and certificates for reading the most books.

Behaviourism is a particular form of psychology, of which B. F. Skinner is the most famous proponent. He worked with rats. He showed that they could be made to do things by altering the contingencies – the consequences for the rat of a given action. Give them some sugar water to suck and they would return to suck more. Give them a small electric shock and they would learn to avoid that area of their cage. Skinner (1963) called this 'operant conditioning'.

Applied to a classroom of children in which some are on task and others less so, the former group would be praised (verbal, non-verbal or written) and possibly rewarded (stickers or merits), and the latter group would be threatened with consequences specifically contrived to be unpleasant. The hope is that these contingencies – the positive and negative ones – will result in the children doing what they are told. For some, this will work.

Some schools believe that using rewards is preferable to using sanctions and opt to take a more positive approach. It's certainly true that children will *say* that they prefer rewards to sanctions. However, there is a significant body of research which shows that rewards and punishments have the same drawbacks when it comes to learning (Kohn, 1999). This is because rewards can act as a punishment when a child does not get the reward and another child does, or when they do not get a reward that they expected. Rewards shift the focus of what a child is doing towards the hoped-for outcome and away from the learning itself.

The aim of all such behaviourist strategies is the same: to persuade children that it's better to do as they are asked/told than to persist in their resistance. Do behavioural strategies work? Yes – on behaviour. We can all be induced to change our behaviour because of an anticipated reward or a feared punishment. We all choose where we park in order to avoid a fine. This apparent effectiveness explains the ongoing popularity of behavioural strategies in schools. However, there are significant drawbacks, particularly when applied to learning, and all the more so for our square pegs.

## The problem with focusing on outcomes

Behavioural approaches assume that the reason we behave in certain ways is because of the outcome we anticipate – good or bad, pleasant or painful. However, there is an important difference between behaviour and learning. If behaviour is the focus, it only matters what you do. It doesn't really matter how you *feel* about what you do. Let's take the COVID-19 pandemic as an example. On a behavioural level, it doesn't really matter if I feel bored, trapped and frustrated by being locked down at home.[2] I will still be less likely to get the virus if I stay inside and keep away from others. I can be furious about it, but following the rules will still help me to stay safe. My feelings are irrelevant to the outcome.

Learning is different. With learning, it matters what you think and how you feel about what you are doing. In fact, it can be argued that what you think actually *is* the learning in many cases. This means that feeling bored, trapped or frustrated while learning is very relevant. Experience tells us that feeling bored with a topic means we will learn far less effectively than when we are interested. There is even research which indicates that using behavioural techniques actually increases our chances of losing interest in what we are doing (Ryan and Deci, 2000).

## Rewards can destroy motivation

Being interested in a topic not only means we learn more effectively, but we also retain more of what we learn (Seli et al., 2016). That is why children passionate about dinosaurs can tell you all about *Tyrannosaurus rex*, even if they can't remember where they put their book bag.

---

2   No prizes for guessing where I am while writing this.

Good teachers know this intuitively, of course. They try to make their lessons interesting by introducing activities that children enjoy. They use word searches, colouring pages, quizzes and the like. But they are in an impossible situation. For a start, these activities may be only tangentially related to the actual topic. It's possible to enjoy doing the colouring but still know very little about the intended lesson. And the ongoing reliance on rewards and sanctions used by so many schools will still not make children more interested in what they are learning in the long term (Pulfrey et al., 2013). Note too that when we use external consequences to alter someone's behaviour, we change their relationship to what they are doing (Pink, 2018). They are no longer doing something because they enjoy it; they are doing it because someone else is trying to make them do it. This actually makes the activity less enjoyable.

Researchers first showed this with children in the 1970s. They rewarded preschoolers for doing an activity they enjoyed – drawing with felt-tip pens. They compared children who were rewarded with stickers to those who were not. They found that the rewarded group drew more pictures when given stickers, but once the stickers stopped coming they drew fewer pictures than the group who had never been rewarded. By introducing an external reward, the researchers had changed the children's relationship to drawing (Lepper et al., 1973).

The problem seems to be that being rewarded – and note that verbal praise isn't as damaging as a physical reward, and unexpected rewards are less damaging than predicted rewards, but they are still damaging (Deci et al., 2001) – fundamentally changes the way in which children relate to an activity. It shifts the emphasis from process to outcome, which means that now it makes sense for children to choose easier activities in order to maximise their rewards, as opposed to choosing something that challenges them (Pulfrey et al., 2011). In addition, it shifts the locus of control. A child who is doing something they enjoy is the one making the choices (intrinsic motivation), but once an adult comes along and starts rewarding them for those choices, it's the adult who is seeking to control the behaviour. The adult takes charge and, in so doing, takes power away from the child.

The moment the adult does that, we have a potential problem with motivation and learning. High-quality motivation requires the learner to be acting from an internal drive, not purely because of external factors such as consequences. And, in contrast to what many schools seem to believe, starting with external motivators makes it less likely that the internal drive will develop.

Two psychologists who have researched different forms of motivation are Richard Ryan and Edward Deci (2017). They break down motivation into six different types which fall on a spectrum. At one end is 'amotivation' – the situation when a person simply refuses to do anything. At the other end is the engaged and curious child, doing what they do because they are passionate about it.

As we move along the spectrum, motivation changes. We are used to simply thinking about intrinsic and extrinsic motivation, but in fact variation is far more subtle. Internally driven motivation isn't just about doing things you enjoy. A child might be intrinsically motivated because they love doing something, but they might also be motivated by a desire to meet a goal or a desire to feel good about themselves. They may choose to do something that isn't enjoyable right now because it will move towards something they value. (For example, many of us exercise not because we really enjoy it but because we want to feel fit or get stronger.) All these types of motivation, according to Deci and Ryan, are of a higher quality than one that is imposed from the outside using rewards and punishments. And higher quality motivation leads to higher quality learning. If we can create an environment which nurtures high-quality internally driven motivation, we can help all children to thrive.

Ryan and Deci called this 'self-determination theory' and identified three key factors in the environment that nurture high-quality motivation: autonomy, competence and relatedness.

*Autonomy* is often misunderstood as being synonymous with independence – children doing things by themselves – but it is actually quite different. In Deci and Ryan's interpretation, it is about a person having governance over their life, knowing that their opinions matter and are valued. Teachers can nurture this through allowing choices where possible, by valuing different approaches to tasks, and through respecting each child as an individual who can be trusted to make decisions.

A school that focuses on control can remove autonomy from children.

*Competence* is not about a learner being rated by an external observer but about how that learner feels about themselves. It's about a child seeing that they can become better at doing something, and, ultimately, having a sense of mastery. Teachers can encourage this by giving genuine positive feedback (note: this is not the same as praise) when they notice a child making progress and in allowing children to engage in activities, wherever possible, where they have strengths. It could involve a teacher or parent showing that they value and take an interest in the things at which a child is competent, whether that is Minecraft, skateboarding or, yes, dinosaurs.

A school that focuses on weakness and deficit – on what the child can't do – particularly in those with learning disabilities, means that child will never feel competent.

*Relatedness* is about connection to other people. Here, teachers and teaching assistants can nurture their relationship with the children in their care by taking time to listen to the child's own concerns by being present with that child and by shifting the focus from control to connection. This might simply involve asking about a child's family and friends or sharing some information about the teacher's own life, which helps the child to see them as a person.

A school that focuses on content before connection is missing an opportunity to improve the quality of motivation and learning in its children, especially its square pegs.

Creating an environment that nurtures high-quality motivation isn't easy, particularly if you are used to implementing behavioural strategies. Behaviour strategies are easier. They don't require an adult to consider the internal world of the child. And, in the short term (useful for politicians and their appointees) they appear to be effective. However, there are many evidence-based reasons to be concerned about the effect of behavioural strategies on learning and, importantly, on the relationship to learning that children take into adulthood.

What is more, there are many examples of successful alternative school models that put children very much in the driving seat when it comes to choosing what and how to learn (Bernstein, 1968; Gray and Chanoff, 1986; Greenberg et al., 2005; Lucas, 2011). Not to mention a body of research on children educated at home, whose parents have chosen not to follow an enforced curriculum but instead have chosen to follow the children's interests – an approach often known as 'unschooling' (Gray and Riley, 2015; Riley and Gray, 2015; Arnall, 2018). Like their counterparts in self-directed schools, these children learn to read, acquire maths skills and go on to formal study when they choose to, typically as teenagers or young adults.

Talking of alternatives, let's go back to our square peg, Hayley:

Hayley's school and parents decided to take a different path, one that prioritises autonomy, competence and relatedness. Her parents stopped rewarding her for reading and instead sought out books on topics that interested her, even when they were too hard for her to read alone. This increased her sense of autonomy, as she herself chose her books, regardless of what anyone else thought. Her parents read them to her until she wanted to read them herself, and discussed the stories with her, showing that they valued her opinion and were not just focused on her 'age appropriate' reading ability.

Instead of writing her name on the board, her teacher instead asked Hayley how she thought she could get her work done in time, thus increasing her sense of collaboration with her teacher. Hayley's idea was that she would do her work using her 'special pen' and turn her desk towards the wall so she had fewer distractions. She also wanted to decide for herself how much she could do each day without being told she was too slow. It was agreed that Hayley would not lose her Golden Time, even if she did not complete her work. Being able to choose how she managed her work increased Hayley's feelings of competence and, as her self-esteem improved, she took more pride in her work and was able to finish more quickly.

Hayley is still a square peg, but the system has adapted to her.

# References

Alivernini, F. and Lucidi, F. (2011) Relationship Between Social Context, Self-Efficacy, Motivation, Academic Achievement, and Intention to Drop Out of High School: A Longitudinal Study, *Journal of Educational Research*, 104(4): 241–252.

Arnall, J. (2018) *Unschooling to University: Relationships Matter Most in a World Crammed with Information*. Calgary: Perfect Paperbacks.

Bernstein, E. (1968) Summerhill: A Follow-Up Study of its Students, *Journal of Humanistic Psychology*, 8(2): 123–136.

Coll, C. G., Bearer, E. L. and Lerner, R. (eds) (2004) *Nature and Nurture: The Complex Interplay of Genetic and Environmental Influences on Human Behaviour and Development*. London: Psychology Press.

Cunningham, I. (2020) *Self-Managed Learning and the New Educational Paradigm*. Abingdon and New York: Routledge.

Deci, E. L., Koestner, R. and Ryan, R. (2001) Extrinsic Rewards and Intrinsic Motivation in Education: Reconsidered Once Again, *Review of Educational Research*, 71(1): 1–27.

Deci, E. L., and Ryan, R. M. (1985) *Intrinsic Motivation and Self-Determination in Human Behavior*. New York: Plenum.

Dick, D. M. (2011) Gene-Environment Interaction in Psychological Traits and Disorder, *Annual Review of Clinical Psychology*, 7: 383–409.

Eliot, L. (2010) *Pink Brain, Blue Brain: How Small Differences Grow into Troublesome Gaps – And What We Can Do About It*. London: Oneworld.

Gray, P. (2013) *Free to Learn: Why Unleashing the Instinct to Play Will Make Our Children Happier, More Self-Reliant and Better Students for Life*. New York: Basic Books.

Gray, P. and Chanoff, D. (1986) Democratic Schooling: What Happens to Young People Who Have Charge of Their Own Education?, *American Journal of Education*, 94(2): 182–213.

Gray, P. and Riley, G. (2015) Grown Unschoolers' Evaluations of Their Unschooling Experiences: Report 1 on a Survey of 75 Unschooled Adults, *Other Education: The Journal of Educational Alternatives*, 4(2): 8–32.

Greenberg, D., Sadofsky, M. and Lempka, J. (2005) *The Pursuit of Happiness: The Lives of Sudbury Valley Alumni*. Framingham, MA: Sudbury Valley School Press.

Hannam, D. (2020) *Another Way is Possible: Becoming a Democratic Teacher in a State School*. Los Gatos, CA: Smashwords.

Kohn, A. (1999) *Punished by Rewards: The Trouble with Gold Stars, Incentive Plans, A's, Praise and Other Bribes*. Boston, MA: Houghton Mifflin.

Lepper, M., Greene, D. and Nisbett, R. (1973) Undermining Children's Intrinsic Interest with Extrinsic Reward: A Test of the 'Overjustification' Hypothesis, *Journal of Personality and Social Psychology*, 28(1): 129–137.

Lucas, H. (2011) *After Summerhill*. Bristol: Herbert Adler.

McGue, M. and Lykken, D. T. (1992) Genetic Influence on Risk of Divorce, *Psychological Science*, 3(6): 368–373.

Paschall, K. and Mastergeorge, A. (2015) A Review of 25 Years of Research in Bidirectionality in Parent–Child Relationships: An Examination of Methodological Approaches, *International Journal of Behavioral Development*, 40(5): 442–451.

Pink, D. (2018) *Drive: The Surprising Trust About What Motivates Us.* Edinburgh: Canongate Books.

Plomin, R. (2018) *Blueprint: How DNA Makes Us Who We Are.* London: Penguin.

Pulfrey, C., Buchs, C. and Butera, F. (2011) Why Grades Engender Performance-Avoidance Goals: The Mediating Role of Autonomous Motivation, *Journal of Educational Psychology*, 103(3): 683–700.

Pulfrey, C., Darnon, C. and Butera, F. (2013) Autonomy and Task Performance: Explaining the Impact of Grades on Intrinsic Motivation, *Journal of Educational Psychology*, 105(1): 39–57.

Rhodes, I. and Long, M. (2019) *Improving Behaviour in Schools: Guidance Report.* London: Education Endowment Foundation. Available at: https://educationendowmentfoundation.org.uk/public/files/Publications/Behaviour/EEF_Improving_behaviour_in_schools_Report.pdf.

Riley, G. and Gray, P. (2015) Grown Unschoolers' Experiences with Higher Education and Employment: Report II on a Survey of 75 Unschooled Adults, *Other Education: The Journal of Educational Alternatives*, 4(2): 33–53.

Ryan, R. M. and Deci, E. L. (2000) Self-Determination Theory and the Facilitation of Intrinsic Motivation, Social Development, and Well-Being, *American Psychologist*, 55: 68–78.

Ryan, R. M. and Deci, E. L. (2017) *Self-Determination Theory: Basic Psychological Needs in Motivation, Development, and Wellness.* New York: Guilford Press.

Seli, P., Wammes, J., Risko, E. and Smilek, D. (2016) On the Relation Between Motivation and Retention in Education Contexts: The Role of Intentional and Unintentional Mind Wandering, *Psychonomic Bulletin & Review*, 23(4): 1280–1287.

Skinner, B. F. (1963). Operant Behaviour, *American Psychologist*, 18(8): 503–515.

Susperreguy, M., Davis-Kean, P., Duckworth, K. and Chen, M. (2017) Self-Concept Predicts Academic Achievement Across Levels of the Achievement Distribution: Domain Specificity for Math and Reading, *Child Development*, 89(6): 2196–2214.

Tenenbaum, H. and Ruck, M. (2007) Are Teacher's Expectations Different for Racial Minority Than for European American Students? A Meta-Analysis, *Journal of Educational Psychology*, 99(2): 253–273.

Tokan, M. and Imakulata, M. M. (2019) The Effect of Motivation and Learning Behaviour on Student Achievement, *South African Journal of Education*, 39(1): 1–8.

van de Vegte, Y. J., Said, M. A., Rienstra, M., van der Harst, P. and Verweij, N. (2020) Genome-Wide Association Studies and Mendelian Randomization Analyses for Leisure Sedentary Behaviours, *Nature Communications*, 11, article 1770.

# Chapter 2

# SCHOOL ATTENDANCE PROBLEMS AND BARRIERS

## Beth Bodycote

---

Our poor boy. Yet, he kept on going … We kept sending him in, telling him he had no choice.

We shamefully and regrettably bowed to the pressure that was placed upon us from all those services that were there to 'help' … We ignored our parental instincts, ignored our intuition and placed pressure on Ben[1] to go to the place that caused him so much anguish.

We had daily morning, after-school, evening and night-time battles. We watched his behaviour deteriorate, his mental health suffer … We watched his spark go out … but still, we kept on pushing. Kids need to go to school, right? The school knows more than us parents, right? He has to go. I need to work, and we all need to pretend this is going to be okay.

So, that is what we did. We used raised voices, we used force, carrying him to the car on occasions, we used consequences, we withdrew privileges … in essence, we punished our son for being unwell. We helped to take him to that place where his world became very dark and scary. Where he could no longer leave the house, or later, even his room. We did that. We taught him that he couldn't trust those people called 'parents', the ones who are supposed to be there to care for you, love you, understand you and support you.

By now, the utter trust I had placed in the school to meet his needs had long gone. I had been the parent that 'accepted' they were doing all they could, the parent that sympathised with a school that had no money, that there were children with greater needs than Ben's. I even attended several parenting workshops that were suggested to me (because, of course, this was all about me and my parenting. And, no, the irony wasn't lost on me that, as a social worker, I had delivered many of these parenting courses to other parents). They didn't help. Of course, they didn't. It wasn't about my parenting. This was about my son being too anxious to attend school.

Ben is a square peg.

---

1   Not his real name.

This is the experience of one parent with a child who was 'not fine in school'. His school insisted that he was, and repeatedly refused to authorise his absences or provide the support he needed. There are many families facing the same predicament in schools across the UK and worldwide. Thousands of them are members of a peer support group called Not Fine in School (NFIS)[2], and some of them shared their experiences with me for my doctoral research.

## Not Fine in School

NFIS was created as a resource for families with children who experience school attendance problems and barriers (SAPB). A private Facebook group for parents lies at the heart of NFIS. In July 2022, it had nearly 30,000 members and was growing at a rate of around 1,000 new members a month. This is an active group with about 60% of members posting or commenting daily. NFIS surveys plus my PhD findings tell us that contact with peers who have lived experience offers by far the most effective source of support, advice and empowerment for parents.

## Researching parental experiences

My PhD study has investigated the experiences of 40 parents who are members of the NFIS Facebook group. Between them they have 29 sons and 18 daughters, all of whom have faced problems and barriers to attending school.

Either currently or previously, almost half of these 40 parents worked in roles and settings with relevance to school attendance (i.e. education, childcare, health, law, social work). I wondered if these parents might have different experiences in comparison to parents who had no 'insider' training, information, experience and contacts; however, it was clear that all parents reported the same issues and problems with locating support and advice. Moreover, all but one of those who worked in education changed career following their experiences of SAPB, citing disillusionment with current systemic issues and practices.

---

2   See www.notfineinschool.co.uk.

# School attendance problems and barriers

For over 100 years, 'school absenteeism' has been studied and understood following dominant clinical and scientific methods and perspectives. Consequently, it has been argued that psychologists and psychiatrists have conceptualised 'school attendance problems' (truancy, school withdrawal, and school refusal) using a medical model approach. This approach focuses on within-child and within-family factors, making links to behavioural, emotional, developmental or psychological issues (Pellegrini, 2007; Birioukov, 2016). Carlen et al. (1992: 62) concur with this argument, observing that terminology such as 'school phobia' and 'truancy' is based on a 'pathological model' that views non-attenders as 'either "mad" ("phobic" and therefore psychologically disturbed) or "bad" ("truant-delinquent" and therefore socially and morally disturbed)', or a third category, '"sad" or "truant as victim"'.

The contribution of more recent studies grounded in sociological and educationalist perspectives has promoted alternative discourses to compete with these clinical perspectives. These researchers argue that the long-standing dominance of clinical research has hindered a holistic understanding of the full context of SAPB. Instead, they have drawn attention to the role of environmental and systemic variables that create barriers to attendance. In 2003, Lauchlan recommended that a multi-disciplinary collaboration was necessary because no strategy had been suggested that was appropriate for all children experiencing SAPB. It was claimed that there had been an inclination to favour certain factors and theories over others: 'In the past, and even today, school-related factors were often played down and de-emphasised by school staff as playing a contributory role to pupils' non-attendance (Elliott and Place, 1998)' (Lauchlan, 2003: 138).

Moreover, Lauchlan argued that the functional approach (Kearney, 2007) to analysing 'school refusal behaviour' had prompted more recognition that schools need to accept some responsibility for children being fearful of attending. Indeed, some have suggested that school absenteeism should be considered a normal avoidance reaction to an unpleasant or even hostile environment (Pilkington and Piersel, 1991; Elliott, 1999; Harber, 2004; Davies and Lee, 2006; Lees, 2014).

It is notable that within the relevant literature, reference is frequently made to the detrimental effects of absence from school, linking it to impacts such as a lack of academic and career achievement, mental ill health and social difficulties. However, it is more rarely acknowledged that for some children and young people school attendance can be equally detrimental. These detrimental reasons for attendance include unmet special educational needs and disabilities (SEND) (House of Commons Education Committee, 2019), bullying (Ditch the Label, 2020), sexual harassment and assault (Lloyd et al., 2020; Girlguiding, 2021; Ofsted, 2021), unsupported physical health needs (No Isolation, 2020), unsupported mental health needs (Mind, 2021), inequality and oppression (Stuart and Walker, 2019) and the impact of strict behaviour policies, especially on students with SEND (IPSEA, 2021).

Significantly, there is a recognition of the importance of schools as places where children and young people need to feel a sense of belonging and a sense of safety in order to attend school without difficulty (Bacon and Kearney, 2020; Riley et al., 2020). In relation to school belonging and safety, Stroobant and Jones (2006) interviewed university students who had previously been 'school refusers'. Within their findings, they suggested that school refusal behaviour may be a perfectly rational response to a disturbing school environment. They argued that rather than the usual response of exploring why a child or young person is school refusing, a more relevant question should be: 'why assume that the child should want to attend school?' (Stroobant and Jones, 2006: 2013).

Exploring the perspective of young people who are non-attenders, Davies and Lee (2006) acknowledge that rather than being a problem for the student, non-attendance is a solution to a problem. They argue that the problem of non-attendance exists for schools, local authorities and the political community. Davies and Lee (2006: 208) approached their research by standing back from the assumption that 'non-attendance is a problem'; they viewed the young people involved as 'self-withdrawers' who 'offer a critique of the school and the system and solve their personal problems by refusal to engage'. They suggested that this self-withdrawal is evidence of a contractual breakdown. The contract being one where the young person attends and complies at school, and in return the school offers 'a safe environment, meaningful and relevant learning, opportunities for association with friends, and dignified and respectful treatment' (2006: 208); the contractual breakdown therefore occurs when a young person does not feel safe, protected, respected or dignified.

More recent perspectives have also challenged where, and how, the problem of absence from school is sited and constructed. Reflecting the perspective offered by Davies and Lee (2006), Knage (2021) suggests that although we frame school absence as the problem, it may not be the absence from school that is problematic. Instead, depending on how a child is engaged while not in school, it is possible they could still be benefiting from learning opportunities and gaining an education elsewhere. Therefore, querying this assumption that absence from school is detrimental, Knage (2021: 12) suggests that 'Absence is not the problem itself, it may only be the sign of one. And sometimes it is actually just we the adults that have a problem with children not being in school.'

Similarly, Frydenlund (2021) argues that absence from school is not the true problem we need to resolve, even though it has been constructed as problematic through its supposedly causal link to other concerns. Frydenlund suggests that this is faulty logic; instead, it is the way people respond to a child being absent from school that creates the negative impacts of school absence. Therefore, he suggests, 'we need to take a closer look at the consequences we make absence have' (2021: 9).

The consequences we force on absent children and their families are evidenced through my own research and the daily interactions that occur within the NFIS groups. These outcomes reflect the beliefs and attitudes towards non-attendance that have developed within society through a process of normalisation and habitualisation (Berger and Luckmann, 1991 [1966]), and in response to over a century of political, clinical and educationalist discourses aimed at control, obedience and punishment for non-compliance (Lawson and Silver, 1973; Carlen et al., 1992; Rose, 2004; Giddens and Sutton, 2017; Kohn, 2018; Fisher, 2021).

## Parental responsibility for school attendance

Put simply, parents have been assigned a legal duty to ensure their children receive a full-time, suitable education through attendance at school or otherwise.[3] If parents decide to enrol a child in a mainstream school, they must then ensure that their child attends all timetabled sessions, unless they are unwell or satisfy one of the other legally acceptable reasons for absence. Head teachers now have the discretion to decide whether the reason provided by a parent for an absence is acceptable and therefore authorised or unacceptable and unauthorised. In effect, this places a legal duty on parents to seek to resolve any attendance problems that occur, and their efficacy in doing so is judged by those around them. If they are considered to be failing in this duty, they are at risk of punitive action through the use of fines and prosecution under criminal law, with the possibility of up to three months in prison and a criminal record.

However, Sheppard (2011) discusses the lack of published evidence indicating that young people's attendance improves after parents are prosecuted for their non-attendance. She observes: 'There is an irony here, in that services are increasingly encouraged to show that their interventions are evidence-based, yet the legislation itself takes no account of the evidence and there is no attempt to seek it' (Sheppard, 2011: 244).

Criticism of the systemic response to school absence was reinforced by Epstein et al. (2019), who conducted a study entitled *Prosecuting Parents for Truancy: Who Pays the Price?* The report aimed to explore the reasons behind children's school absence, the problems experienced by families and parents' views about schools' responses. The findings were critical of systemic support, with parents stating that schools did not understand the difficulties their child faced or fully understand how to be inclusive. It

---

3   See section 7 of the Education Act 1996: http://www.legislation.gov.uk/ukpga/1996/56/section/7.

was noted that SEND discrimination happens repeatedly through sanctions and behaviour management strategies. The impact of shortages of resources was highlighted, with a particular concern being delays accessing support from child and adolescent mental health services (CAMHS). The researchers concluded:

> It is evident that the punitive approach leads to harm for parents, children and vulnerable families. It also appears to be ineffective in getting reluctant and fearful children back into the classroom. The current law is cruel and discriminatory and does not achieve its purpose of reducing the number of children who do not attend school regularly. (Epstein et al., 2019: 5)

## Are all parents of school-absent children guilty of condoning truancy?

School absenteeism has been conceptualised differently over time through the different perspectives of researchers and stakeholders (Lauchlan, 2003; Pellegrini, 2007; Birioukov, 2016). These conceptualisations have carried with them various evaluations of parental motivations and influence. Examples include absence 'due to parental neglect' (Hiatt, 1915: 7), truancy influenced by the 'unwitting and even wilful encouragement of the parents' (Broadwin, 1932: 253) and the influence of 'socially deviant parents who do not accept their responsibilities' (Berg et al., 1978: 447). Warren (1948: 266) observed that 'a neurotic and adoring mother is a common figure in the background', and Hersov (1960: 144) suggested that fathers are most often 'inadequate and passive'. Tyerman (1968: 76) stated that 'any interested parent who wants their child to go to school regularly will rarely have any difficulty over attendance'. Each of these examples demonstrate how clinicians have tended to pathologise parental involvement.

Although the systemic response to SAPB has consistently featured legislation based on this social construction of truancy, I would argue that not all parents fit the commonly held 'parent of a truant' stereotype. This categorisation commonly holds that parents of children who are absent from school have a negative view of education and are disinterested in resolving their children's absence (Heyne et al., 2019). However, it has also been established that the majority of parents do recognise the value of education and the importance of school attendance (Dalziel and Henthorne, 2005).

The literature features a more nuanced consideration of the different types of SAPB. Here, subgroups of parents have been noted who make reasonable efforts to resolve absence from school (Berg, 2002; Heyne et al., 2019), try everything to help their child but are frustrated and feel let down by the 'system' (Reid, 2002) and who try to work in partnership with professionals and services (Dalziel and Henthorne, 2005). These parental subgroups, apparent in my NFIS respondents, have rarely been acknowledged within dominant discourses, which focus on truancy and assumptions that the children and parents are to blame. Such a nuanced approach illuminates what I have called the parents' journeys through SAPB.

## Parents' journeys through SAPB

Overall, the parents' journeys reflect their experience of seeking a resolution for SAPB, in parallel with the predicament of attempting to manage a range of conflicting legal duties, practical dilemmas, emotional reactions and empowering influences. These journeys were described in four contexts, beginning with the parents responding to emerging SAPB, then navigating the systemic context, while also managing the home context. The journey is concluded as parents work towards identifying the most suitable resolution.

## 1. Responding to emerging SAPB

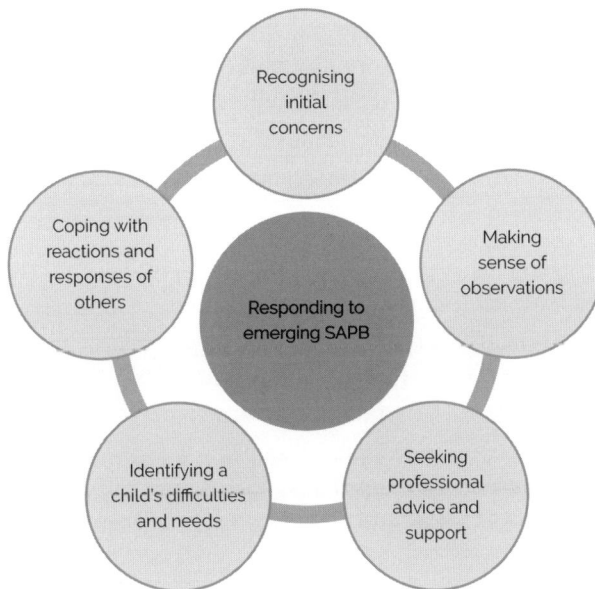

Figure 2.1. Responding to emerging school attendance problems and barriers

The beginning of the journey relates to the early development of the SAPB and describes how the predicament begins to develop. Here, as shown in Figure 2.1, parents recognise initial concerns around attendance and undertake complex interpretations and assessments of children's difficulties to help them identify and understand any underlying triggers or causes. When difficulties continue or increase, parents respond by raising their concerns with frontline professionals (most commonly a teacher and/or GP), hoping to obtain advice and arrange appropriate support for their child's ongoing difficulties.

## Seeking professional advice and support

My findings indicated that parents reported having concerns about 40 of the 47 children prior to the start of the SAPB. Fifteen parents had acted on these concerns about their child's behaviour or development before they were of school age. However, when difficulties then began at school and parents tried to share their concerns with the school, they reported that staff dismissed those concerns, insisting that their children were 'fine in school'. NFIS group surveys also suggest that these difficulties often start at primary or even nursery age.[4]

The study also found that 17 children first experienced attendance difficulties at primary school, while 24 children didn't experience attendance difficulties until secondary school. Again, in most cases, parental concerns were dismissed (with school staff again often responding by saying the child was 'fine in school'). Alternatively, concerns were acknowledged yet went unsupported with no further response. In cases where it was clear that a different setting may be needed, systemic issues meant that no suitable provision was made available for those children. This dismissal of concern and lack of support means that the journey into non-attendance often starts from an unhelpful place.

This is especially worrying at primary level as the research suggests that an effective resolution is easier to achieve if children have access to early help (Kearney and Graczyk, 2014), and that the longer SAPB go unsupported, the more entrenched the child's absence becomes. Without early and effective intervention there can be less chance of a successful return to school (Ingul et al., 2019). In the absence of these interventions, and with the professional dismissal of legitimate concerns, it is not surprising that parents learn early on that they will have to fight to have these concerns acknowledged and to arrange help and support for their child.

---

4   See https://notfineinschool.co.uk/nfis-surveys for NFIS Parent Survey Results from May 2018 and March 2020.

# Identifying a child's difficulties and needs

The factors that influence attendance difficulties are many and complex. The current lack of a widely available effective, comprehensive and triangulated screening tool is a further barrier to early and effective identification of needs, triggers and appropriate responses.[5] The parents who took part in my study attributed their children's SAPB to a range of triggers and influences, summarised as follows:

- **School environments.** Four children were reported to have experienced bullying, while 25 parents attributed their child's difficulties, in part, to the school environment/climate/ethos. Five children's SAPB were linked to the transition between primary and secondary school.

- **Diagnosed mental health difficulties.** Three children gained a diagnosis of depression, 14 children were diagnosed with an anxiety disorder and five children experienced difficulties as a result of traumatic experiences.

- **Special educational needs and disabilities.** Of the 47 children who featured within parents' accounts, 40 had a SEND that had been diagnosed prior to, or during, the period of time described in parental accounts. These diagnoses included everything from pathological demand avoidance to avoidant/restrictive food intake disorder, mutism and having been identified as gifted and talented. A further seven children were awaiting diagnostic assessments for suspected SEND issues.

- **Autism.** Three-quarters of parents (30 out of 40) expressed concerns about autism either as a suspected or diagnosed influence on their child's difficulties in attending school. Four were already diagnosed and four were awaiting diagnosis, but the majority of parents (13) had tried to raise concerns about a possible link to autism, and all had their concerns dismissed by school staff.[6] Only one child was suspected to be autistic and supported in school without a diagnosis.

- **Physical illness.** Fourteen children had experienced physical illness that affected their ability to attend school, including asthma, cystic fibrosis, migraine, continence issues, heavy and painful periods, irritable bowel syndrome, postural orthostatic tachycardia syndrome, Ehlers-Danlos syndrome, hypermobile joints, cerebral palsy, trigeminal neuralgia and chronic fatigue syndrome.

---

5   The School Non-Attendance CheckList or SNACK (https://www.insa.network/resources/questionnaires) and the School Refusal Assessment Scale-Revised (https://www.insa.network/images/Davids_uploads/SNACK_English_with_extra_Covid_item_08-03-2021.pdf) are tools developed by academics, but tend not to be widely used and fail to adequately recognise the impact of school culture and environment.
6   All 13 children went on to receive an autism diagnosis eventually – 10 through the NHS and three through private assessment. Three parents suspected autism traits but had not sought assessments.

# 2. Navigating the systemic context

Figure 2.2. Navigating the systemic context

The core experiences within parents' journeys relate to their ability to access support through the education system, plus any relevant health and local government services (Figure 2.2). These experiences also relate to repercussions affecting the family and home, such as problems with fulfilling employment commitments, financial impacts, and changes and damage to family relationships.

The responses and reactions displayed by professionals, family and friends were central to the development of each parent's journey in terms of both its complexity and emotional impact. One key aspect of the developing predicament related to the parent trying to ensure there was a shared understanding of their child's needs, along with recognition that their child had a valid and significant difficulty with school attendance. Another important aspect related to the family struggling to manage the developing predicament and being in genuine need of advice and systemic support as a result.

## School-based responses

Positive experiences within the education system were mentioned by only five of the 40 parents (12.5%). These positive experiences reflected schools which offered help and support at an early stage. It was empowering if help was provided by professionals who were knowledgeable about SAPB, SEND, mental and physical health needs, navigating policy and legislation, and working in partnership with families and health/local authority services. Children were empowered by being allowed some control within the situation, so they had the flexibility to make small steps of progress with minimal pressure. To facilitate this, schools needed to manage their expectations around attendance data and policies with one-size-fits-all expectations.

The majority of parents in the study described negative school-based experiences, which included a lack of empathy, compassion and interest in assisting parents. Responses were mostly critical, punitive and hostile, and parents reported a general feeling of indifference to their child's situation. The dominant attitude was that children should be forced or coerced to attend,[7] so they could be marked as attending. This included the use of restraint, threats of fines and telling already anxious children that their parents would be sent to prison if they did not attend.

## NHS-based responses

Parents either consulted their GP first or turned to their GP after experiencing a negative response from the school. Participants reported an equal number of negative and positive GP/NHS experiences. With regard to CAMHS, there were three times the number of negative experiences noted than positive. Positive support was offered by NHS professionals who recognised that the child and family needed help, and then went on to advocate for families to source further support. Negative experiences within the NHS mostly related to staff with unhelpful and obstructive attitudes and approaches.

## Local authority responses

There was a single mention of a positive experience with local authority staff or services. Otherwise, parents described their frustration and anger at the lack of support, communication failures and the deliberately obstructive tactics used by local authorities to avoid or delay arranging and funding provision for children. Local authorities regularly failed to follow relevant legislation (e.g. section 19 of the Education Act 1996), which should ensure that any child who is unable to access an education is offered appropriate support or alternative provision.

---

7   Parents were asked in the NFIS surveys about their experience of being pressured to force children to attend school, and the majority admitted they had used force at some point. Significantly, parents also reported that when they had used force, it had rarely helped to resolve the problem and often made things much worse.

## Working relationships

The relationship between professionals and families was central to the progress made in parents' journeys. This was especially significant in schools, as the site of children's difficulties and therefore the focus of interventions. It was crucial for parents and schools to work in partnership to identify and overcome the barriers that were stopping each child from attending. The success or failure of these working relationships depended on the beliefs, reactions and approaches implemented by those involved. The list below sets out the features of professional responses that contributed towards a positive working relationship with families.

- Willingness to listen to family concerns.
- Respecting a parent's knowledge of their child.
- Demonstrating empathy for the child.
- Recognising the limits in their own knowledge.
- Respecting medical practitioner input.
- Consideration that the child may be masking their difficulties.
- Avoiding making assumptions.
- Understanding of attendance difficulties.
- Offering support for mental/physical health.
- Demonstrating knowledge of SEND.
- Following legislation relating to SEND/attendance.
- Prioritising the child's wellbeing.
- Arranging SEND support via an education, health and care plan (EHCP) when needed.
- Providing school work at home (to prevent extra anxiety about catching up).
- Resolving bullying issues effectively.
- Referring to social services for support if needed.
- Referral by CAMHS leading to assessments.
- Referral by CAMHS leading to appropriate support.
- Local authority complying with education otherwise than at school legislation.
- Local authority complying with SEND Code of Practice (2014).
- Working in partnership and co-production with families.
- Effective and reliable communication.

The importance of co-production is discussed in more detail in Chapter 7.

## 3. Managing the home context

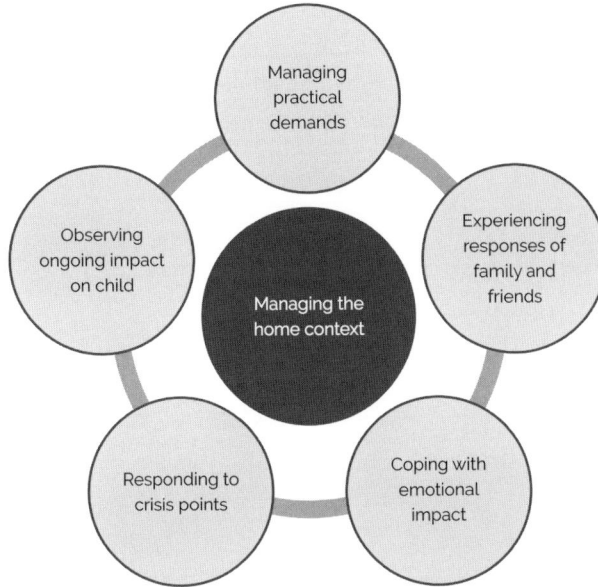

Figure 2.3. Managing the home context

Parents' accounts indicated that the impact on all members of the immediate family was often significant (Figure 2.3). Family relationships were negatively impacted by the daily stress and disruption to routines. Parents expressed sadness and frustration at needing to reduce working hours or give up jobs and careers if the SAPB were not resolved through early intervention. This led to financial losses along with the additional costs involved in seeking help. The situation was often made more difficult by the reactions of other people in the families' social circles, who sometimes made critical or judgemental comments.

As the complexity of identifying triggers or needs and sourcing appropriate support meant that each family's SAPB took many months or years to reach any sort of resolution or conclusion, their circumstances evolved over time (and may continue to evolve in the future). Educational provision often altered as different strategies or types of provision were organised and tried. Children may have attended school with difficulty or been on roll at a school with reduced or no attendance; they may have been home educated or accessed alternative provision. If a child was unwell, mentally or physically, their symptoms may have improved or worsened as circumstances changed. Parents noted their concern for their children and the ongoing impact of this evolving journey – for example, one parent explained: 'As a mum it's been hell. It's been harder than anything I've ever faced in my life, including life-threatening illness. Watching your beautiful, enthusiastic, funny, clever and creative child deteriorate in front of your eyes over a period of time is absolutely heartbreaking.'

Observations such as this indicated how profound the mental and physical changes were in the children. The positive aspects of their personality seemed to diminish and their behaviour often changed radically. It was very clear how the wide range of experiences throughout the journey also had a significant emotional impact on parents, triggering a variety of feelings including isolation, anger, guilt and judgement, with frustration an overarching theme.

# 4. Working towards a resolution

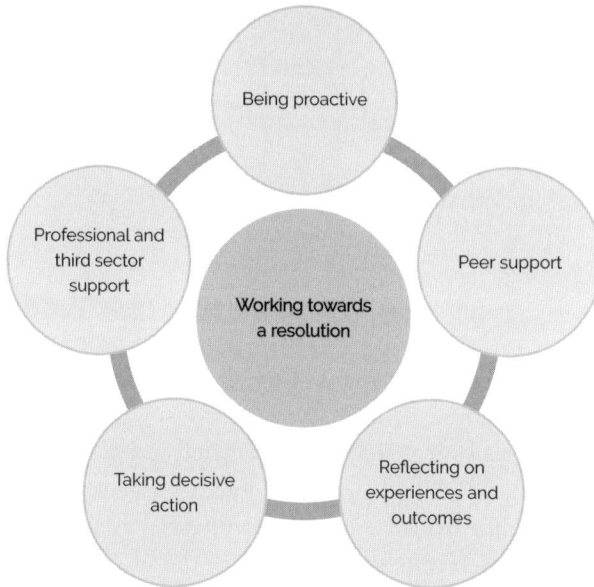

Figure 2.4. Working towards a resolution

This aspect of parents' journeys reflects the impact that the various experiences have on the child and their family, and how these experiences combine to influence the resolution of the SAPB. As indicated in Figure 2.4, the peak of parents' predicament often evolved as they observed further or additional concerns related to their child's health and wellbeing, combined with the ongoing effects of any family-based consequences, crisis points or changes in priorities, plus the emotional impact and any elements of empowerment they had experienced. The overall combined effect of these elements influenced the decisions they took regarding the best way to resolve the SAPB to the benefit of child and family.

## Taking decisive action

When families experienced a build-up of difficulties and concerns, they reached a point where they needed to evaluate their priorities and take decisions and actions to protect the wellbeing of their child, establish the most suitable means available of facilitating an education, and reduce levels of stress within the family home. Parents' accounts featured instances where they experienced a range of factors that contributed to a growing feeling of empowerment. This enabled families to gain a better understanding of their situation, and identify the options they had if school attendance continued to be problematic.

They gained a feeling of control from becoming proactive in sourcing information and increasing their knowledge of relevant factors; gaining access to support from peers, helpful professionals and charities; recognising changes in family priorities; and taking account of children's opinions. The combined influence of observing ongoing impacts on the family, recognising systemic failure, and gaining knowledge about alternative options and the lived experience of others often influenced families to reach a place of resolution.

The following factors influenced this decision-making process:

- Acceptance that a child was genuinely unable to attend a school at that time.
- Acceptance that appropriate help was not available and an ongoing fight for help would be too damaging to child and family, *or* appreciating any help and support that was provided.
- Recognising that prioritising the child's health and wellbeing was in their best interests.
- Deciding to reject the pressure to physically or emotionally coerce a child to attend school.
- Deciding to stop prioritising compliance with cultural expectations over their child's needs.
- Focusing on educational alternatives to mainstream school.
- Changing their thinking and beliefs about mainstream schooling.
- Accepting that academic success is not the only way to become successful and happy as an adult, and that academic success can be achieved outside mainstream schooling.
- Prioritising wellbeing on days when anxiety levels were too high.
- Prioritising a child's emotional wellbeing over their own wellbeing as parents.

- Needing to prioritise factors such as family finances or individual needs.
- Respecting whether the child wants to return to school or has a different preference.

## Outcomes

Within the time period of the study, the outcomes reported for the 47 children were as follows:

- One child returned to their mainstream school and re-established a normal pattern of attendance. (He spent some time at home, too unwell to attend. Then, over an 18-month period, he made tiny steps of progress. The focus was on him feeling safe and in control. He then spent a further six months in a medical needs unit, taking further small steps of progress towards a return to mainstream school.)
- Seven children remained enrolled at mainstream school with reduced/low levels of attendance.
- Six children had a place in a SEND school, arranged through an EHCP.
- Five children were being educated through alternative provision, such as home tuition, online school or hospital school.
- Seven children were being home educated.
- Thirteen children were not able to access any type of educational provision.
- Eight children had reached the age of 16 (of those, four had gone on to college, two were being home educated while taking A levels and two were too unwell to be involved in any educational activity).

Therefore, it is clear that parents eventually achieve a range of outcomes for their children's school attendance problems. Some of these outcomes are sited within the education system, while others reflect a rejection of systemic provision or a failure in systemic support.

So, what can you do to improve things for your students and their families?

- **Listen to parents' concerns and co-produce with them.** Never just assume that a child is 'fine' even if your staff have not noticed any problems in school. If parents are reporting difficulties with attendance, they will have genuine concerns that you need to respond to with respect and an open mind.
- **Absence due to physical and/or mental illness should be authorised.** Families need support rather than counterproductive threats of fines or prosecution. The

legal implications of unauthorised absences will only add to a child's anxiety and substantially increase the difficulties families face, especially given the long waiting times and high thresholds for referrals to NHS specialists.

- **Support mental health issues in children and young people.** The government recommends that schools develop a mental health policy that establishes an environment where young people with anxiety feel supported, understood and able to seek help. This is likely to make them feel safer and more able to attend school.

- **Understand and acknowledge the complexities of this issue.** Recognise the practical and emotional consequences for children and their families.

- **Conduct assessments for SEND.** Many children have an underlying SEND that contributes to their difficulties, which can also include social, emotional or mental health difficulties. This may affect a child's ability to establish friendships and cope with a variety of strong emotions; it may also increase a child's vulnerability to bullying. Remember your duty to use best endeavours and make reasonable adjustments according to the Equality Act 2010.

- **Apply for an EHCP assessment.** An EHCP application is crucial if a school does not have the expertise or funding to fully identify a child's needs or to offer the provision or support a child requires to access an effective education. Parents can also make an application to the local authority for an ECHP assessment, but a joint approach will be the most beneficial way forward.

- **Support referrals to CAMHS and other healthcare professionals.** Where significant health problems occur, schools should facilitate a student's access to more specialist support, including paediatricians, occupational therapy, and speech and language therapy. Unfortunately, long wait times for referrals can compound the problem, but support from schools goes a long way in ensuring that students gain access to necessary treatment.

- **Take action if bullying or sexual assault are reported to you.** There are legal duties on schools and local authorities to safeguard and promote the welfare of children. School anti-bullying policies should set out the actions that will be taken to prevent or address bullying. Ofsted (2021) has produced peer sexual violence guidance for schools and colleges.

- **Provide homework and connections while the student is absent.** Not supplying learning opportunities during absence means a student gets further behind, adding to their anxieties around returning to school. A school's duty to educate does not stop because a student is absent due to illness, SEND (diagnosed or not) or bullying. Schools should notify the local authority if absence due to illness lasts over 15 days (consecutive or cumulative). The local authority then has a duty to ensure that a child receives alternative educational provision while absent (under section 19 of the Education Act 1996).

- **Collaborate to create a child-led support plan.** It is important to ensure that children, their parents and health professionals participate as fully as possible in developing support plans that are flexible, child-led and individualised. Plans must be communicated to all staff and combined with relevant staff training and whole-school awareness. If children struggle to engage, they need patience and an experienced professional to help them access the right support.

- **Be prepared to experiment.** What works for one child won't work for another.

- **Readjust your priorities.** No child will learn when in permanent distress. Always put their emotional wellbeing and mental health first.

- **Reflect on your school culture and ethos.** To what extent is your school a place of safety and belonging for all children, regardless of the personal difficulties they may be facing?

- **Review your attendance policies.** Consider how realistic, inclusive and effective those policies are in supporting and encouraging children who genuinely struggle with attendance. Consider how you promote and reward attendance too, without penalising those who cannot attend.

- **Examine your absence codes.** My survey findings suggest that the code most commonly applied by schools when a child's mental and/or physical health difficulties impacted on their ability to attend school was 'O' (other) unauthorised absence. Yet, there are 23 absence codes suggested by the Department for Education for use in schools, and the appropriate code in this situation is 'I' (illness), which is an authorised absence. Note that in this instance parents can find themselves in a catch-22 situation, with schools asking for specific medical evidence before they will authorise ongoing absences and most GPs reluctant to write a letter stating the child is 'unable to attend school'.[8]

My research gave a voice and legitimacy to the parents in my study as they struggled to achieve what any parent wants – the best for their children. I hope that school leaders reading this chapter will feel encouraged and empowered to support parents in that same battle.

---

8   This suggests that schools doubt the word of parents, further weakening trust and relationships. In fact, the Department for Education advise schools to request medical evidence only if they question the authenticity of the illness reported by parents:

   If the authenticity of illness is in doubt, schools can request parents to provide medical evidence to support illness.

   Schools can record the absence as unauthorised if not satisfied of the authenticity of the illness but should advise parents of their intention. Schools are advised not to request medical evidence unnecessarily. Medical evidence can take the form of prescriptions, appointment cards, etc. rather than doctors' notes (Department for Education, 2022a: 14).

   Note that new guidance will apply from the academic year starting in September 2022 (see Department for Education, 2022b).

# References

Bacon, V. R. and Kearney, C. A. (2020) School Climate and Student-Based Contextual Learning Factors as Predictors of School Absenteeism Severity at Multiple Levels via CHAID Analysis, *Child and Youth Services Review*, 118, article 105452. doi:10.1016/j.childyouth.2020.105452

Berg, I. (2002) School Avoidance, School Phobia, and Truancy. In M. Lewis (ed.), *Child and Adolescent Psychiatry: A Comprehensive Textbook*, 3rd edn. Sydney: Lippincott Williams & Wilkins, pp. 1260–1266.

Berg, I., Butler, A., Hullin, R., Smith, R. and Tyrer, S. (1978) Features of Children Taken to Juvenile Court for Failure to Attend School, *Psychological Medicine*, 8: 447–453. doi:10.1017/S0033291700016123

Berger, P. and Luckmann, T. (1991 [1966]) *The Social Construction of Reality: A Treatise in the Sociology of Knowledge*. London: Penguin.

Birioukov, A. (2016) Beyond the Excused/Unexcused Absence Binary: Classifying Absenteeism Through a Voluntary/Involuntary Absence Framework, *Educational Review*, 68(3): 340–357. doi:10.1080/00131911.2015.1090400

Broadwin, I. T. (1932) A Contribution to the Study of Truancy, *American Journal of Orthopsychiatry*, 2(3): 253–259. doi:10.1111/j.1939-0025.1932.tb05183.x

Carlen, P., Gleeson, D. and Wardhaugh, J. (1992) *Truancy: The Politics of Compulsory Schooling*. Milton Keynes: Open University Press.

Davies, J. D. and Lee, J. (2006) To Attend or Not To Attend? Why Some Students Choose School and Others Reject It, *Support for Learning*, 21(4): 204–209. doi:10.1111/j.1467-9604.2006.00433.x

Dalziel, K. and Henthorne, D. (2005) *Parents'/Carers' Attitudes Towards School Attendance*. Research Report RR61. Nottingham: Department for Education and Skills. Available at: https://dera.ioe.ac.uk/5548/1/RR618.pdf.

Department for Education (2022a) *School Attendance: Guidance for Maintained Schools, Academies, Independent Schools and Local Authorities* (May). Available at: https://www.gov.uk/government/publications/school-attendance.

Department for Education (2022b) *Working Together to Improve School Attendance Guidance for Maintained Schools, Academies, Independent Schools, and Local Authorities* (May; applies from September). Available at: https://www.gov.uk/government/publications/working-together-to-improve-school-attendance.

Department for Education and Department of Health and Social Care (2014) *Special Educational Needs and Disability Code of Practice: 0 to 25 Years* (11 June; updated 30 April 2020). Available at: https://www.gov.uk/government/publications/send-code-of-practice-0-to-25.

Ditch the Label (2020) *The Annual Bullying Report 2020: The Annual Benchmark of Bullying in the United Kingdom, with an Additional Focus on Mental Wellbeing*. Available at: https://www.ditchthelabel.org/wp-content/uploads/2020/11/The-Annual-Bullying-Survey-2020-2.pdf.

Elliott, J. G. (1999) School Refusal: Issues of Conceptualisation, Assessment and Treatment, *Journal of Child Psychology & Psychiatry*, 40(7): 1001–1012.

Elliott, J. G. and Place, M. (1998) *Children in Difficulty: A Guide to Understanding and Helping*. Abingdon and New York: Routledge.

Epstein, R., Brown, G. and O'Flynn, S. (2019) *Prosecuting Parents for Truancy: Who Pays the Price?* Coventry: University of Coventry. Available at: http://covrj.uk/wp-content/uploads/2019/01/PROSECUTINGParents.pdf.

Frydenlund, J. H. (2021) How an Empty Chair at School Becomes an Empty Claim: A Discussion of Absence from School and Its Causality, *Scandinavian Journal of Educational Research*, 66(4): 658–671. doi:10.1080/00313831.2021.1897883

Fisher, N. (2021) *Changing Our Minds: How Children Can Take Control of Their Own Learning.* London: Robinson.

Giddens, A. and Sutton, P. W. (2017) *Essential Concepts in Sociology*, 2nd edn. Cambridge: Polity Press.

Girlguiding (2021) *Research Briefing: It Happens All the Time. Girls' and Young Women's Experiences of Sexual Harassment.* Available at: https://www.girlguiding.org.uk/globalassets/docs-and-resources/research-and-campaigns/girlguiding-research-briefing_girls-experiences-of-sexual-harassment_june2021.pdf.

Harber, C. (2004) *Schooling As Violence: How Schools Harm Pupils and Societies.* London: RoutledgeFalmer.

Hersov, L. A. (1960) Refusal to go to School, *Child Psychology and Psychiatry*, 1: 137–145. doi:10.1111/j.1469-7610.1960.tb01988.x

Heyne, D., Gren-Landell, M., Melvin, G. and Gentle-Genitty, C. (2019) Differentiation Between School Attendance Problems: Why and How?, *Cognitive and Behavioral Practice*, 26(1): 8–34. doi:10.1016/j.cbpra.2018.03.006

Hiatt, J. S. (1915) The Truant Problem and the Parental School, *Bulletin of the Bureau of Education*, 29: 7–35. Available at: https://eric.ed.gov/?id=ED541858.

House of Commons Committee of Public Accounts (2020) *Support for Children with Special Educational Needs and Disabilities: First Report of Session 2019–21.* HC 85. Available at: https://committees.parliament.uk/publications/941/documents/7292/default.

House of Commons Education Committee (2019) *A Ten-Year Plan for School and College Funding: Tenth Report of Session 2017–19.* HC 969. Available at: https://publications.parliament.uk/pa/cm201719/cmselect/cmeduc/969/969.pdf.

Ingul, J. M., Havik, T. and Heyne, D. (2019) Emerging School Refusal: A School-Based Framework for Identifying Early Signs and Risk Factors, *Cognitive and Behavioral Practice*, 26(1): 46–62. doi:10.1016/j.cbpra.2018.03.005

Independent Provider of Special Education Advice (IPSEA) (2021) Our Response to the Government's 'Call For Evidence' on Behaviour Management in Schools [press release] (7 September). Available at: https://www.ipsea.org.uk/news/our-response-to-the-governments-call-for-evidence-on-behaviour-management-in-schools.

Kearney, C. A. (2007) Forms and Functions of School Refusal Behaviour in Youth: An Empirical Analysis of Absenteeism Severity, *Journal of Child Psychology & Psychiatry*, 48(1): 53–61.

Kearney, C. A. and Graczyk, P. (2014) A Response to Intervention Model to Promote School Attendance and Decrease School Absenteeism, *Child and Youth Care Forum*, 43(1): 1–25. doi:10.1007/s10566-013-9222-1

Kohn, A. (2018) *Punished by Rewards: The Trouble with Gold Stars, Incentive Plans, A's, Praise and Other Bribes*, 3rd edn. Boston, MA: Houghton Mifflin.

Knage, F. S. (2021) Beyond the School Refusal/Truancy Binary: Engaging with the Complexities of Extended School Non-Attendance, *International Studies in Sociology of Education*. doi:10.1080/09620214.2021.1966827

Lauchlan, F. (2003) Responding to Chronic Non-Attendance: A Review of Intervention Approaches, *Educational Psychology in Practice*, 19: 133–146. doi:10.1080/02667360303236

Lawson, J. and Silver, H. (1973) *A Social History of Education in England*. London: Methuen.

Lees, H. E. (2014) *Education Without Schools: Discovering Alternatives*. Bristol: Policy Press.

Lloyd, J., Walker, J. and Bradbury, V. (2020) *Beyond Referrals. Harmful Sexual Behaviour in Schools: A Briefing on the Findings, Implications and Resources for Schools and Multi-Agency Partners*. Luton: University of Bedfordshire. Available at: https://uobrep.openrepository.com/bitstream/handle/10547/625043/Beyond-Referrals-Two-Harmful-Sexual-Behaviour-in-Schools.pdf.

Mind (2021) *Not Making the Grade: Why Our Approach to Mental Health at Secondary School is Failing Young People*. Available at: https://www.mind.org.uk/media/8852/not-making-the-grade.pdf.

No Isolation (2020) *The Invisible Children: Serious Illness, Prolonged School Absence and Long-Term Impact*. Available at: https://www.noisolation.com/research/the-invisible-children.

Ofsted (2021) Review of Sexual Abuse in Schools and Colleges (June). Available at: https://www.gov.uk/government/publications/review-of-sexual-abuse-in-schools-and-colleges/review-of-sexual-abuse-in-schools-and-colleges.

Pellegrini, D. W. (2007) School Non-Attendance: Definitions, Meanings, Responses, Interventions, *Educational Psychology in Practice*, 23(1): 63–177.

Pilkington, C. L. and Piersel, W. C. (1991) School Phobia: A Critical Analysis of the Separation Anxiety Theory and an Alternative Conceptualization, *Psychology in the Schools*, 28(4): 290–303. doi:10.1002/1520-6807(199110)28:4<290::AID-PITS2310280403>3.0.CO;2-K

Reid, K. (2002) *Truancy: Short and Long-Term Solutions*. Abingdon and New York: Routledge.

Riley, K., Coates, M. and Allen, T. (2020) *Place and Belonging in School: Why It Matters*. London: National Education Union.

Rose, N. (2004) *Powers of Freedom: Reframing Political Thought*. Cambridge: Cambridge University Press.

Sheppard, A. (2011) The Non-Sense of Raising School Attendance, *Emotional & Behavioural Difficulties*, 16(3): 239–247.

Stroobant, E. and Jones, A. (2006) School Refuser Child Identities, *Discourse: Studies in the Cultural Politics of Education*, 27(2): 209–223.

Stuart, K. and Walker, S. (2019) 'Great Expectations' in the UK Education System, *Journal of Youth Voices in Education: Methods Theory Practice*, 1(1): 3–13.

Tyerman, M. J. (1968) *Truancy*. London: University of London Press.

Warren, W. (1948) Acute Neurotic Breakdown in Children with Refusal to go to School, *Archives of Disease in Childhood*, 23(116): 266–72. doi: 10.1136/adc.23.116.266

# Chapter 3

# A TALE OF THREE FAMILIES

## Tom Quilter

## 1. The Peters Family

Mr and Mrs Peters have a son called Shaun. They love their son and, like most parents, want the best for him. Shaun is 14 years old and has always found following the behaviour policy in school a challenge. He struggles to concentrate and stay at his desk like other students. Shaun is a square peg.

Shaun's behaviour is a challenge to many – but not all – of his teachers, especially Mr Trimble. Mr Trimble has been teaching for 20 years and, like most teachers, wants nothing more than to see all his students succeed. He worries that Shaun's behaviour will impact on the education of the other students. When he tells Shaun to sit down, it makes it worse, as Shaun ignores him, fidgets, stares out of the window and talks to the other students who are trying to concentrate.

Mr Trimble knows how fragile teacher authority is and knows that by ignoring his requests and demands, Shaun is undermining that authority. If it keeps going this way, he will lose control of the whole class and then everyone will suffer.

Ultimately, Mr Trimble uses the evidence and justification he has to ensure that Shaun is awarded a fixed-term exclusion for 'persistent, disruptive behaviour'. The school is very clear that any student breaking its behaviour policy will be treated in this way – they are to be taught a lesson.

When the news is broken to Mr and Mrs Peters they are angry. This is now the sixth time they have been called into school to be told about their son's behaviour. The second they enter the head teacher's office they make their feelings known through their body language and, when they speak, their verbal language. They feel that Mr Trimble is targeting Shaun for the sake of better grades for the rest of the class at Shaun's expense. They are sitting opposite Mr Trimble who is angry with them for being angry with him, when he is simply trying to do what is right for his class: 'After all, Mr and Mrs Peters, I've tried my best for Shaun. I've let him get away with a great deal and given him every chance, but I do have another 30 or so students to think about.'

And now his parents are making it seem like *he* is the one with the problem – in front of the school's head teacher, Mrs Hunter, who is in charge of his appraisal.

Mrs Hunter is looking between both parties from the head of the table. Like all head teachers, she wants what is best for her school and is desperate to find a solution. She knows that she must protect her staff, she knows how badly the school will suffer if another teacher goes on long-term sick leave and she knows that an Ofsted inspection is imminent. She wonders, out loud, whether Shaun might be better educated at home, and that this could be done instead of an exclusion that would end up on his record and affect his life chances. She knows she isn't allowed to pressure someone into home education, but it does seem like the best solution for all.

# 2. The Bashir Family

Mr and Mrs Bashir have a daughter called Leila. They love their daughter and, like most parents, want the best for her. Leila is 12 years old and has an education, health and care plan for her profound and multiple learning disabilities. The plan says she needs routine and structure along with sensory activities such as music therapy. Leila is a square peg.

At a recent annual review, it came to light that the local music therapist from whom the school has previously brought in services has been on long-term sick leave and they haven't been able to find someone to cover at the same cost. Therefore, Leila has not been receiving these sensory activities. Mr and Mrs Bashir are furious. At a meeting in the office of the head teacher, Mr Donaldson, they say that it's the same old story, just like when they fought to have sensory activities included in the plan in the first place. They ask why it always comes down to money.

Mr Donaldson knows they have a point, but he is stuck between a rock and a hard place:'After all, Mr and Mrs Bashir, how do you expect me to get blood from a stone? I do have another 90 or so students to think about.'

But it wasn't just about the money, as the school had known that finding a sensory specialist in their rural area was always going to be a challenge. Since their one local therapist went on long-term sick leave, their only option would have been to bring in a new one from miles away for an hour a day for just one child and at a cost greater than the funding they were receiving from the local authority to cover this service. He had held back this information as he knew, legally, that the school had to provide what was written in the plan. Mr Donaldson was really hoping that things would sort themselves out before anyone noticed.

# 3. The O'Malley Family

My third family, the O'Malleys – just like the Peters and Bashir families – are not real, but everything I have described is. The O'Malleys' son was a square peg, and his parents, when I took on their case, were described to me as 'difficult'. They made complaints about many of my colleagues, copied MPs into their emails and used all the tools at their disposal to challenge the decisions that went against them.

When I was assigned to work with them, my first visit was not without a little trepidation. Over those initial few months, I was expecting to hear that a complaint had been made against me every time I said no to a request. During those meetings, I was at pains to explain how the system worked, how resources were distributed and how places were allocated on a needs-led basis, so they could understand and appreciate the balance between need, services and resources.

A year after my first meeting with the indomitable O'Malley family – a year in which we had carefully and deliberately built a positive working relationship – I was sitting in the kitchen with Mrs O'Malley, sharing a pot of tea as we pulled together a reassessment plan for her son. She asked me a question – I can't even remember what the question was – to which I had responded honestly, 'I don't know.'

'That's why you've been the only person we've trusted enough to stick with,' Mrs O'Malley replied. 'You admit when you don't know something or when you're wrong. So, we trust that when you say you do know, you really do. We believe that you're being honest and that you don't have an agenda.'

Her reply has stayed with me, and is one of the keys to fundamentally improving the special educational needs and disabilities (SEND) system, one that doesn't require a magic wand or a blank cheque. It's a cultural shift. A shift towards relationships with all those involved that are honest, open and transparent. The system may pull and push us – all of us – and rather than fight it, we end up fighting each other. But we all want what is best for the child, despite our different agendas.

Take the Peters family. They arrived angry, but what the school didn't know, because it didn't ask, was why. In fact, before they had even arrived, they were already stressed as a result of having to take even more time off work (this was the sixth meeting, if you remember). Mrs Peters' phone had been buzzing with calls from angry clients she had cancelled that day, and Mr Peters was fuming from the fight he'd had with his wife on the way to the meeting about who would stay home with Shaun if he was excluded.

Most of all, they feel they are not being listened to. They want everyone to understand that Shaun is not being intentionally bad; he just can't sit still for long and has never been able to. Shaun is not being listened to either. He hadn't even been allowed to attend the meetings, despite the important decisions being taken about him. So, even though it will mean a loss of much-needed income from taking time off work again, they feel they have to be there as they are the only ones sticking up for their son. It's them against the majority, and they are damned if they will stand by and let Shaun take the hit. What kind of parent lets their child suffer for the benefit of others?

And what about the Bashir family? What the school didn't know, because it didn't ask, was that Leila had not been sleeping well over the last three months. As a result, Mr Bashir had needed to leave his job, so he could stay up all night with Leila who has no sense of danger. They are under financial pressures now and may even lose their house if they can't keep up the payments.

They had been waiting for a social care assessment for some time, but it hadn't been forthcoming due to capacity issues in the social care team. And now they finally get why Leila hasn't been sleeping! It's because she hasn't been having the sensory activities in school that help her to relax. If they had known, they would have done it themselves at home.

How different might these meetings have gone if a better, more honest, working relationship had been built? For Shaun, if there was a less adversarial relationship between the parents and the teacher, then through that communication they may have seen a pattern in his behaviour – how it was much worse at the beginnings and ends of lessons. If someone had asked Shaun what it felt like when he wasn't sitting down, he might be able, to some degree, to explain the heightened anxiety he felt at those particular times.

If an objective for a meeting, early on (not the sixth) had been to recognise and understand Shaun's rights (not just his responsibilities) and the legal duties of the school, and to empower all parties with this information, then perhaps a calmer conversation could have been taken place, based on exclusion guidance and the need to assess a child's needs as early as possible and before an exclusion is considered. In the real example this story was based on, Shaun was later diagnosed with attention deficit hyperactivity disorder and autism, which went at least some of the way to explaining why he found transitions between activities and classes difficult. He accessed SEND support and an agreement was made between Shaun and his teachers that he was allowed to leave each class five minutes early to arrive, calmly and without disturbing others, at his next lesson five minutes ahead of time and have the chance to settle before the class started.

Unfortunately, the diagnosis and subsequent adaptions all happened at the new school his parents moved him to after the first one took the impactful decision to exclude him. It took Shaun, his parents and his new teachers a lot of time and energy to build a trusting relationship, but it was worth it.

In the real-world example of the Bashir family, the relationship between them and the school was rebuilt, without the need to involve appeals or move schools. Once the school came clean about the problem, the family understood and, between them, an alternative was worked out in which one of the school's teaching assistants underwent training in sensory play activities as a stopgap until more formal provision was re-established.

This is not to say that all breakdowns in school placements, in educational outcomes or attainment for children and young people with SEND should be blamed on the school, college or professionals not building relationships with those with whom they are working. Many do, and do this well. But it is to say that things for all could be hugely improved by a cultural shift away from a closed, adversarial relationship, and towards one where all parties work together to challenge the system through whatever legal, financial and creative means a committed group of people can come up with together.

Creativity is key here to find the cracks in the system to make things happen – a 'where there's a will, there's a way' mentality. It will often take a whole team to support a single family, but sometimes it takes just one person. A 'champion' who can stand up when something is wrong to make sure families and individuals know their legal rights, along with the responsibilities of the services they meet, and who can help them to get the support they need to respectfully but strongly challenge those services, if necessary. Someone who can lead the way in encouraging all parties to be creative in the face of what might look like insurmountable obstacles.[1]

Flexibility is vital too. To be too rigid about every detail and every situation can cause more problems than it solves. When James, who has social, emotional and mental health needs, is feeling too anxious to concentrate, it may be reasonable to agree that he can put his hand up and ask for a time out. For Debbie, who has severe autism and communicates non-verbally, it may be unreasonable to expect this of her. So, any policy that says all students must put their hand up if they need a time out is doomed to fail. All you can do is ask every professional to consider what works and is 'reasonable' for that individual.[2]

And, as seen in my examples above, honesty is at the heart of building effective working relationships too. When you don't know, say so. When you are under external pressures, explain them, without hiding behind them or being patronising. When you get it wrong, say so. And apologise. Ask for honesty in return and listen without judgement when it is given, even if it is hard to take. It's not about egos, quick wins or ticking boxes. It's much more important than that.

We all want what is best for our square pegs. As do the square pegs themselves. Through a creative, flexible and honest approach where all parties – including the child – have a voice and are heard, we can build the relationships that ensure effective collaboration.

---

1   After all, think about how creative we all had to be in the face of the ongoing lockdowns during the COVID-19 pandemic, doing our best to ensure every child received the best education they could at that time.
2   In section 20 of the Equality Act 2010, 'reasonable' is characterised as what a reasonable person would reasonably do (see https://www.legislation.gov.uk/ukpga/2010/15/part/2/chapter/2/crossheading/adjustments-for-disabled-persons). I know …

# Chapter 4

# THE BIG POWER OF LITTLE THINGS

## Ginny Bootman

In my first year of teaching, I realised the difference I had made, as PE coordinator, to a family when a child gave me an end-of-year present. It was a whistle with my name engraved on it as a thank you for the support I had given to help them feel more comfortable at school. And do you know what I had done for that child? I had simply photocopied all his work onto A3 paper because he had fine motor difficulties, and that simple act had made his time at school so much more enjoyable. I understood then that it is the little things that can make the biggest difference, and now, over 25 years later, I still stand by that. Whatever we do, it is never too small to a child. Especially if that child is a square peg.

Early in my career, I really didn't understand the reasons why any child could be experiencing so much trouble fitting into school, even to the point of choosing not to go. I felt that it wasn't part of my remit to ask. I left it to senior leaders. They dealt with it, and I did as I was told. Thinking back, I compartmentalised my role, and I see now that this is so often the case. Job descriptions, siloed training, personal preferences, time constraints and more all conspire to allow us to pass the buck to someone else. I have actually heard someone say, 'That's not on my pay scale,' when asked to perform a task to help a child. For me, back then, I simply saw supporting struggling children as somebody else's remit. In this way, I acted as an observer, not as a facilitator, in the lives of children who needed more.

Now, as a former teacher and head teacher, and the current special educational needs coordinator across four primary schools, I have experienced many instances of children who, for many reasons, struggle or 'fail' to attend school. For example, I have even been an outreach teacher for a child with medical needs as a one-to-one tutor and successfully reintegrated them back into school through a well-thought-out plan. In this way, and through liaising with parents and outside agencies, I have come to understand far better the reasons why individuals have barriers to their learning and their attendance at school, and I know that no one need be just an observer in such cases. We all have our part to play. After all, understanding a child and what makes them tick has got to be the most important part of our job.

Fortunately, we are not alone in this endeavour.

When a child has an unmet need, it is an unmet need for the whole family. Where there is a lack of triangulation between the child, their school and the carers involved, there is going to be confusion and inconsistency. Connection – genuine, open, honest and empathetic – is key.

When working with families, the unmet need can provoke some strong emotions, and I have seen plenty of anger and tears from the individuals involved – child and adult. As professionals, we need the emotional intelligence to see past this, to not take it personally, to not disengage when it starts to feel threatening or uncomfortable, and to resolve to do all we can to unpick the unmet need in others. After all, when emotions run high, what we are really experiencing is another human being saying, 'Help me, I'm struggling.'

I had a child in my class who was very disengaged. He did not perceive school as a safe place for him. I employed all the strategies I had in my toolkit, and we saw improvement through lots of hard work and giving him plenty of time. However, there was a disconnect between school and home, which was brought about by the many differences in approach between the two most significant places in the child's life. It is so difficult to put in place effective long-term strategies when the two most frequented places in a child's life do not share the same values. It took a lot of time, meetings and mutual understanding to address this disconnect, but we got there finally. Especially pernicious was that the parents had been coming from a place of 'Been there, tried that, good luck to you!' – and understandably so, given all they had gone through – and we needed to show them that our suggestions would work before they invested their time and emotional energy in something else.

I say 'understandably' as many parents and carers will already feel like the system has let them down and failed to address their unmet needs before they even get to you. This means they may arrive at your doorstep weary, frustrated and up for a fight. Who can blame them? It is only when they see for themselves that we are all on the same side that connection can take place, not before. All too often, my first meeting with a parent involves the emotional unpacking of previous failures and frustrations. Parents need to be encouraged to do this unpacking and to be given a safe, non-judgemental and empathetic (that word again) space to do it in. Only when this has happened, and we all know where we stand, can we move on. In a first meeting I once had, the parents told me how they had been promised an education, health and care plan for their child but, despite meeting after meeting, it never materialised. It was like the lift in *Dirty Dancing* that never came. Now, as they had come to me, those parents needed to know that we had the strength to do the lift, and to do it well.

Honest and open conversations about unmet needs will also serve to reveal the veracity – or otherwise – of the information the parent or carer believes. Now, that is an interesting one to unpick. There are children who, perhaps wanting to please their parents or get their teachers into trouble, will feed information to them about the school which is factually incorrect. When this happens it's a real spoiler for positive home–school links. I have had examples when a child has said that other children are picking on them, but after monitoring by staff it turned out to be untrue. However, rather than writing off this line of enquiry as a dead end, we need to ask ourselves if stopping bullying is not the unmet need, then what is? It is imperative to look closely into anything a child says to discover what is actually happening, because only then, when home and school both share the true picture, can we do something about it, together. Until this happens, there is going to be conflict.

## With whom do we need to build connection?

As educators, we need to build connection with all those involved with the children in our care – children, parents, teachers and senior leadership team (including the busy head teacher) as well as outside agencies. And notice that I refer to 'building connection'. It is about more than just linking up, attending a meeting or two, or cc'ing someone in an email. Well-built connections entail trust, reciprocity and a mutual desire to collaborate and do whatever it takes to achieve the sought-after outcome. Connection is something that is earned. Once earned, it allows us to challenge our peers professionally, even when it is uncomfortable and even if it involves hearing that our behaviours may be the cause of the problem. As Maynard and Weinstein (2019: 23) state in *Hacking School Discipline*: 'Staff should be able to openly discuss how adult behaviour affects student interactions.'

Trust builds up over time. Once it is firmly established, parents begin to let their barriers down and let us into their world, and then we can truly start that journey together to help the child. It is built by being honest and open, by not shying away from those tricky conversations but by talking them through.

Trust lasts through the highs and lows too, which is just as well, because even with trust and connection in place, no one is guaranteed a happy ending. I remember once that we had all worked together to apply for funding for a child who was very much a square peg. We had done all we could, as well as we could, and now it was a waiting game. One lunchtime, my head teacher approached me carrying a box of Maltesers. By the look on her face, I knew why she hadn't chosen a box of Celebrations. This was commiseration confectionery. Apart from my own disappointment in the outcome, I now faced the added anxiety of having to tell the parents that we had failed, that I had let them down, and to do so without losing their trust for the other battles that lay ahead. As I broke the news to them, their response showed me that, despite the outcome, our approach had been a success. 'If I had been in any other school,' the mother started, 'I would be banging my fist on this table, telling you that you had let my child down. But as it is, you just need to tell me what door we need to bang on together next to get this funding through.'

That response remains in my mind so clearly and makes me emotional even now. Our togetherness and connection were strong enough to get us through a major disappointment, a setback that only served to further strengthen that connection. And do you know what? We did get the funding the next time we applied.

Notice, by the way, my use of the word 'we'. As schools, connection needs to be from everyone and with everyone. We are working as one team to support that child. Get T-shirts made if it helps!

Once you have the precious trust of the parent, a major part of your role is to become an interface between their world and the alien world of systems, agencies, committees and forms. The simplest thing you can do here is to talk them through it all – what is going to happen, why and what next.

Another personal example (after 25 years I have many) to illustrate the point: I was preparing for a joint meeting with a parent and a number of outside agencies when the mother involved asked me if we could have a 'pre-meeting meeting'. She was feeling really nervous, she didn't want to 'get it wrong' and, above all, she didn't want any surprises. We had the pre-meeting meeting, during which we agreed that if she needed any support or help, then, with her permission, I would speak on her behalf. Oh my goodness, you should have seen her at the meeting. She was on fire. She was articulate, putting her points across brilliantly and persuasively, with me simply and virtually holding her hand. She didn't need me to speak for her. She just needed to know that I was there if needed. This experience shows the power of trust and connection that can be built up between home and school.

On other occasions, I am the one speaking up for parents, carers and children (with their permission). Educational talk can be confusing, so my role is often as an interface between home and school, to help others see things from a different perspective in order to get to a solution that works well for everyone.

Another role of the home/system interface person (i.e. you) is to help parents, who understandably want a result 'now', to see that things take time. We will get there but they need to be patient. This is especially true when applying for funding or getting outside agencies involved. By explaining the system, parents better understand the processes involved. It is when we don't take the time to explain the system that this lack of understanding can cause a breakdown in communication and connection.

Of course, this flattening of the hierarchy, as I call it, applies just as much to the children for whom we are fighting. We need to build connection and trust with them too. In this way, we can work to do things *with* them, not *to* them or *for* them.

I remember a child I taught once who trusted no one. She would always push staff away because she had been let down so many times before in her life. Why would anything be different now? Her rejection of adults could be physical as well as verbal. It was a case of getting her retaliation in first: if she rejected the adults in her life, she got there before they could reject her.

To build trust in circumstances like these, I was signposted to the work of Kim Golding (Golding et al., 2021) and Dan Hughes (2006) and have since used the celebrated PACE approach.[1] It was a whole new strategy which appealed to me because of its simplicity and ability to connect with, not blame, others. PACE stands for playfulness, acceptance, curiosity and empathy, and it is an approach that lessens the individual's feelings of being judged and brings about an understanding of the individual child through shared understanding and direct discussion with that child.

One of the first times I employed PACE was with a boy who had 'inadvertently' thrown a ball at another boy's head during playtime. Before I could even begin to challenge him (another example of getting his retaliation in first), he blurted out to me, 'Go on then, shout at me, like they all do. I'm used to it. Let's just get it over with.' However, when I spoke with him and he explained what had actually happened and could see I was listening and not judging, his shoulders – and hackles – went down. I made sure I found out what his likes and dislikes were and would subsequently ask him about them when I saw him in the corridor. Again, these small actions provoked a significant enough change in his demeanour for other members of staff to comment on it. That playfulness, acceptance, curiosity and empathy paved the way for true connection.

A lot has happened since I was presented with that whistle. There have been many changes in the nature of the school system and the agencies involved in supporting children, including our square pegs, to access it to the full. But one thing remains the same: little things can make a big difference.

# References

Golding, K. S., Phillips, S. and Bombèr, L. M. (2021) *Working with Relational Trauma in Schools: An Educator's Guide to Using Dyadic Developmental Practice*. London: Jessica Kingsley.

Hughes, D. A. (2006) *Building the Bonds of Attachment: Awakening Love in Deeply Troubled Children*. Northvale, NJ: Aronson.

Maynard, N. and Weinstein. B. (2019) *Hacking School Discipline: 9 Ways to Create a Culture of Empathy and Responsibility Using Restorative Care*. Highland Heights, OH: Times 10 Publications.

---

1  See Chapter 34 for more on PACE.

# Chapter 5

# WHAT CAN I TELL YOU?

## William Carter

I had many things going on during my school years. I was dyslexic, dyspraxic and autistic,[1] a young carer for my mum and had a complex home life. Because of our situation, my aunt and grandmother were key figures in my life and we were effectively one large family unit. I am also mixed race (British/African), something that many students will tell you makes a difference. It shouldn't, but it does. Yet, for much of my school life, there were few staff who fully understood my circumstances. Many made assumptions, but few took the time to learn the reality.

I was a square peg.

The cry 'We're all individuals!' sounds like a cliché, a joke even, yet nowhere is it more important for this to be taken seriously than at school. Your blanket rules don't work here, not for us. Your lack of flexibility may suit you, but it harms us. If you believe in equality, then you have to embrace flexibility. If you think school should be fair to all, then it needs to adapt to all. Some of us need you more than others, and your stretched resources need to be weighted in favour of those whom, from the start, have so much weighted against them.

In short, a standardised system will never be an equal one. Consistency is the enemy of fairness. Equality of opportunity means that *you* must do the work to adapt, not *us*. Where to start?

## You can't fill children's minds if their stomachs are empty

I was eligible for free school meals. In my school, this meant we had the option of breakfasts and, if we were staying after school for extra tuition, snacks. Good nutrition and a stomach that isn't rumbling are such important foundations for learning. Given the government's focus on post-pandemic lost learning and catch-up (Newton, 2021),

---

1   The later diagnoses of autism and attention deficit hyperactivity disorder were delayed until the second year of my undergraduate studies at the University of Bristol.

it amazes me why this isn't an integral part of national policy, let alone why Marcus Rashford has had such a battle to get those in power to do their job (Weale and Adams, 2020), and why so many great schools have had to step in and feed their children from overstretched budgets.

When I was at school, I was initially only offered a snack on Mondays for my English catch-up session but not, for some reason, on Thursdays during maths catch-up. I was fortunate that my teachers subsequently recognised the difference in energy – and then did something about it.

# Use pupil premium funding to fuel our passions, not your results

Creative outlets that tap into a child's individual talents and passions are vital,[2] all the more so for a child who struggles in our increasingly rigid, overly academic education system. I believe that money invested in nurturing the talents of 'disruptive' children would serve to keep them in school – and keep them learning – saving the inevitable spend further down the line on alternative provision or addressing potential subsequent criminality.

At my school, we were each offered half of our pupil premium money (then £250 a year) to select an educational activity or course of our choosing. I chose Debating Camp and it was life-changing. It not only taught me how to debate constructively, but it also gave me confidence and social tools. Since that time, I have spoken at European Youth Events, at the Parliamentary Assembly of the Council of Europe and European Parliament, at high-level conferences around the world and at the closing plenary of the first ever Commonwealth Parliamentarians Forum at the Houses of Parliament in London.

Another example of how these relatively small amounts can be transformational features one of my closest friends, who was in trouble all the time but who had a passion for music. The school paid him (yes, paid him!) to undertake a special music education course that would enable him to use his passion to pursue a music career. His motivation was both the money (why not?!) and, more importantly, the job that he could see himself doing in the future. He now plays the drums professionally as a touring musician and teaches drumming in schools.

Yet another friend was subsidised to visit the United Nations in Geneva. He developed his passion for international politics that led him to study politics at Oxford. Pupil premium students like me were also given laptops in Year 13 to prepare us for

---

2   See Article 29 of the United Nations Convention on the Rights of the Child: https://www.unicef.org.uk/what-we-do/un-convention-child-rights.

our A levels and to ensure that we subsequently had access to a computer at university.

## You can't 'do' values unless you teach rights

We all know why posters featuring 'British values' have been appearing in our schools since November 2014, even in early years settings (see Department for Education and Lord Nash, 2014). But if democracy is one of these values, then I suggest that it should also appear in the set-up and running of our schools, so that it really comes alive. Equally, the values of liberty and respect need to be shown to all students for them to live beyond the posters on the walls. And if we have posters about values, we also need posters about human rights and children's rights, as well as posters that offer practical support, such as the phone numbers for Childline[3] or national domestic abuse charities.

I remember my citizenship lessons well. Our teachers made us question human rights legislation in every lesson – for example, drawing comparisons between collective, whole-class, punishment and war crimes. On one occasion, the teacher walked into the classroom and ordered us to 'Be quiet!' and then threatened to punish us *all* if even one student made a noise. When there was absolute silence, the teacher pointed out that it was against our human rights for us to be ordered to be quiet, as collective punishment for individual crimes is actually an infringement of international law. They also empowered us to question the moral dilemmas inherent in the school's behaviour policies; policies that would not be supported in any other 'working' environment.

I wonder what might change if we introduced a national charter of children's rights in schools,[4] one that was widely publicised and put up next to the British values poster in every classroom?

## We need to reconsider our policies on rules

There is a difference between policies and rules. One is a set of guidelines that exists for good reason. It is, hopefully, co-produced (doing 'with' those involved) and has buy-in from all those it affects.[5] The other is enforced (doing 'to') and exploits the power imbalance in education. This imbalance can be particularly problematic for square pegs like me. When we receive the message, 'I'm the adult and you're the child,

---

3   It is 0800 1111.
4   See UNICEF's Rights Respecting Schools Award: https://www.unicef.org.uk/rights-respecting-schools.
5   Find out more about co-production and what it means in Chapter 7.

so you'll do as I say,' backed up by the non-explanation, 'Because I say so,' this can light a fuse. You see, at home as a young carer for my mum, I was the one who was the adult. We need to be so careful with the language we use.

We also need to be careful that we separate behaviour from character. I was often late, but just because I was late, it doesn't mean I was bad.

If the rule says 'A letter is sent home for lateness', even when the reasons for that lateness are known, then the rule is the problem.

# Save streaming for Netflix

I have a particular aversion to streaming. I was in the bottom set for every subject from primary school right up until my GCSE years, yet I finished school with the highest number of A*s they had ever had and went on to achieve a first-class degree at Bristol University. Schools are invited to university open days, but because it's usually only the top students who are picked to go, those in lower sets are rarely given the opportunity. A case in point: my academic record meant I wasn't chosen to go on a universities trip to the United States, but here I am, a Fulbright scholar at the University of California, Berkeley – the number one public university in the world.

The problem with streaming is threefold. Firstly, it isn't about academic streaming, it's about separating academic students from those with challenging behaviour. Secondly, the best teachers end up teaching the top sets when, in reality, it's the students struggling in the bottom sets that most need those teachers. Thirdly, if you tell a child they aren't good at something, they will live up to the label and eventually give up. I read avidly now using my text-to-speech software, but none of my teachers would believe me if I told them, since it was almost impossible to make me read back then. I had come to hate it because my dyslexia made so many subjects unbelievably hard, but now that I have the right support, my love of reading has flourished.

Of course, there are more issues to consider when we do support struggling students. I found that once I achieved 'pass' grades, support was taken away from me. In this way, 'just good enough to pass' becomes the marker of success and a sign that a school has done enough to feel good about itself. But who defines success, and is good enough actually enough? One student's success might be very different to another's, and that is okay. The most important thing is to identify what success means *on an individual basis* and do everything you can to help a student fulfil those goals.

# School can be something we escape to, not from

Many students, particularly those like me who had caring responsibilities at home, value the opportunity to use spaces like the school library to get their homework done or simply escape. Our school had an open-door policy for all students on Saturdays, between 10am and 2pm. Students could bring in a sibling and meals were available using pupil premium funding. When we stayed late for extra tutoring, not only did we get a snack (even eventually in maths), but some staff would ensure that younger siblings from other schools could also stay later.

At one point, it felt like half the school was staying until 5pm, taking advantage of all the after-school activities on offer, with the majority of the exam year students coming in on Saturdays and at half-term. This not only kept us out of trouble, but it also provided much-needed – and free – childcare for many families.

Although much of the school had to be shut down at some point, due to cleaning and safeguarding issues, the school made sure that the conference rooms next to the reception and school entrances were open. You had students staying there until 7pm and even 11pm close to exam seasons – Monday to Sunday. It was made clear, even in the earlier secondary years, that the school's facilities were designed for students, and it was for the school to put the effort in and make it work. Just opening up conference rooms to offer people a place to study or read past normal operating hours, and then making sure a staff member can call home or call the student to make sure they got home safely, can make such a difference in the lives of young people.

# Scared learners are not good learners

I had so many obstacles that got in the way of school. One I remember vividly was the gangs that often hung out on street corners on the way home. If I wanted to stay late in the winter months, for sport or extra tutoring, I would spend most of that time worrying about my walk home. The school understood this – let me repeat, my school *understood* this – and laid on minibuses to local transport hubs, so that students like me could benefit from all school had to offer *and* get home safely.

Another example of the understanding, creativity and action I witnessed was in the case of a Year 7 student who was being badly bullied during their first term at school. When this started to impact on his attendance, as well it might, the school helped him to get a bicycle, take a cycling proficiency course and then let him leave five minutes early each day. That simple gesture allowed him to avoid the bullies, and his attendance shot back up again.[6] Putting in a system whereby the front and back school gates were used at different times by different age groups also helped to avoid much of the older-students-intimidating-younger-students behaviour too.

## All work and no play

When our AS levels were done, Wednesday afternoons became about sport or creativity. Lesson time was set aside for non-academic activities that didn't fit the 'knowledge-rich' curriculum. Students were given the freedom to choose what they wanted to do (and staff learned not to make demands of, or resolve issues with, a child who was already adrenaline-fuelled through sport or play; as we know, the neuroscience tells us that they are unable to process demands then anyway[7]).

The great thing about finding a time in the curriculum for such freedoms is the way it offers solutions for the mental health problems that come from internalising difficulties, as well as the behaviour problems that come from externalising them. The ability to run out your anger or take yourself away to a calm space are vital coping strategies. Yet, too many behaviour management policies turn to isolation booths rather than calm, reflective spaces. There is a reason why isolation has been banned in New York prisons (Closson, 2021) – it isn't good for your mental health!

So, there you have it: what I can tell you to help you help the square pegs in your school. Be flexible. Mould the school to the child. Know what fairness and equality – and the rights that go with it – really mean. And help your square pegs to discover the passion that reveals to them – and those around them – just what they are really capable of. And know that for dyslexic kids, the difference between a life of underemployment, unemployment or even imprisonment could be the provision of a laptop, a Dictaphone or an audiobook.

If we are honest in our desire to make schools reflect the professional workplace, then let's be clear that workplaces have a statutory responsibility to ensure open access, accessibility and a disability-friendly environment.

Instead of trying to inspire our dyslexic/dyspraxic/autistic young people with stories of neurodiverse students who have beaten the odds and are now achieving great things, why don't we try to reduce the odds against them, so that it isn't the few who make it but the many. Let's stop aggrandising struggle and, instead, focus on eliminating barriers.

---

6    I am not suggesting we ignore bullying and simply work around it, but in this case, it was a quick-win solution that gave him a much-needed feeling of emotional safety and bought time for the bullying to be addressed.

7    See more on this in Chapter 27.

Maybe then, when you next tell students that some of the most amazing business people, creatives and scientists have a learning difference, young people will believe in themselves – and not feel guilty about their own educational experience of being a square peg squeezed into a round hole.

And if you take away anything, remember this! If students are to stay in school later or on the weekends as part of a 'catch-up' strategy, make sure they are fed, that any siblings are taken care of and – more than anything else – make sure they can get home safely and with confidence. And if you genuinely want that child to succeed, particularly if they are a young carer, then send them home with some food too, so they don't have to stay up even later, cooking for a family member.

I went from being a student who couldn't read or write properly at 13 to a first-class politics student, a Fulbright scholar and PhD student at 23. It wasn't my motivation that changed – it was access.[8]

# References

Closson, T. (2021) New York Will End Long-Term Solitary Confinement in Prisons and Jails, *New York Times* (1 April). Available at: https://www.nytimes.com/2021/04/01/nyregion/solitary-confinement-restricted.html.

Department for Education and Lord Nash (2014) Guidance on Promoting British Values in Schools [press release]. Available at: https://www.gov.uk/government/news/guidance-on-promoting-british-values-in-schools-published.

Newton, P. E. (2021) Learning During the Pandemic: Quantifying Lost Learning (12 July). Available at: https://www.gov.uk/government/publications/learning-during-the-pandemic/learning-during-the-pandemic-quantifying-lost-time--2.

Weale, S. and Adams, R. (2020) Marcus Rashford in 'Despair' As MPs Reject Free School Meal Plan, *The Guardian* (21 October). Available at: https://www.theguardian.com/education/2020/oct/21/marcus-rashford-in-despair-as-mps-reject-free-school-meal-plan.

---

8   If you want to learn more about my journey and views, check out my interview on Ian Wright's *Everyday Heroes* podcast (https://podcasts.apple.com/gb/podcast/dyslexia-breaking-educational-barriers/id1549385121?i=1000521211585) or my interview on ITV's *This Morning* entitled 'Boy Who Overcame Severe Dyslexia Now Studying for a PhD' (https://www.youtube.com/watch?v=KLnUjgM7Pvk).

# Chapter 6

# MASLOW, RELATIONSHIPS AND SQUARE PEGS

## Maddi Popoola and Sarah Sivers

---

*Education must develop every child's personality, talents and abilities to the full.*

Article 29, United Nations Convention on the Rights of the Child (1989)

---

As educational psychologists, it is our job to help those young people who, even before the COVID-19 pandemic, were struggling with the four Ds – disadvantage, dissatisfaction, disconnection and dissociation. There have always been such children and there always will be; they are our square pegs. As educators, it's our job to celebrate them too. These children inspire us to be innovative, flexible and, most importantly, inclusive in all education settings. They also encourage us to consider and question the wider system in which we all operate and the way such a system and all its component parts interact to support or hold back these children.

In short, we can learn a great deal from our square pegs.

## The hierarchy of needs

A core part of our job as educational psychologists is gaining the views of children and young people and finding out what life is really like for them. For example, during the pandemic we carried out surveys to explore the experience of this particularly different and difficult time (Popoola and Sivers, 2021), mapping the themes from nearly 3,000 respondents directly onto Maslow's hierarchy of needs (see Figure 6.1).

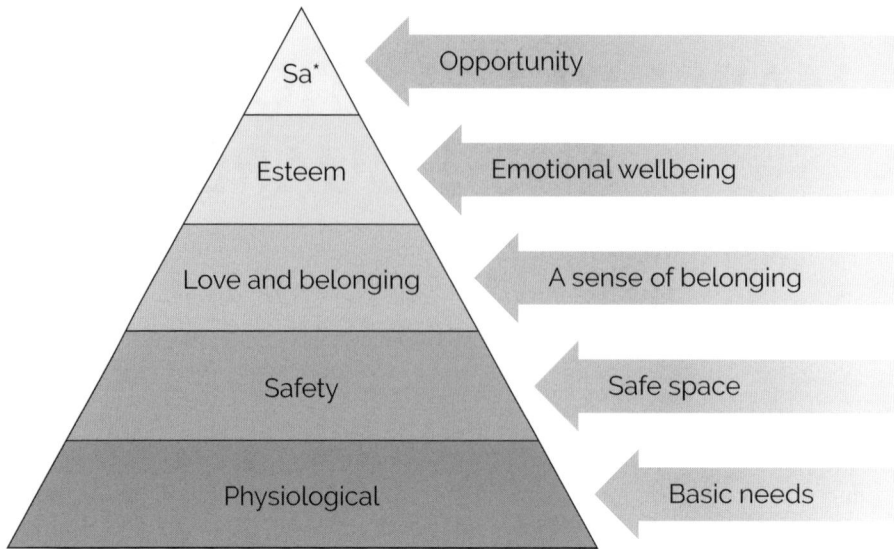

*Self-actualisation

Figure 6.1. Hierarchy of needs and education (adapted from Maslow, 1987 [1954])

The way these needs build and interlink through our findings offers powerful insights for school leaders, teaching staff and parents, which stretches beyond the pandemic and can be of benefit to all children and young people – especially our square pegs.

# Basic needs

Food, shelter, air and sleep – these are the physiological needs that must be met before we can engage in 'higher order' experiences such as thinking, problem-solving or relating. We cannot concentrate or focus when these basic needs are not met, not only because we are preoccupied with the physical sensations of hunger and discomfort but also the consequent feelings of fear, shame and vigilance.

Because of this, it is incredibly important to monitor and evaluate how well a child's basic needs are being met in an educational setting (as well as at home), and this is always the starting point for examining that child's behaviours. A process developed by Dr Sandra Kempsell, an educational psychologist at Nottingham City Council, adapts Maslow's hierarchy into an assessment tool which identifies key gaps along with potential 'quick wins' (see Table 6.1).

**Table 6.1. Physiological needs and interventions (Kempsell, 2018)**

| Questions to consider | Quick wins |
|---|---|
| Does the pupil often seem hungry or not having enough to eat? | Breakfast club, daily free and hot school lunch, food vouchers sent home, ensuring eating environments are warm/clean. Do you have alternative eating environments for pupils with sensory processing needs? |
| Does the pupil often seem tired? Are you aware of any difficulties with sleeping? | Access to support services that can help parents with sleep routine, family support and targeted support. |
| Are learning environments conducive to supporting concentration? Do they meet a pupil's basic physiological needs? | What is the temperature in the room? Do pupils have enough personal space? Are chairs and tables positioned so that all pupils can see, hear and engage with peers and teaching? |
| Does the pupil have any ongoing health/medical needs/diagnosis? | Ensure regular liaison with families, check medical appointments are being attended, ensure a multi-agency approach to meeting needs, utilise pastoral care systems and family support workers. |
| Does the pupil's hearing/vision need to be checked? | Ensure access to the school nurse. |
| Are there concerns about the pupil appearing clean and well presented (e.g. appropriate clothing/material resources)? | Financial support for school uniform, ensuring pupils have warm outerwear/ coats, socks and shoes that are the correct size. |

Note that educational staff need their basic needs met for their own wellbeing too. Working in education means long hours, missed lunches, insufficient sleep, stress and possible personal health needs being sidelined because of busy schedules. Effective leaders look to the basic needs of everyone involved, including themselves.

# Safe spaces

Remember how unsafe we all felt during the pandemic, especially at the beginning? How unsafe might your square pegs feel all of the time? Schools committed to all of their children and young people can and should provide a safe space for them. We know that this is not always the case and work needs to be done to ensure a country-wide ethos of physical and emotional/psychological safety in all of our educational settings.

The link between safety and relationships (and fear and the breakdown of relationships) cannot be underestimated here, and we know that relational trauma requires relational and trauma-infused approaches to support repair (Treisman, 2018). Relational trauma refers to experiences of multi-layered ongoing stress and disruption in close relationships, something that can be intergenerational and span wider contexts, such as schools and community relationships.

A trauma-informed approach can create a space that develops empathy and wellbeing in a school, but note that it is not a programme or intervention for 'those kids'. It works when it is part of a school-wide ethos and culture, one that acknowledges the different experiences and unique nature of all. This starts with systems and policy. In our experience, school leaders can empower staff through the inclusion of all staff and pupils in developing new ways of managing and interpreting behaviour based on empathy, understanding and meeting the emotional needs of the whole community. Table 6.2 shows what this might mean in practice.

Table 6.2. Different behaviour models and approaches

|  | Punitive/ rule-based model | Behaviourist/ consequence-based model | Relational/ developmental model |
|---|---|---|---|
| Children are … | responsible for their actions. | learning. | developing, error prone and highly responsive to environment. |
| Main means of behaviour management is … | fear. | consequences. | relationships. |
| Boundaries are to … | indicate right and wrong. | make standards clear. | try to meet everyone's needs. |

| | Punitive/ rule-based model | Behaviourist/ consequence-based model | Relational/ developmental model |
|---|---|---|---|
| Rules should be … | enforced without exception. | clearly communicated. | developed together and adapted where needed. |
| Behaviour is something to … | control. | manage. | interpret. |
| Consequences are … | sanctions and punishments. | ways to shape behaviour. | a last resort, only used within a process of repair. |
| 'Inappropriate' behaviour is … | wrongdoing and deliberate. | learned. | a sign of an unmet need, difficulty coping or lack of knowledge. |
| The causes of difficulties are … | lack of compliance and insufficient discipline. | learned poor responses and lack of appropriate reinforcement. | mostly in the environment, relationship-based and developmentally appropriate. |
| Solutions lie in … | the child. | adjusting consequences. | understanding what the behaviour tells us about the child and their need. |
| Children who don't manage should be … | excluded or fixed. | helped and given intervention. | understood and included. |
| Policy effectiveness is measured by … | compliance. | behaviour change. | wellbeing. |

It is relatively easy to create physical and emotional safe spaces for both pupils and staff, spaces that are integrated into the school system and not just provided in reaction to a crisis. After all, an ethos of safety has a preventative effect too. In our work, we have experienced safe spaces that have supported video-enhanced reflective practice, work discussion groups for staff to share challenges and solutions, individual and group therapeutic sessions for children, and the process of transitioning from whole-school behaviour to relationship policies.

# A sense of belonging

We will hear more about the importance of belonging in Chapters 16 and 17. Feeling safe is a precursor to this. Once in a space of safety, an individual can look around, explore that space and hopefully find a sense of belonging there. Sadly, even though they may feel physically safe, our research has revealed that square pegs often feel they don't belong, perhaps due to difference or feeling 'othered' (Popoola and Sivers, 2021). This, they felt, had an impact on their wellbeing as well as their ability and desire to engage with school.

There has been much recent research exploring and demonstrating the importance of belongingness in a school setting (Bonnel et al, 2019; Korpershoek et al., 2020), revealing the positive impact a sense of belonging can have on a range of social, emotional and academic skills. A sense of not belonging or not feeling comfortable in school is often a barrier to school attendance, so careful thought needs to be given to how schools can ensure all pupils feel as though they belong.

One way we have found useful to consider the issue of belonging is through the idea of role theory (Bonnel et al., 2019). In this approach, we are encouraged to consider whether there is a range of roles or identities pupils can take up, try out and experience in school, or whether there is only a small choice of options. Bonnel et al. found that when there is a diversity of pro-school roles – that is, the opportunity to try out different experiences, not just those with a purely academic focus – this can have a positive impact not only on social and emotional wellbeing, but also on engagement with school and the general health of pupils. This also means that a school should embrace cultural diversity, thus minimising the way in which any child (or adult) can feel disenfranchised, ostracised or othered by the system.

Roles are not just about 'being' but also 'doing'. To what extent are young people, especially the square pegs in our schools, involved in making decisions about their lives? A Public Health England review states:

Involving students in decisions that impact on them can benefit their mental health and wellbeing by helping them to feel part of the school, college and wider community and to have some control over their lives. At an individual level, benefits include helping students to gain belief in their own capabilities, including building their knowledge and skills to make healthy choices and developing their independence. Collectively, students benefit through having opportunities to influence decisions, to express their views and to develop strong social networks. (Public Health England and Department for Education, 2021: 19)

This links back to the ideas of Bonnel et al. (2019) about ensuring a range of roles for pupils in school and how strong social networks – relationships – are a key element in ensuring emotional wellbeing.

# Emotional wellbeing

At the very core of learning and wellbeing in school (and life in general) are relationships. This includes the sense that there is someone who cares, who thinks about you and likes you, even when you are not always doing likeable things.

The interconnection between emotional wellbeing, mental health and relationships cannot be underestimated. Research has provided clear evidence that 'Children with higher levels of emotional, behavioural, social and school wellbeing, on average, have higher levels of academic achievement' (Gutman and Vorhaus, 2012: 3). There is also evidence to suggest that whole-school approaches to promoting wellbeing have a positive impact on non-academic outcomes for pupils, such as mental health, motivation, engagement with school and self-efficacy (Gutman and Vorhaus, 2012; Lindorff, 2020).

The wellbeing of children and young people also needs to be considered systemically in education, not as something that is addressed as a pastoral 'add-on'. After all, the very structure and processes of education can create, or exacerbate, wellbeing difficulties in children and young people.

As educational psychologists, a major element of our work is to promote the importance of relationships to support all areas of a child's development. There is a perception that this is only needed in primary education, but it is just as important, if not more so, for secondary-age children. Learning relationships are complex and combine many profound experiences such as 'giving and receiving, reciprocity, dependence, growth and conflict' (Rustin, 2011: 2). This way of thinking moves us from the notion of education as the input of knowledge towards a concept of learning as a relational act.

There is now widespread recognition that school plays a vital role in supporting the mental health and resilience of children, based on research and understanding of the neuroscience underpinning relational practises (Public Health England and Department for Education, 2021). For example, developments growing out of the pandemic have seen increased awareness of a variety of approaches to support all those in school. Educational psychology services across the country have been leading on emotional wellbeing projects, working alongside schools to embed the eight principles that contribute to good practice as represented in Figure 6.2 (see page 85).

By considering these factors as quality markers for wellbeing and mental health practices in schools, we can start to see a system in which the square pegs – or, indeed, any shaped peg – are accommodated in school, not adapted or rejected. Such a change starts with the system; and the system starts with the leaders. For example, what is your school doing to embed an ethos that means every child is included, relationships are at the forefront of policy and behaviour can be understood for what it may be communicating? As you seek answers to this important question, remember that you can draw on the support of educational psychologists like us. Many educational psychologists have moved away from working at the level of the individual child and are working systemically with leadership teams to support and challenge, guiding them through the process of changing the system so that it meets the needs of the whole school community.

Talking of leaders, there is a growing body of research that focuses on the importance of their wellbeing too. For example, a recent feasibility study has explored how a group-based acceptance and commitment therapy programme can help (Hayes et al., 2012; Gillard et al., 2021). You are not alone in this important work, and there are people to help you.

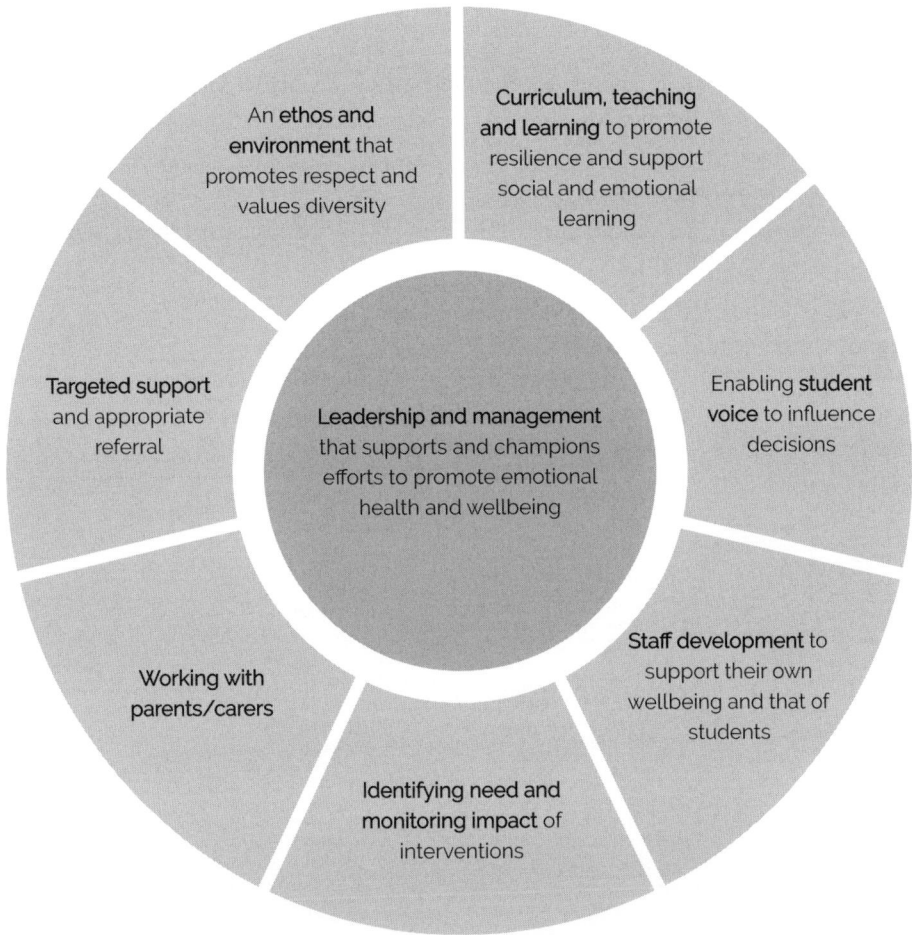

Figure 6.2. Eight principles to promoting a whole-school and college approach to emotional health and wellbeing (Public Health England and Department for Education, 2021: 9)

# Opportunity

The aftermath of a pandemic that changed everything is a perfect time for systemic innovation in school, and the pupils and teachers we speak to are prepared to be innovative, dynamic and creative. Rather than simply passing academic exams, we are ready for a system that instils real skills for the future. One young person explained to us that they wanted to learn 'how to manage money, how to get a job, how to pay bills and how to buy a house'.

As well as such life skills, there has been a great deal of work highlighting what young people need to succeed in a life beyond school. In our work with schools, it has been helpful to distil the various studies and papers on the topic into Table 6.3, which combines core knowledge, competencies, personal qualities and those all-important values – an aspect that can often be omitted when we look at 21st century skills.

Table 6.3. Twenty-first century skills
(adapted from World Economic Forum, 2015: 4)

| Core knowledge | Competencies | Qualities |
|---|---|---|
| 1. Literacy | 1. Problem-solving | 1. Curiosity |
| 2. Numeracy | 2. Creativity | 2. Initiative |
| 3. Science | 3. Communication | 3. Resilience |
| 4. ICT | 4. Collaboration | 4. Adaptability |
| 5. Financial literacy | **Values** | 5. Leadership |
| 6. Cultural and civic literacy | Important to the individual and guide beliefs | 6. Social and cultural awareness |

To what extent does your school offer children and young people the opportunity to learn, practise and develop these vital attributes?

# Conclusion

Our hope is that every square peg can find their place in an education system that guarantees them a safe space and a sense of belonging. We want them to be immersed in an education process that speaks to them, makes them feel motivated and gives them joy. And, referring back to Article 29 of the UN Convention on the Rights of the Child – 'Education must develop every child's personality, talents and abilities to the full' – our hope is that educators can have the freedom to be dynamic, flexible and creative to achieve this, and that the role of relationships is universally acknowledged as the key driver in academic success and emotional health. That is why we do what we do, and why we know our job is not yet done.

# References

Bonnel, C., Blakemore, S-J., Fletcher, A. and Patton, G. (2019) Role Theory of Schools and Adolescent Health, *Lancet Child & Adolescent Health*, 3(10): 742–748.

Gillard, S., Dare, C., Hardy, J., Nyikavaranda, P., Rowan Olive, R., Shah, P. et al. (2021) Experiences of Living with Mental Health Problems During the COVID-19 Pandemic in the UK: A Coproduced, Participatory Qualitative Interview Study, *Social Psychiatry and Psychiatric Epidemiology*, 56(8): 1447–1457.

Gutman, L. M. and Vorhaus, J. (2012) *The Impact of Pupil Behaviour and Wellbeing on Educational Outcomes*. London: Department for Education. Available at: https://www.gov.uk/government/publications/the-impact-of-pupil-behaviour-and-wellbeing-on-educational-outcomes.

Hart, A., Blincow, D. and Thomas, H. (2007) *Resilient Therapy: Working with Children and Families*. London: Brunner Routledge.

Hayes, S., Strosahl, K. and Wilson, K. (2012) *Acceptance and Commitment Therapy: The Process and Practice of Mindful Change*, 2nd edn. New York: Guilford Press.

Kempsell, S. (2018) Roots of Inclusion [unpublished Nottingham City Council Educational Psychology Service document].

Korpershoek, H., Canrinus, E. T., Fokkens-Bruinsma, M. and de Boer, H. (2020) The Relationships Between School Belonging and Students' Motivational, Social-Emotional, Behavioural, and Academic Outcomes in Secondary Education: A Meta-Analytic Review, *Research Papers in Education*, 35(6): 641–680.

Lindorff, A. (2020) *The Impact of Promoting Student Wellbeing on Student Academic and Non-Academic Outcomes: An Analysis of the Evidence*. Available at: https://oxfordimpact.oup.com/home/wellbeing-impact-study.

Maslow, A. H. (1987 [1954]) *Motivation and Personality*, 3rd edn. New York: Harper & Row.

Popoola, M. and Sivers, S. (2021) Hearing the Voices of Children and Young People: An Ecological Systems Analysis of Individual Difference and Experiences During the Covid-19 Lockdown, *DECP Debate*, 177 (March): 21–25.

Public Health England and Department for Education (2021) *Promoting Children and Young People's Mental and Wellbeing: A Whole School or College Approach*. Available at: https://www.gov.uk/government/publications/promoting-children-and-young-peoples-emotional-health-and-wellbeing.

Rustin, M. (2011) Passion in the Classroom: Understanding Some Vicissitudes in Teacher–Pupil Relationships and the Unavoidable Anxieties of Learning. In R. Harris, S. Rendall and S. Nashat (eds), *Engaging with Complexity: Child and Adolescent Mental Health and Education*. Abingdon and New York: Routledge, pp. 1–20.

Treisman, T. (2018) *Becoming a Trauma-Informed Organisation: Practices and Principles*. London: Winston Churchill Memorial Trust. Available at: https://media.churchillfellowship.org/documents/Treisman_K_Report_2018_Final.pdf.

World Economic Forum (2015) *New Vision for Education: Fostering Social and Emotional Learning through Technology*. Available at: https://www.weforum.org/reports/new-vision-for-education-fostering-social-and-emotional-learning-through-technology.

# Chapter 7

# STEPS TO 'WITH'

## Ellie Costello and James Gillum

Co-production means delivering public services in an equal and reciprocal relationship between professionals, people using services, their families and their neighbours. Where activities are co-produced in this way, both services and neighbourhoods become far more effective agents of change.

Boyle and Harris (2009: 11)

In the 1970s, the Chicago Police Department moved from patrolling neighbourhoods on foot to putting its officers in police cars. Crime went up. Professor Elinor Ostrom from the University of Indiana was brought in to explain what had gone wrong. She introduced the term 'co-production' to the lexicon of public services. In a nutshell, 'the term aimed to explain to the police why they need the community as much as the community needs them' (Mason-Angelow, 2018: 5).

In its simplest terms, effective co-production is a philosophy of practice firmly rooted in the values of community, transparency and authenticity. It flourishes when you place your service users – families, children and young people – alongside your team as joint and equitable stakeholders to help develop your school, strengthen relationships, increase belonging and improve outcomes. It's already well-established in community policing, academic research, disability rights, healthcare and youthwork, and there are many examples of great practice.[1] At the centre of co-production is the trust and courage to take decisions 'with' the children and families who need your professional help the most – your square pegs. And when it comes to co-production, we refer to those service users as experts by experience, or EbEs, which reflects their equal value in this process.

It's important to make the distinction between co-production and all those activities that are not co-production: co-design, engagement and consultation, for example, as

---

1 Recognised frameworks include Involve (https://www.nihr.ac.uk/health-and-care-professionals/engagement-and-participation-in-research/involve-patients.htm), Think Local Act Personal (https://www.thinklocalactpersonal.org.uk/Browse/Co-production) and Amplified (https://www.youngminds.org.uk/professional/consultancy-and-service-design/case-studies/amplified).

outlined by the ladder of co-production.[2] This ensures that everyone shares the same language and frame of reference from the start.

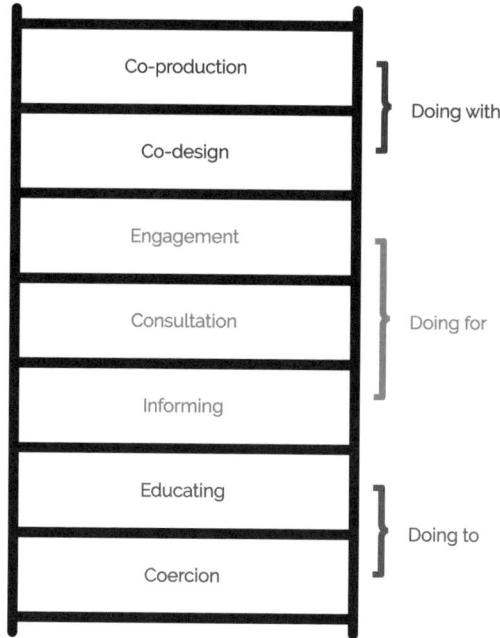

Figure 7.1. The ladder of co-production

To help you as you make the move to consider, adopt or further embrace this idea, we have drawn up a number of key pointers to reflect on. These are not 'top tips', as there are as many scenarios as there are family circumstances, but they are designed to help you reflect on your current – and, we hope, future – practice.

## Be brave and open to change

- Co-production isn't meant to be easy or comfortable. Co-production partners are your critical friends, pioneers and champions. If it doesn't feel awkward sometimes, you aren't doing it right!

- Be prepared for unusual communication styles, zero filters and some blunt conversations. Parents and carers – your EbEs – won't always tiptoe around the issues and will often speak with a directness that can be unnerving.

---

2   The ladder was originally created by members of the National Co-Production Advisory Group – see https:// www.thinklocalactpersonal.org.uk/co-production-in-commissioning-tool/co-production/In-more-detail/ what-makes-co-production-different.

- Conflict is normal, rupture is expected and it's necessary, because when you hit that zone you know you have a very engaged, invested and determined co-production team going through its paces – and that is when you start to see real innovation.

- Having difficult conversations is never easy, but harnessing active listening – truly, authentically, openly listening to hear without judgement – will rapidly forge stronger connections. The act of being listened to, of feeling heard, is incredibly powerful, and is such an undervalued tool in building relationships and communities.

- When tension emerges over conflicting ideas, agendas or expectations, it's vitally important to be prepared to change and embrace flexibility.

- Start with a blank piece of paper rather than a pre-formed agenda.

- It's important to be open to the fact that views might need to change as new information or ideas emerge.

- Co-production will not be possible if neither side is willing to have a go at doing something different. If it isn't possible to change a particular way of working, what else could be changed instead?

- Experimentation is key. Be brave. Mix things up. Try something new. All can be invaluable when starting to facilitate co-productive practice.

## Prioritise relationships

- The principle of co-production relies on equitable partnerships.

- View co-production as a long-term relationship, not a one-off task.

- Complex problems need time to resolve. In the interim, it's important to focus on the quality of the relationship.

- Keep things informal so that all partners can feel relaxed and able to participate. Not everything needs to be discussed in a meeting; sometimes a phone call or a chat over coffee is better.

- When you build relationships effectively, you will discover a psychological safety in your practice that allows everyone the freedom to speak without fear of recrimination, judgement or shame and to stay together 'in flow'.

- Consider providing professionals with the opportunity to act as coaches and facilitators to service users.

# Empower others

- You might already have examples of co-production between staff and students – for example, a youth or student council, a special interest group or a club. Or maybe it's through a vertical year group or house or with a good, active, integrated parent–teacher association or parent governors' team. This is a great start, but make sure it's co-production you offer, not consultation or engagement.

- Allow children and young people equal voice in the process. Give them the opportunity to lead and explore options alongside parents, carers and colleagues; it can be enlivening.

- Choose who will be the point of contact for the family and give them the authority to use their judgement and make decisions.

- If you are the leader, take a back seat early on.

- Put someone in the driving seat who doesn't look like the expected leader in the room.

- Encourage risk-taking and creativity.

- Ask your assembled experts what areas they think need to be addressed; this can be illuminating.

- Use small break-out groups to your advantage.

- After starting with that blank sheet of paper, continue the drafting process, iterating, editing and reviewing together, including between meetings. This is really important to help maintain those bonds of engagement and agency.

- Celebrate the assets of users and the community rather than focusing on the deficits.

- Build the skills of those involved.

- Broker a true partnership with shared responsibility between professionals and users.

- Support, connect with, learn with and reflect with individuals other than the usual suspects.

- Develop forums for users and professionals to connect and share their expertise.

- Make sure that professionals *and* service users are viewed as equally crucial to successful delivery.

# Agree the scope of co-production

- Use co-production whenever and wherever you are developing services and policies. Bringing together professionals and service users on an equal footing is the best way to maximise the chances of success.
- Agree the scope of the co-production activity or discussion, with all involved.
- Recognise that co-production cannot address everything at the same time.
- Be aware that some things may need more senior input or fall beyond the scope of the current discussion.
- It's okay to start a meeting with lines such as, 'Can you help me to understand how things look for you?' or 'Are you able to share your frustrations with me so we can address them together?'
- If you are using co-production to resolve a conflict, naming it is a good place to start.

# Recognise professional vulnerability

- Co-production is about learning to be comfortably uncomfortable, at the edge of our comfort zones.
- Ensure professionals know it's okay to come away from a meeting without answers or to admit 'I don't know'.
- It's okay for professionals to express their feelings.
- Acknowledge that a solution might not be possible immediately. This doesn't mean co-production has failed.
- If you are actively including those 'hard to reach' families who have possibly disagreed with parts of the discussion, recognise that hearing them talk about the cause and effect of your or the system's negative impact can be really hard for professionals.
- Coming face to face with a family's adversity, trauma or distress, particularly if this has been compounded and impacted by service failures or gaps in provision, can feel incredibly challenging.
- At times of stress or tension, we can find ourselves retreating into firmer, more rigid and more formal interactions. It's an understandable response to feeling threatened.

■ Humility, honesty and transparency go a long way to repairing ruptured relationships.

■ The power of an apology when working with vulnerable families or diverse stakeholders should never be underestimated.

# Build in supervision

■ Co-production and compassion can be emotionally demanding, and professionals will probably have to deal with heightened emotion (theirs and others').

■ They will need space to debrief and reframe, with support.

■ Supervision can be an essential part of co-production, particularly if we are working on a gnarly problem or individual issue for a family.[3]

■ Formal supervision offers a safe and reflective space. It supports the supporters to build and maintain the capacity they need to co-produce, co-design, lead and thus reach vulnerable families and communities.

■ Good supervision is impartial, confidential and essential. It can help to build capacity and resilience, support mental health and wellbeing, and assist with compassionate, holistic and community-focused practice.

■ Supervision done well can also be a useful way to experience containment, reciprocity and connection.

■ Staffroom chat or a meeting with a superior untrained in supervision won't replace professionally trained supervision.

# Review and revise where necessary

■ Just because a plan has been agreed, it doesn't mean that co-production is complete.

■ Be open when it hasn't been possible to do something.

■ Review, revisit and revise plans; reviews increase the likelihood of people sticking to them and circumstances change.

■ A regular temperature check after meetings is also good ('How was that for you?'), or offering an open door or mode of communication for EbEs to flag concerns or share feelings if the direction of travel is becoming policy-led rather than person-led.

---

3   There are providers, practitioners and professionals who offer supervision training or provide direct supervision.

- It's okay to say something like, 'I understand it was important for you that we resolved this. I'm sorry we weren't able to come to an agreement today. I'd like to find a way to do that. Let's take some time to gather our thoughts and regroup next week.'

- Be alert to individual needs and be prepared to learn from the lived experience of your families.

- Bear in mind that one family's experience may not be representative of all families. Each family is unique and each person within each family holds their own particular view and unique experience.

- When in doubt, remember that simple is best.

Embracing co-production is so important, particularly for those families who are often under the radar. Courageously enabling trusted conversations to find those solutions that arise when we authentically listen in order to hear and remain flexible, open to change and willing to work *with* those who need our help, leads to better outcomes for all.

## References

Boyle, D. and Harris, M. (2009) *The Challenge of Co-Production: How Equal Partnerships between Professionals and the Public Are Crucial to Improving Public Services.* London: NESTA. Available at: https://neweconomics.org/uploads/files/312ac8ce93a00d5973_3im6i6t0e.pdf.

Mason-Angelow, V. (2018) *A Guide to Coproduction.* Bath: National Development Team for Inclusion. Available at: https://www.ndti.org.uk/assets/files/Coproduction_Guide.pdf.

# Chapter 8

# LESSONS FROM A 999 CALL

## Edward Pearson

To misquote the late great partnership of Liverpool Football Club icons Bill Shankley and Bob Paisley, education isn't a matter of life and death. It's more important than that.[1] What is interesting is how many lessons from the world of emergency medical care have something for educators striving to offer the best level of support, in challenging circumstances, for the children and young people who really need them.

1   It might be 'just another call' for us, but for the people involved it is both memorable and potentially life-changing. *Remember the human impact of what is going on and your part in it.*

2   Polls globally often reveal 'paramedic' to be one of the world's most trusted professions. Teachers appear high on the list too. *That is a big thing and worth remembering in all our interactions.*

3   You would be surprised how many call-outs we attend where all is not what it first seems. *Take the time to listen and be creative as you evaluate all options before you act.*

4   We are all underfunded and facing increasing pressure to see as many people a day as possible. *Never allow the care we offer to be compromised by a lack of time.*

5   Every call-out involves a moral dilemma. Where do you best focus your time and energy? Who gets the ambulance first? *Do all you can to find out all you can so that nothing important is missed when decisions are made.*

6   A doorstep diagnosis will lead to what we call a 'big sick/little sick' response, but the patient sitting quietly on the sofa may be the sickest of all. *Look beyond your first impressions, especially at what is not being said.*

7   Whenever I hear a parent say, 'They're just not right,' I know I need to get the child off to hospital pretty damned quick. *A parent may not know what is wrong, but they will know something is not right. Listen to them, hard.*

---

1   In an interview in 1981, Shankly commented: 'Someone said, "Football is more important than life and death to you," and I said, "Listen, it's more important than that"' (quoted in Lloyd and Mitchinson, 2008: 123).

8   The next person we listen to is the child, engaging with them at an appropriate level physically, verbally and emotionally, and earning their trust. *Listen to the child and prove to them you are hearing.*

9   Shared decision-making means we involve everyone present in choices about the care we provide. We may give differing weights to the views of different individuals, but a consensus means no one feels left out. *Take the time to ensure everyone feels at least heard when decisions are being taken.*

10  The number one complaint we receive from the public is about crew attitude. I think this happens when that crew did not take the time to listen. We are all human – and often tired, hungry and wet too – and most people know how overstretched the NHS is. *People will often forgive the things outside your control but not what you can control – and that is your attitude. Show you care and get it right.*

Part II

# LAW AND THE SYSTEM

# Introduction

One of the problems with the education system in England – brought sharply into focus during the COVID-19 pandemic – is that we have a complex interplay of non-statutory guidance, statutory guidance and law. This is perfectly demonstrated by a letter that Square Peg and Not Fine in School received from the Department for Education in October 2019 when we initiated a legal challenge around attendance.

The Department for Education letter confirmed that

> The use of the absence and attendance codes are not mandatory but they enable schools to record and monitor absence in a consistent way. They are also used for collecting statistics through the school census system. The absence and attendance codes are detailed in the department's guidance on school attendance.[1]

This is true, in that this guidance is non-statutory. However, separate school census guidance – which *is* statutory – requires all schools to submit pupil attendance data via these same codes.[2] So, the use of the codes may not be mandatory, but schools must by law submit pupil data against these same codes.[3]

In their research report, *School Exclusion and the Law*, Lucinda Ferguson and Naomi Webber (2015: 38) conclude:

> It is thus non-lawyers who implement the law, particularly school management teams, with the support and guidance of LA [local authority] officers. … the law affords significant discretion to non-lawyers, particularly headteachers, in terms of how they interpret and apply the law. It is also clear that headteachers and parents misunderstand the law on exclusion. … In addition, headteachers also disregard particular legal requirements, principally if they consider that the 'best interests' of the affected pupil and others in the school lie elsewhere. … school culture has a role to play in determining the likelihood that a particular pupil will be excluded.

It is highly likely that the same principles are true of non-attendance, with the added complication that the child or family is the 'instigator' of the absence, rather than the

---

1   See https://img1.wsimg.com/blobby/go/a41082e1-5561-438b-a6a2-16176f7570e9/downloads/DfE_Letter-of_Response_to_Square_Peg_NFIS_Auth.pdf?ver=1658927264156.
2   See https://www.gov.uk/guidance/complete-the-school-census/find-a-school-census-code. The submission of the school census returns, including a set of named pupil records, is a statutory requirement on schools under section 537A of the Education Act 1996.
3   Not every code is included in the school census, and there is nothing to stop a school creating its own codes.

school, and so parents find that their right to an education their child can access is often denied.

It is therefore crucial that school leaders understand the full implications of the school policies that can create issues for square pegs, and that they challenge their local authority when directives are unlawful. They can then use the full force of the law and guidance to ensure appropriate support for those children whose only crime is that they don't fit the system.

## References

Ferguson, L. and Webber, N. (2015) *School Exclusion and the Law: A Literature Review and Scoping Survey of Practice*. Oxford: University of Oxford. Available at: https://papers.ssrn.com/sol3/papers.cfm?abstract_id=2523194.

# Chapter 9

# SYSTEM FAILURE

## Marijke Miles

There is an irony at the heart of any discussion about the way in which the system, especially an underfunded and overstretched one, can fail the children and young people it must serve best. While we seem to be happy to take the credit for our successes, it is easy to blame the system when things don't work. But if we want to try to find a better way of working as school leaders at a local level, we have to accept that people create systems, and that people are therefore responsible for changing them to overcome their flaws. I have been searching for these improvements for 25 years, and I have not yet lost my optimism or my belief that I can make a difference and that I have a part to play in it all.

Here is another irony: for most of us, what makes the human race so beautiful is its exquisite diversity. You never hear of anyone going into the woods and complaining that the trees aren't more like each other or that the pebbles and shells on the beach aren't all the same. As a seaside girl, I keep this thought close to my heart every time I am faced with a new challenge to the norm. And yet we have to accept that sometimes we find the extent of human diversity problematic and end up putting our energies into either trying to minimise the differences that exist or pretending they aren't there. However, when we embrace – welcome even – diversity at a personal and professional level, it frees us up both to take responsibility for and take heart in the changes we can enact to make our system better for the children and young people struggling with that system. For our square pegs.

At a neurological level, our brains like to put things into boxes – 'neural templates' as they are called – so we know where we stand in an unpredictable world. We make assumptions, jump to conclusions and create patterns, even when none are present. We continually update, refine and nuance these internal constructs, which we use to interpret and respond to the world as we encounter it. As we get older, it's easy for these neural algorithms to become fixed, but we owe it to our families, let alone ourselves – if the adage 'use it or lose it' is anything to go by – that our thinking should continually change, evolve and – God forbid – mutate to reflect our ever-widening experience of an ever-changing world.

Human beings also like to organise themselves into systems because this is a logical and sensible thing to do. Everyone needs to know where they stand in relation to everyone else and what they need to do or not do to get by. And, of course, this needs to be scalable. So, we need systems and we need people to fit the systems – or where would we be?

Herein lies the problem for our square pegs. Firstly, by their very nature, they don't fit into an existing scheme or structure, beyond a very general framework. More importantly, we encounter these children and their families with our own mental maps already in place, so we start to compare them with our known professional taxonomy. Subconsciously, we are already strategising about how we 'fix them' to make them fit the system.

A piece of advice I often give to emerging leaders facing a particularly challenging meeting is to make it clear to the protagonists that they won't be making a decision or offering a solution in that meeting. Even if there is only a delay of a few hours, what I am trying to enable new leaders to do is *really* listen and observe and, yes, *feel* what the actual issues are – something that can only be done properly when you put aside the mental noise that comes from always trying to seek a solution and that surreptitious scrolling through of a metaphorical Rolodex of known situations, scenarios and solutions that comes with it. As the famous saying goes, 'it is tempting, if the only tool you have is a hammer, to treat everything as if it were a nail' (Maslow, 1966: 15–16).

Our professional formation only serves to create and strengthen our mental constructs, something that is, broadly speaking, desirable. They give us frames of reference from which to hone our professional interpretation, responses and interventions. The concern is when they remain fixed and are, if anything, strengthened by the number of cases or encounters that match them. This can lead to over-reliance and the law of the instrument prevails, as the hammer-and-nail adage is known. This is all the more evident in an overstretched system with excessive caseloads and the constant drive for greater efficiencies.

But, let's not forget, humans create inhumane systems – and humans can do something about it.

## Distribution, delegation and distillation

A lot has been written about effective and courageous leadership, especially in schools. It's fascinating that in education we have long since jettisoned 'management' in favour of the entirely different concept of 'leadership', whereas in nearly all of the partner services for our most complex children and families, management is still the prevailing terminology and therefore permeates the culture. It would be a whole chapter in itself to make the distinction between the two (and, of course, there are managers in partner agencies who are also leaders).

Why is this difference important? If you manage the system, then your job is to ensure that it works as effectively as possible. Leaders, on the other hand, can only lead if they have the agency to adapt and change the organisation as required. By definition, a good leader needs to be more flexible in their thinking, more ready and more confident to evolve and adapt their mental models, and therefore more ready to really perceive and respond to the needs of the square pegs before them. What marks a good leader? Someone who ensures high-quality supervision from excellent practitioners (this is not the same as a good manager), who espouses a no-blame culture (different from a no-mistakes one) and who models sincere professional and cross-discipline curiosity, respect and cooperation, putting relationships first (see Chapter 25).

It is worth bearing in mind too that, for schools, this all-encompassing wraparound care for children and their families is relatively new and still problematic for those teachers who see their job as teaching, end of. Indeed, across the world, teachers in many systems have no duty of care to children other than to teach them. Espousing the practices and approaches of caring and clinical disciplines is a new step for schools, and we all need to remember this.

What is more, in my opinion, in order to be liberated to think fully about a specific family or case, we need to take the fear of accountability out of situations and imbue lead professionals with the confidence to do what they think is right. A common issue in schools is that the roles most likely to encounter complex case work – class teachers, tutors and teaching assistants, for example – are often too distant from the most senior leadership. The staff making decisions on a day-to-day basis find themselves accountable, yet with little or no supervision from the leaders who are more experienced or, when it comes to bending the system, the most able to deviate from agreed procedures. This is a consequence of having to generalise and standardise policy and procedure, distilling it to its most base components so that anyone can deliver it across an organisation, regardless of size: 'When A happens, do B. There is no C.'

## Learning from other agencies

It has taken me a long time to realise one essential truth about being a head teacher: compared to more junior colleagues, I have pretty much a free rein when it comes to being pragmatic and creative in the way I deal directly with children and families in complex circumstances. I sink or swim on my decisions, but they are my decisions to make. This realisation is not without its apprehensions, but a leader hiding behind a dubious system is a cop-out that is in no one's interests.

Once I had realised this, I started to think about what it would take to facilitate this level of confidence and autonomy throughout the pastoral and leadership structure in my school. The answer soon became clear. It was to bring in a colleague with a strong

supervision background, a level of senior experience and accountability, and yet someone who had relative liberty from ultimate personal accountability for head teachers
(i.e. Ofsted). I made the decision to recruit a very senior social worker into my leadership team as an assistant head teacher.

Yep, this is a brave – and expensive – solution because it diverts funds away from the
core business of teaching and learning, but it has proven well worth it in so many ways.
It is becoming more common for schools to engage social workers or para-social workers but usually at relatively low grades. I am talking about bringing into an organisation
a social worker at assistant head teacher level who answers only to the head teacher
and who is directly challenging and supervising them as well as co-constructing policy
and actions.

I can honestly say that it's the best thing I have ever done for myself, my colleagues and
my children and families, and I would do it again and again (and have done).

One of the benefits of working this closely, for over 12 years now, with colleagues from
a social care background is a fluency in the mysterious lexicon of social work. This
sounds so obvious, but truly to speak to each other in our own 'language' builds trust
and understanding which directly benefits families. Add to this an empathetic understanding of each other's metrics and constraints and the right level of professional
challenge, and we have transformed the effectiveness of the partnerships which can
then genuinely support the families who need us.

Throughout the school and beyond, rigorous and effective supervision takes place,
building confidence, deepening experience and improving the fluidity in our thinking.
This in turn means that the staff who look after my families, at all levels, have begun
to experience an authentic sense of autonomy, the freedom to be creative and solution-focused, not to mention – and this is something we don't think about enough
– the emotional gratification that comes with seeing things through to their conclusion. Such a reward for their investment encourages ongoing emotional and
intellectual engagement when the next situation arises, along with that all-important
appropriate level of personal responsibility for making things better.

We have found this set-up to be incredibly productive as a senior leadership team,
facilitating a healthy and dynamic forum for respectful professional challenge and
dialogue. And because we have established this well-rehearsed routine *within* our
community, we have now developed far more effective skills to use it when facing
outwards, leading to better partnerships and more productive solutions and support
for families when they really need it.

For example, rather than kicking off professional conversations with, '*They* ought to
be doing something', where 'they' is any agency or organisation that isn't us, we are now
able to see and understand the constraints at play which, in turn, brings us round to
the position where we acknowledge that *we* are best placed to take whatever action we

were previously thinking someone else should be taking. Having an 'outsider on the inside' also helps us stick to our moral compass whenever the 'What would Ofsted say?' tea party comes up. By having a master practitioner in an allied discipline, we can better seek solutions that balance our accountability to our families with the external frameworks and scrutiny we face.

## A word about safeguarding

Talking with the families of some of my square pegs recently, I was asked the question about the coverall term 'safeguarding' being brought into every conversation about school attendance. Of course, school absence can be indicative of risk in certain situations, but it has started to become axiomatic that an inability to force a child to attend school *must* be a safeguarding issue. Conflating these two terms is dangerous, as we saw during the pandemic, where 'vulnerable' came to imply 'at risk' and was applied indiscriminately to all children with education, health and care plans, for example, causing deep hurts and insult to children and families.

What was most revelatory about that conversation was the fact that the others in the discussion literally had no idea how high the stakes have become for families, where reaching out for help can quickly seem to snowball to a point where the family is placed under scrutiny, or where even a small delay in reporting a safeguarding issue can result in a disciplinary process for a member of school staff.

Having blame and shame hanging over us all is an incredibly unhelpful starting point, leading to a sense that 'It can't be my fault if it's your fault' or 'If it's not your fault, it must be my fault. And I'm not having that!' To help, we need to make clear the distinction between accountability and liability, and this is especially true when we are talking about school attendance.

In cases of difficulties with square pegs attending or accessing the physical site of a school, this is all the more problematic as 'high' attendance is sanctioned as a sign of a 'good' school. It is a situation that does not lay the groundwork for positive conversations between families and schools, especially when listing the reasons for non-attendance is such a blunt instrument (see Chapter 2). To remedy this, I have occasionally drawn on consultant psychiatrists in child and adolescent mental health services to provide letters to the effect that a certain condition or presentation would make it extremely difficult for a young person to attend school regularly, if at all. In this way, we have been able to diffuse some of the anxiety for the different parties around responsibility for school attendance, thus enabling more productive and creative dialogues. We do, however, need much wider recognition of the fact that children and young people can be, and often are, too unwell to access school on site on given days and for periods of time. And, that this does not need professional confirmation, any more than sickness and diarrhoea do, if we respect the assessment of responsible and loving parents.

## Can I borrow your specs?

You know when you go to the opticians and they painstakingly add and take away different lenses to bring your eyes into perfect focus to determine the prescription you need? I am often reminded of this when considering the less effective aspects of our inter-agency work. Rather than all of us simply sticking to our bit of the challenge (like the blind man feeling just one part of an elephant and proclaiming it a snake), multi-agency working should borrow each other's professional lenses to layer on their own, to refine again and again the perception of a family or situation until it finally comes into full focus. Note that the 'taking away' part is just as vital as the 'adding to'. We are dealing with dynamic, not fixed, situations, and just as what might work for one family might not work for another, what worked once for a family might not work next time. Despite our overstretched caseloads, we must avoid the 'one hit' phenomenon, where a view is formed from a single encounter or experience. As I mentioned earlier, the brain is quick to make cognitive leaps, all the more so when a single event forms 100% of our perception of a situation.

Crucially, this multilayered approach will also give us the confidence to really listen to parents, to question their views curiously and respectfully, and, of course, to be receptive to their critique of our views. It can be challenging to be faced with a parent who has had to become a powerful advocate for their child, and it is a natural urge to try to control that which makes us anxious. But if we have, at least in part, freed ourselves from the blame-based and fault-driven thinking about complex case work, then we should not be daunted by a parent who has had to become a 'confident champion' for their child (O'Connor et al., 2021).

## How to achieve this?

The will for partnership working absolutely starts at the top of the organisation. The most senior leaders, and ideally the head teacher, need to believe that it is *their* business to deepen their understanding of the work of other agencies, especially social care. The children's services team banner has to start to mean something.

One way to achieve this is to really understand equivalency of roles and to communicate and share at that level. There are some very enlightened colleagues in social care who have invited head teachers to attend strategic meetings, for example, and who have in turn attended senior leadership meetings to compare and contrast the organisational conventions and contentions.

Consider how to harness, even on a part-time or consultancy basis, the long-term skills and experience of an expert social care practitioner as part of your leadership team. Both times, this is how it started for me – an ad hoc, tentative arrangement that bloomed into a must-have. The rich rewards of this will be felt throughout your organisation and beyond, and all involved will understand your commitment to effective interagency working.

Another way, especially but not necessarily if you have a senior social worker in post, is to work with universities where social workers are trained. My schools have particularly benefited from having teams of social work students on placement, supervised in both cases by outstanding social care practitioners on my senior teams. Like teaching placements, there is a small amount of compensation in administration and supervision for each student, but there are enormous gains to be made in other ways too. Firstly, in capacity and the amazing contribution student social workers can make to children and families during their time with you. Secondly, the way in which hosting them can bring alive a curiosity and appreciation for their work, their professional culture and their formation across the community. And, finally, from a systems point of view, you now contribute to helping form rounded social work practitioners with a genuine perspective on how schools work and how they can work with us. They develop a familiarity with our lexicon and our restrictions and frustrations, which can form a career-long sympathy for, and synergy with, education staff in their multi-agency working.

I also recommend emotional intelligence coaching for all involved. This is all the more important where children with complex needs or complex situations provoke powerful and challenging feelings in all of us, from despair, impotency and incompetence to pity, anger and grief. The quickest route to dodging the bullet of these disturbing emotions is to transfer or project them onto others. We are all only human, and acknowledgement of this tendency as well as gentle and supportive deflection or diffusion of such behaviours can be so helpful in ensuring that working relationships, both in the moment and over time, can be safe, trusting and effective.

Returning to the start, systems can be good or bad, but they are created by, operated by and sustained by people. That said, we cannot 'fix' the system overnight, but we, as schools and leaders, can reframe our relationship with it and our relationships with the others within it. We do not need to let ourselves or our children and families become victims of its shortcomings. As leaders, we have far greater agency and more assets available to us to improve outcomes than we perhaps imagine. And when we change our thinking, everything changes. Try it. You won't regret it.

# References

Maslow, A. H. (1966) *The Psychology of Science: A Reconnaissance.* New York: Harper & Row.

O'Connor, A. B., Carpenter, B. and Coughlan, B. (2021) Confident Championing: A Grounded Theory of Parental Adjustment Following a Child's Diagnosis of Developmental Disability, *British Journal of Learning Disabilities,* 49(1): 1–12.

Chapter 10

# TWO HEADS ARE BETTER THAN ONE

## Jane Pickthall

Q: What do you call a head teacher who doesn't have a school building and who very rarely gets to meet the pupils on roll, despite being fully accountable for their outcomes?

A: A virtual school head.

I should know; I am one.

There are 150 of us across the country, supporting just over 65,000 5–18-year-olds who have found themselves in the care of local authorities, many of whom will be square pegs. Teachers supporting the education of children in care have existed for many years, but virtual school heads only became a thing in 2014. If you don't already have a well-established relationship with your virtual school head (or heads, as we work across local authority areas), I urge you to make the link, as per the title of this chapter. We are pretty well networked due to the transient nature of some of our pupils, so if you need details of a neighbouring virtual school head, your local authority's virtual school head can help. Local authority websites should include details too.

In 2018, we were given a role to provide information and advice around previously looked-after children who had found a permanent home through adoption, a special guardianship order or a child arrangement order (Department for Education, 2018a, 2018b). We don't have the same corporate parenting responsibility for this cohort and the pupil premium plus goes directly to schools, as long as the pupils are recorded on the school census. For this part of the role we cover only the schools in our local authority, but it isn't just schools that can seek our support and advice – social workers, independent reviewing officers, carers and parents can get in touch as well.

Then, in 2021, we were also given strategic oversight of all children with a social worker (ever), following the Department for Education's Children in Need Review (2019; see also Department for Education, 2021). This aspect of the role is about supporting schools and social workers to ensure both understand the importance of education and create the stability and trauma-informed environments these pupils need to succeed.

# So, you are a real person, not a computer?

If you thought being a school head was a lonely job, spare a thought for virtual school heads. We lead a school that only exists as a database, a 'virtual roll' of children and young people in the care of a local authority that may differ from their school's local authority. For example, I had one pupil who had moved to live with an aunt in Australia but who remained looked-after. His pupil premium plus money went on after-school scuba-diving lessons!

Our role is to monitor how the children in care are all doing through personal education plans and via regular data collection. We have a statutory responsibility, like you, to 'promote the education of looked-after and previously looked-after children' (Department for Education, 2018a, 2018b), but each virtual school head is likely to do this slightly differently, depending on the size of team, the local landscape and the nature of the local authority. It's a strategic role, but when a crisis occurs, we are also there on the ground trying to resolve whatever the problem is and get the right support in place. It's our job to ensure that education is seen as a high priority across children's social care and that schools are equipped to meet the needs of our shared pupils.

I am aware that as I describe what we do in my local authority, it is likely to be slightly different in yours. The principles remain the same, though: we are concerned with improving the outcomes and life chances of some of our most vulnerable pupils.[1]

# Don't believe the data

The national dataset for the educational outcomes of looked-after children looks bleak, but I have spent a lot of time unpicking it to get beneath the headlines. Thanks to two pivotal pieces of research by the Rees Centre at the University of Oxford (Sebba et al., 2015; Berridge at al., 2020), we now know which factors have the greatest impact on the educational outcomes of children in care and children in need. Whilst there is no guarantee of success if all the factors that impact most on academic achievement are in place, it does help to guide the work of a virtual school through careful selection of schools, support around mental health and emotional wellbeing, and promoting stability at school and home.

---

1  I really don't like the word 'vulnerable', especially since it has taken on a particular significance during the COVID-19 lockdowns. In the midst of a dangerous pandemic, these children were being told they should be in school. Many questioned why they weren't being kept safe at home and hated being treated differently to their friends. That said, some did enjoy the smaller class sizes and one spoke warmly to me of how the teachers were being more 'canny'. I heard from another virtual school head of a boy who misheard the word 'vulnerable' and thought he was going to school because he was 'valuable'. In many ways he was right.

Unfortunately, the list of factors that most impact on positive outcomes does not describe the vast majority of such children. Many care-experienced children simply don't have the stability they need at home or school, they haven't had the therapeutic support needed to address their past trauma and around 50% have identified (let alone unidentified) special educational needs and disabilities. The good news is that between mainstream schools, virtual schools, children's services and mental health services, we can do something about many of these factors. This is exactly what I have been tackling in my local authority, and my efforts are starting to make a difference.

My virtual school sits within a broader multi-agency team which includes nurses, counsellors, educational psychologists, an occupational therapist and a small team of teachers. We are co-located and work in a transdisciplinary way, meaning I have access to nearly all the information, advice and expertise I need across a desk or at the end of an email. We are very much a point of contact when help is needed. Whilst you might not have everyone so easily accessible, all these people exist in your local authority or health provisions, and they are there to help. We say it all the time, 'schools can't do everything'. In the case of our most complex children, I would agree, and you shouldn't have to do everything. However, there are many things you can do as a school that will make a huge difference.

Consider what it is like to be a child in the care of the state. It's really important for school leaders to understand what life is like for their individual pupils as there is no such thing as a 'typical' child in care. These children really benefit from having friends in high places, so if you can find some time to build a relationship and find out about their ambitions, favourite subjects, the books they like to read and what is important to them, it really helps. I have known school leaders find time to provide tea and biscuits, play a game of chess or send a holiday postcard to help develop that important connection. I have worked with hundreds of children in care and/or with a social worker over the past 20 years, and each one has their own story and a unique personality that has helped them to manage, cope with and, ultimately, survive the adversity they have been through. I will agree that sometimes these strategies don't always work so well in a school environment, but it's important to remember that there may have been a time when these strategies did succeed in getting a child's needs met, perhaps even keeping them alive.

## Mind the gap

Imagine trying to concentrate on learning when you don't think your mother is safe at home as you are not there to protect her from her violent partner. Many of our looked-after children have significant gaps in their knowledge simply because they were not always able to access learning, even if they were in school. It's not that they don't have the ability. It's just that they have holes that need filling, ideally by a compassionate teacher who can reteach the missing bits. In my virtual school, we have a reading recovery teacher who does just that. She goes back to basics and gives children the gift of reading and a way back into learning in the classroom. Since we have taken this approach, our literacy outcomes match those of non-looked-after children at Key Stage 1.

I also have a secondary maths teacher who works with our Key Stage 3 pupils to assess their gaps using the Sandwell Early Numeracy Test,[2] and reteaches the missing mathematical principles. This was key to our GCSE strategy when the curriculum changed and numerical grades were introduced and modular exams removed. We also noticed that the questions in the maths paper placed a greater reliance on working memory. Many of our children have poor working memory skills, linked to past trauma, which impacts on certain sections of the brain (see Chapter 32), so we undertook specific work to develop these skills.

The work of a virtual school head is very much about finding ways to accelerate progress and promote approaches that meet the specific needs of looked-after children. Virtual school heads have argued for years that looked-after children often need a different approach to their non-looked-after peers; in 2020, the Education Endowment Foundation and What Works for Children's Social Care revisited a range of trials and proved me right (Sanders et al., 2020). They found that certain interventions worked better for looked-after children than other supposedly successful interventions, which could in fact have a detrimental impact on progress for this group. It's worth taking a look at these reports to ensure the interventions you are using in your school are the ones that are most effective, especially now there is so much focus on 'catch-up' due to the COVID-19 pandemic. The researchers found that interventions that involved improving communication with parents and carers were beneficial[3] and projects that supported reading in the home[4] and those focused on literacy gaps[5] all had a greater impact on pupils with a social worker. Further trials are currently underway to strengthen this evidence base.

An analysis of the national data set throws up something else too – a worrying trend that the highest achieving looked-after children are making the least progress at Key Stage 4. I was listening to a care-experienced person talking recently about how 'average' was seen as 'good enough' for her, yet she had always been a high achiever prior to entering care. Good enough is not enough when a child has the ability to achieve better (as Will Carter so eloquently describes in Chapter 5). Flight paths and trajectories can really work against those children in care who perhaps didn't do so well in their early assessments. A SATs score from when a child was aged 7, living in an

---

2   See https://www.gl-assessment.co.uk/assessments/products/sandwell-early-numeracy-test.
3   See Save the Children's Families and Schools Together (FAST) programme: https://www.savethechildren.org.uk/what-we-do/child-poverty/uk-child-poverty/in-schools/fast#!.
4   See the Supporting Parents on Kids Education in Schools (SPOKES) programme in Plymouth: https://www.plymouthias.org.uk/parenting-programmes/supporting-parents-on-kids-education-in-schools-spokes.
5   See the Vocabulary Enrichment Intervention Programme (Styles et al., 2014) and the Catch Up Literacy intervention: https://www.catchup.org/interventions/literacy.php.

abusive environment and unable to access classroom learning is not a fair indicator of future achievement. We must all remember to look beyond the prediction, and with some children well beyond it.

Perhaps the low aspirations some schools may have for looked-after children comes from the very term used to describe them, often shortened to LAC. Children tell me they really don't like it as it makes them sound 'lacking' and might be contributing to the negative connotations sometimes associated with children in this position. We have even heard school leaders using these negative connotations to argue why they don't want to admit a child to their schools. There was a time when every article in the *TES* that mentioned a looked-after child was accompanied by a picture of a sad or angry child or a youth in a hoodie. It was one of the things I tackled as chair of the National Association of Virtual School Heads, and thankfully clouds with ladders started to appear instead. Of course, there are children in care who are sad, angry and struggling, and given what they have lived through it's hardly surprising, but most I know are hard-working, desperate to belong, resilient and charming.

## We can't take away the events of the past but we can support the recovery

To meet the thresholds for children's services involvement, a child needs to have been through some pretty traumatic life events, even more so if they have spent time in care. This means that even if you don't know the finer details of the abuse, neglect or loss a child has experienced, you can imagine how frightening and traumatic it must have been. Very few children are in care because of their own behaviour; it is the behaviour of the adults around them that brings a child under the watchful eye of children's services. Adults have let them down, failed them, caused harm that can last a lifetime and broken their trust. We can't take away what has happened in the past, as much as we would love to, but we can help a child to rebuild the trust of adults and learn to feel safe. Dr Karen Treisman talks about 'every interaction being an intervention,'[6] and this is so true.

As we have seen elsewhere in this book, the impact of childhood trauma can be devastating and can present as very distressing behaviour. In my virtual school, we believe in trauma recovery and post-traumatic growth. We have seen it happen, given a period of stability, supportive adults and the right therapeutic support. I have been in my role long enough to see primary school pupils we have worked with mature into confident and capable young adults. It's the best feeling in the world. I am as proud as any parent of each and every one of them. It's not always easy and it's certainly not quick, but if you stick in there, the rewards are unbelievable.

---

6   See https://www.youtube.com/watch?v=8pBkXbCP3Q4.

Always bear in mind, then, how schools can be transformative places. Where to start? Do you have a 'no shouting' policy, for example? And did you know that in the 2020/2021 academic year, 70,763 fixed-term exclusions occurred due to a child shouting at an adult (Department for Education, 2022[7])? When an adult shouts it can take a child back to how they felt living in a household where domestic abuse was a daily occurrence. I know because I have had big burly lads telling me just that. They get flashbacks to that time when they felt scared.

Some remember how raised voices were a precursor to physical violence either towards another family member, or worse, towards themselves. If a child has witnessed domestic violence, they will be all too familiar with the victim/perpetrator relationship and so do all they can to avoid being that victim again. Keep an eye out for members of staff who use raised voices as there is an increased risk of a child responding with aggression to protect themselves. Sadly, I have known it happen all too often, and the child is then sanctioned, with a possible exclusion, because they have reacted instinctively to shield themselves from harm.

You and your staff are in the fortunate position to show children that adults can be kind, caring and safe. You have the power to change perception, build trust and give the child the opportunity to see the world in a very different way.

## What is going on inside that brain?

The trauma recovery approach we use in my virtual school is based on a neurodevelopmental model which reflects how the brain develops in early childhood. When children have experienced developmental trauma, there are often interruptions in the way their brains have developed that require work to strengthen and enhance the parts most impacted by the trauma.[8] It's useful to teach children a basic understanding of their brain, too, as it helps them to understand why they respond in the way they do. In my virtual school, we have developed a series of lesson plans on psycho-education to help pupils as young as 6 learn about the brain's stress response, different emotions and the window of tolerance.

Drawing on brain research that shows how the brainstem (our 'downstairs brain' as it is referred to in Chapter 27) is where our survival response sits, note that many children with a trauma history can easily find themselves back in survival mode. It is also the part of the brain that helps us to regulate and can impact on sensory responses, so we have an occupational therapist who works with children to provide specific activities, also known as sensory diets, which help them with self-regulation and make them

---

7   For data on permanent exclusions and suspensions in England for the academic year 2020/21 see https://explore-education-statistics.service.gov.uk/find-statistics/permanent-and-fixed-period-exclusions-in-england.
8   This is discussed in more detail in Chapter 27. See also Lyons (2017).

better able to manage in a classroom. Some children can get sensory overload with activities such as playtime, trampolining or even walking down a busy corridor. This is an area that many schools overlook, but it can make a huge difference to behaviour.[9]

Next we consider the limbic system which is linked to emotions and relationships. Navigating relationships can be hard if you have been harmed within and by relationships. Peer relationships can be a challenge here, too, as looked-after children can be at a different developmental stage than their chronological age and may share interests with younger children. They can be easily influenced and long to be part of a group, even if that group does not have their best interests at heart.

An added complication for children in care is around what they choose to tell their peers about their circumstances at home. Friendships can be fraught as a child in care doesn't always want others to know this, which can lead to feelings of shame as they can't be honest. Children can be cruel, and bullying is a sad feature of the lives of many looked-after and adopted children. 'Your mother doesn't love you' is a regular taunt. If a care-experienced child does lash out at another child, it is always worth checking what was behind it, as it is often linked to nasty comments. The more a school creates an ethos that values individual difference, supports friendships and takes a restorative approach, the easier it is for care-experienced pupils to thrive.

We use our educational psychologists to support this work using interventions such as Theraplay,[10] which is a nurturing, playful programme designed to build trust, self-esteem and attachments between an adult and child or a group of children or young people. It can be used at home with parents or carers and in schools with support staff. We also use programmes such as Friends Resilience,[11] which is endorsed by the World Health Organization and the Department of Health and Social Care. There are four schemes of work from Key Stage 1 through to adult, which support a reduction in anxiety, help to develop coping strategies and build resilience. The programme promotes the values of kindness, gratitude and bravery, encouraging pupils and parents to develop self-help skills.

Consider, too, the relationships with adults in the school. These can make or break a child's time there. If one good thing comes out of the COVID-19 pandemic, it is the relationships that have been built by staff and the 'valuable' pupils who have still been attending school. Even those who have been studying at home felt valued when staff phoned regularly to check how they were getting on, demonstrating that they were being 'kept in mind'. I know how precious time is in schools but even two minutes a day can make a big difference.

---

9   Sometimes these behaviours can be mistaken for autism, but if a child has a trauma history it is much more likely to be linked to this. The Coventry Grid provides a useful comparison between behaviours associated with attachment/trauma and autism – see https://drawingtheidealself.co.uk/the-coventry-grid.

10   See http://www.wp.theraplay.org/uk.

11   See https://friendsresilience.org.

Once the brainstem and limbic system are happy, then, and only then, can we think about the thinking brain, the neocortex, where formal school learning happens. Sometimes the pathways here are weak and need strengthening, otherwise there is a risk that the child remains in the more survival-driven parts of the brain. It's important to recognise which part of the brain the child is operating in and support the child where they are at.[12] A child in survival mode will first need time to regulate and feel safe. A child focused on the adult in a classroom, rather than the task, will need more support with feeling safe in their relationships before they can fully access learning. So often staff expect a child to be able to reason whilst they are 'offline', but to enable those rational conversations to take place, a child first needs to regulate and then be with someone they trust, before there is any chance of understanding what has been behind the behaviour.[13]

## Shame vs guilt – why conventional behaviour management approaches might not work

Most behaviour management strategies in schools rely on pupils feeling a sense of guilt when they do something wrong, so they won't do it again. They also rely on pupils being able to rationalise behaviour enough for the threatened sanction to prevent the behaviour happening in the first place. For some pupils this will be enough, but a one-size-fit-all approach can never work in a school where a significant proportion of the children have experienced adversity. By applying the rules in this way, it will be the children who have experienced trauma who will be further disadvantaged.

The exclusion rates nationally for children in need[14] show they are almost three times more likely to be permanently excluded than their peers. Although the numbers for looked-after children permanently excluded are small, the fixed-term exclusion rates are worryingly high, with over 11% experiencing at least one period of fixed-term exclusion (Department for Education, 2020a). Exclusions are felt very keenly as a rejection, building resentment and decreasing trust, not to mention the further loss of learning opportunities. Virtual school heads work hard to reduce exclusions, and I am proud to say that I have had only one permanent exclusion of a looked-after child in the past 15 years.

Shame trumps guilt, so for a child to be able to feel the latter they need not to be feeling the former (Brown, 2012). Children who have grown up in abusive and

---

12  See, for example, the Neurosequential Model of Therapeutics, which was developed by Dr Bruce Perry: https://www.neurosequential.com.

13  Remember Dr Perry's three Rs – regulate, relate and reason – and you might add a fourth, repair (Bombèr, 2020). This entails making everything right again, whether that is the physical repair of damage to property or the emotional repair of a broken relationship.

14  A social services categorisation.

neglectful households can often feel a huge sense of shame. Their internal belief is that they themselves are to blame for their circumstances, that *they* are the mistake. Where guilt can enable us to recognise that 'I made a mistake', to externalise the situation to what we did, not who we are, shame causes us to put up our defences to protect us from feeling so bad. It's what Dan Hughes and Kim Golding (Golding, 2015) call the 'shield against shame':

- Denying doing whatever we are accused of.
- Blaming others.
- Minimising the scale of the incident.
- Raging and diverting anger towards the accuser.

Unfortunately, these responses make the matter worse and usually lead to even greater consequences. It's all too easy for a minor misdemeanour to escalate into something major, so be mindful of this when you are unpicking an incident and deciding how to deal with it. Does there always need to be a sanction? A consequence, yes, but always a punishment? If the purpose of discipline is about teaching someone to change their ways,[15] then making pupils feel even worse is not going to change anything; it will only reinforce their sense of shame. So many school sanctions involve shaming pupils – the grey cloud at the end of the rainbow, names on the board, public admonishments – so, imagine how this feels for the child who already thinks they are a mistake. These pupils need time, safe relationships and understanding to reduce the shame and increase acceptance. Many care-experienced children have already experienced rejection. They know when rejection is heading their way. Threats of exclusion make a child feel very insecure and can lead to pre-emptive behaviours that are even harder to deal with. When a lack of stability at home is all-too familiar, school stability is even more important.

We differentiate in our teaching and learning, so why not in our behaviour system? It's not about letting pupils 'get away with' poor behaviour, it's about understanding where the behaviour comes from, taking time to understand it, offering opportunities to repair things and, in so doing, taking the shame away. After all, these children's lives have been punishing enough.

## No fresh starts

'A fresh start will be good for them.' This is rarely the case for a pupil who has experienced developmental trauma. For children and young people who take such a long time to build trust with an adult, starting somewhere new is a real challenge. Leaving

---

15 Although in some schools it is clearly used *pour encourager les autres.*

behind established peer friendships and adult relationships, and sometimes family connections and roots, then having to fit into established friendship groups can be tough, especially for those pupils who have struggled with peer relationships previously. Having to tell their story from scratch can be fraught with anxiety and shame, particularly when they don't know who can be trusted. Scared about being bullied, having to lie, denying who they are for risk of judgement – it's a really difficult situation for a care-experienced child and should be avoided as much possible.

In an attempt to avoid exclusions, schools sometimes opt for a 'managed move' – the chance to try out another school, with a built-in exit strategy if it doesn't work after a period of between six and ten weeks. This approach puts pupils under enormous stress and, more often than not, it fails. It doesn't give them enough time to settle into a school, build trust with new teachers, adapt to curriculum changes and make friendships. A child in this situation is placed under tremendous scrutiny and every hiccup diminishes the likelihood of success. I don't allow this approach for looked-after children in my authority, and our authority-wide Keeping Children in School policy (North Tyneside Council, 2021: 7) has really supported this approach, with all school leaders working towards the common goal of reducing exclusions and managed moves for all pupils.

Instead, I work with my school leaders to provide additional support, opportunities for assessment and training for staff to help schools hold on to my pupils. In my authority, that can mean extra funding and/or access to an educational psychologist, occupational therapist, counsellor or teacher. We work in partnership, alongside the child's social worker and carer, to identify what the child or young person needs, but it is often the pupils themselves who can explain what they need most accurately.

# Getting the support right and that four-letter word

The cure for bad relationships is good ones. There is no quick fix, but there is plenty that can be done here. Even though I know all too well how tight budgets are, with a bit of creativity and flexibility there are many ways to maximise the support available:

- Only use staff who want to do relationship-based work.
- Use the staff who are bigger, stronger, wiser and kind – these children need to feel safe and respond best to adults who have clear boundaries, confidence and warmth. Humour, done kindly, helps too.
- Make sure staff have their own houses in order, so they have room in their heads and hearts for pupils who have experienced trauma.

- Allow staff to access specialist training in attachment and trauma.

- Keep support flexible and make it available as and when needed. One member of staff can be a key adult to half a dozen pupils using this approach.

- Provide staff doing this work with 'supervision' (see Chapter 7) to avoid the risk of secondary trauma and burnout.

- Make sure pupils have not just a key adult but a small team of staff around them, a group who are almost like a family within the school. This reduces the impact of staff changes, minimises over-reliance on one person and allows more staff to get to know the pupil better. A senior leader should be part of this team.[16]

Relationships matter. When care-experienced adults look back at their experience, they often talk about the lack of love they felt within the care system (Felitti et al., 1998). When most schools are so focused on safeguarding practice, it can be hard to imagine how they can show their love for their pupils, especially for those who need it most, but it can be done. I remember working with a great pastoral lead who would make it explicit that he needed to keep pupils safe, but at the same time there were times when only a hug would do. He would say, 'Come here and I'll give you one of those sideways hugs,' and he would stand hip to hip with a child and put his arm around their shoulder and squeeze. Scotland's Independent Care Review (2020) mentions the word 'love' 52 times, showing the importance of it in its ambition for the Scottish care system. You may have heard paediatric neurologist Dr Andrew Curran describing the neurobiological imperative for love (see Chapter 26). Increasingly, people are talking about the role of 'professional love', especially for children and young people in the care system. Even if we can't always tell them how precious and important they are to us, we can demonstrate it in our actions:

- Give them our time and attention.

- Take an interest in them.

- Find joy in their company.

- Demonstrate care and kindness to them.

## Two heads really are better than one

I hope this chapter has been insightful, but please remember that you will have your own virtual school head in your local authority (in England at least) who can offer further support. Together, we can ensure that we are providing opportunities for our most 'valuable' square pegs to grow, develop and secure positive futures. We can't take

---

16  For more on this model, see Louise Michelle Bombèr's *Team Pupil in School* (2016), one of five books in the Attachment Aware Schools Series.

away the past for these pupils, but we can shape the future with kindness, patience, understanding and, yes, love.

# References

Berridge, D., Luke, N., Sebba, J., Strand, S., Cartwright, M., Staples, E. et al. (2020) *Children in Need and Children in Care: Educational Attainment and Progress.* Available at: http://www.bristol.ac.uk/media-library/sites/policybristol/briefings-and-reports-pdfs/Final%20Report%20Nuffield.pdf.

Bombèr, L. M. (2016) *Bridging the Gap for Troubled Pupils* (Attachment Aware Schools Series; 5 vol. box set). Duffield: Worth Publishing.

Bombèr, L. M. (2020) *Know Me to Teach Me: Differentiated Discipline for Those Recovering from Adverse Childhood Experiences.* Duffield: Worth Publishing.

Brown, B. (2012) Listening to Shame [TED Talk] [video] (1 March). Available at: https://brenebrown.com/videos/ted-talk-listening-to-shame.

Department for Education (2018a) *The Designated Teacher for Looked-After and Previously Looked-After Children: Statutory Guidance on Their Roles and Responsibilities* (February). Available at: https://www.gov.uk/government/publications/designated-teacher-for-looked-after-children.

Department for Education (2018b) *Promoting the Education of Looked-After Children and Previously Looked-After Children: Statutory Guidance for Local Authorities* (February). Available at: https://www.gov.uk/government/publications/promoting-the-education-of-looked-after-children.

Department for Education (2019) *Help, Protection, Education: Concluding the Children in Need Review* (June). Available at: https://www.gov.uk/government/publications/review-of-children-in-need/review-of-children-in-need.

Department for Education (2020a) *Outcomes for Children Looked After by Local Authorities in England, 31 March 2019* (26 March). Available at: https://assets.publishing.service.gov.uk/government/uploads/system/uploads/attachment_data/file/884758/CLA_Outcomes_Main_Text_2019.pdf.

Department for Education (2020b) Permanent Exclusions and Suspensions in England: Academic Year 2018/19 (30 July). Available at: https://explore-education-statistics.service.gov.uk/find-statistics/permanent-and-fixed-period-exclusions-in-england/2018-19.

Department for Education (2021) *Promoting the Education of Children with a Social Worker: Virtual School Head Role Extension* (June; updated June 2022). Available at: https://www.gov.uk/government/publications/virtual-school-head-role-extension-to-children-with-a-social-worker.

Felitti, V. J., Anda, R. F., Nordenberg, D., Williamson, D. F., Spitz, A. M., Edwards, V. et al. (1998) Relationship of Childhood Abuse and Household Dysfunction to Many of the Leading Causes of Death in Adults: The Adverse Childhood Experiences (ACE) Study, *American Journal of Preventive Medicine*, 14(4): 245–258.

Golding, K. (2015) Connection Before Correction: Supporting Parents to Meet the Challenges of Parenting Children Who Have Been Traumatised Within Their Early Parenting Environments, *Children Australia*, 40(2): 1–8.

Independent Care Review (2020) *The Promise* (February). Available at: https://www.carereview.scot/conclusions/independent-care-review-reports.

Lyons, S. (2017) The Repair of Early Trauma: A 'Bottom Up' Approach. Available at: https://beaconhouse.org.uk/wp-content/uploads/2019/09/Repair-of-Early-Trauma.pdf.

North Tyneside Council (2021) *North Tyneside Children and Young People's Plan, 2021–2025.* Available at: https://my.northtyneside.gov.uk/sites/default/files/web-page-related-files/Final%20Children%20and%20Young%20people%20Plan%20%282021-2025%29..pdf.

Sanders, M., Sholl, P., Leroy, A., Mitchell, C., Reid, L. and Gibbons, D. (2020) *What Works in Education for Children Who Have Had a Social Worker: Summary Report.* Available at: https://whatworks-csc.org.uk/wp-content/uploads/WWCSC_what_works_education_children_SWs_Feb20_A.pdf.

Sebba, J., Berridge, D., Luke, N., Fletcher, J., Bell, K., Strand, S. et al. (2015) *The Educational Progress of Looked After Children in England: Linking Care and Educational Data.* London: Nuffield Foundation. Available at: http://www.education.ox.ac.uk/wp-content/uploads/2019/05/301411.pdf.

Styles, B., Stevens, E., Bradshaw, S. and Clarkson, R. (2014) *Vocabulary Enrichment Intervention Programme: Evaluation Report and Executive Summary* (October). London: Education Endowment Foundation. Available at: https://www.nfer.ac.uk/publications/EFTR03/EFTR03.pdf.

Treisman, K. (2021) *A Treasure Box for Creating Trauma-Informed Organizations: A Ready-to-Use Resource for Trauma, Adversity, and Culturally Informed, Infused and Responsive Systems,* 2 vols. London: Jessica Kingsley.

# Chapter 11

# SHOW ME YOU KNOW ME

## Chris Bagley

---

Go to lesson one, English. I can't do it, feel thick, get really angry and sometimes mess around. Lesson two, science, even worse. Literally no idea. Lesson three is maths which is like my worst lesson. The teacher hates me 'cos I always get rude 'cos I just can't do it or am just bored. Basically, I fail almost all week apart from PE, which is cool, and it makes me so angry 'cos there's nothing I can do.

---

This is how 13-year-old Sam described his school life to me.

Sam is a square peg.

## What do the statistics say about school exclusion?

In 2018/2019, 7,894 children were permanently excluded from school in England and Wales (Department for Education, 2020). The numbers decreased in the years 2019/20 and 2020/21 due to the COVID-19 pandemic.[1] However, the increase over time is stark. In 2013/2014, 4,949 permanent exclusions were reported (Partridge, 2019) and, hence, a worrying increase of almost 3,000 was recorded over a short period of five years. According to the recent Timpson Review (2019), 78% of permanent exclusions issued were to students who either had special educational needs and disabilities (SEND), were classified as in need or were eligible for free school meals. A disproportionate number were living in care. Young people from Gypsy, Roma, Traveller, Black Caribbean and Mixed White Caribbean backgrounds were considerably more likely to be excluded than other groups. Official figures are a significant underestimate as they do not account for the many young people who are yearly subject to 'off-rolling' and other forms of illegal, hidden exclusion (Ofsted, 2019).

---

1   For data on permanent exclusions and suspensions in England for the academic year 2020/21 and previous years see https://explore-education-statistics.service.gov.uk/find-statistics/permanent-and-fixed-period-exclusions-in-england/2020-21.

Having spent many years working as a psychologist in a youth offending team, child prisons and pupil referral units, what is abundantly clear to me is that young people like Sam who are kicked out of school are those in most need of help. In some quarters, there are ongoing attempts to stoke a narrative that school exclusions occur solely to keep staff and children safe. It's asserted that our schools are potentially unsafe due to dangerous reprobates and violent youths. The data do not support this. By far the most common reasons that young people are excluded are 'persistent disruptive behaviour' and those catalogued under an elusive 'other' category (Department for Education, 2021). Systemic factors created by hostile government policies make things difficult too.

There is much that we can do, though.

## What happens for young people that leads to their exclusion?

No child wants to be in trouble. Persistent disruptive behaviour, consciously or unconsciously, serves a purpose. It shows us that something is not working, persistently. This purpose grows from the invisible consequences of an infinitely complex maze of genetic and environmental interactions. It is not possible, as some claim, to know the behaviours that are 'chosen' and those that are beyond conscious control, simply by looking at them. As psychoanalyst and physician Gabor Maté (2010) reminds us, choice is not absolute.

In my experience, most young people who present with 'challenging behaviour' are trying to belong. They are vying to survive in an education environment that does not work for them. For example, there is a reason why many excluded teens have SEND. Often, they are desperate to fit in socially in a context where they feel constantly judged for being 'thick', 'hyper', 'stupid' or 'dumb'. These words come up constantly in my work with children who have been socialised to develop negative core beliefs about themselves, often from a very early age. Combine SEND with living in care, and you have a particularly toxic combination in a school system where results are prioritised over connection.

How could a child with learning difficulties, an unstable sense of self, an understandable fear of being 'unwanted' and a perception of inferiority live in this context without becoming distressed?

Sam's story is not unusual. Anyone who has genuinely listened to our square pegs will have heard this story over and over. When a young person does not believe they can succeed academically, they will seek validation in other ways, perhaps by moving closer to young people who are similarly 'othered' by the system. Teen development is exceptionally complex and peer relationships are a primary driver of behaviour. As cognitive scientist and expert on the adolescent brain, Sarah-Jayne Blakemore (2018: 24) says, 'Adolescents are more likely than younger children to compare themselves with others and to understand that others are making comparisons and judgements about them.'

Adolescents report higher levels of embarrassment and often overestimate the extent to which others are evaluating them compared with younger children and adults. Teens who struggle to cope in school are often developing a sense of self that is framed by feelings of not being 'good enough'. Imagine what it's like for a young person who knows they are miles behind their peers academically, and is in a state of panic about judgement by others. These are the children I see, week in, week out. They can become progressively more hypervigilant, anxious and low. In some cases, they externalise this distress through 'disruptive behaviour'. Teachers are often in the impossible situation of observing – and being on the receiving end of – these behaviours, without having the time, emotional space, training or curriculum flexibility to respond.

Of course, there are occasions of physical or verbal assault, but, even in these cases, there is always a context to consider. Assaults do not occur in a vacuum. And, again, in many situations staff do not have the time, resources or flexibility to act preventatively. Nobody denies the importance of keeping students and staff safe, and in extreme circumstances a young person might need immediate removal from the school site. But steps can always be taken to minimise the distress of a child subject to that exclusion.

## What psychological processes are relevant in relation to exclusion?

Psychological distress is consistently higher among children who have experienced exclusion when compared with their non-excluded peers (Ford et al., 2018). Importantly, there is a bidirectional association between psychological distress and exclusion. In some cases distress can make exclusion more likely, and in others exclusion itself increases distress.

One essential psychological construct to consider is the need for 'belongingness' (Baumeister and Leary, 1995) (see also Chapter 6). We all need to feel connected to others via safe, consistent, reciprocal relationships. Exclusion ostracises those children in society who are most in need of relational security, and being ostracised has long-term emotional consequences. As Baumeister and Leary (1995: 508) explain, 'being accepted, included, or welcomed leads to a variety of positive emotions (e.g., happiness, elation, contentment, and calm), whereas being rejected, excluded, or ignored leads to potent negative feelings (e.g., anxiety, depression, grief, jealousy, and loneliness)'.

The pain caused by social ostracisation is deeper and lasts longer than a physical injury. Professor Kipling Williams, who has conducted numerous studies around the impact of ostracisation, puts it thus: 'Being excluded is painful because it threatens fundamental human needs, such as belonging and self-esteem … Again and again research has found that strong, harmful reactions are possible even when ostracized by a stranger or for a short amount of time' (Purdue University, 2011; see also Williams and Nida, 2011).

Human beings are social animals. This has an evolutionary basis, as maintaining social bonds promotes survival (Over, 2016). According to Baumeister and Leary (1995: 497), much of what we do is done in the service of belongingness, which is a 'fundamental human motivation'. It is essential for us to develop (a) frequent, positive interactions with the same individuals, and (b) engage in these interactions within a framework of long-term, stable care and concern. People who lack belongingness are at significantly greater risk of involvement in criminality (Ben-Zeév, 2014). Which brings us back to Sam.

# Sam's story

Sam lives in South London, and I have known him for many years. Growing up, he was surrounded by domestic violence and emotional abuse. He is a good egg with a cracking sense of humour, and is truly resilient in the face of huge challenges. He is great at football, and in this context has excellent leadership skills and social intelligence. But he struggles. His birth father is in prison, and he views the world (and the people in it) as threatening. Sam is constantly hypervigilant and has difficulty regulating his emotions, forming trusting relationships, focusing in class and conforming to school rules. Sam always struggled with academic study, and home was not a safe, nurturing place in which to learn. He muddled through school until Year 10 when the increased academic demands became overwhelming. He became progressively more anxious, developing a perception of himself as 'stupid' and 'hyper', eventually resulting in permanent exclusion for 'persistent disruptive behaviour'. A few months later, Sam came my way again through a court-sanctioned referral order following a knife offence.

The popular press has Sam down as a delinquent, excluded from school for poor behaviour and a perpetrator of knife crime. Such headlines ignore the fact that Sam is also an abused, neglected, traumatised child with serious learning and language difficulties.

Following his exclusion, Sam – totally isolated, ashamed and riddled with an all-encompassing feeling of worthlessness – had found somewhere else to belong. He always was, and still is, a good egg. But it was his motivation to belong, a fundamental human need we all share, that drove Sam to seek another community – one that took him down a path that ended in violence. He 'substituted' new relationships for those lost and was drawn to other young people with similar experiences, just like ex-pats in a Hong Kong bar. What is more, research shows that external threats increase the human tendency to form strong bonds (Baumeister and Leary, 1995).

Diane Reay, professor of sociology of education at the University of Cambridge, in her furious critique of the UK education system, describes young people like Sam as 'educational collateral damage' (Reay, 2017: 142). We have created a system that inflicts harm on children, then holds them individually responsible when things go wrong.

## The link between youth violence and exclusion

Careful readers of the previous section will not be surprised to learn that there is a very strong relationship between school exclusion and youth violence. The Ministry of Justice (2013; see also Ministry of Justice, 2014) reports that of 15–17-year-olds in young offender institutions (child prisons), 88% of young men and 74% of young women had been excluded from school at some point. According to the Home Office (Smith and Wynne-McHardy, 2019), young people who have been excluded are six times more likely to carry/use a weapon than those who have not been excluded. The following factors correlate most significantly with youth violence: gender (males), early puberty, maltreatment (physical, sexual, emotional abuse), parental drug use, poor relationship with parents, number of siblings, school exclusion, truancy, being a victim, feeling unsafe in a neighbourhood, feelings of isolation, risk-taking tendency and self-control issues. These are often called 'risk factors'. Alongside other factors, exclusion often exerts a strong influence on the mental health and life outcomes of thousands of children.

It's impossible to assert the exact influence of exclusion, as the interrelationship between risk factors is complex and impossible to disentangle. I know that almost every child I have worked with in the youth justice or pupil referral unit system has been excluded from school, and *all* of them cite it as a prominent, negative factor in their story. Analysing correlational data is about considering how numerous social forces interact. Every child and every social context is different, yet we know that school exclusion can be a hugely impactful event that exists in a chain of causality. Whilst no single factor such as exclusion can be shown to *cause* youth violence, it is hugely significant for many young people, and this is why it is so highly correlated. Young people like Sam are both victim and perpetrator.

Our challenge is that, after a certain age, there is a narrative shift and teenagers cease to be victims who are at risk and begin to be defined as the risk factors themselves (Levell, 2021).

# The international picture

There are many in England who perceive that school exclusion is a self-evident, essential facet of our education system. Yet, in Scotland, a cultural shift has taken place in recent years (Cole et al., 2019). Viewing behaviour as a form of communication is now central to education policy edict and exclusions have reduced drastically. In many European nations, such as Italy, Finland and Portugal, alternative provision – schools where children are often sent once excluded and segregated from their mainstream peers – is not a thing (Boyle and Topping, 2012). Fully integrated mainstream schooling is taken for granted (Bagley, 2021).

The Scottish government has taken steps to prioritise 'better relationships' in their educational approach.[2] Yet in England, strict behaviour management policies – characterised by removal rooms (isolation rooms/internal exclusion) and in-school behavioural units – have been promoted.[3] There is no official expectation that schools should focus on belongingness or building relationships. Note, then, that England is an outlier here, and is a place of enormous exclusion and marginalisation compared with similar nations.

The alternative provision sector is expanding exponentially, sometimes in unregistered schools (IntegratED, 2020), and people are literally making money from the marginalisation of children. Why? At first glance, there are two ways we can interpret this:

1   Assume that there is something uniquely amiss with English children which means they are inherently more challenging, out of control or dangerous than those elsewhere. These children *must* be excluded because they can't be educated alongside their peers. Evidence at home and internationally, comparing the behaviour of English children to others, debunks this pernicious myth (Jenkins and Ueno, 2017; Rhodes and Long, 2021). This assumption is implied by those who constantly reinforce the 'right to exclude' or the concept of 'preventable exclusions', a phrase that presumes many are inevitable.

---

2   See https://education.gov.scot/education-scotland/scottish-education-system/policy-for-scottish-education/policy-drivers/better-relationships-better-learning-better-behaviour.
3   The government is currently analysing feedback from a consultation held in 2021 on behaviour management strategies, in-school units and managed moves – see https://www.gov.uk/government/consultations/behaviour-management-strategies-in-school-units-and-managed-moves-call-for-evidence.

2   Accept that there are significant, deep-rooted problems with the English education system which underpin the exceptional levels of exclusion and marginalisation. Given that contention one is absurd, we are left to examine the reasons why exclusion and marginalisation are so prominent in England.

## What are the underlying reasons for exclusion being so common in England?

A number of systemic factors are at play:

◼ Inflexible curricula and rigid success criteria. Student success and worth are measured solely by exam results, and teachers are forced into a straitjacket that makes inclusion extremely difficult. As asserted by Stephen Ball (2003: 224), 'authentic social relations are replaced by judgemental relations wherein persons are valued for their productivity'. Senior teachers are under extreme pressure to enhance the results of students, monitored by Progress 8 at secondary level and the ever-present shadow of league tables. In this context, when a child is presenting with challenging behaviour, is it surprising that senior teachers consider exclusion as a valid option? The stakes are high, but the children who suffer are always the most needy.

◼ Accountability measures, policed by Ofsted, alongside the positioning of schools in a competitive market, prompt some schools to treat young people as commodities. The accountability and competition ideologies incentivise some to prioritise their needs over individual student needs in order to compete. Recent research by Zancajo and Bonal (2020: 1) found that 'market-oriented policies that enhance competition and choice tend to produce negative effects on equity by boosting school segregation and social stratification'. In essence, when the futures of children are placed in the hands of the market and a system of competition, the least 'marketable' children are pushed out and marginalised. They are treated as 'human unsaleable goods' (Parfrey, 1994: 119).

◼ To contain young people who push back against this coercive system, a growth in punitive behaviour policies has triggered an increase in sanctions, segregation and ostracisation for children who struggle to comply (Graham, 2018). What is interesting is that after decades of punitive behaviour policies, exclusion has not reduced – rather it has increased significantly. A reminder: whilst data indicate that permanent exclusions decreased in 2019/2020 and 2020/2021 (5,057 and 3,928 respectively), this is expected given the COVID-19 pandemic and consequent school closures and limited attendance. Hence, it is not valid to compare years 2019/2021 to previous (or subsequent) years. Figures are not yet available for 2021/2022. Crucially, no research evidence – ever – has been presented in support of the punitive approach. It is thoroughly ideological. Zero tolerance, in particular, is psychologically illiterate. Ask yourself: if zero tolerance and inflexible behaviour policies are so effective, why are more and more children being excluded from mainstream schooling?

# What can we do?

There are clear steps that school leaders can take to prevent the marginalisation of young people, like Sam, who do not fit neatly into the education system – the square pegs. This is challenging, given that exclusion is incentivised and strict behaviour policies are promoted by the government and its favoured pugilists.

It is possible, with the right mindset, careful resourcing and an understanding of psychology, to make things work. The six suggestions below are drawn from the real-life examples of Sam and another boy I have worked with, Jamie, at the start of Year 10. They have similar histories and ways of relating and responding to their social worlds. Sam, as we have heard, was permanently excluded at the end of term one, but Jamie made it through his GCSEs and went to college. It's important to observe that, even with the additional interventions outlined below, Jamie always found things difficult. There were many ups and downs, but staff persevered with their approach and, ultimately, he made it. It can be done.

## 1. When they push you away, hold them closer

The knee-jerk reaction in many societies, and especially in England, is to isolate and exclude those who fail to follow the rules. This is heavily ingrained in our school culture. For some, perhaps a short, sharp shock such as a detention will scare them into obeying, but the situation is far more complex for Sam, as we have seen. Young people like Sam, with low self-worth and little faith that adults are trustworthy, can perceive rejection as massively threatening. It can trigger entrenched fears about being worthless. They are often hypervigilant, prone to overreacting and sometimes externalise their distress by acting out in lessons or in their social relationships with peers. They may behave in a way that prompts others to confirm a negative belief they already hold about themselves; a belief that they are no good, unloveable. Hence, any form of exclusion or forced isolation can have a profoundly negative impact, far outweighing the misdemeanour they may have committed. As was the case with Sam, we need to remember that those who push back hardest need to be held closest, hard though we might find that at times.

Sam was craving closeness above all else. He needed to be seen, heard and understood. He wanted people to 'get' him and recognise that, whilst he was trying, school was incredibly hard for numerous reasons. In reality, he was subject to a mounting schedule of disciplinary sanctions – detentions during and after school, detentions on Saturday mornings(!), detentions for not making it to other detentions, fixed-term exclusions, regular isolation (internal exclusion), being sent to adjacent schools to remove him from site for the day, and more. Within just a few months, Sam was utterly immersed in the negative story about who he was. He was left feeling unwanted, unsuccessful and unvalued, and he gradually pulled away even from the teachers he had previously trusted. It left him alienated, mistrustful and depressed. He tried to cope in the beginning, but, as his behaviour issues escalated, he eventually gave up. On top, Sam was then blamed for this.

An alternative approach might have involved a mounting schedule, not of sanctions, but of relational interventions. This is what happened with Jamie in a nearby school. Rather than a gradual increase of segregation from others, he was immediately allocated a teacher/mentor who:

■ Met Jamie for a mentoring session twice weekly. He checked in and genuinely listened to Jamie's thoughts and feelings, allowing him to get things off his chest in an appropriate space with a trusted adult. Knowing that mentoring sessions were there, where he could offload and convey his frustrations and anxieties, was vital, otherwise he would simply offload in class, triggering the inevitable consequences.

■ Acted as a conduit between Jamie and his teachers, engaged in restorative conversations to build (and when necessary rebuild) fractured relationships with staff. This allowed both teacher and student to engage in mediated conversations and develop an understanding of how to work together successfully. This was particularly important in scenarios after Jamie had been removed from class or subject to a detention, when he might feel ostracised without subsequent remedial work.

■ Liaised with external agencies and drew on wider networks to support and coordinate a response. This included the youth service, social worker and me. We were able to work together to establish Jamie's needs and implement interventions with his consent.

■ Pulled together messages of success from all teachers, via email, sharing these with Jamie weekly and also with his family. This supported Jamie to focus on when things were going well in a context where his overriding self-perceptions were of failure and unworthiness. This helped him to positively re-evaluate his sense of self. Jamie was good at so many things, but he needed help to notice them in a life where criticism was the norm.

Of course, the above interventions are time-intensive but they do work. They can be done. When a child feels they are valued, wanted and belong in a school setting, they become less hypervigilant and more resilient when things inevitably become difficult.

## 2. Student–teacher remedial work

Things can escalate quickly in schools when student–teacher relationships break down. Very often, when I consult with teachers, some will assert, 'They are fine in my lessons,' whilst others complain, 'They are rude and oppositional in my lessons.' So, which statement represents the truth? There is a huge risk of systemic myths developing about children that represent, at best, a partial evaluation of what is really involved. Hugely complex social interrelationships occur in classrooms that involve individual students, teachers, groups, environmental factors (space, time of day, content of lesson, etc.). In many cases, when a child 'misbehaves' and is subsequently sanctioned, little exploration is made as to *why* a behaviour manifested in *that* lesson with *that* teacher and at *that* time. Often, things can be resolved when teacher and student come together and have an authentic, honest conversation about what underpinning factors were at play. Through such conversations come better relationships, trust, understanding and social consonance.

Sam's experience of relationship breakdown with a number of his teachers eventually led to his exclusion for persistent disruptive behaviour. As his distress escalated, Sam became further and further isolated from his class teachers and spent much of his time in alternative spaces, such as the inclusion room. Naming a room for exclusion the 'inclusion room' is, of course, deeply ironic. Eventually, the response was to remove him entirely from all classes to 'work on his behaviour'. Little effort was made to proactively rebuild relationships with the minority of staff for whom conflict was the norm. The approach was all about removal rather than reconnection, thus exacerbating Sam's emotional crisis.

In Jamie's case, the situation was managed differently. His mentor was given time twice a week to spend 30 minutes with Jamie. The mentor was able to communicate with his teachers, to humanise Jamie, to explain his complex history and to inform them about his emotional state. He reminded teachers about Jamie's strengths, needs and the helpful strategies they could employ, as described on a pupil passport, which was created alongside Jamie. Most importantly, the mentor facilitated restorative meetings with Jamie and his teachers, when necessary, which led to greater understanding, more authentic relationships and a sense of shared ownership around what to do when things became challenging. Backed up by the evidence, which clearly shows that positive teacher–student relationships significantly reduce risky behaviour across contexts (Rudasill et al., 2010), the school named this a 'show me that you know me' approach. Jamie felt immeasurably safer with teachers when he knew they understood him and recognised the difficulties he faced. Through closer relations came calmer behaviours.

## 3. Be curious

When a child presents as 'challenging', 'oppositional' or 'persistently disruptive', consider what this communicates. This is a chance to bring together key staff, the family and the young person to explore the child's experiences. How is the child feeling about their schooling? Are they coping socially, emotionally and academically? In secondary schools, a useful approach can involve:

- Regular consultation with the young person and family. A teenager's sense of self is in a state of flux as their brain grows and their capacity for introspection develops. They are often not aware of how their behaviours manifest and need support from non-judgemental adults with whom they have built trust to explore why certain environmental triggers are significant. When necessary, it can be helpful to access support from external professionals such as educational psychologists, speech and language therapists and/or occupational therapists to facilitate this process of exploration. Perhaps the child has unrecognised learning difficulties, sensory needs or speech and language challenges? Are things going on at home that are impacting on the young person? Ask questions. Be professionally inquisitive. Keep the young person and their family in the loop in terms of any discussions in which they are not directly involved.

- TeachMeets. These are weekly opportunities for staff to come together, led by the special educational needs coordinator (SENCO) or senior teacher, to discuss a specific young person and plan collaboratively how best to support them. In my experience, these work best at lunchtime (with free snacks provided!), but can also be effective at the beginning of the day or after school. TeachMeets develop shared ownership of interventions to support a child, alongside creative strategising, teacher empowerment and co-agreement of next steps. They can be a very powerful tool.

- Bring in external professionals as a form of prevention, not reaction. Very often, educational psychologists and other professionals are asked to get involved with young people 'at risk' of exclusion only once they have already received months of detentions, isolations and fixed-term exclusions. If a child is persistently finding it hard to cope, there are likely contributing factors that are not visible or difficult to identify, and external professionals can help to unravel things.

# 4. Create opportunities for competence and autonomy

This is no easy task in an education climate with its obsessive focus on standardisation and top-down curricula priorities. However, we know from decades of research around self-determination theory that feeling competent and autonomous are fundamental human needs.[4] Imagine you are a child who struggles to access the academic curriculum. Your day is characterised by lesson after lesson, day after day where you perceive yourself as less than your peers; you are placed in bottom sets and learning is a chore at which you fail repeatedly. In innumerable sessions with young people, they have shared the profound psychological impact of this. It's crippling. Crucially, it is not possible for a human being to experience positive mental health in a context where they feel incompetent and lack autonomy. Young people can become demotivated, sometimes even amotivated, by a curriculum that leaves them feeling unintelligent and devoid of choice. It is critical for schools to find opportunities, for at least some of the week, for a young person to experience competence and autonomy.

In Sam's case, the minimal autonomy offered by the school timetable progressively decreased when he began to struggle. He was offered increasingly narrow learning opportunities with a focus on core subjects, which he found exceptionally difficult and demotivating. Sam felt a profound lack of control over his life, minimal autonomy and an overwhelming sense of incompetence. His motivation to engage with school-based tasks was virtually non-existent outside of design and technology and PE, where he perceived himself competent. Eventually, he was removed from classes and was tasked with completing worksheets in a room with non-specialist staff, devoid of all opportunity to feel competent or autonomous. After a while, this became untenable. When he was excluded, his anxiety had reached fever pitch, and this was manifested in his anger and opposition.

For Jamie, things looked different. The SENCO, mentor, parent and I worked together to establish his views around what aspects of school were more or less manageable. Overtly drawing on self-determination theory, his core timetable was reduced and he was able to spend time, alongside a small cohort of other students, working on a project of his choice. He chose to build a wardrobe, supported by a fantastic design and technology teacher who met him once a week at lunchtime to support. For 20% of his week, Jamie was 'off timetable'. The negotiation was challenging; some senior teachers did not feel this was appropriate given the pressures of standardisation. However, in the end they agreed to be flexible. Ironically, the most positive experience Jamie reported at the end of Year 11 was the two 30-minute sessions a week he was able to spend with the school caretaker, doing odd jobs and taking responsibility for working on tasks independently. Unlike Sam, alongside feelings of belongingness, he developed a sense of competence and autonomy, which meant his fundamental human needs were met.

---

4   See https://selfdeterminationtheory.org/topics/application-basic-psychological-needs.

## 5. Managing the process of exclusion

If a child is involved in an extreme incident that requires them to be removed from the school roll, followed by a change of placement, there are ways of managing this that can reduce the distress of the young person and family. If a young person is permanently excluded, they need to maintain a sense of self as worthy, valuable and wanted. This is challenging, but it can be attained by:

- Maintaining a relationship with the student and family and helping them with the process. Ensure that they are aware of the procedures and next steps; stay in touch with them. Ostracising a child and family and leaving them with nowhere to turn can lead to isolation and confusion, which can have a hugely detrimental effect on the emotional wellbeing of the whole family.

- Presenting the young person with some choice and autonomy around what happens next. Ensure that their views are taken into account to help them perceive some measure of control, thus meeting their fundamental human needs.

- Recognising that an adult may have to leave work to care for a child who is excluded. For some, this can be hugely challenging and lead to 'deep exclusion' (Daniels, 2011: 38) – that is, a wide circle of impact and multidimensional effects that impinge on whole families, both economically and socially. There is often a strong sense of shame felt by a young person and their family. They need support and a multi-agency response is crucial.

- Liaising closely with the local authority and external professionals, such as the exclusions officer, education welfare and support agencies, such as educational psychology, and when appropriate, social services. Remember, outside the family context, schools know young people better than anyone and, hence, need to be on hand to smooth the way for this difficult transition.

- Clearly explaining that the exclusion is not a rejection of the child but an acknowledgement that some of their behaviours were unsafe. It is critical that the child's character and behaviour are overtly separated in conversation to avoid alienation, disaffection and the development of a negative self-perception. Otherwise, core beliefs can take hold around being 'bad', 'unwanted' or 'unworthy' that become all-consuming. These can become a self-fulfilling prophecy if not managed with the utmost delicacy.

- Providing a rigorous information package to the receiving education provision so they are aware of the young person's strengths and needs, and highlighting interventions that have previously been successful.

## 6. Building a learning community and conditions of care

Working with young people with additional needs, particularly those with traumatic backgrounds and complex learning difficulties, is exceptionally hard work. Shifting school cultures to encompass some of the ideas above takes time, patience and the promotion of a school community where reforms are made with the consent of those involved. The systemic changes introduced in relation to Jamie were co-developed over a number of months. They were slowly and carefully negotiated with his mother, his teachers and a range of other stakeholders. Whilst it is never possible to co-develop a school culture that every single member of staff thoroughly accepts, there are many well-documented cases of success.[5] A shared purpose around working with the most vulnerable children can support a collegiate environment where staff come together in a mutually supportive fashion.

As identified earlier, prevailing ideologies around education in England make it hard for schools to foster communities of care and respond to children who don't fit the mould. Regardless, some do so successfully. It can be done. Their approaches are drawn from observing great practice and using a knowledge of psychology and human development to co-create environments that make inclusion possible. There are no simple, quick-fix solutions. To help our square pegs, we need to be flexible and pay attention to their fundamental psychological needs. If school leaders create a climate of shared ownership and promote curiosity, consideration of what behaviour communicates and nurture student belongingness and self-determination, then the outcomes can be magical.

Ask Jamie.

## References

Bagley, C. (2021) Alternative Education Provision: An Exclusive English Myth, *Byline Times* (17 February). Available at: https://bylinetimes.com/2021/02/17/alternative-education-provision-an-exclusive-english-myth.

Ball, S. J. (2003) The Teacher's Soul and the Terrors of Performativity, *Journal of Education Policy*, 18(2): 215–228.

Baumeister, R. F. and Leary, M. R. (1995) The Need to Belong: Desire for Interpersonal Attachments as a Fundamental Human Motivation, *Psychological Bulletin*, 117(3): 497–529.

---

5   Michael Fullan's book, *The New Meaning of Educational Change* (2016), is a great starting point for those wishing to action meaningful cultural change. It is possible, as many rich examples and studies demonstrate, to create a dynamic, responsive school community in which teaching staff, students and families have a common stake around inclusion.

Ben-Zeév, A. (2014) Why We All Need to Belong to Someone, *Psychology Today* (11 March). Available at: https://www.psychologytoday.com/gb/blog/in-the-name-love/201403/why-we-all-need-belong-someone.

Blakemore, S-J. (2018) *Inventing Ourselves: The Secret Life of the Teenage Brain*. London: Doubleday.

Boyle, C. and Topping, K. (2012) *What Works in Inclusion?* London: McGraw-Hill Education.

Cole, T., McCluskey, G., Daniels, H., Thompson, I. and Tawell, A. (2019) Factors Associated with High and Low Levels of School Exclusions: Comparing the English and Wider UK Experience, *Emotional and Behavioural Difficulties*, 24(4): 374–390.

Daniels, H. (2011) Exclusion from School and Its Consequences, *Psikhologicheskaya nauka i obrazovanie* [Psychological Science and Education], 16(1): 38–50. (In Russian, abstracted in English.)

Department for Education (2020) Permanent Exclusions and Suspensions in England: Academic Year 2018/19. Available at: https://explore-education-statistics.service.gov.uk/find-statistics/permanent-and-fixed-period-exclusions-in-england/2018-19.

Department for Education (2021) Permanent Exclusions and Suspensions in England: Academic Year 2019/20. Available at: https://explore-education-statistics.service.gov.uk/find-statistics/permanent-and-fixed-period-exclusions-in-england/2019-20.

Ford, T., Parker, C., Salim, J., Goodman, R., Logan, S. and Henley, W. (2018) The Relationship between Exclusion from School and Mental Health: A Secondary Analysis of the British Child and Adolescent Mental Health Surveys 2004 and 2007, *Psychological Medicine*, 48(4): 629–641.

Fullan, M. (2016) *The New Meaning of Educational Change*, 5th edn. Abingdon and New York: Routledge.

Graham, L. J. (2018) Student Compliance Will Not Mean 'All Teachers Can Teach': A Critical Analysis of the Rationale for 'No Excuses' Discipline, *International Journal of Inclusive Education*, 22(11): 1242–1256.

IntegratED (2020) *Annual Report 2020*. Available at: https://www.integrated.org.uk/2020/12/20/integrated-annual-report-2020.

Jenkins, A. and Ueno, A. (2017) Classroom Disciplinary Climate in Secondary Schools in England: What is the Real Picture?, *British Educational Research Journal*, 43(1): 124–150.

Levell, J. (2021) The Commission on Young Lives: The 'Conveyer Belt from Vulnerable Children' to 'Criminal Gangs'… [blog] (13 September). Available at: https://jadelevell.com/2021/09/13/the-commission-on-young-lives-the-conveyer-belt-from-vulnerable-children-to-criminal-gangs.

Maté, G. (2010) *In the Realm of Hungry Ghosts: Close Encounters with Addiction*. Berkeley, CA: North Atlantic Books.

Ministry of Justice (2013) *Transforming Youth Custody: Putting Education at the Heart of Detention*. CP 4/2013. Available at: https://assets.publishing.service.gov.uk/government/uploads/system/uploads/attachment_data/file/181588/transforming-youth-custody.pdf.

Ministry of Justice (2014) *Transforming Youth Custody: Government Response to the Consultation*. Cm 8792. Available at: https://consult.justice.gov.uk/digital-communications/transforming-youth-custody/results/transforming-youth-custody-consultation-response.pdf.

Ofsted (2019) *Exploring the Issue of Off-Rolling* (May). Available at: https://www.gov.uk/government/publications/off-rolling-exploring-the-issue.

Over, H. (2016) The Origins of Belonging: Social Motivation in Infants and Young Children, *Philosophical Transactions of the Royal Society of London. Series B: Biological Sciences*, 371(1686): 20150072.

Parfrey, V. (1994) Exclusion: Failed Children or Systems Failure?, *School Organisation*, 14(2): 107–120.

Partridge, L. (2019) School Exclusions Are a Social Justice Issue, New Data Shows, *RSA* [blog] (6 August). Available at: https://www.thersa.org/blog/2019/08/exclusions.

Purdue University (2011) Pain of Ostracism Can Be Deep, Long-Lasting, *ScienceDaily* (6 June). Available at: https://www.sciencedaily.com/releases/2011/05/110510151216.htm.

Reay, D. (2017) *Miseducation: Inequality, Education and the Working Classes*. Bristol: Policy Press.

Rhodes, I. and Long, M. (2021) *Improving Behaviour in Schools: Guidance Report*. London: Education Endowment Foundation. Available at: https://educationendowmentfoundation.org.uk/education-evidence/guidance-reports/behaviour.

Rudasill, K. M., Reio, T. G., Stipanovic, N. and Taylor, J. E. (2010) A Longitudinal Study of Student–Teacher Relationship Quality, Difficult Temperament, and Risky Behavior from Childhood to Early Adolescence, *Journal of School Psychology*, 48(5): 389–412.

Smith, V. and Wynne-McHardy, E. (2019) *An Analysis of Indicators of Serious Violence: Findings from the Millennium Cohort Study and the Environmental Risk (E-Risk) Longitudinal Twin Study*. Research Report 110 (July). London: Home Office. Available at: https://www.gov.uk/government/publications/an-analysis-of-indicators-of-serious-violence-findings-from-the-millennium-cohort-study-and-the-environmental-risk-e-risk-longitudinal-twin-study.

Timpson, E. (2019) *Timpson Review of School Exclusion*. CP 92. London: Department for Education. Available at: https://www.gov.uk/government/consultations/school-exclusions-review-call-for-evidence.

Williams, K. D. and Nida, S. A. (2011) Ostracism: Consequences and Coping, *Current Directions in Psychological Science*, 20(2): 71–75.

Zancajo, A. and Bonal, X. (2020) Education Markets and School Segregation: A Mechanism-Based Explanation, *Compare: A Journal of Comparative and International Education*, 50. doi:10.1080/03057925.2020.1858272

# Chapter 12

# WHAT GOES WRONG

## Dan Rosenberg

With a few exceptions, there is little wrong with the legal framework for education in schools in England. Its implementation is another matter entirely.

Education law is a relatively wide field, so I will focus on those elements most likely to have a bearing on the education and treatment of our square pegs. It's not my role here to set out the law in detail or reference relevant legislation and case law, but to use the legal principles to set out a framework to help avoid the common mistakes and poor practice that I have often seen when dealing with children who have complex needs.[1] I will seek to deal with the common misconceptions and errors made by schools (and local authorities), which can have the consequence of either making a bad situation worse for the child or the school (often both) or externalising the problem and passing it on to others.

As a lawyer acting for parents and pupils, I only tend to see things that have gone very wrong. I have acted for countless children who have self-harmed and even attempted suicide as a result of their experiences at school. I have acted for numerous children who have been discriminated against and bullied. I have acted for many children with special educational needs who did not have those needs met. I have dealt with large numbers of exclusions, both lawful and unlawful, and have come across most methods (I think) of seeking to game the system employed by schools to improve results without necessarily having to take steps to improve the quality of the teaching.

And, of course, all of these issues tend to overlap because, as this book attests, it's often a highly complex situation.

While the substantive law relating to education is strong, there are structural weaknesses in the system caused in particular by its fragmentation since 2010. Since then, local authorities have often had no control over the actions of local schools, which sometimes act in what the school's leadership perceives to be the interests of the school or academy chain rather than those of the children or the wider local community. It is hard to see this as anything other than a structural problem in the national system.

---

1   If readers are looking for an accessible book setting out the law in more detail, a very useable textbook is Hannett et al.'s *Special Educational Needs and Disability Discrimination in Schools: A Legal Handbook* (2017).

The tension between academies and local authorities arises when each seeks to avoid either responsibility to or the provision of resources for children with difficulties. For example, I have acted in many cases relating to the permanent exclusion of very young (Key Stage 1) autistic children from schools. The story normally goes like this:

1   The local authority does not provide sufficient material, financial and/or expert support in the first place. More 'evidence' is required to prove a problem exists and that all necessary steps have been taken to solve it.

2   Unsupported, the school deals with the child in an inappropriate way, often involving the use of isolation or restraint.

3   The child becomes repeatedly distressed and the school then seeks to address the problem through a permanent exclusion.

4   This provokes outrage on the part of the local authority. The school generally sticks to its guns and the child generally does not remain at the school.

5   The child eventually starts elsewhere, often after time out of school, having had a fairly dire experience and also having lost any friends they may have made. It does not set them up well for a future in school, and problems then often persist throughout education with implications for life beyond.

My experience tells me that race and class are often, but not always, a factor in these scenarios. Gender almost always comes into it: 90% of permanent exclusions in primary schools relate to boys (Department for Education, 2021).

Let's look at some of the detail here.

## Special educational needs and disabilities

There is a very well-developed framework for the assessment and provision of education for children with special educational needs and disabilities (SEND). The Children and Families Act 2014 only came into force relatively recently, and it has no inherent flaws. Similarly, the legislation requiring schools to have special educational needs coordinators and make provision for children with SEND (including those without an education, health and care (EHC) plan) has been in place for some time. For the most part, the *Special Educational Needs and Disability Code of Practice* (Department for Education and Department of Health, 2015) is written in accessible language and has few flaws. Yet still things go wrong. Children with difficulties do not get the help they need and instead can be punished, isolated and excluded. Why is this?

There are factors outside a school's control at play here, of course. Lack of resources is a major factor, for example. Budgets have been cut, often meaning that insufficient support is provided at an early stage. In this way, more of what little budget there is ends up being spent on fewer children with more expensive needs. Other factors such as recent medical advances mean that children born very prematurely or with complex medical conditions are surviving in greater numbers. But this is a book about the factors that are in a school's control, and there are plenty of those to consider.

It is clear that schools can exacerbate problems for square pegs. Sometimes, they do not seek the assistance that is required and do not take a proactive enough stance, often passing the full responsibility to parents to take the lead in ensuring their children get the help they need. Race and class often loom large here too. Many middle-class parents may be relatively adept at seeking support from professionals for their children and will approach staff in the 'right way', thus ensuring that referrals and requests are made on their children's behalf. Other parents are often told that there is 'no point' in seeking support, as the needs are not 'severe enough', so won't meet the 'criteria' of the relevant body. It's true that those parents who shout the loudest, and can work the system, tend to be heard above those who are less articulate and assertive. It should not be like this.

Let me share an example from a case I was involved with to highlight my point. It relates to a 12-year-old Black boy from South London who had been permanently excluded from school for his behaviour in class. He was a square peg. Following a speech and language therapy assessment, it was evident that he was in the bottom centile for both receptive and expressive skills. Communication skills – or a deficit thereof – was actually the issue here, but it had been assumed that he was just 'naughty'. Schools often err in favour of not seeking an EHC needs assessment from their local authority at an early stage because they believe it will be rejected, and parents are not told that they can request these themselves. Furthermore, it is often believed that enough 'evidence' has to be compiled before any request can be made. I have seen numerous cases where building up that evidence has taken a number of years, and I have seen records showing children going from struggling Year 7s, when assessments were being discussed, to excluded Year 9s, who have been groomed and exploited by criminal gangs. Often, just one assessment would have been all it took to reveal a serious problem, as was the case with my 12-year-old client from South London.

Local authorities often demand that all manner of criteria are met and a multitude of forms completed before a school can request an EHC needs assessment. Some even have limits on the number of requests that individual schools can make. None of this is lawful. Bizarrely, many local authorities effectively require all manner of individual assessments to be undertaken before an EHC needs assessment request can even be made. We see turf wars developing because local authorities want to push the cost of an educational psychology assessment on to an academy chain, for example, and they effectively stipulate (whether formally or informally) that an educational psychology assessment is required from a school before a request can be made. Schools are often reluctant to spend money on such assessments and, meanwhile, nobody is identifying what the child's actual problems are and what is needed. The same applies to speech and language therapy assessments.

Schools need to be bolder at making these requests of local authorities, particularly with young children, and local authorities need to be more open to these in return, in order to avoid what are initially SEND issues becoming behavioural issues. It rarely ends well, especially when you consider that, in so many cases, more expensive consequences are then required further down the line – namely, interventions such as pupil referral units, special schools and, of course, the risk of children ending up on a path that leads towards school refusal, antisocial behaviour, criminality and/or serious emotional health problems.

# Exclusions

The law on exclusions is clear. They can only be for behavioural reasons, and unofficial exclusions (such as sending students home for the rest of the day) are unlawful, always.

The statutory guidance on exclusions is, insofar as the decision to exclude is concerned, also relatively robust (Department for Education, 2022b). It makes direct reference to the need to ascertain what underlying problems a child may have and to consider any SEND, and what can be done to address these first. It makes clear both that permanent exclusion is the last resort and also that permanent exclusion should not be used for children with EHC plans. In such instances, an emergency annual review should be called with the local authority instead. Despite this, a child with an EHC plan is 1.6 times more likely to be excluded. A child on SEN support (without an EHC plan) is more than three times as likely to be excluded (Department for Education, 2021). Other issues, including bullying, must also be explicitly taken into account in any exclusion process.

If there is nothing intrinsically wrong with the law and the guidance, then why is it that our square pegs are excluded so often? And, importantly, what should be done instead?

Unfortunately, the reasons why exclusions are happening are deep-seated. Firstly, classroom management is much easier if the 'difficult' child is not in the class. Excluding them is a ready (and cheap) way of dealing with the problem, temporarily insofar as a fixed-term exclusion is concerned and permanently (for the excluding school at least) in respect of a permanent exclusion. A zero-tolerance approach to behaviour management, which has found favour with the Department for Education in recent years, and is to a significant degree reflected in their non-statutory behavioural advice to schools (Department for Education, 2022a), has increasingly been adopted by academy trusts.

Of course, some schools do make great efforts to ensure that underlying problems are identified and resolved, with appropriate support and resources put in place for the children who need them. However, I am aware that many schools do not take that approach and use (and are encouraged to use) rigid behavioural policies, which can be disastrous for many, if not most of the children facing difficulties at school. This is the case for those who have diagnosed issues such as attention deficit hyperactivity disorder, autistic spectrum disorder or some other neurodivergence, or those who have experienced adverse childhood experiences or problems at home. It is all the more devastating for children who have specific undiagnosed problems, particularly relating to language and communication.

Where a school has concerns about a pupil's behaviour, it should try to identify whether there are any causal factors and intervene early on to reduce the need for a subsequent exclusion. Unfortunately, this does not always happen.

Early intervention to address underlying causes of disruptive behaviour should include an assessment of whether appropriate provision is in place to support any suspected SEND. If the underlying SEND has not been identified, because the appropriate assessment has not taken place, then an assessment of the most appropriate provision is simply not possible. Identification of any SEND needs to happen as early as possible with steps taken quickly to ensure that the appropriate support is put in place. Very often, this involves provision to support communication issues to deal with the frustration that such problems can cause.

If the legislation and guidance in respect of lawful exclusions is for the most part helpful, then why are children being unlawfully excluded?

Effectively, an exclusion that does not follow the legislation or guidance is an unlawful – illegal –exclusion. Indeed, it is something that Ofsted inspects against under the 2019 Inspection Framework (Ofsted, 2021) because unlawful exclusions are almost always also a form of gaming.

Included within the broad umbrella of unlawful exclusions are the other means that a school may use to improve their results – and their standing. Off-rolling is one of the most common of these. There are criteria that set out the basis on which a child can be removed from the school roll,[2] and doing so without regard to these defined categories is, again, unlawful. Pressurising parents to withdraw their children from the school – another strategy I have witnessed – is also (yes, you have guessed it) unlawful. Pressurising a parent to withdraw their child from school, combined with a threat of permanent exclusion if they fail to do so, is explicitly prohibited. It has, up until now, been a relatively regular occurrence. It remains to be seen whether the new exclusions guidance (Department for Education, 2022b), with its very explicit warnings to head teachers that Ofsted will judge schools that off-roll as inadequate, will finally make the practice too risky for schools to pursue. One would hope that it does.

---

2   These are set out in the Education (Pupil Registration) (England) Regulations 2006.

Other mechanisms to remove children from schools and sidestep the statutory framework are also unlawful. For example, 'managed moves' can be a good idea to give a child a fresh start,[3] but there has to be agreement from the parents. It is not permissible to argue, as one head did, that it was a managed move and, as she was 'the management', that the child was going to remain in isolation at the school until such time as the parents agreed to the move. Under the new exclusions guidance, that would have led to a referral to Ofsted and a finding that the school was inadequate. Seeking to keep children down a year if they wish to remain at the school (on the basis that they are almost certain not to agree to this) is unlawful, as are any policies that make progression from one year to the next conditional on either good behaviour, attendance or academic attainment.

# Bullying

It is unfortunately a fact of playground life that children who are a bit 'different' will run the risk of being the victims of bullying. Bullying in school should not happen but it does. All schools are required by law to have and implement an effective anti-bullying policy. Some schools manage this better than others. Not having an effective anti-bullying policy, or not implementing it, is almost certain to be indirectly discriminatory, as those with protected characteristics (for example, those with a disability or who are from a minority ethnic group[4]) are much more likely to be on the receiving end.

Apart from their legal obligations here, schools need to be alive to the fact that they are likely to mirror society as a whole; if racism is endemic in society, it will be reflected in our classrooms and playgrounds (and staffrooms[5]), particularly if that prejudice is normalised and seen as acceptable among a significant proportion of the population (as is the case to a large degree with discrimination towards Gypsy, Roma and Traveller children). They also need to be alive to the fact that when children are singled out for extra support, that too can lead to bullying. One case that sticks in the memory related to a child with special needs who went to the school's 'hub' for extra assistance and was taunted as 'hubman'.

Bullying very often leads to retaliation by the bullied. Those who are bullied, particularly if they have communication issues and are not as adept at expressing themselves, can be more likely to hit out. This is likely to lead them down yet another path of disciplinary sanctions, isolations and exclusions.

---

3   See Chapter 10 for more discussion on managed moves and their unintended consequences.
4   I struggle to recall a Traveller child for whom I have acted who has not been verbally abused at school.
5   It is, of course, not only the actions of the children in schools that we need to consider. Despite exhibiting exactly the same behaviours, a White 4-year-old may be perceived as 'boisterous' and a Black 4-year-old 'challenging'.

Not only does bullying need to be dealt with, but the mere fact that a child is being bullied may often be an indication that there is unmet SEND. Children are very adept at picking up on difference.

# Behaviour and behaviour management

Schools have always had the ability to discipline pupils to keep order in the classroom. Lines and detentions have been around for many years; caning and other abuses thankfully went out decades ago.

While physical punishment is no longer allowed, mental punishment is. And it has serious effects, particularly on our square pegs. Even those who have may have shown resilience up to this point may crack under pressure from what has in recent years become a pernicious form of such systems of control – isolation.

Prior to 2010, there was guidance on the use of internal isolation in schools (Department for Children, Schools and Families, 2009). It was not perfect, but it made very clear that it was a last resort. The Department for Education subsequently removed this guidance and the use of isolation grew in an unfettered way, including such practices as the use of isolation booths. Subsequent behavioural guidance on such practices (e.g. Department for Education, 2016) was extremely weak and offered no effective safeguards.

In effect, isolation has been an off-the-books means of excluding children from classrooms. Unlike the data on exclusions, the data on internal exclusions does not go to the Department for Education or the local authority and is not publicly available. There was not even a requirement (or recommendation) that it went to school governors. It could be argued that the children who are repeatedly isolated are essentially 'sacrificed' for the greater benefit of the school. While not outlawing the practice, the government's new behaviour guidance (Department for Education, 2022a) has significantly tightened up the use of isolation, which is now termed 'removal'.

The guidance makes clear just how serious a sanction it is, the factors that should be considered by a head teacher before it is used, and the undesirability of using it repeatedly or for long periods. There are also strong recommendations on the collection and analysis by schools of data relating to its use, including its impact on children with protected characteristics. It is hoped that this new guidance will make a significant difference, in particular to those 'square pegs' who, in the absence of any proper guidance, were being repeatedly placed in it.

Some schools 'flatten the grass' by subjecting children to short-range shouting and screaming, with exclusions becoming a tool to ensure compliance for such misdemeanours as slouching or not looking forward in assemblies. This may be effective at improving overall average GCSE results, but at the expense of a minority of children who simply cannot cope with the treatment to which they are subjected. Schools that have a policy of nurturing each blade of grass are more likely to help those children succeed, and at the very least not fall apart or disengage from education entirely. It may be harder. It may take longer. It may require more resources or that existing resources are spread more thinly. Ultimately, it depends on what the aims of the school are and what those running it are seeking to achieve.

The effects of such practices on the mental health of children are unsurprising. I have seen too many GPs, paediatricians and child and adolescent mental health service (CAMHS) practitioners having to write letters to schools pleading for them not to use isolation for particular children.

Another tool that goes unmonitored is the use of restraint. Unbelievably, a school does not need to tell parents that their child has been restrained. The recent Equality and Human Rights Commission (2021) report makes clear that training on restraint is inadequate and that far more careful monitoring is required. At the time of publishing, these recommendations have been accepted and new legislation and guidance is awaited.

# School refusal and prosecuting parents for children's non-attendance

Parents are under a duty to ensure that children of compulsory school age are receiving suitable education. If they do not comply they can be prosecuted. This sounds simple. The complications arise when the demands being placed on the child are simply too much and they find themselves unable to attend.

The first point to note here is that schools should do everything possible to avoid matters getting to this stage in the first place. Parental concerns must be taken seriously, even if the child seems 'fine at school' (a phrase often replayed by parents after their child has reached crisis point). Specific needs must be identified early, as I have highlighted above, and provision must be put in place to meet them. Bullying must be tackled. Academic pressure needs to be considered and evaluated. Reasonable adjustments must be offered. Oppressive behaviour policies, and in particular the use of isolation (removal as it is now termed), need to be rethought, especially when it leads to children becoming reluctant to attend school. The often justified gang-related fears of parents need to be dealt with, especially within a pupil referral unit or alternative provision setting.

Where the problem is anxiety, it needs to be identified swiftly and de-escalated before it becomes too entrenched. Resources, time and effort need to be deployed before it gets worse, in collaboration with the child's family. As soon as a child stops attending, it becomes an educational emergency and needs to be seen as such by the parent, the school and all others involved with the child. The school may well be able to assist before matters deteriorate further, but parents often report that their early concerns were dismissed and that the proposed reintegration plans are unworkable.

Efforts need to be made to try and understand the child's concerns and take steps to resolve them, bearing in mind that many children cannot articulate their fears and no amount of asking will produce answers. Many of these children already have low self-esteem – they desperately want to attend, they just can't – so berating by frustrated adults is unlikely to prove helpful. A punitive or tick-box approach here can easily lead to a child missing months, if not years, of education, not to mention an all-too-common breakdown in the relationship between family, school and local authority. Many parents resort to home education, which is a form of off-rolling when it becomes a last resort rather than a positive choice.

If the matter has not been resolved swiftly, particularly if anxiety is driving the school refusal, then the situation is liable to become even more complex. Assistance from CAMHS or other professionals with relevant experience is likely to be required, and the sooner the better (CAMHS caseloads notwithstanding). And, apart from in those rare circumstances where there is genuinely no underlying problem, prosecution really does not help.[6] All it succeeds in doing is criminalising large numbers of struggling parents, usually mothers (Epstein et al., 2019).

Even if a suitable education is deemed to be on offer by the local authority, which (whether the parent likes it or not) will almost always be the case in a school refusal situation, the question will be whether it is 'reasonably practicable' for the child to access it. If this is not the case, the local authority is obliged to provide suitable education under section 19 of the Education Act 1996. Of course, whether it is reasonably practicable for a child to attend is often in dispute, although if the child is involved with CAMHS and they are of the view that it is not reasonably practicable, then the answer is clear. Similarly, if CAMHS takes the view that the child could and should be attending, and sets out the steps that need to be taken for that to happen, then it is equally clear. The problem arises when they are not involved or when the support being offered falls short of what is needed.

The obligation under section 19 of the Education Act 1996 falls on the local authority, even if they knew nothing about the child previously and all the engagement has been with the school (particularly if it is an academy). This is one of the areas where the effects of the fragmentation of the education system since 2010 are felt most urgently, and significant buck-passing (and financial wrangling) often take place. The law is clear, however, that responsibility lies with the local authority where it is not reasonably practicable for the child to attend the provision.

---

6   The only way in which prosecution can be of use is that it often encourages a parent to seek external help, sometimes resulting in legal action against schools and local authorities as a result of their lack of assistance for the child, or the involvement of CAMHS or some other such agency that the school should have brought in months or even years before.

The traditional view of school refusal is thankfully changing, so that it is increasingly being seen as a problem with the school environment and culture – the education system itself – and less a problem within the child or family. In many cases, it may be best understood as a stress response to problems caused by a rigid and pressured system; in which case, policy responses need to reflect this.

Whether our square pegs face suspensions, exclusion (internal or external) or extended non-attendance, it is clear that the policies and responses we have used for many years have not reduced these problems; in fact, for some groups of square pegs, the problem is now worse. Perhaps it's time that we rethought our approach. If we create an education system that works for the square pegs, it will most likely work for all children.

# References

Department for Children, Schools and Families (2009) *Internal Exclusion Guidance*. Available at: https://dera.ioe.ac.uk/712/1/DCSF-00055-2010.pdf.

Department for Education (2016) *Behaviour and Discipline in Schools: A Guide for Headteachers and School Staff* (January). Available at: https://dera.ioe.ac.uk/25117/1/Behaviour_and_Discipline_in_Schools_-_A_guide_for_headteachers_and_School_Staff.pdf.

Department for Education (2021) Permanent Exclusions and Suspensions in England: Academic Year 2019/20 (29 July). Available at: https://explore-education-statistics.service.gov.uk/find-statistics/permanent-and-fixed-period-exclusions-in-england/2019-20.

Department for Education (2022a) *Behaviour in Schools: Advice for Headteachers and School Staff* (September). Available at: https://www.gov.uk/government/publications/behaviour-in-schools--2.

Department for Education (2022b) *Suspension and Permanent Exclusion from Maintained Schools, Academies and Pupil Referral Units in England, including Pupil Movement: Guidance for Maintained Schools, Academies, and Pupil Referral Units in England* (July). Available at: https://www.gov.uk/government/publications/school-exclusion.

Department for Education and Department of Health (2015) *Special Educational Needs and Disability Code of Practice: 0 to 25 Years. Statutory Guidance for Organisations Which Work with and Support Children and Young People Who Have Special Educational Needs or Disabilities* (January). Available at: https://www.gov.uk/government/publications/send-code-of-practice-0-to-25.

Epstein, R., Brown, G. and O'Flynn, S. (2019) *Prosecuting Parents for Truancy: Who Pays the Price?* Coventry: Coventry University. Available at: http://covrj.uk/wp-content/uploads/2019/01/PROSECUTINGParents.pdf.

Equality and Human Rights Commission (2021) *Restraint in Schools Inquiry: Using Meaningful Data to Protect Children's Rights*. Available at: https://www.equalityhumanrights.com/sites/default/files/inquiry-restraint-in-schools-report.pdf.

Hannett, S., McColgan, A. and Prochaska, E. (2017) *Special Educational Needs and Disability Discrimination in Schools: A Legal Handbook*. London: Legal Action Group.

Ofsted (2021) Education Inspection Framework (updated 11 July 2022). Available at: https://www.gov.uk/government/publications/education-inspection-framework/education-inspection-framework.

# Chapter 13

# WE KNOW WHAT YOU'RE DOING

## Mike Charles

---

If your actions inspire others to dream more, learn more, do more and become more, you are a leader.

John Quincy Adams (attrib.)

---

On arriving at the hotel, I noticed that the manager had a familiar face, one I could not quite seem to place. He remembered who I was, however, as he identified himself as having once been a client of mine. As a boy, he was in his own words 'written off' due to what turned out to be the wrongful belief that he was severely cognitively impaired. He did not, in fact, have global developmental delay at all. He was a young man who had a range of specific learning difficulties that required bespoke intervention – support that I helped to secure for him. This intervention went on to make a massive difference to his life, leading to a discovery of talent that he had not even realised himself.

He was a square peg.

It was then that I realised how few things are more motivating than discovering that your professional intervention made a real difference to a young person's life.

As we saw in Chapter 12, the law is quite clear when it comes to how schools can help their square pegs. The trouble is that not only can it be accidentally – or intentionally – misunderstood and misapplied, but the practices to which this leads can soon start to become established. If other schools are doing something in a particular way, then it must be the right and lawful way to do it, even if it is not. No wonder lawyers in the field of education law are currently facing unprecedented levels of demand – a striking reminder that all is not well in the world of our square pegs.

So, let's look at these errors with a view to eradicating them, helping all pupils to access the education they deserve and, if it helps, the promise of doing busy education lawyers like me out of a job.

# Error 1: Schools are on their own

It is true that a school owes a duty of care to its pupils. This obligation includes the requirement to use its best endeavours to ensure that a child's special educational needs and disabilities are met. In practice, this means that a school is expected to do everything that a reasonable person would be able to do in the circumstances. It is a strong obligation, and the test in determining whether the duty has been met is an objective one. It requires the party with the burden to take all necessary practical action, aside from having to take action that might cause it to suffer substantial detriment, such as significant financial loss. However, before seeking to justify failing to comply with the duty, the school will be well advised to also consider its responsibilities under the Equality Act 2010, which, of course, include the duty to avoid unlawful discrimination as well as its 'reasonable adjustment' duties.[1]

This level of responsibility can be daunting, but be reassured, no school is alone here. There are support mechanisms available, including the duty that befalls the local authority to support the school in meeting these obligations. The fact is that a local authority has the power, and indeed arguably a responsibility, to ensure that all schools are sufficiently resourced by making available to them whatever goods and services may be required. Although the power to make available these services might be part of the discretionary powers open to a local authority, meaning that it is not of itself duty-bound to do so; nevertheless, the local authority might still be acting unlawfully if it ignores the basic duties that the law will require it to follow in order to support schools in this regard. This would be particularly so, if a child is left without adequate support and suffers a loss as a consequence.

For example, these basic rules require the local authority decision-maker to properly understand the nature of the powers it has, and the need to ask itself the right questions. It may also include the duty to consider actually exercising that power, as opposed to claiming that it is policy-bound to refuse to do so. It should never delay in making the decision, and in doing so, it will be bound to take reasonable steps to inform itself of all the relevant facts. To be specific, if a child requires certain provision that the school is inadequately resourced to provide, and without which the child's welfare may be compromised, the council might still find itself obligated to provide it, whether the child holds an education, health and care plan (EHCP) or not.

It is worth remembering that a failure to act in a manner that corresponds with common sense may render the council vulnerable to a legal challenge either by the school or by a parent through the process of judicial review.[2]

---

1   See https://www.legislation.gov.uk/ukpga/2010/15/part/6.
2   Judicial review is the rule of law in action, providing fundamental and inalienable constitutional protection. It is the court's way of enforcing the rule of law by ensuring that all public bodies are never treated as being in effect 'above the law'.

# Error 2: Guidance is law

Section 77 of the Children and Families Act 2014 obliges the secretary of state in England to issue, and sometimes if necessary revise, a code of practice (e.g. Department for Education and Department of Health, 2015).[3] The aim is to give guidance to local government and schools about the exercise of their functions under the Acts. It is common for public authority action to be the subject of policy of this kind.

The code of practice is supposed to be advisory, assisting the decision-making process, but it must never be regarded as superior to law. Thus, if any part of the guidance conflicts with statutory duties and the definitions provided by case law, the law will always come out on top. Yes, there is a duty to have regard to the guidance, but this must never be interpreted as being in all cases bound by it. Basic public law principles include the obligation to avoid policy dictating the outcome in every case. The requirement is to have regard to guidance, interpreting it accurately, but also departing from it when it is just and right to do so and giving the reasons for this departure.

However, in the absence of a considered decision that there is a good reason to deviate from guidance, the statutory guidance, found within the code of practice, must be followed. The rules are well explained by reference to the judgement of the court in Lord Browne-Wilkinson's decision on *R v Secretary of State for the Home Department ex parte Venables and Thompson*:

> the person on whom the power is conferred cannot fetter the future exercise of his discretion by committing himself now as to the way in which he will exercise his power in the future ... By the same token, the person on whom the power has been conferred cannot fetter the way he will use that power by ruling out of consideration on the future exercise of that power factors which may then be relevant to such exercise.[4]

# Error 3: A bright child does not need the protection of a plan

It is assumed by many that the evaluation of a child's academic progress is the only real test to determine whether that child might require the protection of a legally enforceable plan. Yet, even academically very able children may have additional needs

3   See https://www.legislation.gov.uk/ukpga/2014/6/section/77/enacted.
4   [1998] AC 407.

requiring support (and, yes, even the protection of a plan). Dual or multiple excep-tionality, as it has come to be called, occurs when a child displays excellent learning potential but, at the same time, has special educational needs due to some form of disability. The Children and Families Act 2014 defines special educational needs and disabilities as existing when a child has a learning difficulty or disability which calls for special educational provision to be made for him or her. A person is said to have a learning difficulty if he or she 'has a significantly greater difficulty in learning than the majority of others of the same age' or 'has a disability which prevents or hinders him or her from making use of facilities of a kind generally provided for others of the same age in mainstream schools or mainstream post-16 institutions.'[5] For example, a child with severe mental health issues may very well qualify even if they appear to be at an academic level expected of those of the same age. Psychiatric input is capable of demonstrating an educational need, but it is generally a question of fact for a local authority – and, ultimately, a tribunal – to determine. Educational needs can lawfully be given a broad meaning – for example, a child's disability might require substantial adult support throughout the child's time at school.

Controversially, it is important to realise that whilst one-to-one support from a teach-ing assistant or similar may be a necessary part of the support toolkit, it should not – and cannot – be a cheap catch-all solution for children with SEND. We have seen a sharp rise in the argument for the use of teaching assistants in SEND cases, with many parents correlating the potential success of their child with the number of assis-tant hours allocated. It is hardly surprising then that most appeals to tribunal will involve an argument over the degree of teaching assistance that a child might receive within their statement or EHCP. A common argument used by local authority expert psychologists tasked with resisting the claim is to quote Blatchford et al. (2012) (see also Webster et al., 2013). This strategic weapon designed to outmanoeuvre a parental appeal basically advocates that the more support children get from teaching assistants, the less academic progress they actually make. So, whilst the specificity of support hours is crucial in an EHCP, the employment of a teaching assistant who has not undergone appropriate training is not.

The argument presented by local authorities against the use of teaching assistants is, in any case, misleading. Blatchford's study should not be quoted as a basis for refusing teaching assistance but rather as a warning against, or in relation to, the way in which teaching assistants have come to be deployed in class. They also reported that little training is provided to teachers in how to manage teaching assistants and warned against them being used as a substitute for teachers. Indeed, it is not even lawful to do so. The Blatchford study was therefore not seeking to advocate against one-to-one support. On the contrary, a well-trained one-to-one assistant, applying their skills correctly and in the appropriate way, has a material part to play.

---

5   See https://www.legislation.gov.uk/ukpga/2014/6/section/20/enacted.

# Error 4: The wording of a plan should remain flexible to avoid overly committing the school to one particular approach

This is a very common statement heard in a various forms across the country. Too often, I find myself reviewing statements and EHCPs that lack the requisite detail and specificity to be meaningfully enforceable. The law is quite clear that such documents are to *specify* the special educational provision that a child needs.

A number of cases have dealt with this issue, but I believe the cases described below, both endorsed by the Court of Appeal, neatly explain the true position in the eyes of the law.

*L v Clarke and Somerset* (as approved by the Court of Appeal in *E v London Borough of Newham*[6]) states: 'The real question … is whether [the statement] is so specific and so clear as to leave no room for doubt as to what has been decided and what is needed in the individual case.'[7] Very often, specification of hours per week will no doubt be necessary and there will be a need for that to be done.

And in *R (IPSEA) v Secretary of State for Education*: 'It follows that any flexibility built into the statement must be there to meet the needs of the child and not the needs of the system. But the needs of the child cannot be seen in a vacuum.'[8]

These authoritative statements issued by the Court of Appeal indicate clearly that in the majority of cases, clear specification and quantification of provision to indicate the frequency and duration of particular provision will be required.

There is some limited scope for flexibility in an EHCP, but such flexibility can only relate to circumstances where (a) it is the needs of the child, rather than the needs of the system itself, that requires such flexibility and (b) there is sufficient specificity around the 'flexible' element that allows for the necessary provision to be delivered.

For example, an EHCP might specify that a speech and language therapist must provide one hour of direct speech and language therapy to a child to target an expressive language difficulty. In this way, the child's rights are assured. However, it would perhaps be inadvisable for the plan to specify exactly how the speech and language therapist should go about such therapy or the strategies they should use. The reason for this is that they are, by definition, a qualified and registered Health and Care Professions Council (HCPC) therapist who will have had all the requisite training necessary to assess, diagnose and provide therapy for the child's speech and language therapy needs.

---

6   [2003] EWCA Civ 9.
7   [1998] ELR 129 [15].
8   [2003] EWCA Civ 7 [14]–[16] at [15].

It is vital for practitioners (and parents) to recognise that greater detail in an ECHP is not the enemy. On the contrary, it can often be far more helpful to school staff, particularly those not in specialist schools, to have very clear parameters and instruction as to the provision they are making for the child during a given week. It is far easier to follow clear and unambiguous instructions through an EHCP than vague and ambiguous instructions which may leave all parties dissatisfied.

As to what 'specificity' and 'quantification' mean in practice, a good rule of thumb is to ensure the following is recorded:

- **What**. What provision is required (e.g. direct speech and language therapy, social skill groups, additional numeracy lessons)?

- **Who**. Who is going to deliver this provision? What qualifications do they need (e.g. qualified and registered HCPC speech and language therapist or teaching assistant with training and experience in assisting children and young people with expressive language disorders)? The recommendation should ensure that the level of qualification specified is sufficient to deliver the provision required.

- **When**. How frequently will these sessions take place and how long should each session be? These recommendations should be specified by the requisite experts involved in the case, but often a minimum frequency and duration should be stated (e.g. 30 minutes direct speech and language therapy provided by a qualified and registered HCPC speech and language therapist on a weekly basis).

- **Where**. Unlike the preceding three questions, this question is normally answered by simple confirmation that the provision will occur in school. However, if the provision needs to happen in a specific environment within the school (e.g. on a one-to-one basis outside of the classroom or in a small group of four to six pupils in a separate room), then the statement or EHCP needs to specify this. Again, the greater the detail provided, the easier it will be for the school and staff to follow this instruction.

Keeping the above questions in mind when reviewing a draft EHCP and proposing these questions back to the local authority can be a vital tool for parents and practitioners to ensure they fully understand what is expected of them and what the child needs. Once the parties are in no doubt about what is required, not only will they have complied with the requisite statutory thresholds but they will also, more importantly, be able to ensure that the child gets the support they need to thrive in education. There can be no more important factor than that.

# Error 5: The annual review is not the place to decide whether to make amendments to an EHCP as this is a decision for the local authority

Like many of these common misstatements, it would be laughable were it not so widespread. Too often, my clients have attended annual reviews when, for whatever reason, a misguided staff member has advised them that the annual review was not the appropriate occasion for them to raise their proposals. This could not be further from the true statutory purpose of these meetings, which is precisely to review what has occurred over the past academic year, the content of the ECHP or individual development plan and to decide whether any amendments are required.

This is plainly specified in the relevant regulations. For example, in England, where a child and young person has attended a school or other educational institution, it is specified in the Special Educational Needs and Disability Regulations 2014 that:

> where the child or young person attends a school … the local authority must ask the head teacher or principal of the school to prepare a written report on the child or young person, setting out that person's recommendations on any amendments to be made to the EHC plan, and referring to any difference between those recommendations and recommendations of others attending the meeting.[9]

Although, ultimately, it is the local authority's decision whether or not to adopt the amendments recommended (as confirmed by Regulation 20(10)), it is an essential ingredient of the annual review that the content of the EHCP is reviewed and any amendments proposed and discussed between the parties present. For most children and young people, the annual review will represent the first opportunity in 12 months for the multidisciplinary teams required by their EHCP or individual development plan to get together and discuss their progress. These meetings are a fantastic and essential opportunity for the parties to share knowledge and work together in support of the child or young person.

In my practice, I strongly advise all parents and practitioners to make sure they prepare their contributions to the annual review ahead of time, set these out in writing, and then enhance them with open conversation and discussion at the meeting itself. In my experience, practitioners are often very helpful in these meetings, but, where there is an unlawful implication that the annual review is not the vehicle to discuss

---

9   See Regulation 20(7) at https://www.legislation.gov.uk/uksi/2014/1530/pdfs/uksi_20141530_en.pdf.

changes to the plan, it can stop progress in its tracks. Indeed, positive, detailed and thoughtful discussions about the child, their progress and possible improvements are essential components of the annual review to ensure that accurate, high-quality amendments can be proposed to the local authority.

It is, of course, difficult within one simple chapter to identify all the mistakes that are made when it comes to supporting our square pegs. These are a few of the most common, but by making small changes to practice based on an accurate assessment of what is legally required, we can make a positive difference and help to create outcomes in which dreams may be fulfilled. We must do what is right rather than be misled by inaccurate information, which then makes us part of the problem. True leaders, whatever our role, will never be part of the problem.

# References

Blatchford, P., Webster, R. and Russell, A. (2012) *Challenging the Role and Deployment of Teaching Assistants in Mainstream Schools: The Impact on Schools. Final Report on the Effective Deployment of Teaching Assistants (EDTA) Project.* London: UCL Institute of Education. Available at: https://discovery.ucl.ac.uk/id/eprint/10096860.

Department for Education and Department of Health (2015) *Special Educational Needs and Disability Code of Practice: 0 to 25 Years. Statutory Guidance for Organisations Which Work with and Support Children and Young People Who Have Special Educational Needs or Disabilities* (January). Available at: https://www.gov.uk/government/publications/send-code-of-practice-0-to-25.

Webster, R., Blatchford, P. and Russell, A. (2013) Challenging and Changing How Schools Use Teaching Assistants: Findings from the Effective Deployment of Teaching Assistants Project, *School Leadership & Management,* 33(1): 78–96.

# Chapter 14

# WARRIOR MOTHERS AND FATHERS

## Luke Clements and Karine George

> If you take everything away from a person in my position when the only thing you have left to lose is your loved one, your sanity and your reputation, we have nothing left and we become very dangerous.
>
> A mother (Clements, 2020: 93)

Have you ever dreaded a meeting with the family of one of your square pegs? Such parents and carers are often described as 'challenging' or 'difficult', but many have learned, through hard experience, that this is the only way to be noticed and to effect positive change for their children. Imagine how it feels to be wanting the best for your child, but to then have not only the system but also the law fighting you.

With many square pegs facing barriers to attendance, parents can be subject to the threat of fines, prosecutions and safeguarding scrutiny. It is important that school leaders understand how this situation has arisen and the consequences for 'difficult' families.

Under section 17 of the Children Act 1989, 'Provision of services for children in need, their families and others', a child shall be taken to be in need if:

a   he is unlikely to achieve or maintain, or to have the opportunity of achieving or maintaining, a reasonable standard of health or development without the provision for him of services by a local authority under this Part;

b   his health or development is likely to be significantly impaired, or further impaired, without the provision for him of such services; or

c   he is disabled,[1]

---

1   See https://www.legislation.gov.uk/ukpga/1989/41/section/17, para. 10–11. For the purposes of this Part, '"development" means physical, intellectual, emotional, social or behavioural development; and "health" means physical or mental health'.

The Act goes on to state that a child is disabled (in legal terms) if 'he is blind, deaf or dumb or suffers from mental disorder of any kind or is substantially and permanently handicapped by illness, injury or congenital deformity or such other disability as may be prescribed'.

There is no requirement for the mental disorder to be substantial or permanent, for there to be a severe learning disability or for there to be challenging behaviour which poses a significant risk of harm. There is not even the requirement for a formal diagnosis.

Sadly, disabled children and their families are one of the most severely disadvantaged groups in the UK, as evidenced by the recent Cerebra report (Clements and Aiello, 2021). The research underpinning this report considers from a legal perspective the experiences of disabled children and their families of the process by which their needs for care and support are assessed by children's services authorities in England. The researchers did this by examining the assessment protocols of 143 English children's services authorities (23, para. 3.02) and running a survey with 92 English parent/carer-led support organisations (23, para. 3.04).

The report throws up two serious issues: (1) the narrow and imprecise way in which disabled children are assessed and (2) a default position that assumes parental neglect and safeguarding concerns. Now imagine you are a parent trying to do the best for your child, asking for help from a group of professionals who assume that the biggest risk to your child is *you*. The most extreme example of this is probably an accusation of fabricated or induced illness (FII), or what was formerly Munchausen syndrome by proxy. In a Not Fine in School (2020) survey, 23% of respondents (152 parents) whose children were persistently absent had been accused of FII.

This default position is something we call 'institutionalising parent–carer blame', and even the national guidance for assessing disabled children (Department for Education, 2018) is arguably unlawful as it stands, with its focus on safeguarding. It also fails to address the distinct assessment and support needs of disabled children for whom there is no evidence of neglect or abuse.

What is more, unlike the national guidance for the assessment of disabled adults, it contains no requirement that those assessing the needs of disabled children have any expertise or experience in a particular condition in order to ensure the needs of the disabled child are accurately identified.

Consider the following evidence that Clements and Aiello's (2021: 4) report has brought into the open. How might it impact the conversations you have and the decisions you make going forward?

Of the 143 local authority assessment protocols identified:

+ None contained a clear explanation that a different approach should be taken concerning the assessment of the needs of disabled children where the referral was not accompanied by evidence of neglect or abuse;

+ 80 per cent required the assessor to confirm if the 'child's bedroom has been seen' (para 4.18) regardless of whether there was any evidence to suspect that the child was being neglected or abused;

+ 87 per cent referred to the need of seeing (or communicating with) the children alone (para 4.19) regardless of whether there was any evidence to suspect that the child was being neglected or abused;

+ None gave guidance to assessors concerning the need for cogent grounds to exist before seeking to see a child's bedroom or seeking to interview a child in the absence of their parent.

Policies of this nature interfere with the fundamental rights of families to respect for their private and family lives and their home (para 5.40) and are discriminatory in that they treat disabled people and their families in the same way as people whose circumstances are materially different (para 5.34).

On top of this, 'Local authorities are routinely denying disabled children and their families the right to have their eligibility for statutory support services assessed. Services such as: parent carer's needs assessments, direct payments and long-term support packages including, for example, respite care (para 2.04)' (Clements and Aiello, 2021: 5).

There is clearly an urgent need to update the guidance and make meaningful changes, such as, for a start, improved training and more in-depth and specific knowledge and experience for assessors.

## Influence on teacher training and continuing professional development

This faulty guidance is inextricably linked with school attendance and filters through to teacher training and continuing professional development (CPD). Training in attendance often highlights that students who are absent (whether non-attenders or excluded) are heading for the school-to-prison pipeline; they are the ones wandering the streets, exhibiting antisocial behaviour, getting pulled into gangs and the victims or perpetrators of knife crime (Shearing, 2022). Targets of 96% attendance and higher are common in many schools because of the link that has already been made between attendance, attainment, truancy, street crime, antisocial behaviour and safeguarding. It's full-time attendance or the school-to-prison pipeline (plus the possibility of abuse and neglect). It's the reason why head teachers are given targets supported by strict disciplinarian policies. Every part of the system feeds into this and serves to pulls the strings ever tighter.

The leap between attendance and solving antisocial behaviour, attainment and attendance is far too simplistic, neglecting other key issues, like the child who arrives at school with a disabling level of anxiety which interferes with the normal daily activities that most children and their parents take for granted. When there is nothing physical to see with a child, it's often more difficult for others to understand. So, in the interim, head teachers often find themselves conflicted in their obligation to the policies, procedures and accountability mechanisms that exist and the families they wish to help. Situations are rarely black and white, yet the guidance dictates that they apply a standard set of generic rules and regulations to every child. It's no wonder that it seems like head teachers and these parents are often pulling in different directions, especially when it comes to attendance.

Which brings us back to those 'difficult' parents. For those of us who do not live with disadvantage and have the space to practise 'slow thinking' (Kahneman, 2012: 41), one of its invaluable benefits is that it keeps us polite when we are in fact very angry and stops us blurting out distasteful remarks or using offensive language. Slow thinking provides us with 'resistance to self-destructive temptation' (Mullainathan and Shafir, 2013: 63), and in times of stress it stops us snapping and saying what we are actually thinking. For lawyers, slow thinking does not stop us from writing the furious and exceedingly blunt email, but it does stop us from pressing the 'send' button (generally). We know that we need to calm down, review and tone it down the next day when we have regained some sense of self-control. However, if you live with disadvantage 24/7 and are hemmed in by clusters of problems – and even being blamed for them – your reserves of 'mental effort' (Clements, 2020: 92) may be so depleted that you just press that button. As the mother we met at the beginning of the chapter goes on to say, 'I think nothing about sending letters and emails trying to tell our life, as it's not a story' (Clements, 2020: 93).

## Difficult parents

It is not unusual for a lawyer to be briefed before a meeting that such-and-such a parent is 'a very difficult person, you know'. Remembering why they are difficult is essential for us all. Being enmeshed in a dysfunctional social justice system – ostensibly created to support them – is what has made them difficult.

What is troubling is the lack of insight by those responsible for shaping these systems; systems that create difficult, angry people who have no compunction about pressing the send button at 2am; people who do not like the combative person they have become; people who are suffering a form of post-traumatic stress disorder created by years of sleepless nights and shell-shocked by the behaviour of a heartless system (Clements, 2000: 93); families who are pushed beyond endurance, beyond extreme anxiety for their child and have absolutely no qualms about saying exactly what they think.

Although there are 'warrior parents' of both sexes, mothers, in particular, experience hostility when they push back strongly against incompetent, unresponsive public sector systems. Research conducted by Rona Epstein at Coventry University into the offence of truancy (effectively persistent absence – see Chapter 2) found that women are disproportionately pursued for this offence, and that the punitive approach when a child struggles to attend school leads to harm for parents, children and vulnerable families (Epstein et al., 2019). This approach also appears to be ineffective in getting reluctant and fearful children back into the classroom, and therefore does not achieve its purpose of reducing the number of children who do not attend school regularly.

All too commonly, mothers advocating for their children are categorised as 'unwomanly' and 'hysterical', raising troubling questions about their ability to be 'fit' parents. Helen Lewis uses the phrase 'difficult women', and from our experience this provides a much more accurate assessment of their nature and their approach:

> The Difficult Woman is not rude, petty or mean. She is simply willing to be awkward, if the situation demands it; demanding, if the occasion requires it; and obstinate, if someone tries to fob her off. She does not care if 'that's the way it's always been done'. She is unmoved by the suggestion that it's 'natural' for women to act a certain way or accept a lower status. (Lewis, 2020: 327)

Of course, there are many mothers who lack the skills and networks necessary to enable them to secure their children's essential needs. In this context, Janet Read (2000: 119) has described the constant danger of marginalisation that 'poor women' and mothers from minority ethnic communities experience when fighting to have their disabled children's needs fully represented, but who lack the necessary skills to do this and 'have to live with the knowledge that they could not make it happen no matter how hard they tried'.

To close, let's revisit Clements and Aiello's (2021) report and ask you, again, to imagine that you are the parent of a disabled child and you are desperate for help. You know that those assessing your child lack training, experience and any understanding of your child's particular disability. You are trying to understand why people seem more interested in your fitness as a parent than your child's needs. And you are subject to assessment visits at short or even no notice. During one of these visits, the assessor asks first to see your child's bedroom and then to speak your child alone. What would you say? Yes or no?

# References

Clements, L. (2020) *Clustered Injustice and the Level Green*. London: Legal Action Group.

Clements, L. and Aiello, A. L. (2021) *Institutionalising Parent Carer Blame: The Experiences of Families with Disabled Children in Their Interactions with English Local Authority Children's Services Departments*. Leeds: Cerebra and University of Leeds. Available at: https://cerebra.org.uk/wp-content/uploads/2021/07/Final-Parent-Blame-Report-20-July-21-03.pdf.

Department for Education (2018) *Working Together to Safeguard Children: A Guide to Inter-Agency Working to Safeguard and Promote the Welfare of Children* (July). Available at: https://www.gov.uk/government/publications/working-together-to-safeguard-children--2.

Epstein, R., Brown, G. and O'Flynn, S. (2019) *Prosecuting Parents for Truancy: Who Pays the Price?* Coventry: University of Coventry. Available at: http://covrj.uk/wp-content/uploads/2019/01/PROSECUTINGParents.pdf.

Kahneman, D. (2012) *Thinking, Fast and Slow*. London: Penguin.

Lewis, H. (2020) *Difficult Women: A History of Feminism in 11 Fights*. London: Jonathan Cape.

Mullainathan, S. and Shafir, E. (2013) *Scarcity: Why Having Too Little Means So Much*. London: Penguin.

Not Fine in School (2020) School Attendance Difficulties: Parent Survey Results (March). Available at: https://notfineinschool.co.uk/nfis-surveys.

Read, J. (2000) *Disability, the Family and Society: Listening to Mothers*. Buckingham: Open University Press.

Shearing, H. (2022) Covid in Schools: Inquiry Launched to Find 100,000 Pupils Absent in England, *BBC News* (19 January). Available at: https://www.bbc.co.uk/news/education-60054253.

Chapter 15
# FLEXISCHOOLING

## Alison Sauer

Full-time school can be very stressful for some pupils – for example, those who have suffered trauma at school (such as bullying), those who are not neurotypical and those who have anxiety or sensory processing difficulties. Flexischooling, a long-established but not yet widespread practice, can be a solution to this, especially for those in secondary school.

Flexischooling is a bespoke mixture of on-site and off-site, typically parent-led, provision which can meet the needs of a pupil experiencing difficulties in attending school. It can also lessen, or even eliminate, any disruptive behaviour in the classroom caused by their difficulties, and over time it can potentially lead to full-time attendance on-site.

Of course, it is not only suitable for those with difficulties attending school, but it can also be a positive choice enabling a child to benefit from a mixture of provision and more time with their family.

Flexischooling should not be confused with a part-time timetable. The latter is a temporary provision of part-time education, which from a legal point of view can be only a short-term intervention.

Flexischooling is full-time provision with some of that provision occurring off-site. It is an arrangement between the school and the parent and never requires the permission of the local authority, regardless of whether the school is local authority maintained or not.

Therapy and treatment for various conditions are often obtained through the school for those attending. If a child is deregistered in order to be home educated, then the therapy may be difficult to obtain or even cease completely. Flexischooling can enable these provisions to continue whilst providing a personalised education for the child. Additionally, if there are safeguarding concerns about the family or there is a common assessment framework or support team alongside the family in place, then flexischooling allows a continuation of the same professional oversight.

One challenge of flexischooling is the effect on the school of the attendance code. If the register is marked for the off-site session as an 'authorised absence' it will affect the school's attendance figures.[1] In my experience, most schools use this code. However, despite the Department for Education's rather confusing guidance on the issue, if schools mark the pupil as being 'educated off-site', inspectors are more often than not happy with this, as long as the various regulations are met.[2]

Whatever attendance code is used, good practice dictates that a contract should be drawn up between the school and the parent. This will allay confusion and misunderstanding as it can clearly identify the duties and responsibilities of both parties. Flexischooling should be seen as a partnership in the provision of education for the pupil, and so good practice is also to have a termly meeting with parents to discuss progress and content.

Choosing the attendance code is important – and problematic for many schools – because of the unhelpfully blinkered view, discussed elsewhere in this book, that all attendance issues are safeguarding issues. Of course, any school has a duty to take reasonable steps to safeguard a pupil attending an activity off-site with a third party, but a parent is not a third party. In flexischooling, the pupil is merely returned to the care of the parent, as with all pupils at the end of the school day. To decline to even consider flexischooling on safeguarding grounds is, therefore, a nonsense.[3]

# References

Humphreys, P. with Sauer, A. and Dyke, E. (2019) *Flexischooling: A Guidebook for England and Wales.* Shrewsbury: Educational Heretics Press.

---

1   However, if the pupil was not attending school, such a coding will improve these figures.
2   Regulation 6 (para. 4) of the Education (Pupil Registration) (England) Regulations 2006 describes off-site education as an 'approved educational activity', which is either:
   a   an activity which takes place outside the school premises and which is—
      i   approved by a person authorised in that behalf by the proprietor of the school;
      ii   of an educational nature, including work experience under section 560 of the Education Act 1996 … and a sporting activity; and
      iii   supervised by a person authorised in that behalf by the proprietor or the head teacher of the school; or
   b   attendance at another school at which the pupil is a registered pupil.
   See https://www.legislation.gov.uk/uksi/2006/1751/regulation/6/made.
3   Further information on flexischooling can be found in Humphreys et al. (2019), and the files section of the Flexischooling Practitioners UK Facebook group where there are a number of informative factsheets.

Part III

# RELATIONSHIP

# Introduction

In compiling this book, a common thread came up time and time again from our contributors. It relates to the concept of relationship – between educators and pupils, between school leadership and staff, between parents and school staff, between peers. Without relationship, issues can quickly escalate; strong relationships are the foundations on which issues can be aired, discussed and resolved. But relationships must be earned. They exist only with trust, honesty and transparency. They require effort, and as we observe in the Introduction, 'Genuine relationships are the only ones that genuinely count.'

Relationship ties in with a sense of belonging, akin to family. It's crucial that both children and staff feel a sense of belonging in their school (or other educational establishment), and that the school has its own clearly defined role within its local community. In this way, external skills can be harnessed for the benefit of all, and the school and its staff are connected not just to its pupils but also its families and local networks. In a conversation with me for this book, Karine George talked about a time when volunteers from the local police station would accompany the school on trips, or come in to help specific pupils with their homework (effectively mentoring them to keep them out of trouble).[1] Dave McPartlin of Flakefleet Primary (Chapter 30) told me that if he found himself out of a job, he knows that his local community would rally round to support him as a way of thanking him for the food parcels he delivered during the pandemic. In Chapter 24, Andy Sprakes from XP talks about 'crew', and in Chapter 21, Stone Soup is a 'family'.

Children are not homogenous robots on an in-one-end-out-the-other-end school conveyor belt. They are all (thankfully) unique and individual, with their own lives outside school and their own worries, talents and passions. Building strong relationships with them and their families – and thus authentically knowing them – is the starting point for ensuring that no child is a square peg.

---

1   See Karine's views on teacher training and continuous professional development in Chapter 14.

# Chapter 16

# FROM SPACES TO PLACES

## Sarah Johnson

Understanding what it means to 'belong' is a cornerstone of ideas around inclusive education. Inclusion and belonging can be seen as having a symbiotic relationship. Without one you cannot have the other.

So, what does the research tell us about belonging in a school environment, especially when it comes to understanding – and improving – the lives of our square pegs?

## What does it mean to belong?

To feel like you belong is to appreciate that you are part of something bigger, that you are an integral member of the wider community. Belonging is frequently referred to in a range of literature, and perhaps most recognised for educators through Maslow's seminal work on the hierarchy of needs (see Chapter 6). As we will see, Maslow argues that without the need for 'belongingness' being met, humans are prevented from developing beyond the basics. This includes the ability to achieve self-actualisation, under which we may put 'doing well at school'. Belonging and learning, from this perspective, go hand in hand.[1]

For researchers Baumeister and Leary (1995: 497), building on Maslow's ideas, belonging necessitates two emotional components: 'the need for frequent, affectively pleasant interactions with a few other people' and that 'these interactions must take place in the context of a temporarily stable and enduring framework of affective concern for each other's welfare'. In other words, belonging comes from positive relationships built over time. There are no quick wins here. A key feature of these relationships is that they must be stable (at least in part) and foster mutual pleasantness. 'Pleasant' encapsulates ideas of kindness, mutual respect, and gentleness.

It's worth highlighting too, within the structures of schooling that a child will experience a range of relationships that shift and change, whether that is during the span of a school day or across the longer context of school years and key stages. Every student

---

1 This is sometimes referred to as 'Maslow before Bloom' in reference to Bloom's taxonomy, although Maslow has stood the test of time better than Bloom.

within the school space must manage interactions with their peers, peers' families, teachers, support staff, canteen staff and pastoral staff as well as senior leaders. This is a socially demanding task for some individuals (not just children). What is more, different spaces within the school demand a whole set of different interactions, from the formal learning space of classrooms to the hallways connecting those spaces and on into the playground. Whilst an individual may feel 'settled' and that they 'belong' in one space, it doesn't mean they will feel the same in a different area within the school space or with the different individuals they find there.

We see then that as our thoughts, feelings, environment, and relationships change, so too does our sense of belonging. Furthermore, Riley et al. (2018: 3) suggest that belonging should be situated within notions of identity and self: feeling that you are safe and that you fit in.

All the theories touched on above, and many more, highlight how we should view belonging as being something that takes the active participation of all involved to make it a reality.[2] Riley et al. (2018) further suggest that belonging can be seen as a transition from our being in a 'space' – somewhere without community, somewhere we are passing through – to the idea of a 'place', somewhere we are connected to in a meaningful way. Given recent changes in a school's accountability to its community from local to national – through its place in a multi-academy trust, for example – to what extent are we still creating a sense of genuine community to which young people can and want to belong?

It is also worth bearing in mind that people who self-report strong feelings of belonging also report better psycho-social measures of wellbeing, noted to have long-lasting effects (Slaten et al., 2016: 1). Of course, the flipside is that experiences of not belonging are associated with a range of negative outcomes: 'Of note in associated belonging research is the relationship between school belonging and academic achievement, mental health outcomes and maladaptive behaviours' (Slaten et al., 2016: 4).

The above sentence should be especially considered when we are looking to exclude children or move them to forms of alternative provision, although Riley et al. (2018) argue that schools are in a strong position to support all children in developing a sense of belonging. The key, as ever, is strong, knowledgeable and compassionate leadership. The researchers go on to suggest three key areas for 'unlocking possibilities':

1   Recognition that each child and adult that enters the school gates brings their own story.

2   Using the wider community to support belonging beyond the school gates.

3   Appreciation that belonging is not fixed, but enacted and re-enacted every day. (Riley et al., 2018: 11)

---

2   For example, check out Allen and Kern (2017: 6).

Riley et al. (2018: 27–28) further recognise that belonging is a particular challenge for schools, and that a person's sense of belonging is shaped by a multitude of factors: personal experiences, histories, external events and what happens on a day-to-day basis in school.

All of the above associate a sense of belonging with a particular locale, the one that lies within the school gates. How, then, do school communities develop a sense of belonging in the context of children who experience barriers to attendance or who demonstrate behaviour that is not consistent with school rules? Here, I suggest that we see belonging as being beyond the spatial domain. Rather, we need communities to see children as the responsibility of all. This would be evidenced through activities such as the deliberations of in-year fair access panels, governors' discipline committees (assessing whether or not an exclusion is fair and proportionate) and transition meetings between primary and secondary schools. The children discussed in these gatherings are not the responsibility of one school or one provision, but the collective, shared responsibility of the wider community, which includes schools, the local authority, health, social care and others where necessary.

## School communities and belonging – beyond individual factors

To sum up this brief chapter on the all-important topic of square pegs and belonging in schools, consider that Allen and Kern (2017: 104) argue that an alternative framework is required. As we have seen, a multiplicity of factors can lead to – or inhibit – belonging, factors that they suggest form part of a 'bio-psycho-socio-ecological model of school belonging'. Figure 16.1 illustrates this more complex model, with the student at the centre and other factors radiating out from the individual to the microsystem (relational factors) and then the macrosystem of wider political and cultural implications.

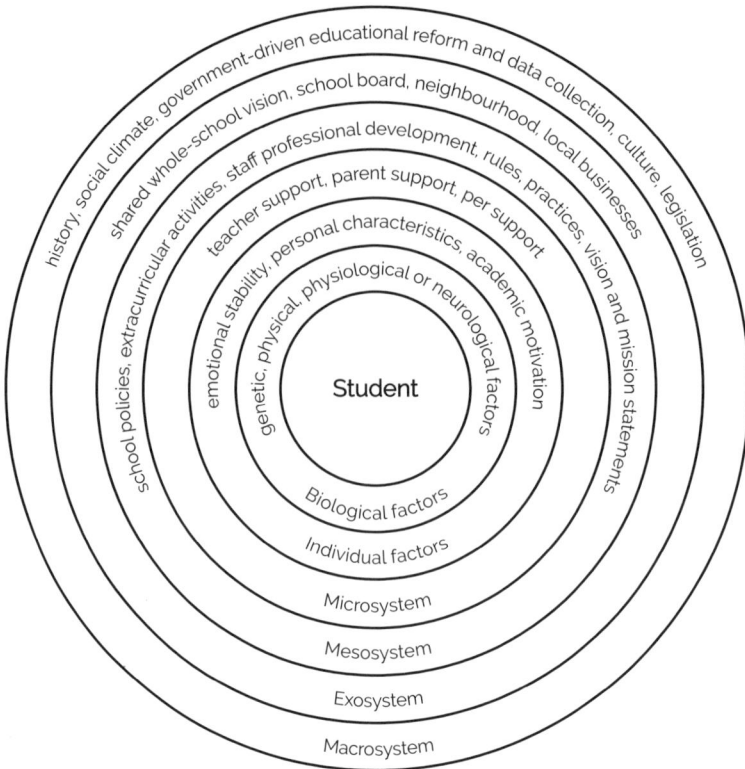

Figure 16.1. The bio-psycho-socio-ecological model
of school belonging (Allen and Kern, 2017: 104)

Note, too, the prominent part that biological factors play in this model, and then consider some of the particular challenges of the square pegs in our schools. To genuinely support them, we need to look beyond the obvious and do our professional best to ensure they learn to be happy, wherever and whomever they are.

# References

Allen, K-A. and Kern, M. L. (2017) *School Belonging in Adolescents: Theory, Research and Practice.* Singapore: Springer Social Sciences.

Allen, K-A., Vella-Brodrick, D. and Waters, L. (2018) Rethinking School Belonging: A Socio-Economic Framework. In K-A. Allen and C. Boyle (eds) *Pathways to Belonging: Contemporary Research in School Belonging.* Leiden: Brill, pp. 191–218.

Baumeister, R. F. and Leary, M. R. (1995) The Need to Belong: Desire for Interpersonal Attachments as a Fundamental Human Motivation, *Psychological Bulletin*, 117(3): 497–529.

Maslow, A. H. (1968) *Toward a Psychology of Being.* New York: Van Nostrand Reinhold.

Riley, K. C. (2022) *Compassionate Leadership for School Belonging*. London: UCL Institute of Education. Available at: https://discovery.ucl.ac.uk/id/eprint/10146072/1/Compassionate-Leadership-for-School-Belonging.pdf.

Riley, K. C., Coates, M. and Martinez, S. P. (2018) *Place & Belonging in Schools: Unlocking Possibilities*. London: UCL Institute of Education. Available at: https://www.ucl.ac.uk/ioe/sites/ioe/files/place-and-belonging-unlocking-possibilities.pdf.

Slaten, C. D., Ferguson, J. K., Allen, K-A. and Dianne-Vella, B. (2016) School Belonging: A Review of the History, Current Trends and Future Direction, *Educational and Developmental Psychologist*, 33(1): 1–15.

Slee, R. (2019) Belonging in An Age of Exclusion, *International Journal of Inclusive Education*, 23(9): 909–922.

# Chapter 17

# THREE KEY QUESTIONS ABOUT BELONGING

## Kathryn Riley

---

'Belonging' is that sense of being somewhere where you can be confident that you will fit in and feel safe in your identity.

Riley et al. (2018: 3)

---

Schools that are places of belonging are great places to be for all young people, including our square pegs. Young people experience a sense of connectedness, perform better academically and come to believe in themselves more; their teachers feel more professionally fulfilled; and their families feel more accepted.

So many children and young people start school with enthusiasm and curiosity, and then seem to lose interest along the way or find themselves dismissed or excluded. Findings from research in many parts of the world suggest that a lack of school belonging, and experiences of being sidelined and rejected, create a downward – but avoidable – trajectory for too many youngsters.

A sense of belonging is a complex emotion and is triggered by a range of factors. Young people's sense of school belonging is shaped by their histories and their lived everyday realities, how schools respond to those realities and what happens to them when they enter the school gates (Riley, 2017).

Let me suggest three important questions for you to think about. They are designed to help schools understand more about the part they play in ensuring that all children and young people experience a sense of physical and emotional safety – key aspects of belonging – and come to conclude that their school life is meaningful and worthwhile.

## 1. What do you see?

Life outside the school gates can be tough for children (Riley, 2013). *Does the school understand what is going on in the community? Is the school connected to the local communities? Do young people see themselves represented within the school?*

Life inside school can be tough too. *Do young people feel they are protected from bullying and harassment? Do they feel connected to the school? Do they experience the academic pressure as supportive?*

## 2. What do you know?

Schools need to be encouraged to look afresh at what is happening by looking through the 'prism of place and belonging'. Only then will they understand their role in working to remedy the situation for our square pegs. The number of young people who feel they don't belong in school is rising and is nearly one in three (Allen and Kern, 2019). School exclusion becomes both a personal and social issue, with young people from socio-economically disadvantaged communities twice as likely as their more advantaged peers to feel that they do not belong in school and four times more likely to be excluded (Fair Education Alliance, 2017). Those who are excluded then seek belongingness elsewhere, finding it in many ways, including self-harm, gang membership and forms of extremism (Riley, 2022). The excluded frequently become the exploited.

We also know from the evidence on belonging and inclusion that actively addressing a sense of school belonging can close the achievement gap by between 50–60%, with the benefits lasting well into adulthood (Allen et al., 2018). What is more, along with improved academic achievement, young people who feel they belong in school tend to be happier and more confident (Riley, Coates and Allen, 2020).

## 3. What do you do?

A sense of belonging is manifested in the ways in which staff and students listen and respond to each other and talk about each other (Riley, 2013). In the classroom, the relationship between young people and their teachers is the most significant factor in terms of whether they have a sense of school belonging. Across the wider school environment, belonging is nurtured through compassionate leadership at all levels and through an inclusive culture. And, of course, beyond school, young people's feelings about school belonging are linked to whether their families feel welcome and whether their school understands the realities of its community.

What I have learned from my own research and development work on school belonging, in many countries and contexts, is that schools which actively pursue this important aspect of school life share a number of common features. Staff *and* students feel they belong. They are heard and seen for who they are. They have a sense of agency – a belief that what they do makes a real difference (Riley, 2019). A sense of belonging is manifested in relationships at all levels and can be seen in the ways in which staff and students talk to and about each other (Telford and Wrekin Council, 2019; Riley and Mendoza, 2020).

There is little in these schools about 'tough' sanction-based behaviour policies which depend on exclusion and social isolation (Allen et al., 2020). Any interventions are characterised by relational approaches that value individuals.[1] Behaviour policies are owned by everyone. Staff and students know what they are, have helped to shape them and think they are fair.

When it comes to belonging, we know that what works are intentional, purposeful and positive interventions (not one-off reactions) that are clearly understood across schools and the wider school system, and which aim to create the conditions for school belonging (Riley, 2019). This approach is supported by place-based, compassionate and intentional leadership which listens to and involves staff, young people, families and communities (Coates, 2018; Riley et al., 2018; Riley, Mendoza and Galdames, 2020; Smylie et al., 2020; Riley, 2022). Compassion, intent and purpose will help all children – and especially our square pegs.

Video materials and resources on school belonging are available at: www.theartofpossiblities.org.uk.

# References

Allen, K. A. and Kern, P. (2019) *Boosting School Belonging in Adolescents: Interventions for Teachers and Mental Health Professionals*. Abingdon and New York: Routledge.

Allen, K. A., Kern, M. L., Vella-Brodrick, D., Hattie, J. and Waters, L. (2018) What Schools Need to Know About Belonging: A Meta-Analysis, *Educational Psychology Review*, 30(1): 1–34. doi:10.1007/s10648-016-9389-8

Allen, T., Riley K., and Coates, M. (2020) *Belonging, Behaviour and Inclusion in Schools: What Does Research Tell Us?* London: National Education Union. Available at: https://neu.org.uk/media/13036/view.

Coates, M. (2018) *It's Doing My Head In*. Woodbridge: John Catt Educational.

Fair Education Alliance (2017) *Report Card, 2016/17*. Available at: http://www.faireducation.org.uk/report-card.

---

1 Exclusions are rare in such schools and responses to challenging behaviour are usually along the lines of, 'Why did you do that?', 'How do you feel?', 'How do you think other children or your teachers feel?' and 'What do you think we should do?'

Riley, K. (2013) *Leadership of Place: Stories from Schools in the US, UK and South Africa*. London: Bloomsbury.

Riley, K. (2017) *Place, Belonging and School Leadership: Researching to Make the Difference*. London: Bloomsbury Academic.

Riley, K. (2019) Agency and Belonging: What Transformative Actions Can Schools Take to Help Create a Sense of Place and Belonging?, *Journal of Educational & Child Psychology*, 36(4): 91–103.

Riley, K. (2022) *Compassionate Leadership for School Belonging*. London: UCL Press. Available at: https://discovery.ucl.ac.uk/id/eprint/10146072/1/Compassionate-Leadership-for-School-Belonging.pdf.

Riley, K., Coates, M. and Allen, T. (2020) *Place and Belonging in School: Why It Matters Today. Case Studies*. London: National Education Union. Available at: https://neu.org.uk/media/13026/view.

Riley, K., Coates, M. and Martinez, S. P. (2018) *Place & Belonging in Schools: Unlocking Possibilities*. London: UCL Institute of Education. Available at: https://www.ucl.ac.uk/ioe/sites/ioe/files/place-and-belonging-unlocking-possibilities.pdf.

Riley, K. and Mendoza, M. (2020) *Leading in a New Era: Compassionate Leadership for Place and Belonging. A Research Inquiry*. Available at: https://www.theartofpossibilities.org.uk/docs/NewResearch2.pdf.

Riley, K., Mendoza, M. and Galdames, S. (2020) *Cross-Sector & Interdisciplinary Perspectives on School Belonging & Exclusion. A Discussion Document. What We Know; What We Need to Know; and What Needs to Change*. London: UCL Institute of Education. Available at: https://theartofpossibilities.org.uk/docs/NewResearch3.pdf.

Smylie, M. A., Murphy, J. and Seashore Louis, K. (2020) *The Practice of Caring School Leadership*. Thousand Oaks, CA: Corwin Press.

Telford and Wrekin Council (2019) *Telford and Wrekin Belonging Strategy*. Available at: https://www.telfordsend.org.uk/downloads/file/1251/belonging_strategy.

# Chapter 18

# MOVING ON

## Lorraine Petersen, Andrew Cowley and Fran Morgan

Transition implies a move to the unfamiliar. It can be a scary time for anyone, let alone our square pegs. Children and young people go through many transitions during their educational journey – from home to school, from school to school and, ultimately, from school to whatever lies beyond. Getting it right is a vital part of a child's development, helping to avoid issues further down the line, and should not be seen as something that merely 'happens'. Getting it right is a win for everyone.

The keys to success in any transition – and we will look at just five here – are preparation, managing expectations, involving all the relevant people and thinking of it as a journey rather than a destination, one that involves children, practitioners and parents working together.

## Transition 1: Home to school or nursery

The first transition point for a very young child will be leaving their home, hopefully a safe and secure environment, to start their educational journey in an early years setting. This might be to nursery or straight into reception, but that separation from home (and usually from mum) can initiate long-term problems if it's not managed carefully. This is particularly true if a child is summer born, as there is undue pressure on parents to apply for a place in their child's fourth year, even if they have only just turned 4, something that is simply too soon for some children.[1]

There is a world of developmental difference between a child who has just turned 4 and one who is almost 5. And if that same child has been with a parent at home until the start of reception, then that transition may require extra care. This is a time when staff need to collaborate with parents, look out for their square pegs (particularly the 'invisible' ones), make sure any needs are identified quickly, accurately and comprehensively

---

1    In 2015, the then schools minister, Nick Gibb, announced the government's intention to give summer-born children the right to start reception at the age of 5. Five years later, the Department for Education (2020: 4) published *Summer Born Children. Starting School: Advice for Parents*, stating: 'We remain committed to making that change when a legislative opportunity is available.' We are still waiting ...

and then addressed, supported and reviewed. One of the most effective ways to do this is by investing in that all-important relationship with parents, passing information to and inviting information from them, and making them part of their child's educational life from the very start.

# Transition 2: Early years foundation stage to Year 1 and on through primary

Since the introduction of the updated Early Years Foundation Stage Statutory Framework in September 2021, the expectation is that a child arriving in a Year 1 setting is met with a much more formal and prescriptive curriculum. To make this transition smoother for all concerned, it helps if children continue to have access to the sorts of physical resources they had in reception – sand, water and construction tools, for example – with opportunities to learn through first-hand play-based experiences.

The stronger the relationship a setting has with parents and carers, the better a child can be supported in the journey up through the school – and this is all the more important in these first few years. Transitions should be given due attention, not simply allowed to happen. Building in sufficient time for children to get used to the change of teacher and environment is an investment that will certainly save problems later on, particularly for those children known to struggle most with change. If the transition is from an infant to a junior school, then this necessitates extra preparation for a smooth handover. It's worth noting from Not Fine in School surveys that the roots of future attendance and behaviour difficulties tend to start at primary.[2] How a school responds – or fails to respond – can send a child down a path that is hard to come back from.

# Transition 3: Primary to secondary

When we talk about transition, the move from primary to secondary is the one that usually springs to mind. It's a huge cliff face for so many of our square pegs. The differences go way beyond the obvious (see Table 18.1) and it seems like a glaring omission that there is no consistent evidence-based government guidance for our primary and secondary schools on the matter.

There are so many pitfalls for new Year 7 students, from remembering to bring all their resources each day to moving between lessons, topping up their lunch credit and

---

2   See https://notfineinschool.co.uk/nfis-surveys.

catching the bus home. But, if anxieties are minimised and the transition is well managed, there are just as many benefits: more trust between the young person, parents and school; reduced anxiety for all concerned; fewer attendance and behaviour issues; clearer lines of communication; quicker identification of any problems; and less staff time needed to resolve concerns.

Whilst every secondary school will run a transition programme, it needs to be more than a day showing children where the toilets are and laying on some 'show lessons'. Transition often causes anxiety, and this needs to be addressed head on and never simply dismissed as a rite of passage that everyone goes through because 'It didn't do me any harm.' Think also about whether children come from primary schools spread far and wide or whether the particular cohort coming through has above average, or higher than previous, numbers of children eligible for free school meals or those with special educational needs and disabilities (SEND).[3] Make sure you are taking into account the heightened anxieties thrown up by the pandemic too. Don't simply focus on 'lost learning' and 'catch-up' but on their experiences of that time – good and bad.

Waiting until a child is in Year 6 is too late. This transition is arguably the most important in a child's educational life, and it needs to be well planned and organised. Good working relationships developed over time between primaries and secondaries ensure that children are prepared well in advance. The more staff can work together throughout a child's primary years, the better, with this collaboration reaching its crescendo (but not necessarily stopping – see below) in the Year 6 summer term at primary, so it blends seamlessly into the Year 7 autumn term at secondary.

If physical visits are difficult then get creative about visualising what life at the new secondary school will be like. Take a leaf out of Steve Brice's book, for example. He is a head teacher in Manchester who built his school in *Minecraft* over three weeks, with the help of his daughters, in order to provide engaging virtual tours for Year 6 students (Newsround, 2020). The added advantage of digital transition tools (e.g. virtual tours and maps, vox pops from teachers and current Year 7 students, even footage of a typical school day or those common trigger points like first thing each day or moving between lessons) is that an anxious young person can watch them in their own time, with whomever they wish and as many times as they wish.

It can help to treat Year 7 as a 'transition year', taking all that is good from primary education and using it to ease the child into the secondary way of working without losing impetus or direction. Once in secondary schools, it's great if primary teachers can continue to keep in touch with their previous Year 6 cohort, liaising with secondary staff where helpful.

It's true that many schools identify the SEND children at this stage and provide extra care during transition, but often it's only those with an education, health and care plan

---

3   We know that these children are disproportionately represented in absence and exclusions data.

(EHCP) as there are so many more on SEN support. Even combined, these children still only represent a handful of the square pegs, and the extra attention SEND children receive would most likely benefit a far wider group of children and help to prevent problems further down the line.

One of the key obstacles that secondary schools face is building strong relationships with families. Strong home–school ties are almost a given at primary, as help is needed for activities such as reading, swimming and fundraising. Keeping parents at arm's length to help students become independent more quickly may work for some, but rarely does it work for our square pegs. Parents with concerns can often feel like they are not being heard and children can find themselves very anxious, sometimes with their needs going unsupported. This can continue until it reaches crisis point. As you will read elsewhere in this book, the sooner needs are met, the better. It is vital to demonstrate honesty and transparency to parents, to build clear lines of communication, to manage expectations and to extend an open invitation to get in touch if they have concerns.

# Transition 4: Post-16 and the transition to adulthood

Planning for post-16 transition has to start early. Offering opportunities and support throughout the secondary school years will help all children to find their right path as they choose GCSE subjects and post-16 settings. For those with an EHCP, the Year 9 annual review will be key, particularly now that plans can support a young person up to the age of 25.

For some young people, post-16 education and training will represent an opportunity to go in a less academic direction and to make more personal choices about their ongoing education. For some, a continuous school environment will work well; for others, the independence and more equal power balance between staff and students at a sixth-form college will suit them better. Some will thrive if challenged academically; others will find new passions via vocational training.

What this means is that the best support we can offer is personalised, comprehensive, creative advice on the opportunities open to them, perhaps arranging visits to companies, bringing in speakers and encouraging students to do their own research. We also need to keep lines of communication open with parents, especially where there is conflict between what the young person wants and what the parents think is best for them.

# Transition 5: Transition to a new school outside the normal transition process

Transition to another school is difficult for any child, as friendship groups will already exist in the new school and a newcomer is by definition singled out. It is all the harder when that child has left behind their friends in the previous setting. There is no clearer indicator of a positive and compassionate school than when a new child is welcomed warmly by classmates and staff.

In these sideways transitions, for whatever reason, staff need to be alert to any degree of social marginalisation. Classrooms (like staffrooms) have a pecking order, and a new arrival may find it difficult to fit in and end up excluded. Equally, there may be children in the class who, for a number of reasons, may be challenged by the arrival of someone from outside their known group of peers. Both should be action points for the class and the school, particularly if any bullying or behaviour involving fighting or other aggressions are seen or reported. How these situations manifest themselves and how they are addressed are key indicators of how well a values-led culture is embedded in the fabric of the school.

Regardless of the transition, there are common characteristics that will help to make it a success:

- Managing expectations and minimising unfamiliarity. Time and patience are key here.
- Actively listening to the child and their parents/carers, so that any concerns can be quickly addressed.
- Seamlessness so that the gap between one setting and another is an exciting step, not a daunting canyon.
- Thinking creatively about transition. Use technology, make it engaging and make sure it works for all children.
- Check back regularly to see how it's going for all concerned. Make sure lines of communication are clear and invite – don't wait for – concerns.
- Watch the quiet ones. They are often the students who drop into crisis with no visible warning. With children working hard to stay under the radar at school, it's often parents who spot the signs first.

Invest in transition. Done well, it mitigates against many issues further down the line – issues that end up costing everyone a great deal of time and money, and worse. Done well, it makes every transition a move in the right direction, especially for our square pegs.

**Table 18.1. Creating a smooth transition between Year 6 in primary school and (a few weeks later) Year 7 in secondary school**

| Primary | | Secondary | Ideas |
|---------|---|-----------|-------|
| Average 281 pupils (Staufenberg, 2018). | | Average 948 students (Staufenberg, 2018) but can be upwards of 2,000. | Think about creating smaller cohorts within the school, even within large year groups, so children have a better sense of belonging and support. |
| One class teacher 90% of the time, possibly a teaching/ learning support assistant. Lunchtime supervisors. | | One form tutor for about 45 minutes per day? Head of year occasionally, plus approximately 13 teachers for different subjects. | Carve out extra time for that all-important informal catch-up with students (ideally daily). This is an opportunity to notice whether someone is struggling or to provide an environment where problems can be aired. |
| Smaller building, same classroom. | Six weeks of summer holiday | Large, often complex estate of buildings. | Be creative with maps and signage. Think digital too. Try to minimise the amount of moving around that Year 7s have to do as they get used to their new environment – not getting to the next classroom on time is often a huge source of anxiety. |
| Staff in the playground at break times. | | No staff around during break times and lots of 'hidden corners'. | Could Year 7s have their own space outside? Could staff be available to show their faces (in an informal walkabout) during break times, particularly in those hidden corners? |
| A Year 6 child is a big fish in a small pond. | | A Year 7 child is a very small fish in a lake of much bigger (and scarier) fish. | Make sure older children don't victimise the new Year 7s. Can they be incentivised to act as 'buddies' instead? Find other ways to shield Year 7 square pegs from the vastness of a secondary school and minimise their anxiety. |

| Primary | | Secondary | Ideas |
|---|---|---|---|
| Independence is encouraged, but a broken pencil or lost glue stick rarely has severe consequences. | | Independence is often promoted via strict rules, to the point where a forgotten ruler can result in a detention. This instils fear in any child who is already anxious. | Don't increase the anxiety of Year 7s who just a few weeks ago were enjoying a familiar, and hopefully nurturing, primary environment. Forgetting something is another huge and unnecessary source of anxiety. Laying down the law from day one isn't compassionate and only serves to make the square pegs more anxious. |
| Parents are encouraged to come in and help with reading, swimming and so on. | Six weeks of summer holiday | Parents are often kept at arm's length from day one. | Collaboration and relationships are key to addressing concerns early, as well as identifying the right support and interventions. You are better off investing in getting parents onside from the beginning. Bear in mind that some will come with baggage from their experiences with previous schools and the education system; accept that this is understandable and don't take it personally. |
| School knows the child from age 4–5 and will have a wealth of knowledge about them. | | School doesn't know the child until age 10, so there is no first-hand knowledge of their earlier years. Some secondaries prefer to make their own judgements about their Year 7 intake and may not prioritise primary school information as much as they should. | Listen to parents and pay attention to any reports from primary schools. It's a major parental concern that a child who has already had difficulties will enter secondary school and face the same battles all over again, with no one having due regard to their concerns or their child's previous history. You can still make your own judgements, but life will be much smoother if you start with the knowledge that already exists. |

| Primary | | Secondary | Ideas |
|---|---|---|---|
| Nurturing environment, with a more play-based pedagogy. | Six weeks of summer holiday | More formal, academic environment and pedagogy. | The curriculum will necessarily be increasingly academic, but it can still be taught in a creative way. Some schools combine departments to dream up projects that are far more engaging for students whilst still delivering the national curriculum. Work with primaries to develop projects that can create continuity between Years 6 and 7. Develop a Year 7 primary-based environment whereby students stay in the same class with the same teacher (primary-trained) for the majority of lessons, maybe going to PE, art and so on with specialist teachers. This really helps the new Year 7s as they don't have to get to know lots of new teachers and constantly move around the school. |
| Parents of a child with SEND are often able to build strong relationships with class teachers and special educational needs coordinators. | | Parents of a child with SEND may struggle to build a strong relationship with a bigger SEN team or the many different SEND/ attendance-related roles within the school and local authority. | Make sure lines of communication are clear and that parents have been introduced to all relevant staff and understand the distinction between roles. For children with SEND, it will be beneficial if one staff member remains the main point of contact between school and family. |

| Primary | | Secondary | Ideas |
|---|---|---|---|
| For many parents, any problems develop whilst their child is in primary. | Six weeks of summer holiday | For many parents, problems are already apparent, making them anxious about transition from the outset. | Take the time to invite all parents into school, introducing them to staff and explaining policies (and the reason for them). Manage expectations and work to eliminate the power imbalance that often exists between school and parents. Recognise that some will have had bad experiences of schools themselves. |
| If primary went well, there are seven years of familiarity and trust. | | Secondary is all new, so this trust needs to be built/earned. | You can't expect or demand trust. Your actions will speak far louder than any marketing spiel at an open day or on your website. If parents trust you, they will be more ready to collaborate, help you to support their child's educational journey and forgive any slip-ups that happen along the way. |

# References

Department for Education (2020) *Summer Born Children. Starting School: Advice for Parents* (September). Available at: https://www.gov.uk/government/publications/summer-born-children-school-admission.

Department for Education (2021) *Statutory Framework for the Early Years Foundation Stage: Setting the Standards for Learning, Development and Care for Children from Birth to Five* (31 March; effective 1 September). Available at: https://www.gov.uk/government/publications/early-years-foundation-stage-framework--2.

Department for Education and Gibb, N. (2015) The Admission to School of Summer Born Children [letter] (8 September). Available at: https://www.gov.uk/government/publications/summer-born-children-nick-gibbs-letter-about-school-admissions.

Newsround (2020) Minecraft: A Head Teacher Used the Game to Create a Virtual Secondary School Tour for Kids Joining Year 7 (12 July). Available at: https://www.bbc.co.uk/newsround/53373921.

Staufenberg, J. (2018) DfE: Schools Get Bigger as Pupil Population Increases by 66,000, *Schools Week* (28 June). Available at: https://schoolsweek.co.uk/dfe-schools-get-bigger-as-pupil-population-increases-by-66000.

# Chapter 19

# AN OUTSTANDING CULTURE

## Lucie Lakin

In 2013, when the inspectors told us that the behaviour of our pupils was outstanding, we probably weren't as bothered as we could have been. No disrespect to those fine public servants at Ofsted, but that label just wasn't what drove or shaped our work. We were more concerned about whether there was an inspection team out there that could handle the innovative approach embodied within our school community.

Now, nearly eight years on, a growing number of schools are aware, in theory at least, of topics such as trauma-informed practice, adverse childhood experiences and the importance of relationships with pupils, their families and staff. This has been highlighted further with the COVID-19 pandemic, where so many schools have understood that relationships must be at the heart of any attempt to 'catch up', 'level up' or 'close gaps'.

I say 'in theory' because adopting the practice seems to provoke feelings of trepidation and reluctance, so let me briefly outline our journey in the hope that it may inspire others to embark on theirs.

Carr Manor Community School, an all-through, inner-city Leeds comprehensive, was much like any other. We had the same battles, statistics and challenging square pegs as other schools, but we realised that doing more of the same and expecting things to improve was madness. Our community deserved better, and so we set out to live by four simple, closely guarded and visibly upheld values:

1  Know our children well.

2  Partners in learning.

3  Enjoy and achieve.

4  Character for learning.

There is no 10-point plan or fancy diagram to explain our achievements, just these values matched by a consistent commitment to include every family, to give every child every chance and a willingness to go the long way around when needed.

Teachers love a silver bullet, but the truth is that there isn't one. There is just a series of decisions, approaches and strategies, which all contribute to building a culture that fosters positive relationships and the great behaviour and achievements that result. Let me highlight some of the key areas where such decisions were taken.

## Exclusions

Our first key decision was to take the option to permanently exclude any child off the table. Why would we throw out a child presenting challenging behaviour, with potential safeguarding risks, and send them down the road for other children, other staff and other families to manage? Anyway, if behaviour can be addressed simply by starting somewhere else, it implies that the behaviour was telling you more about your school than the child.

'Ah!' I hear you tweet, 'Carr Manor wants children sitting next to attackers and bullies!' Er, actually, I don't want *any* children in *any* school in that situation. If 'let them carry on' or 'kick them out' are the only two possibilities a group of professionals can come up with, then I suggest we need to spend more time broadening the understanding of the professionals rather than narrowing the options and opportunities of the children. After all, there is always another way.

Of course, Carr Manor doesn't work in a vacuum, and our community includes other schools across the city too. We have worked to build partnerships with all eight local secondary schools, which are now equally committed to a no permanent exclusions strategy.[1]

## Coaching and staff circles

Our second decision was to build relationships relentlessly and routinely. More than just something for a website or lanyard, we decided to make relational practice the cornerstone of what we do, rooted in routines, structure, habits and behaviours that explicitly build social capital and community.

For example, we start every Monday morning with 'staff circles'. These are groups of six to eight staff from across the primary and secondary phases and our resourced provision – a mixture of teaching and non-teaching staff and all management and leadership levels. Staff check in on how their weekend has been and what they are focusing on for the week ahead, as well as discussing and debriefing as necessary.

---

1   All eight are graded at least good by Ofsted, with four also awarded outstanding for behaviour, welfare and personal development.

This means that by 8.45am on a Monday, every member of staff has spoken and been listened to – and as a human being, not just as a staff member with a job to do. Every adult in the school has made a connection to the school community and the school agenda. These sessions are often filled with laughter and excited chatter as the adults sincerely and genuinely take an interest in each other, professionally and personally. The wider understanding each colleague has of how the organisation works and the various roles staff undertake generates not only a more empathetic and knowledgeable workforce, but also one that is more engaged and connected. We have had the lowest staff absence for work-related stress in the city for years, and continue to have low levels of absence generally – trend-bucking that we put down to all the relationship-building work prioritised across the school.

Our coaching programme follows on from these staff circles. It is a central strategy for building and maintaining a sense of community and strong relationships with staff, pupils and families. Developed over 15 years, the coaching model involves all adults in the school – teaching and non-teaching staff – each of whom is responsible for a small vertical class of between eight and twelve children in Years 1 to 5 and Years 6 to 11. As coaches, they also liaise with parents to support pupil learning, especially when children are confronting difficulties. All in all, these 'family groups' meet three times a week for check-in, check-up and check-out sessions – that is a total of 4,680 minutes a year devoted to coaching! They form the central contact point for our children and ensure that all children are listened to, that they receive and give (through peer mentoring) support, that they are listened to, that they are known and belong.

# Learning relationship agreements

Another easy decision to make was that, despite what some may claim, being a compassionate school did not mean we would be any less academic. Like any school, we believe academic qualifications are incredibly important. It's just that we have higher ambitions than grades being the be-all and end-all of school life. Yes, our children leave with great grades, but we are also dedicated to ensuring that they leave with the interpersonal skills and character development that will allow them to put those grades to best use.

To help us in this goal, we ensure that classroom routines and expectations are underpinned by the restorative principles of high challenge and high support.[2] The bar is always set high for *all* pupils, from *all* backgrounds and of *all* abilities, including our square pegs, even as the support required to meet those challenges varies from pupil to pupil and from time to time across a school year. Our community understands that

---

2   There are many practitioners of restorative justice. Mark Finnis is just one; for more information see Finnis (2021).

equity is more important than equality, and we do our best to ensure that every child has the support needed, when it's needed, to meet any challenges they may experience.

As part of this process, pupils sign a learning relationship agreement at the start of a new class or year. This live document notes how the group has agreed to learn together and manage its relationships to benefit all learners. In this way, children are accountable for their actions and understand the active, not passive, role they must play as a learner in a group setting. This is not about pupils setting the rules; it is about the adult being able to engage with pupils meaningfully about learning environment expectations. It offers pupils the ability to understand why there are behaviours and habits to be adopted by all, and so they behave because they know why and how, not out of any sense of fear-generated compliance.

## Special educational needs and disabilities, inclusion and safeguarding

We knew that we needed to be efficient and smart in supporting our many square pegs, thinking beyond the traditional models of small-group intervention, one-to-one support and the like. Such a model also relied on hitting a particular threshold of need before any intervention is triggered and money made available. This feels counterintuitive to us because we know – and as you will read elsewhere in this book – that the earlier we support a pupil in need, the better for all concerned.

We knew, therefore, that we needed to work preventatively and proactively, and, with this in mind, we employed a team of non-teaching support and pastoral staff. These year managers and pupil support workers ensure that the children receive the intervention, challenge and support they need, when they need it. We also employ a safeguarding team made up of a range of specialists, including specially trained social workers, a counsellor and a mental health expert.

## Curriculum

Our curriculum has been a labour of love. We recognise that academic success is underpinned by high levels of literacy and numeracy, and our efforts in developing a primary phase and becoming an all-through school has instilled in us an appreciation of the impact that good reading skills, strong core mathematical knowledge and high levels of oracy can have on a child's progress and achievement.

That said, we border on the evangelical when it comes to the need for all pupils to access a broad, rich, wide-reaching and bespoke curriculum.[3] We want them to be ready for the modern world. We want them to have empathy, compassion, imagination and curiosity. We want them to understand and respect our past and be equipped for, ambitious and optimistic about their future.

At primary, this translates into a wide range of subject specialisms taught by secondary-trained staff with a golden thread (not a suffocating blanket) of literacy and numeracy woven throughout. We have regular inspiration days where children tackle a big question that piques their curiosity about the world around them and broadens their interests, knowledge and horizons. And we love to trip – trips to the seaside, trips to museums, trips to the supermarket to buy baking ingredients. We work hard to root the learning in *their* world, whilst simultaneously stretching their frame of reference and widening their appreciation and understanding of the wider world around them.

At secondary, we maintain the same dedication to a broad curriculum. The world of GCSEs lives at Key Stage 4. Key Stage 3 is filled with proper experiences of subjects that nourish the soul and sharpen the mind; for example, art, technology, music, dance, drama and two languages are all taught explicitly throughout the year. No 'We did an art day last term, I think?' here! It's a sincere and genuine commitment to a broad and balanced curriculum.

In Year 9, the pupils select a 'study school' to attend on a Monday. Apart from their coaching session, their whole Monday is spent here, pursuing a specialised programme of learning that focuses on a group of subjects and their link to pathways, destinations and employability. Guest speakers, trips to work environments and small seminar groupings enable pupils to try out areas of the foundation curriculum which help them make informed choices going into Key Stage 4.

In Years 10 and 11, the children attend an afternoon pupil development programme. This is a blend of lectures and small group seminars that are designed to prepare pupils for the world of work or further training. From politics and the democratic process through to finance, university applications and budgeting, this programme enables pupils to develop their knowledge and understanding of areas that matter to them.

What underpins this curriculum is our flexibility. If there is a choice the pupils can make, we offer it. If we can embed the learning in the real world, we do it. If we can bend the curriculum to connect to their needs and interests, we make it happen. And we review and change the curriculum every year and for every cohort to make sure we never ask, 'What will this do for the school?' but always, 'What will this offer for the child?'

---

3   Not that we were too smug when Ofsted finally caught up with our thinking in the 2019 iteration of the education inspection framework.

# Impact

We ask ourselves all the time, 'Does this have impact?' Because we know that what works for one group may not work for another, we know that we will need to adjust our resources and our planning to meet the needs of each group as they come into view. In this way, we throw out the idea of a school as a lottery, postcode or otherwise, where, if you are lucky, you fit in.

To make all of this work, we need a staff team that understands, believes in and lives the school's priorities.[4] We regularly reflect as a whole school on why we do what we do, reaffirming our mission and aims in the process. We may change our practice, but the goal always remains the same, driven by our four values.

What is more, our parents trust us and choose us, so they tell us, because of our commitment to building, repairing and maintaining relationships. They see that their children make great progress not only as pupils but also as people.

When other schools ask us how to raise their own behaviour to outstanding, as they so often do, we always reply that they should stop trying. Truly outstanding behaviour comes not from chasing an external goal but creating a culture in which all children want and choose to behave, one that is built first and foremost on relationships.

# References

Finnis, M. (2021) *Independent Thinking on Restorative Practice*. Carmarthen: Independent Thinking Press.

Ofsted (2019) Education Inspection Framework (updated 23 July 2021). Available at: https://www.gov.uk/government/publications/education-inspection-framework.

---

4  They should – over 10% are former pupils!

# Chapter 20

# WHAT'S THE ALTERNATIVE?

## Dave Whitaker

If mainstream schools are to learn from special and alternative provision (AP), then we must first address the misconceptions that exist and, in doing so, challenge school leaders to have the confidence in an alternative approach.

The first challenge is to embrace the sort of relational practice that is at the heart of what we do in AP, an approach bolstered by high-quality specialist knowledge. This might mean rewriting behaviour policies or even making a wholesale cultural shift to fully embrace this new way of thinking and working.

Why is this important? Well, neuroscience tells us that if a child feels understood then they will grow in confidence, and increased self-esteem will lead to improvements in learning (Curran, 2008) (see Chapter 26). This is what we do in special schools and AP, and it's something that is wholly accessible and achievable in a mainstream setting. It may need brave leadership, a commitment to change and ongoing support, and professional learning, but ultimately you will create a school where everyone has a place and the happiness of all (pupils and staff) becomes the bedrock of your culture.

Carl Rogers (1961) introduced us to the concept of unconditional positive regard – something of huge importance to our square pegs. It is undeniably the best place to start your cultural change. As a psychologist, Rogers took a humanistic approach, and being non-judgemental was at the heart of his work. Imagine the impact of such an approach in a school! Acceptance and empathy then become the drivers for change and underpin the operational model of relational practice. Working in this way means that we don't instinctively look for compliance and enforce conformity through strict sanctions and a no-excuses culture.

So, before we proceed, ask yourself one simple question: are you looking for compliance and conformity, or do you want children to feel accepted? If the answer is acceptance, then your behaviour policy, staff training programme, values and culture all need to allow it to happen. If you want compliance, then you probably gave up with this book somewhere near the beginning.

There are two major pillars at play here. They are evident every day in the culture of special and AP schools and are easily adopted in a mainstream setting.[1]

## Acceptance

Everyone, including you and me, needs to feel part of something (for more on the importance of belonging see Chapters 6 and 16). But many children struggle to find acceptance in a group, in a school or even in a family. Unconditional positive regard can provide the foundation for acceptance. The children in your school need to feel accepted and understood. Acceptance allows them to build self-esteem and to trust others. We must not assume that acceptance happens automatically at school, even for the most well-rounded children with supportive families and happy childhoods.

Some schools demand conformity as a prerequisite for acceptance. They demand behaviour before belonging, even though for many children that is the reverse of what is needed. It often becomes a wall that is difficult to break down for those who struggle to understand their place in school.

As adults, with the power to influence acceptance, we must not let our preconceptions of conformity prevent our acceptance. We must be highly aware of children who may be struggling to feel accepted. If we do not spot this, then we are in danger of letting pupils slip through the net. They may develop school-based anxiety or even stop attending. If children stop attending school because they don't feel accepted, it will be very difficult to repair the damage and get them back. This can lead to long-term school refusal, high levels of anxiety and significant problems with transition to the next phase of education.

## Empathy

It is important that we do not mistake empathy for sympathy. Sympathy is a feeling of pity or sorrow for another person. Yes, this has its place, but empathy is what helps with unconditional positive regard.

Empathy allows us to understand another's feelings and identify with them. Genuine empathy can be challenging, and it's something with which many people struggle. Avoiding pity and putting ourselves in the place of the other person is a much more powerful stance.

---

1   The text in this chapter has been adapted from Whitaker (2021).

Using empathy to influence the behaviour policy of your school means that you can look at behaviour as a *symptom* of a child's emotional response. Emotions and feelings drive the behaviour of a child, and therefore it is those causal factors that will lead to unwanted behaviours.

We then have choices to make. We either punish the behaviour or attempt to deal with the emotions and feelings. Punishing the behaviour is easier, but does it work? The simple answer is no – at least for many children and particularly those more complex children with complicated lives and a history of trauma, anxiety or adverse childhood experiences.

The basis for any behaviour changes in a school must begin with the behaviour of the adults. Setting the cultural tone is a serious responsibility and will have a long-lasting impact on children's lives. Never underestimate how important your behaviour is and how it is perceived by the children and your colleagues. Your values, in a person-centred profession like education, should be your fundamental beliefs and therefore drive your behaviour. They should be the guiding principles that steer every relationship and interaction you have, whether that is with a child or a colleague.

In specialist settings, it is well known that every interaction you have with a pupil has an impact. Essentially, the interaction is also an intervention – and therein lies your first challenge – but it is also something you can use to help you make connections and build relationships. We have hundreds of personal interactions a day, each one of them influencing our response and our behaviour. If we, as adults, react to the tone, manner and style of another adult's interactions, then why would that be any different for children? To be clear, it's not any different. Children will respond to you depending on how you present yourself, the tone of your voice, your body language and what you say.

The second challenge that special and AP schools offer you is to think beyond a behaviourist approach predicated on the use of rewards and sanctions. Put simply, the behaviourist approach sees behaviour from an observational perspective: a judgement is made on whether that behaviour is appropriate and therefore acceptable. In essence, we assume that the behaviour is a choice that is being made and that rational decisions are influencing the individual's responses. Behaviourist approaches rely very much on an external view of a person's actions and ignore the internal emotions, feelings and thinking that lead to the behaviour. This approach emphasises right from wrong, seeing everything as black or white.

So, why should we look any further than this simple binary approach? It would be unfair to say that it doesn't work at all, it just doesn't work for everyone. Children are complex, after all. If we take the easy approach, there will be unintentional consequences and some children will fail, be excluded (either formally or informally) and disappear. In some schools this is considered acceptable. It is not an unintended consequence but an accepted, and often lauded, method of working with a clear eye on league tables and inspection reports in a system that prioritises league tables and inspection reports.

In AP and special schools, we have reset the default position and we don't immediately look to sanction. This is a mindset that is achievable in mainstream settings. We look beyond the behaviour and become interpreters: we look to find and understand the emotions and feelings that drive the behaviour.

The third challenge is not to hide behind the money argument. It is not about the money. Yes, specialist settings are better funded than mainstream schools and, yes, they enjoy the luxury of small class sizes. However, 100% of their cohorts have complex needs and therefore require an intensity in practice that does not necessarily exist in mainstream schools. Resourcing is always a challenge, no matter what school we work in, but it must not become a barrier or even an excuse to prevent cultural or behavioural change.

The fourth challenge, and this is important for any school leader, is to ensure that there is no trade-off between educational standards and adopting the sorts of practice I am describing. If you accept and embrace this new way of working, do not think that this will be at the expense of educational standards, GCSE results, SATs scores or Ofsted judgements – no matter what Twitter says.

Finally, relational practice is not being soft on naughty kids. It is not about letting them get away with unacceptable behaviour over tea and biscuits. Being kind is a challenge because it is by far the harder option. It takes courage.

Adopting a relational approach to inclusion and behaviour policy requires rigour, and achieving behavioural and cultural change necessitates high standards. If you can allow yourself to dispel the myths, ignore the misconceptions and rise to the challenge, then you can be really optimistic about creating a cultural shift that embraces the work of special schools and AP. Defining your values, living them every day and committing to a new way of working will inevitably lead to a change in school culture that will allow all pupils – not just the square pegs – to feel understood, safe, accepted and unconditionally loved.

# References

Curran, A. (2008) *The Little Book of Big Stuff About the Brain: The True Story of Your Amazing Brain*. Carmarthen: Crown House Publishing.

Rogers, C. R. (1961) *On Becoming a Person: A Therapist's View of Psychotherapy*. Boston, MA: Houghton Mifflin.

Whitaker, D. (2021) *The Kindness Principle: Making Relational Behaviour Management Work in Schools*. Carmarthen: Independent Thinking Press.

# Chapter 21

# THE STONE SOUP FAMILY

## Kerrie Henton

Stone Soup Academy lies behind a big black door on an old narrow street in the centre of Nottingham. We are an award-winning alternative provision free school, one of the first in the country. We meet the needs of up to 100 young people who have been either excluded or are at risk of exclusion from mainstream education. We reflect national statistics, with 70% of our cohort being male and 85% of our cohort in Years 7–11. We are judged to be outstanding, but we think that we are broader and richer than this. I am the principal.

I am embarrassed now, thinking back on my life in mainstream schools as a vice principal, that I didn't really give much thought to those students struggling to exist, grow and learn within our inflexible walls – our square pegs. I realise, on reflection, that I was only concerned with results and focused on 'the many'. Those students who were failing to engage and were causing problems were an inconvenience, something in my peripheral vision.

Stone Soup is where I learned to focus on the square pegs rather than the many.

We are a family, and like a real family we believe that one mistake does not define any one of its members. We believe that there is always another day, another chance, another opportunity to prove that anyone can be amazing.

We reward positivity. In 2020, we celebrated the success of one of our alumni achieving a first-class honours degree and another in Year 11 signing a life-changing contract with a professional football club. These successes are wonderful, but success is also the hundreds of individuals who have been nudged by our unconditional positive regard on to a new life path.

We address the language used within the academy, both written and spoken, to ensure that it reflects our focus. For example, celebration evenings have replaced parents' evenings to ensure we spend the time talking about what the students are achieving rather than what they are not. Our 'seven refrains' serve to change the nature of our conversations and help our students to make better choices, whilst continuing our relentless focus on the vision of 'Creating Unimagined Future', which is the golden thread that runs through our academy:

1  We will always try to show relentless positivity (but not toxic positivity, which is forced rather than authentic).

2  We will always be unfailingly ambitious for you.

3  We will always try to respect and understand you.

4  We will always try to be kind and caring in our approach to you.

5  We will always find creative ways to engage you in your learning through what we teach and how we teach it.

6  We will always celebrate your successes.

7  We will always be here for you, even after you have left.

We have built up impressive links with local and national businesses and deliver long-term work experience at HMRC, Crowne Plaza, John Lewis and Nottingham City Council. Students work in established businesses, gaining a qualification alongside work experience. They also access future employment from these links.[1]

We let these businesses know we care about them, too, by sharing their collaboration with us on our website, talking about them in our newsletter and promoting what we do and how they help us whenever possible.

We work closely with the police, bridging the gap, expelling myths about policing and challenging how many of our young people see them. We also work with the NHS and deliver workshops about positive relationships.

We have set up a Stone Soup Award which assists past students financially who might be struggling to find work. One former student had been temping as a school cleaner since leaving us, and in the course of his work had witnessed the impact of teaching assistants. He decided that was what he wanted to do, and we are now funding him to achieve his dream.

We help students who have been involved in crime to turn their lives around. One was supported throughout his time in prison, coming back to us on his release and gaining qualifications.

We interact with our students in term time, during holidays and at weekends. We often constitute the main 'family' that many of our students have. With us, they receive love, they release their anger, they talk and are listened to, and they are encouraged to achieve.

---

1  There is more on the importance of links with business in Chapter 38.

We go above and beyond. During the pandemic, we delivered and collected student work from home, we stood outside their houses to sing 'Happy Birthday' to them and we gave aid to families in need. We continue to care and make a difference.

We live by our vision – creating unimagined futures – and we don't just do this for our students and their families. We do it for all the staff as well.

At Stone Soup, I have learned that we can make a difference to such students – and in huge ways. It is a superpower that I could have used when I was in mainstream education. My biggest regret is that I didn't realise the difference we could have made at the time.

# Chapter 22

# SUPPORT (NOT PUNISHMENT)

## Adele Bates

---

**Ahmed's story (part 1)**

Ahmed has not been to school for three weeks. One day he arrives, late, looking dishevelled and makes his way to maths. You, a senior leader, spot him in the corridor. After noticing he is here, late, you see that he is wearing trainers …

---

Ahmed is a square peg.

The punishment systems in our schools are modelled on the criminal justice systems of our society, justice systems that go way back, as the Secret Barrister (2018: 7) explains:

---

We are yet to find a society that does not have rules surrounding the behaviour of its members and sanctions of their transgressions. Agreeing social imperatives and taboos, and enforcing them through shunning, appears to be instinctual behaviour in cooperative primates, and the notion of a codified criminal law can be traced back to Bronze Age Mesopotamia and the Code of Ur-Nammu in 2050 BC.

---

Of course, the rules (and consequences) may have changed since then, but it is a good place to start in order to better understand the practice, purpose and effectiveness of punishment. It helps us to understand why the organisation – be it state, company or school – sees fit to punish the individual. Again, in the words of the Secret Barrister (2018: 7): 'To commit a crime is to break a law that offends not just those directly affected, but strikes at the heart of our communal values so deeply that we agree that organized, coercive action is required to mark the affront.'

The values and organisation systems a society decides to live by are exemplified by, and then reaffirmed by, the actions we deem to be punishable. This is how we judge other societies. For example, I pass negative judgements on the countries in which I might be killed for being married to my (same-sex) wife, and take pride in the fact that I am from a country that does not do this (currently). Citizens from those other countries may well judge my country in a poor light for exactly the same reason. In addition, the commonly regulated decisions about which actions are punishable are often linked to our attitudes towards personal safety. For example, I feel safe knowing that to possess an unlicensed gun in the UK is illegal.

That said, some of the self-same laws may, at times, make me feel unsafe. Police powers to physically handle peaceful protestors (as we saw on Clapham Common in March 2021 – see Campbell (2021)) can result in unnecessary violence and discrimination towards certain minority groups to whom the power could be practised with disproportional force as a result of negative bias. My Black teenage pupils at a peaceful protest are five times more likely to be on the receiving end of physical violence from police officers than my White pupils (Grierson, 2020). Same laws, different outcomes.

How might this play out in a school setting with our square pegs, those children and young people who are also in the minority or on the periphery, and who may be subject to the unconscious bias of the adults – and even their peers, in school?

What this suggests is that the rhetoric around punishment as being 'clean', 'clear-cut' and 'no nonsense' – and therefore positioned as the more 'favourable', 'results-led' or 'successful' approach to breaking the rules – needs to be considered far more carefully. Just as there is no one-size-fits-all approach when it comes to helping children and young people adapt to the school environment, there can be no one-size-fits-all system for dealing with those who are struggling to fit in. To ignore this is to ignore the complexities and diversity of the human condition, especially when it comes to children. Also of significant concern is that this approach means we put disproportionate power in the hands of a minority group and out of reach of others. Who, then, gets to decide what is punishable – of what are we zero tolerant? And who do those decisions affect the most?

As we already know from Chapter 1, what has been described as a traditionalist approach to behaviour management (the threat of sanction or reward) and control (the use of sanction or reward) draws on B. F. Skinner's theories of behaviourism. As we are dealing with immature humans, not rats, there is clearly more to it than this. We need to consider such approaches through a far more complex lens.

For example, research has found that in communities with a high level of trust, punishment was an effective tool for maintaining cooperation. However, in communities where trust was low, punishment was less effective (Balliet and Van Lange, 2013). As you consider the impact of your behaviour policies on pupils, consider too the prevalent levels of trust in your school.

Rewards, despite being the go-to carrot dangled in many high-profile schools, also have their complexities. Not only can they become tokenistic, especially as children get older, but they require that children actually give a toss. They also rely on the all-seeing eye of a teacher – who is subject to normal human unconscious biases – to constantly assess what is often the invisible effort of all pupils. In your school, who are the ones most regularly receiving merits, for example, and why? Who are the ones rarely or never on the receiving end, and why?

Punishments – and lack of reward – can also reinforce a negative perception of a pupil, class, ethnicity or even an entire school, and a child's own self-belief can become intrinsically linked with negative behaviour. This can even be used as a badge of honour in itself: 'I'm the kid with the most detentions in Year 3!' And then there are the occasions where failures in learning, perhaps linked to unsupported or even undiagnosed special educational needs and disabilities (SEND) or social, emotional or mental health (SEMH) issues, are mistaken for 'bad behaviour' and duly punished. Data from studies such as the Timpson Review (2019: 10) back up this picture, revealing that 78% of excluded pupils have SEND, are classed as 'in need' or are eligible for free school meals, and that Black Caribbean boys have a disproportionately large permanent exclusion rate.

In a school setting, traditional behaviourist approaches to the management and control of the student body may well work, but mainly for the round pegs. For those who have trouble fitting in, for any one of a whole host of reasons, such approaches can not only fail to address the problem, but they can also make that problem worse.

And things are about to get a whole lot worse for Ahmed.

Ahmed's scenario is based on any number of Ahmeds, Arminas, Andrews and Anelkas I have taught. It is clear what should happen next. The school policy is to apply consequences and punishments equally and to all pupils. Your written behaviour policy is clean, clear-cut and Ofsted approved. This means that you, as a senior leader, will have to sanction Ahmed for not just one but the whole hat trick of misdemeanours he has committed before even getting to class – attendance, punctuality and uniform.

But what is really going on here, and what would punishing Ahmed do?

Let's pick up Ahmed's story again, but we will begin with the other protagonist – you, the senior leader.

---

**Your story**

The evening before the incident, you stayed up until late redoing the marking for two of your teachers who were not in line with your department's new marking policy. This morning you have already dealt with three other behaviour issues, and are on your way to a departmental meeting about the marking that you still didn't get to finish. You already feel tired and frustrated, and understandably have little patience left. Your general mood and facial expression express this overtly. It's not yet 10am.

You 'greet' Ahmed by checking that he has registered his presence on site before telling him that he shouldn't be wearing trainers and that he will receive a C1[1] for uniform plus another C1 for lateness. You remind him that if he picks up another C1 today, then he will be on a C2 and there will be a phone call home, along with a detention.

What are you doing here? Maintaining high expectations is what you are doing. You are following – and being seen to follow – established and agreed school protocols. It is clear, though, that Ahmed has not read the memo as he tells you to 'F*ck off and mind your own business,' thus winning himself another C1 and hence the promised C2. Personally upset by Ahmed's behaviour, you take him to his head of year. You wish it didn't have to be this way, but you know Ahmed has given you no other choice.

---

### Ahmed's story (part 2)

That morning, Ahmed's 'friends' have set him the task of selling more weed, so he decides that going to school might be a good place to go to shift some. He proudly puts on his new trainers (they are his only shoes that fit him) and, after making sure his younger sisters are at school, makes his way slowly to his own school and his maths lesson. This is when you stop him in the corridor. He can tell already that he is in trouble by your expression, and realises that he shouldn't have bothered coming back to school at all.

The first thing you mention, crossly, is whether he has registered. The second thing you mention, more crossly, are his trainers. This sets Ahmed on edge. He is starting to panic that you might confiscate them, and so he grows angry and aggressive towards you. He is also aware that if you find the weed, he will be in even bigger trouble. He tries to be hard like his older mates and decides that telling you to 'F*ck off and mind your own business' will do the trick. Rather than allowing him to go to his lesson, you escort him to the head of year's office where you leave him sitting outside, agitated and nervous, for nearly half an hour as the head of year is teaching a cover lesson. It's still not yet 10am.

Eventually, after checking the coast is clear, Ahmed makes a run for it, deciding there are easier ways to sell his weed and that staying in school just creates more trouble for him.

---

Ahmed is clearly a cause for concern, and following its own punishment-centred approach, the school can only escalate things: isolation booths, fixed-term exclusion,[2] permanent exclusion. Yet, none of these sanctions will lead Ahmed any closer to an

---

1   Or five behaviour points or whatever consequence system you use.
2   Fixed-term exclusion has gone back to the old name of 'suspension' at the time of going to press.

education – the education that is his right to receive. What can a school do that both ensures adherence to the rules that school society expects but also leads him towards, not away from, that education?

What if we start with seeing the bigger picture and, without judgement, seek to understand Ahmed?

---

### Ahmed's story (part 3)

Ahmed has not been to school for three weeks because he has been left in charge of his two younger sisters. His parents are away, and whilst older cousins and aunties visit and often bring food, he has become their main carer. He is unsure when his parents will return and they have left him £60 to look after them. Feeling lonely and scared about getting things wrong with his sisters, but also frustrated, he seeks solace with his best friends – these are young men in their twenties who recently befriended Ahmed. For small favours – passing messages around the neighbourhood, delivering packages and occasionally selling weed – they buy him things that he couldn't otherwise afford. Like new trainers. His friends have bought him these gifts, but they have also said things like, 'Don't do my head in though bro' or we'll take them back.' This worries him, so he makes sure he does what they ask as best he can when his sisters are at school. Having these friends makes him feel better, and he often meets up with them at night once his sisters are asleep.

Ahmed does not feel that he belongs at school. School does not know his parents aren't at home – no one has asked so he hasn't told them. Recently school rang the home phone. Ahmed suspects that he may be in trouble, so he speaks in Bengali and pretends to be his dad (neither parent speaks English), repeating, 'I Ahmed Dad. Ahmed ill,' until they put the phone down. The teachers and other pupils seem to have very different lives to him and he struggles to see how schoolwork relates to his life. He believes he is not clever. His mum supported him a lot with reading and writing when he was little, and his Bengali is fluent, as is his Urdu and Arabic. She also taught him maths, but it was always a different way to how he was being taught at school. He enjoyed some parts of primary school, but since he started secondary school he can't wait to finish. He has also decided that if his friends can give him nice things for the jobs he does, he won't need exams anyway.

---

Ahmed's story is long and richly revealing. Ahmed's life is not clean or clear-cut. It does not fit into a simple behaviour system, and there are complex issues at play, including acting as a carer, being groomed by a gang and being part of a minority ethnicity who are more likely to be discriminated against, both systemically and through hate crime. Every individual factor in young Ahmed's life – and the intersection of them all – affects his behaviour.

What if we start with seeing the bigger picture and, without judgement, seek to support Ahmed?

**Your story (alternative ending)**

This time, the night before you meet Ahmed, you had a decent meal, spent some quality time with your family and slept well. There have been a few issues with your departmental staff switching over to the new marking policy, so you have been asked to find a couple of examples of where the issues lie and will bring them to a meeting later that day to discuss and identify the next steps you need to take. Earlier, you have been involved in a few small altercations with a couple of pupils. However, thanks to your own self-care, training and the support you feel from your team, you are calm and robust enough to de-escalate the situations quickly and enable the pupils to swiftly return to their learning.

You greet Ahmed warmly. You see his dishevelled appearance and note that it is worse than last time you saw him (noting too that you haven't seen him in a while). In contrast, you can see that he has expensive-looking new trainers, wonder where they may have come from and make a mental note to ask him once he is settled. At that point, you will also address the issue of school shoes. You tell Ahmed how good it is to see him and that you have missed his sarcastic comments in your lessons. You see him smile. You have a meeting now, but as you have not seen Ahmed for several weeks, and knowing that pastoral have said that he has been ill, you promise that you will catch up with him later.

To ensure that he doesn't get lost in a 'corridor wander', you walk with him to his maths lesson, talking with him as you do, and watch as he settles into his lesson. At break time, you seek him out. You notice him standing closely to some younger pupils, who you don't think are his usual crowd. As he walks away, you intercept him with a smile, asking him to come and help you with the new-fangled projector in the hall as he is 'good with these things'. He moans, but you can see that he is pleased to have been asked, especially as it means he misses the first bit of personal, social, health and economic education.

In a safe, unthreatening environment, and whilst Ahmed concentrates on a neutral task, you are able to discover what is going on. When Ahmed seems to forget that he was supposed to have been ill, you are careful not to show judgement but to show him you care and have concerns. You empathise with him having to look after his sisters and wonder if there are any ways that school can help to make it easier for him. You know there are safeguarding issues to follow up with colleagues, and mention to Ahmed that you will need to pass these things on, but that he is not in any trouble. You compliment his trainers and ask where they have come from. He seems reluctant to tell you at this stage, so you leave it, but you do introduce the question of his school shoes. You know there is a small fund to help pupils with uniform and you promise to look into it, reassuring him that no one else needs to know this information. In the meantime, you write him a note for other teachers about his trainers. Sensing that Ahmed is feeling uncomfortable with how much he has shared, you turn the topic to the rest of his day and the latest Grand Prix, something you know he enjoys.

On leaving him to his day, you follow up the safeguarding concerns and speak to his head of year. You put a support plan in place which enables you to check in with Ahmed daily for the foreseeable future, and if he doesn't make it into school, you plan a home visit for next week. You also seek out a teaching assistant, who you know speaks Bengali, to see if she can help you with parent–school communication. You ensure that she will be paid additionally for these extra skills and her time. At the end of the day, on the school gate, you give a nod to Ahmed, reaffirm how good it was to see him today and note that you are looking forward to having him in your lesson tomorrow. Tomorrow, Ahmed comes in again. You are able to gently and effectively implement your support plan and safeguarding concerns.

Rules are easy. Compassion takes effort. That said, in the current climate, taking a more flexible approach to school rules can get *you* into trouble. Sometimes, depending on your school, you might balance implementing the C1, C2, C3 behaviour policy with your supportive and understanding approach. For example, perhaps you could discuss with Ahmed the C1 punishment for the uniform infringement alongside the solution of ensuring the school helps to fund new shoes for him and the note for other teachers. You can explain how he could prevent smaller punishments like this in the future – for example, signposting support services he may not be aware of – all whilst explaining that the C1 will still have to be in place. If he shows resistance, you could introduce the concept of 'appeals' to Ahmed, and even say that you would support this if he were to do it in a formal and appropriate way, making the whole incident a learning moment in itself.[3] Then systematically, you can revisit the behaviour policy yourself, discuss with colleagues and leadership whether the approaches to behaviour are still fit for purpose and workable, and whether changes need to be made.

This is where there is a real opportunity to involve pupil voice too, particularly from pupils 'known' for their behaviour. When I support schools with cultural shifts around behaviour, one of the most powerful and long-lasting experiences comes during the pupil consultations in which the young people with the most behaviour issues are interviewed by senior leaders. The pupils always suggest ideas to improve behaviour that no adult has considered.

Support, building relationships, listening and adapting – these are often lazily labelled as 'soft' or 'fluffy' options, but it is, in fact, the much harder approach. Support requires us to admit that everyone is different. That square pegs need more than round holes. Support requires us to admit that we might not be doing things right by every pupil. It makes us reflect on our culture and ethos. It means that we might have to learn from challenging children, apologise and start again. Support means that we have to consider context, nuance and complexity. It makes us ask, should the same rules and consequences apply whilst, for example, a pupil is going through a move to care? Or has a diagnosis of autism? Or is going through a global pandemic? Or all three? Support means we may well have to address our moral dilemmas and reconsider what

---

3   Amnesty International UK provides many free education resources for teaching concepts around justice that I heartily recommend – see https://www.amnesty.org.uk/education-resources.

equality really means, that we consider what can we do to help make Ahmed's life equal to other children in his school.

*But, Adele, how?*

Firstly, know that it can be done. There are schools doing it (even though those applying stricter traditional and populist approaches may grab all the headlines).

Secondly, know that an approach which prioritises care is not a free-for-all. Yes, children can be 'naughty' to test the boundaries, have fun and wind up the supply teacher. That is why we have systems and boundaries in place. Rules, routines and boundaries are essential because they make us feel safe; they let us, as a community, live according to our values; they guide us in our interactions. Moreover, for square peg pupils (or staff), they create a place of safety that might not exist elsewhere. For pupils with a chaotic home life, school may be their calm place. Knowing that certain violent actions in school will have consequences makes some young people feel safe from themselves.

Of course, good teachers know the difference between occasions when a quick 1, 2, 3 and reminder of expectations is needed, often done skilfully with just a look, and occasions when there is an unmet need that requires investigation. What they want is the autonomy to use the right tool in the right context, something they can't do in an intransigent system, one that is fuelled by the fear of adults and children alike.

Thirdly, know that your behaviour policy is always a work in progress. Things will never be perfect. We will never get behaviour 'right' because our pupils, our schools, our communities and our world are ever changing. Take the pressure off yourselves to be rigid or traditional or to see flexibility as a weakness.

Fourthly, lead from your values. Deciding whether the wrong uniform attracts a verbal warning, a C1 or litter-picking duty at break time is, in reality, arbitrary. What is more important is that your systems match the values you celebrate in your school and come from a place that the majority respect and believe in. The best punishment systems I have seen across mainstream and specialist SEMH schools have linked the consequence to the misdemeanour and allowed for restoration to take place. For example, in one school, if a pupil defaced school property, they had to fix it or help the caretaker to do so, no matter how long it took. During this physical reparation, there were conversations that reflected on the incident and allowed the adults and pupil to understand what happened and why, all concluding with an action plan of what steps were needed next to continue leading the child towards their education.

Finally, and arguably most importantly, reflect on the emotional wellbeing of staff. Square peg pupils, by their very nature, can be harder to teach within a system where they don't fit. They require more patience, understanding and time. So does fighting, subverting or even changing that system. We cannot do this work alone, and we cannot do this work when we are run down. We have a responsibility to put self-care and support for staff at the top of the agenda. That way, we can be the best possible educators for square pegs like Ahmed, where and when we are most needed.

# References

Balliet, D. and Van Lange, P. A. M. (2013) Trust, Punishment, and Cooperation Across 18 Societies: A Meta-Analysis, *Perspectives on Psychological Science*, 8(4): 363–379.

Campbell, L. (2021) Met Police Criticised for 'Deeply Disturbing' Handling of Clapham Common Vigil – As It Happened, *The Guardian* (13 March). Available at: https://www.theguardian.com/world/live/2021/mar/13/reclaim-these-streets-vigils-womens-safety-uk-latest-updates.

Grierson, J. (2020) Black People Five Times More Likely to Have Force Used on Them by Police, *The Guardian* (17 December). Available at: https://www.theguardian.com/uk-news/2020/dec/17/black-people-five-times-more-likely-to-be-subjected-to-police-force.

Secret Barrister, The (2018) *Stories of the Law and How It's Broken*. London: Pan Macmillan.

Timpson, E. (2019) *Timpson Review of School Exclusion*. CP 92. London: Department for Education. Available at: https://www.gov.uk/government/consultations/school-exclusions-review-call-for-evidence.

# Chapter 23

# PURPOSE, HOPE AND THE CRACKS IN THE CONCRETE

## Debra Kidd

The two boys at the back of the class are starting to get fizzy. A pen has been thrown across the table and voices are starting to rise. I have done the eyebrow thing, and I am about to do the voice thing, when a young voice echoes across the room: 'Oi! Stop being unprofessional. We're Skyping the UN in half an hour. Now, crack on.'

The 12-year-old team leader clicks her fingers, shakes her head and returns to her work. And the boys do crack on. They crack on so much that they don't mind when our call to the UN[1] overruns into lunchtime. They are keen to share their ideas and don't want to have their moment cut short. In fact, they have been keen to share their ideas for the past few weeks, to the extent that they have set up their own charity and have been staying behind after lessons to get the job done. They are what we might call 'invested' in their work. A visitor asks, 'These are top set kids, right?' and is astonished when I point out they are a mixed-ability Year 8 class.

Let me take you back a few months. We are sitting around a meeting room table, a motley crew of English, science and maths teachers limping towards the end of term. Not everyone from all three departments is there – just those who put themselves forward to try out a cross-curricular project, and are probably now regretting it. The year is 2010. We have not yet been Gove'd. It still feels like we live in a creative world of opportunity. But we are scratching our heads and mumbling a lot.

'So, we're combining maths, English and science? How will that work?'

'I don't know anything about maths.'

'I can't write for toffee.'

'How can we connect them?'

So we start with simple questions: 'What would we normally be teaching that term?' It turns out that in English we would be doing writing for specific purposes and audiences, so it's pretty context free. Similarly in maths – they are 'doing' data handling. It's

---

1   My dad. In his garage.

only science that seems to have specific content that needs to be taught – waterborne diseases. Which means that our next question is: 'Who in the world needs to be able to write well and use data to understand and communicate about waterborne diseases?'

Often, when you are open to creative possibilities and ask the right questions, the stars align. It happened on the way into work that morning. There was a news item about Haiti where, months after the devastating earthquake, the World Health Organization was warning of a second impending disaster. Almost a million homeless and displaced people had been living under tarpaulin with no sanitary facilities since the earthquake. All their waste had been going into ditches and latrines built on the hillsides surrounding the camps. Existing sewage and water systems had been severely damaged by the earthquake and the situation was becoming dire, especially with the rainy season coming. A waterborne disease catastrophe was unfolding …

Fast forward. Some Year 8 classes (but not all since not enough staff wanted to work in this way to allow us to do it with the whole year group) are gathered in a science lab. Their English, maths and science teachers are present. They are given name badges and the room is set up for a conference. They are welcomed into the 'story' – one with a real-life context – and for the next few weeks they will be trainee aid agency workers. When they go to science lessons they will be working at the Centre for Disease Control. When they go to maths they will be attending training sessions at the Office for National Statistics, where they will learn how to use data to make sense of their learning in science. When they come to English they will be working with a public relations agency to learn how best to communicate a message to an audience. They will use their training to plan interventions for people in Haiti, putting together a crisis action plan and producing texts and presentations to help people better understand what to do about waterborne diseases. We are clear that this is not 'real', that we are working within the confines of a story, but the situation is real. And they are in – square pegs and all.

Over the next few weeks we see kids willing to go the extra mile, or three. It's not just that they start to manage each other's behaviour or that they are willing to put in extra time. They take the work out of it just being a story and develop projects to raise real money for real people. 'We can't just pretend to help,' said one child. 'This is really happening.' They do all this 'extra' work in their own time, and in class time they work efficiently and effectively with wholehearted commitment.

We notice three things as they go along: behaviour improves, attitudes to learning improve and vocabulary improves (they are striving to sound like professional adults). And, at the end of it all, when the work starts coming in, we also notice initiative. Some work is translated into French ('That's what they speak over there, Miss') and some into infographics with little to no words on them ('There's a high level of illiteracy among the population there, Miss'). They are doing everything we asked of them and more, much more. It's no real surprise – not for the teachers and kids involved, anyway – when the Haiti kids outperform their peers in the end-of-year tests. They have lived this knowledge inside and out. They have invested. It has mattered to them. And making things matter should be the business of school.

It has long been known that having a sense of purpose is a key element of motivation (we heard about this in Chapter 1), leading to improved performance. We know from research in the world of work that it matters (Pink, 2009) and also from research into early childhood and play (Zosh et al., 2017). Indeed, for learners of all ages it is one key component identified by the Organisation for Economic Co-operation and Development as critical for generating the motivation to learn (Boekarts, 2010).

In the Haiti example, all this small group of teachers had done was to find a way of wrapping curriculum content into a context that offered these young people a chance to feel their learning had a sense of purpose – a sense of being a part of something bigger than themselves, their classrooms and their curriculum. It didn't take a great deal of effort to set up, once the initial ideas started flowing, but it had a significant impact on learners. As teachers, we spend a lot of time thinking about the opportunity cost of activities. Will the pay-off in learning be worth the effort put into setting up tasks and activities? Will we be able to evidence our impact? In this Haiti project, we knew that the benefits outweighed the costs.

So, why isn't every school in the country working in this kind of way, especially with the square pegs, the ones struggling with school in its more traditional form?

It's hard to understand, unless you work in schools day in, day out; how the relentless changes imposed on the profession – the high levels of surveillance, the increasing disconnect from the altruistic sense of purpose that propelled many young teachers into the profession, the workload and the admin – all serve to erode our capacity to imagine alternative possibilities. Whatever the motive for such a system (and I can think of a few), it drives wedges between adults and children, where the needs of adults (to produce results to satisfy a professional development target, performance-related pay objective or inspection) sit in conflict with the child's need to be seen, to have their emotional and social needs met, to be known and to belong.

There is too little time to attend to such needs when chasing the data becomes the overriding point and purpose of education.

That is not to say that exam grades don't matter, but if they are all that matter then we lose sight of a future in which a child's happiness might rest not on their maths grade but on their capacity to make good choices, to build positive relationships, to speak with conviction and confidence, to feel they have a place in the world and the capacity to effect change in that world. Where their sense of who they are and how they belong might sit outside a national curriculum – in an artistic realm, a vocational realm, an altruistic realm. Failing to attend to these ways of being is one outcome of a system that is centred around all children performing the same tasks on the same day, regardless of circumstance.

But it really doesn't have to be that way.

Even in this system – one of the most oppressive and micro-managed we have ever seen – there are possibilities if you look; if you want to look. I call it pedagogical activism (Kidd, 2014) – finding those cracks in the concrete through which the weeds can grow – and turning your classroom into a place where learning becomes collaborative, empowering, hopeful and purposeful. Where we don't simply 'deliver' a curriculum or go through an examination syllabus, but offer a curriculum of hope (Kidd, 2020).

In planning a curriculum of hope, the teacher strives for a learning experience which is not just rich in knowledge but also in humanity. It rests on a conception that lasting human happiness and contentment is connected to what Martin Seligman (2012) refers to as a 'meaningful life' – one in which we feel connected to others and to a sense of purpose. As such, the curriculum is designed around five key pillars:

1  **Coherence.** Things connect to each other – a child can see how their learning in this year connects to what went before. They can see big ideas and concepts joining up. They can see the point of what they are doing. It's all starting to make sense.

2  **Credibility.** The curriculum is rich in knowledge, and this knowledge incites curiosity and fosters an interest in the world. The knowledge builds in such a way that the child feels they are gaining a sense of mastery over their learning. They begin to feel competent and confident.

3  **Compassion.** The curriculum fosters compassion in the child along with a solution-focused attitude, so that agency and self-belief can sit alongside empathy. It is also compassionate towards the child, meeting their emotional as well as intellectual needs. A compassionate curriculum would never remove a child from activities like art and sport for extra English or maths. Never.

4  **Creativity.** The child is placed in situations where they need to use their resourcefulness and creativity to apply their learning to new and interesting contexts. Children and young people use their imaginations and are immersed in stories and problems to develop their capacity to develop creative solutions.

5  **Community.** The child is rooted in their community, and learning also happens beyond the school walls – in museums and galleries, local businesses, natural spaces and anywhere else learning could happen. In turn, the community is welcomed into the school to share its collective expertise with children, and those same children are valued enough to be invited to find solutions to problems within their communities and to offer assistance to those in need.

A curriculum of hope engenders a belief that the world can and will be a better place because we will make it so. What I have witnessed in many settings and with all ages is that when this is the case, schools become a place our square pegs run to, not from.

## References

Boekarts, M. (2010) The Crucial Role of Motivation and Emotion in Classroom Learning. In H. Dumont, D. Istance and F. Benavides (eds), *The Nature of Learning: Using Research to Inspire Practice*. Paris: OECD Publishing, pp. 92–112.

Kidd, D. (2014) *Teaching: Notes from the Frontline*. Carmarthen: Independent Thinking Press.

Kidd, D. (2020) *Curriculum of Hope: As Rich in Humanity as in Knowledge*. Carmarthen: Independent Thinking Press.

Pink, D. H. (2009) *Drive: The Surprising Truth About What Motivates Us*. Edinburgh: Canongate.

Seligman, M. (2012) *Flourish: A New Understanding of Happiness and Well-Being – and How to Achieve Them*. New York: Free Press.

Zosh, J. M., Hopkins, E. J., Jensen, H., Liu, C., Neale, D., Hirsh-Pasek, K., Solis, S. L. and Whitebread, D. (2017) *Learning Through Play: A Review of the Evidence* [white paper]. Billund: LEGO Foundation. Available at: https://www.legofoundation.com/media/1063/learning-through-play_web.pdf.

# Chapter 24

# CREW, EXPEDITIONS AND RELATIONAL PROXIMITY

## Andy Sprakes

Everyone in the school, and even out of school, is family.

Student, XP School

XP is a school designed from scratch, with square pegs firmly front and centre. Whilst the model across both its schools (XP and XP East) is a free school one, borrowing from the principles of High Tech High and Expeditionary Learning schools in the United States, XP remains in the mainstream system and is constrained by the same agenda, guidance and dictates as other state schools.

In fact, on average across its schools, 22.3% of students have special educational needs, 4% have an education, health and care plan, 31% are on free school meals and 4% are looked-after children – statistics all significantly above the national average. And, yet, overall absence for XP remains well below average (in 2018/2019, 3.8% against a national average of 5.5%, with persistent absence at 5.9% against a national average of 13.7%[1]) and with only one exclusion in the last eight years. Fixed-term exclusions are amongst the lowest in the borough. What is more, XP has had an outstanding rating from Ofsted for several years.[2]

So, how does XP tick all the boxes? Some argue that it's because class numbers are small, but research suggests that it's the quality of the teaching that makes more of an impact than class numbers (Department for Education, 2011) and, after all, children can not want to be in a class for many reasons. For us, there are two key characteristics of our work that really stand out when it comes to supporting all children, not just our square pegs: the idea of 'crew' and a curriculum focused on what is called Expeditionary Learning.

---

1   See https://www.compare-school-performance.service.gov.uk/school/140964/xp-school/secondary.
2   At the time of writing, XP East is designated as requires improvement (Ofsted, 2021), despite being rated outstanding for personal development, good for behaviour and attitudes, and good for educational provision. However, Ofsted has agreed to reinspect.

# 'We are crew' and relational proximity

Character traits are part of XP's DNA. It's a culture where staff and students genuinely care about each other, believe in each other and want each other to succeed. That is community in the truest sense of the word. And crew is about the whole XP community. It disrupts the power imbalance that often exists between staff and students, building belonging, trust and relational practice. If you are going to make any difference to young people's lives, you have got to know who they are, and we understand that great relationships enable (but don't necessarily result in) good teaching.

Children become part of the XP crew in Year 7 when they all participate in an Outward Bound trip.[3] Here, the foundational principles of crew – being supportive, honest and challenging – are introduced and authentic relationships between staff and students are forged.

> It's much more than a form class that I've had in other schools, because it's so much smaller and a lot more intense, and we have the time and the space to explore the relationships that we need to build.
>
> Year 7 tutor, XP School

There is clear evidence in XP classrooms of the benefits of prioritising such bonds from the outset, but objective research backs up our investment in this approach too.

The Relational Schools Foundation measures and improves the quality of relationships in schools and employs a number of validated survey tools, including the Relational Proximity Framework.[4] This measures the distance in the relationship between two people or organisations, generating data to show how well each party engages with the thinking, emotions and behaviour of the other. Relational proximity is defined in terms of five main domains, all of which are present to greater or lesser extents in interpersonal or inter-organisational relationships: communication, time, knowledge, power and purpose. The higher the score for each domain and its various drivers and features, the higher quality the relationships being demonstrated, the richer the experiences and the better the outcomes all round.

When the team measured XP's Outward Bound experience and its subsequent experience of building crew back at school, the relational proximity score was shown to be higher than the organisation's benchmark average in every relationship pairing:

▪ Teachers with students – 83% (20% above average).

---

3   The Year 7 trip is organised with the Outward Bound Trust – see www.outwardbound.org.uk; subsequent trips are bespoke to XP.
4   See https://relationalschools.org/about/relational-proximity-framework.

- Students with teachers – 78% (13% above average).
- Students with peers – 64% (15% above average).

In the words of Dr Robert Loe, director of the Relational Schools Foundation:

> After four days we were seeing relationships that were more robust than in many schools in the UK after four months. An environment of belonging had been created where young people could feel attached, could feel secure, and could begin to thrive academically and socially … We know that public policy, or organisational change, can either increase relational distance or overcome it. What is vital to understand here is that the work of XP was so uncomplicated in its design and execution. It was delivered within a framework of stretched budgets and existing resources. What is represented here is a shift in mindset in how education can be conducted.[5]

A few months after this study, the original XP school received its first Ofsted judgement and was found to be outstanding in all areas. Its report highlighted the significant academic progress of the students, which Ofsted (2017: 7) attributed in part to the belief that 'there is no "ceiling" to the standards that pupils can reach'. They also highlighted how disadvantaged students often outperformed their peers 'because staff and leaders know these pupils very well'.

## Cross-curricular expeditions

Great relationships, important as they have proven to be, are not enough. It's what you use them for that matters. At XP, relationships help individuals but individuals make up the community – a community that then comes together through activism, leadership and equity. The curriculum drives this approach, delivered predominantly through cross-disciplinary learning expeditions (rather like the example given by Debra Kidd in Chapter 23). Cross-curricular expeditions connect subjects within highly relatable projects that engage students in a way that is simply not possible through individual subject lessons. Notice, too, that despite the inherently competitive nature of the system – there must be losers for there to be winners – this is about working together for something bigger than an individual's test scores or university application or the school's place in the league tables.

The concept behind this approach is that students produce something that has a genuine purpose and will help to make the school/community/town/country/world a better place. It's founded on engaging students with powerful knowledge that affects

---

5   See https://xpschool.org/we-are-crew-film.

positive social change. In this way, students not only learn about their place in the world, but also, importantly, they are compelled to question it – and from there to change it.

Learning is experience rich,[6] with tightly structured expeditions to ensure that each student can produce beautiful work, and wherever possible we tap into the local community too. In this way, we not only help each student to find their passion, but they also work to improve their community – an alternative take to the view of social mobility that says you get yourself educated in order to leave your home and family behind.

# A three-dimensional curriculum

XP's expedition-driven curriculum centres on three important strands:[7]

1  **Stewardship of our world: the climate emergency.** Changing the world is all well and good, but we need to save it first. Students develop the subject knowledge to understand what is going on and what needs to be done in the face of this existential threat, and also the leadership skills to make a difference.

2  **Stewardship of our community: social justice.** We live in an unequal world, where systems, structures and governance protect the interests of the few at the expense of the many. Students uncover and confront inequities of race, gender, identity and class through the curriculum and use this knowledge to affect social and cultural change. Again, we want our students to be leaders of this change.

3  **Stewardship of ourselves and each other: diversity and belonging.** At XP, we know our community is stronger because of our differences. This is, therefore, a key strand that runs through many of our expeditions, allowing students to deepen their empathy and understanding of the value of difference and non-conformity. Our students know about the interplay between equality, equity and fairness.

# Agents for social change

At XP, we want our students to become compassionate citizens, so we set out not only to develop their personal cultural capital, but also to give them opportunities where they can impact positively on others, in and beyond the school. We nurture and

---

6   Which means, yes, we cover knowledge, but it is always for a purpose.
7   It is important to note that each dimension is reliant on and symbiotic with the others.

develop an understanding of how kindness, empathy and concern for others defines us, both as individuals and as part of society.

Walking our own talk, we are intensely mindful of ensuring that all students, regardless of background, will enjoy opportunities that they might otherwise be denied because of societal barriers. Indeed, we made a pledge when the school first opened that fieldwork – including visits to museums, art galleries, theatres and universities, which feature in every expedition, as well as engaging with experts – would be funded by the school. The curriculum is actively constructed to address any deficit in knowledge and experience that might exist because of disadvantages in the school community.

## The creativity of being human

We believe that representing our lives through the crafting of beautiful work defines our common humanity and resonates across boundaries. Focusing on creativity lifts us beyond the ephemeral and the transient and provides us with a sense of value, meaning and worth.

XP students are encouraged to produce beautiful work of their own as they grow their character and achieve the levels of academic success they do. Creativity sits at the heart of the curriculum; students' craft books, films, information boards and campaigns all allowing them to creatively apply their knowledge as they seek to bring about social change. In this way, we work together to create a legacy of honourable work that transforms not only their lives but also the lives of others.

## It's alright for you ...

We have our detractors. Any school that steps out of line always does. So, yes, it's true that XP has the benefit of being a free school, designed from a blank sheet of paper, and has deliberately small class sizes and a growing and expanding trust, albeit only with partners who align with its values. We are massively oversubscribed.[8] But we are still a school. We have the same constraints and opportunities as any school. There is no magic or sophistry involved. We have a clear idea of education's purpose and how we will achieve it. We believe education to be a social act, and we seek to create a community of square pegs, round pegs, all pegs. And any school can do that.

---

8    XP Gateshead is the most oversubscribed school in the North East and is only in its second year. XP School is
      fourth in the country and XP East ninth.

XP means being part of a team, we're all in the same boat, on the same page, and if someone falls behind it's our responsibility to make sure they're on the same level as us.

Student, XP School

# References

Department for Education (2011) *Class Size and Education in England: Evidence Report.* DFE-RR169. Available at: https://assets.publishing.service.gov.uk/government/uploads/system/uploads/attachment_data/file/183364/DFE-RR169.pdf.

Ofsted (2017) XP School: School Report (12–13 July). Available at: https://files.ofsted.gov.uk/v1/file/2726187.

Ofsted (2021) Inspection of XP East: School Report (12–13 October). Available at: https://files.ofsted.gov.uk/v1/file/50175139.

Chapter 25

# AGENCY, AUTONOMY AND THE CAGE

## Georgina Newton, Rhia Gibbs and Dave Harris

God, grant me the serenity to accept the things I cannot change, courage to change the things I can, and wisdom to know the difference.

Reinhold Niebuhr, The Serenity Prayer

Consider a cage. It imprisons and restricts (and keeps you safe). When you picture it, what do you see? The metal bars or the space between? What if we pointed out that a cage is more space than bars? More air than metal? Would that change how you pictured it? If we focus on the bars then we see the restrictions, the limitations, the things that hold us back (whilst making us feel safe). When we look at the space between the bars, we see possibilities, opportunities, the things we can do (and how wanting safety can hold us back too). We will never escape through the bars, but we may do through the space.

Think about how you and your colleagues see your work at school. Do you focus on the restrictions (and, heavens knows, there are plenty of those), or do you see the possibilities hidden in plain sight among the limitations? Do you see the many ways you can better help the square pegs in your school, whether a child is on free school meals, of ethnic minority origins, a looked-after child, has a special educational need or disability, is dealing with a bereavement or loss, or any number of other reasons that a child doesn't fit into the round hole allocated to them? Or do you see the things you can't do because of all the things you have to do, not to mention the lack of money and time to do them?

In 2020, the National Foundation for Educational Research found that teachers enjoy their work more when they have a sense of autonomy. They are also better able to manage their workload and more likely to stay in teaching when they feel they have agency – the power to change things for themselves. Unfortunately, though, teachers have a lower level of autonomy than many professionals, despite their new 'freedoms',[1] and this might be contributing to the burnout and attrition we see in the workforce (Worth and Van den Brande, 2020).

# Autonomy vs agency

When people hear the term 'autonomy' they often confuse it with agency, but they are false synonyms. In a nutshell, autonomy is what you give; agency is what you take. You can have autonomy without agency ('you're free to do nothing') and agency without autonomy is risky ('better to seek forgiveness than ask permission'), but ideally the two should go hand in hand. Like rights and responsibilities.

For teachers, autonomy goes well beyond being able to plan their own lessons and deliver their own curriculum, as there are so many other ways they can be given autonomy in order to act fully as agents in the education of every child. When children are not fitting in and need extra care and support – something different, bespoke and beyond the norm – this is where autonomy and agency come together in school to transform lives. We have seen it time and time again through the examples in this book.

Start, then, with a question: *to what extent do teachers in my school have autonomy?* Consider the approach that Timpson, shoe menders extraordinaire, employs to empower its staff to do whatever it takes to ensure the customer is satisfied: 'The Timpson ethos is to provide great customer service and to do this we operate an "Upside Down" management style. We believe the best way to give great customer service is to give freedom to the colleagues that serve customers.'[2]

Biesta et al. (2015) describe how in some schools teacher agency is seen as undermining how a school operates, whereas in others it is seen as a vital criterion for success. How does your school see it? And why? How much freedom do the staff have to do whatever it takes to help the child who needs exactly that – whatever it takes? Not, 'What is in the policy?' Not, 'What do the other children get?' Not, 'What have we always done?' Something extraordinary that only a teacher who knows a child extraordinarily well will know.

The second questions is: *if staff have at least some degree of autonomy, to what extent do they feel confident about using that autonomy?* Perhaps they feel scared about leaving the safety of the cage for fear of reprisals or getting it wrong? Or maybe they simply don't

---

1   'Greater freedom and independence were promised to primary and secondary schools today as Secretary of State for Education, Michael Gove, invited all schools to apply to become academies' (Department for Education and Gove, 2010).
2   See https://www.timpson.co.uk/about-timpson. They also have only two rules for their staff: 'Look the part' and 'Put the money in the till'.

feel confident enough to go off-piste, perhaps through lack of training or experience, or even practice at enacting for themselves?[3] Or perhaps they just don't have the time?

Great school leaders are astonishing magicians, making something from nothing and conjuring up time (and often money) from thin air. How? As with the cage, it all depends on how you look at things.

In a job that will always be a complex struggle against the unknown, it can be easy (i.e. safe) to focus on what is known. The syllabus. The lesson plans. The grades. What the inspectors want. Attendance. Timetables. Roles and responsibilities. Fridays. All the various parts of school life that make up the whole. In this way, we can more than adequately fill the school day and most of the evening too. Despite what is written on most, if not all, school websites about focusing on 'the whole child', it is easy to see the schools that actually focus on the parts at the expense of both staff autonomy and the young people they serve. For example, can you hand on heart say that your school is about more than exam results if:

- The first email received in the morning is about assessments and grades?

- Most topics in the morning briefing are also about assessment and grades?

- Many of the posters in the entrance and on every classroom wall, either implicitly or explicitly, talk about assessment and grades?

- Assessment and grades are the standing items on every meeting?

- Assessment and grades are the focus of school reports?

- Assessment and grades are the rationale behind most of the homework set?

Few schools want to be an exam factory, and even fewer would admit it if they were, but if you look like an exam factory, operate like an exam factory and sound like an exam factory, then it's time to face facts, because only then can you do something about it.

In a school where staff have the opportunity *and* ability to do whatever it takes to help *all* their children, a focus that goes well beyond the component parts – the bars of the cage – you will see many, if not all, of the following:

- A reporting system that recognises a genuinely broad set of skills in the students.

- Rewards are given for a wide range of skills, not just academic prowess.

- The 'model' students depicted on the walls are not just the academic elite (with the odd local Olympian thrown in).

- Agendas for meetings are structured with wellbeing near or at the top.

---

3   To stop an elephant from running away, you stake its leg when it is young so it can't run. This belief stays with it into adulthood.

- Communications with parents are frequent and do not focus on exam success.

- The trap of advertising the great historical exam results is avoided.

- The non-academic successes of students are recognised on an equal footing alongside the academic ones.

- There is a positive risk-taking atmosphere in the staffroom, where autonomy meets agency.

- Staff who take positive risks for the benefit of students are acknowledged and praised, regardless of the outcome.

- Good practice in all aspects of the job is recognised regularly and there is an atmosphere of sharing.

- There is trust between leaders and staff.[4]

- The development of academic excellence is not the principal task in staff job descriptions.

- The website has a recognition of the whole child and is not dominated by exam results or university entrance successes.

- The tone of voice in external communication is always friendly, supportive, positive and unequivocally welcoming for *all* families.

- The emphasis for teachers is not about curriculum delivery but about engagement and investment (what Independent Thinking Associate Hywel Roberts (2012) memorably refers to as 'botheredness').

- Any learning walks are focused on student engagement and curiosity, not on rigour, discipline and predetermined perceptions of what good behaviour looks (and sounds) like.

- A section of every briefing is focused on the positives.[5]

- There is a culture of 'thank you', where even little positives are acknowledged, not just from the head teacher to others but from all staff towards one another.

- Staff feel that school leaders truly realise their job is huge and challenging and instigate 'no-work weekends', set time limits on email communications and focus at least some INSET time on teamwork and fun.

- Wonder and curiosity are part of the daily life of the school, not just for students but for teachers and parents as well.

- Staff say good morning to students (and each other) at the start of the day.

- Most staff are visible, smiling (genuinely) and accessible at the end of the day.

---

4  If you are a leader, do what you say you are going to do, every time.
5  Stone Soup Academy, an award-winning alternative provision setting in Nottingham (see Chapter 21) dedicates a section of its weekly Friday afternoon gatherings to 'sunshine moments', during which every member of staff (no exceptions) relates something a student has done that week of which they are proud.

Perhaps, on reading such a list, you might question how staff will end up with more time by having even more to do. And there is the rub. If you see being at the school gate as an unnecessary addition to an already thankless list, then it will be pointless and negative. Such an attitude (looking at the bars) means that you are sure to miss the opportunities (the space) to interact positively with students and colleagues; interactions that will pay dividends in terms of relationships, behaviour, attendance, wellbeing and, yes, exam results, further down the line.

Schools where staff have both the autonomy and agency to focus on their reason for being – on why they do what they do and on the success (in its broadest sense) of their young people – tend to be memorable places. They make you smile as you walk through the door. All the staff (including non-teaching ones) exude a positivity about what they do and why they are doing it. These schools still have the same ridiculous workload as everyone else, the same bizarre assessment criteria, the same unhelpful quality assurance processes, the same often unnecessary bureaucracy, the same number of hours in the day and just as many square pegs as the school down the road. But somehow they rise above it and remind themselves that educating every child *is* the job – and it is the most important job in the world.

# References

Biesta, G., Priestley, M. and Robinson, S. (2015) The Role of Beliefs in Teacher Agency, *Teachers and Teaching*, 21(6): 624–640. doi:10.1080/13540602.2015.1044325

Department for Education and Gove, M. (2010) Gove: 'Teachers, Not Politicians, Know How Best to Run Schools' [press release] (26 May). Available at: https://www.gov.uk/government/news/gove-teachers-not-politicians-know-how-best-to-run-schools.

Roberts, H. (2012) *Oops! Helping Children Learn Accidentally*. Carmarthen: Independent Thinking Press.

Worth, J. and Van den Brande, J. (2020) *Teacher Autonomy: How Does It Relate to Job Satisfaction and Retention?* Slough: National Foundation for Educational Research. Available at: https://www.nfer.ac.uk/teacher-autonomy-how-does-it-relate-to-job-satisfaction-and-retention.

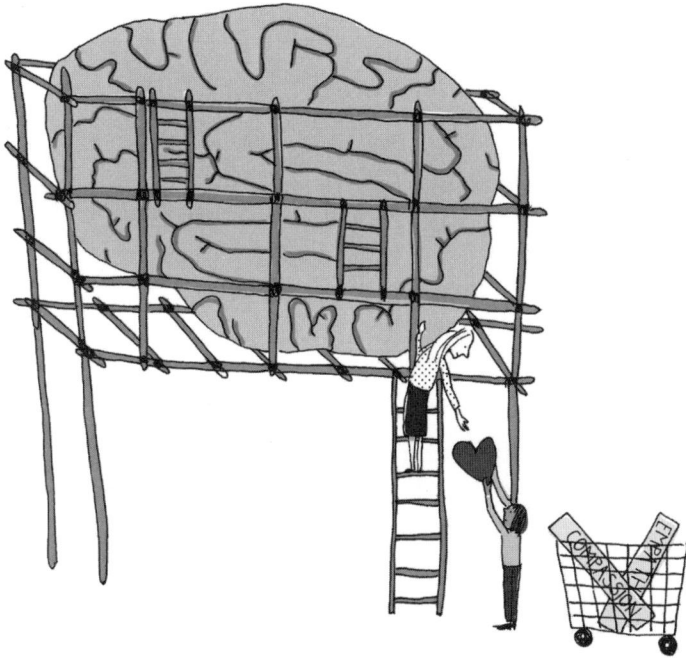

Part IV

# MENTAL HEALTH
# AND THE BRAIN

# Introduction

There has been an extraordinary amount of research and media attention about the mental health of today's children and young people, yet the statistics continue in free fall. It's true that we have had a pandemic, but this was happening long before. Underfunded services lie at the heart of the problem, but the solutions proposed by the government fall largely on the shoulders of our education system (along with responsibility for social care, safeguarding, knife crime and terrorism).

There are several aspects to this part of the book. The way we think and learn should be a central component of the education system, but it isn't. It's shocking that children are hardwired to learn whatever they need to know and what interests them, yet the education system quickly knocks this out of them, relying on fixed learning frameworks, predefined definitions of success and an ever-narrower curriculum. The spectrum of mental health ranges from happiness and contentment through to trauma and everything in-between. We seem to have taken the joy out of learning, whether that means valuing the importance of play or tapping into individual talents and passions.

No child can absorb information if they are in distress, and bums on seats does not mean that children are engaged and learning. As adults, we are well aware of the physical impact of stress on our bodies, yet we put our young square pegs through extraordinary levels of stress on a daily basis. And their ability to cope at school will be directly affected by things outside the school gates – from peer pressure to worries about family finances and worse. It's no wonder that the prevalence of poor mental health among children is rising exponentially.

Many people think of trauma in terms of a particularly harrowing event, like experiencing domestic abuse or watching someone being killed. But one child's threshold for trauma will differ from another's, and repeated exposure to stressful situations can also lead to trauma. It's highly likely that if we actually had the resources to do the assessments, then many more children would be diagnosed with trauma now than in the previous generation. Learning about trauma – its consequential behaviours and how to respond – is one of the most powerful resources at your disposal. And it will benefit all staff and students, not just those with a trauma profile.

# Chapter 26

# THE NEUROBIOLOGY OF LEARNING

## Andrew Curran

As someone who has spent most of his working life as a paediatric neurologist specialising in the square pegs no one else wanted to look after, I have huge sympathy for these children, their parents and their wider family. For most, it is my experience that they spend day after day after day pushing against a system that rarely delivers a fraction of what they need by way of understanding and support. And when they do find that one individual, that one champion, who will go the extra mile for them, the relief often reduces them to tears.

So, what can any of us do to genuinely help? Something that is not just a sticking plaster, like a learned script or a rigid set of procedures, but something that means we truly connect, listen, become involved, sensibly and professionally, and actually help?

Throughout my professional career, this has always started with one very simple word – *understand*. I don't mean in that superficial way where you simply gather the facts with a concerned look on your face, but where you have listened – really listened – and absorbed and thought and then checked your thoughts with the child and the family and then acted. And then, once you have acted, you again reflect with the child and the family on what you have done, so you can explore how it can be improved. This extra mile is usually not resource heavy or costly. It almost always comes down to the sensible giving of self in order to make a difference. And, as we have heard elsewhere in this book, choosing not to hide behind the system.

Where does understanding start in an educational environment? For me, as someone who has studied the neurobiology of the human brain for over 30 years, it starts in the place where there is the least difference between square pegs and ordinarily developing children. It starts with the core neurobiology that needs to be involved for learning to occur.[1]

---

1 Of course, there are differences at a cellular and neurobiological level between an ordinarily developing child and many square pegs. The neurobiological mechanisms that underpin learning may not work as well if the child has significant genetic or other underlying problems with their brain functioning. However, the basic principles to optimise their learning remain the same.

We have seen that learning is heavily influenced by psychology (see Chapter 1), so now let's look at it from a neurobiology perspective. Learning occurs when the specialist learning nerve cells are bathed in the correct types and concentrations of neurochemicals. Paramount among these is the neurochemical dopamine. Dopamine is the neurochemical that becomes deficient in the tragic condition of Parkinson's disease. It can be considered as the oil that makes the brain work smoothly and efficiently. It is also *the* key neurochemical for learning. Its core function is to promote the creation of connections between nerve cells. These are called synapses, and you will probably have heard of them in the context of brain plasticity. It is by forming connections between nerve cells that we learn, a process in which the learning becomes hardwired into our brains. When we remember what we have learned, we fire up the nerve cells that we connected together when we first learned that particular piece of information. When the nerve cells are fired up, they are able to transmit the information they have stored to our thinking brain. And we remember.

The production of dopamine is 93% under the control of the emotional brain (Curran, 2008). The technical term for this network in our brains is the limbic system. It is where we do all our work linked to our emotions. It is also where we process reward.[2]

Reward in humans can be very complex. What is rewarding for you may not be rewarding for someone else. This is particularly true for our square pegs. It is why understanding each individual for who they are is so important, square peg or not. With understanding comes the knowledge of what that person finds uniquely rewarding. Always remember that reward can often be a very simple thing. Most children – again, square pegs or not – will find sincere one-to-one interaction with an adult they respect rewarding, often hugely so. That respect, even when it builds in small increments, will be a natural occurrence if you genuinely work to understand the child. (And remember: if each child in your class is experiencing reward just by being with you, then you are certainly going to experience reward by being with them.)

We know that experiencing reward, or the anticipation of reward, are potent stimuli not only for the brain to release dopamine but also, and this is so clever, to release the right concentration of dopamine to the right nerve cells at the right time. This is true in all children, although the effect of the dopamine may vary depending on the genetics and other functional issues underlying the totality of a particular square peg. Again, understanding remains key. Someone who is a slower learner will still have their learning optimised by experiencing reward or anticipating reward, regardless.

The mechanism by which nerve cells are combined with connections to hardwire learning into the brain is almost magical,[3] and the complexity of the network that is

---

2   I am talking much more than stickers and merits here, of course.
3   Under a microscope, the result of this growing out and connecting of nerves is a remarkable thing to watch. Check out this video on YouTube: https://youtu.be/m0rHZ_RDdyQ.

formed is breathtaking. For you as a teacher, all you have to do is create the right environment for the child to learn, and their brain will automatically do the rest.

Obviously, creating the right environment is another complex concept. After all, an environment that optimises your own learning may be very different from one that optimises learning for another individual, particularly if they happen to be a square peg. Children with autistic spectrum disorder, for example, often have hyperacusis – very sensitive hearing. What for you is a quiet, settled classroom can for them be a collection of distracting and off-putting noises that make concentration extremely hard.

Once again, understanding each individual will, in most cases, provide the answer as to why their learning is not optimised and what to do about it. For example, for the child with hyperacusis, the provision of some form of ear defenders (providing the young person can cope with that sensation) may be all that is required.

Clearly, understanding is at the heart of this book, but how do we go about understanding, so to speak? For me, as a neurobiologist, the first step to understanding others is to understand yourself and, to this end, my advice is to look at attachment theory.

Put simply, we are all formed of two main ingredients: our inherited neurobiological potential and the environment we experience from the moment of birth. How these two interact creates the you that you are now.

This creation of you happens in exactly the same way as all learning: nerve cells in your brain wire together to form networks that are your thoughts, feelings and actions, including how you move physically. In an ideal world, of course, the environment you experienced from birth would be one where the main adult figures – your mother and father, probably a grandparent or two – would understand exactly who you are in terms of your genetic potential. With this understanding, combined with masterful skill and wisdom, they would then nurture you gently, harmoniously and with sensible boundaries to become the person truly inherent in your genetic potential.

Except, it rarely happens in that way. Whilst there has been debate for centuries over nature versus nurture, it's an inescapable truth that all caregivers around a child will, to a lesser or greater extent, exert their own hopes and dreams on that child. And, in some cases, this will shape that child's future.

Why is this so important? The person that each and every child in a class experiences in a teacher is that combination of various parts in varying degrees of disharmony with that teacher's genetic potential. Some of these parts may be helpful to each child's learning, but some may, in fact, introduce barriers to this. And remember that each child in a class will have their own share of attachment disharmonies too. A simple example could be that they might come from a family whose parents were badly let down by the education system themselves, and who may be unintentionally sabotaging your attempts to provide their child with a very different learning experience.

Understanding remains the key, therefore, not only to optimising each child's experience of you, and hence their learning, but also to becoming aware of disharmonies within ourselves which may be interfering not only with how well we support learning in our classrooms but even with many aspects of our broader lives.

Disharmony in a classroom setting often comes out through the behaviour of the humans in the room – yours and theirs – so it is important to look at behaviour through a neurobiological lens as part of our drive for deeper understanding. Of course, whilst the full-blown meltdown of a young person with autistic spectrum disorder is very obviously a detriment to learning, not only for that child but for the rest of the class, it is worth remembering that the underlying neurobiology of behavioural problems is present in all of us. It's just that some individuals are able to exert more control, or self-regulation, than others.

Put simply, pretty much all of our behaviours have elements of input from two structures in our brains called the amygdalae. These are relatively small, one in each hemisphere, and sit in a part of the brain called the temporal lobes. The temporal lobes are central to our limbic system – our emotional brain.

Your amygdalae's job is to evaluate the environment for threat or reward and to respond in one of just three ways – take it, hit it or run away from it. Interestingly, in adults, it is usually the right amygdala that is doing this non-stop surveillance, something that is part of our basic survival instinct dating back millions of years. In the classroom, however, such responses lack the level of sophistication required for successful behaviours in modern human society.

Your amygdalae have another very specific ability which is also problematic in society. They can switch off your thinking brain and take control of your basic survival brain to ensure you respond as quickly as possible – that is, without stopping to think. A square peg in the middle of a full-blown meltdown will not have much thinking brain available for a reasonable discussion. This is why time-out techniques should be used first. Only once you have a calmer – or preferably calm – child to talk to can you start a quiet, thoughtful and non-judgemental discussion to help them work out why they were triggered in that way.

Talking of triggers, be aware that in many cases there may be no identifiable trigger. So, rather than asking, 'What happened?' a discussion that serves to support the child in becoming aware of their own experiences immediately prior to the meltdown can be far more productive. For example, asking a child with significant autistic traits what they *feel* is typically not useful. Indeed, one of the main neurobiological systems that doesn't work well in people with autistic spectrum disorder is the system that is required for you to name your emotions correctly. Instead, ask the child to talk through the changes they experienced as they transitioned from being calm to being in full meltdown. Typically, these include, 'feeling hot', 'feeling restless' and 'feeling itchy' – sensations almost certainly caused by the increasing activation of their amygdalae. It is at the point that these start that early intervention has the best chance of success.[4]

It is also important to remember that *your* amygdalae can be in a constant state of excess arousal, too, if you are feeling stressed yourself. A teacher's stress, if it impairs their behaviour, will transmit itself to the children in their classroom. This can be a significant barrier to learning, as it will be increasingly hard for that teacher to be the relaxed, loving, listening and, where necessary, gentle but firm leader they need to be.

This is a chapter about how an understanding of simple neurobiology can help us to get the best out of the square pegs in our classrooms. But it is also about how we need to get the best out of ourselves to achieve that. The most important person in any classroom is the teacher. The teacher is the dominant adult, and children are programmed to look up to and defer to that adult. If you are the adult in the room, look after yourself. Lead a full and healthy life, rest well, exercise regularly and, above all, find time every day to just be you for you. Being your best you is one of the most important lessons we can share with children and young people, especially our square pegs.

## References

Curran, A. (2008) *The Little Book of Big Stuff About the Brain: The True Story of Your Amazing Brain*. Carmarthen: Crown House Publishing.

---

4   Some teachers have successfully implemented a strategy that involves holding up an orange card, for example, to indicate that things are tipping in the wrong direction. Other warning signs might work for you, including making sure that any teaching assistant in your room is on board.

# Chapter 27

# GREEN WITH MOMENTS IN AMBER

## Helen Andrews

We cannot understand how to help our children stay regulated in the classroom without having an understanding of how the brain and nervous system work. As an experienced clinical psychologist, I call on the work of Daniel Siegel and Stephen Porges to find ways of making sense of these complex systems in an understandable way.[1]

Our starting point is understanding that we have brain cells (neurons) not only in our head but also around our heart and along our gut – we really do have heartfelt feelings and gut feelings. These three systems work together, along with the rest of our nervous system (particularly the vagus nerve) to provide cues about safety and regulate us accordingly.

To simplify the complex structure of the head brain, we can view it as having a downstairs and an upstairs (see Figure 27.1).

The *downstairs brain* contains structures such as the cerebellum and brainstem, where functions essential to life are based (maintaining body temperature, blood pressure, heart rate, automatic breathing rate and sleep/wake cycle, as well as balance, posture and even some speech production), and the limbic area – the emotional centre of our brain, which is also key in memory formation and learning, hormone production and our main stress response and also our drive for social relationships. The downstairs brain is focused on survival, and one of the important strategies it employs is to constantly scan the environment for signs of threat. It is particularly sensitive to things that are new, have changed or are obviously dangerous.

When we are born, the downstairs brain functions relatively well. It uses its earliest experiences to ascertain how safe the world is and sets its sensitivity levels accordingly. As infants are completely dependent on others for their survival, they have the skills to elicit caregiving with a cry that is hard to ignore. Physical closeness and feeding then helps to calm the young baby. Infants are also very attuned to the nervous system of

---

1   See https://drdansiegel.com/hand-model-of-the-brain and https://www.stephenporges.com.

their carers, and feel calm or threatened alongside those caregivers. This is a two-way process that helps us to evaluate risk. Calm parents are more likely to have calm babies, and vice versa. This is known as co-regulation.

The *upstairs brain* is more of a work in progress for a child. The emotion-focused, holistic, intuitive right hemisphere develops first, receiving information from the downstairs brain, the heart and gut. Then the language centres of the left hemisphere, which is more logical and linear in its processing of information, become more active. Last to mature is the prefrontal cortex, behind the eyebrows, at the front of the brain.

The prefrontal cortex is the centre of executive function and working memory, so it helps us to process complex information, make decisions and change our mind based on new information. It is also key for impulse control. It is clear that young children do not have a well-developed prefrontal cortex – they struggle not to call out in class and often act without thinking. Self-control develops gradually with age and experience. As with any newly acquired skills, children are best able to demonstrate impulse control and good working memory when they are regulated and calm; when stressed we lose our newest learned skills first.

We can start to rely more on our prefrontal cortex as we work our way through the primary school years, but maturation is not a straight line. Puberty and adolescence are a period when significant brain changes are happening, which aren't fully completed until our early twenties. As teenagers prepare to lead independent lives, different social priorities take over, with peers becoming more influential than parents and teachers. During this reorganisation, there is also a period when young people lose their facial emotion reading skills and are more likely to interpret someone as being hostile when they are not. Not only are connections being formed now but others are being pruned, especially in the prefrontal cortex, as the brain learns to become more efficient in its decision-making processes. This can lead to poor impulse control, risk-taking behaviours and less organised thinking – the stereotypical teenager.

Now let's think about what happens when the nervous system is under stress.

Think of stress as the consequence of a demand being placed on us that is not easily accommodated by the resources we have. Resources here might refer to our level of skill, our past experiences, the environment we find ourselves in or internal factors like illness, fatigue or neurodivergence.

When we can meet the demands placed on us, especially when we feel connected to those around us, then stress is minimal. Our nervous system is regulated, we feel calm and our natural heart rate is actually slightly lowered (by the vagal brake – more on this later). Our brain is working at its best and in an integrated way. In this state, both despite and because of the stress we are experiencing and how we are dealing with it, we are open to learning.

Young children live more in their DOWNSTAIRS brain. Under stress of any Kind, we are all – especially children and young people – more likely to tip from UPSTAIRS to the DOWNSTAIRS parts of the brain

The UPSTAIRS or forebrain includes the prefrontal cortex 3, which is responsible for thinking, planning, learning and decision-making. Crucially, it takes 25 years to develop fully.

3

2

1

The DOWNSTAIRS brain includes the limbic region 2 (including the amygdala), which centres around attachment and emotion. It also includes the hind brain and brain stem (or primitive brain) 1, which focuses on survival and is responsible for sensory motor input, and the respiratory and digestive systems. It is here that the fight, flight or freeze response originates.

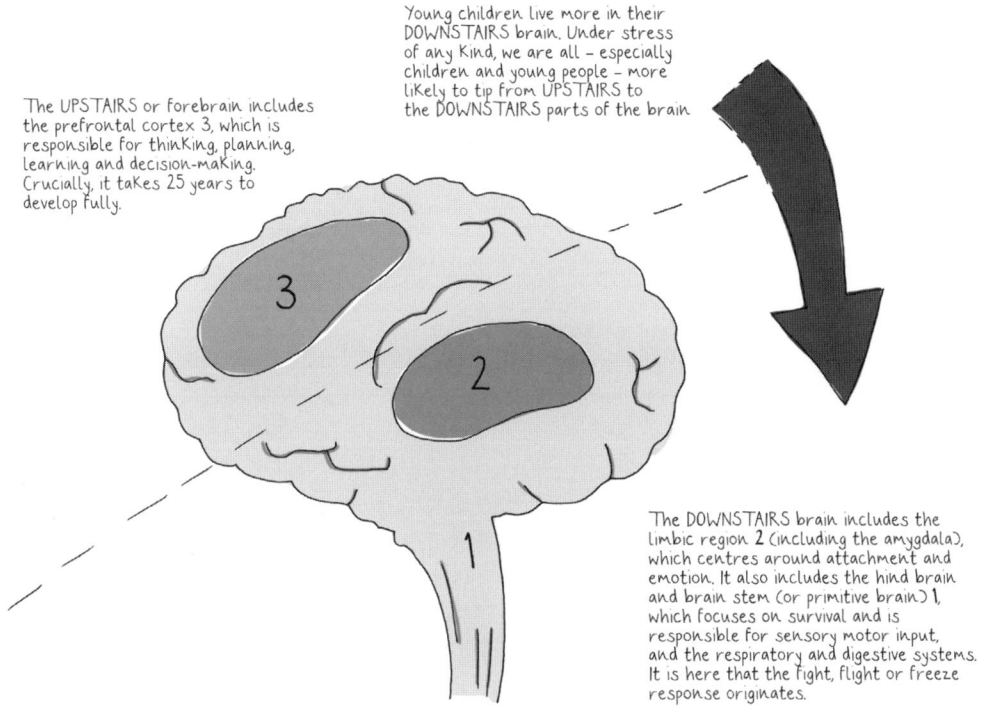

Children and young people's brains develop from the bottom up- 1, 2, then 3

Figure 27.1. Children and young people's brains develop from the bottom up – 1, 2 and then 3

When stress levels have increased, but still feel manageable, the individual may become aware of an uncomfortable feeling of agitation or notice that they are worrying, but the brain is still integrated and working as a whole to manage the situation. You may notice this agitation in your pupils; they might get noisier or start rocking or fiddling in an attempt to self-soothe.

Another stress regulation strategy the brain employs is proximity-seeking behaviour – seeking physical closeness and reassurance from those with whom they feel safe. That is why children may become more demanding when they are struggling. It's also why we see separation anxiety when children are dropped off at school. It can also be one of the reasons why attendance can fall when children find school difficult: there is a strong biological pull to stay at home with a person who helps them to feel safe.

The good news is that we can use this knowledge to our advantage preventatively. Having a key worker system in the early years, allocating teaching assistant time, having the class teacher check in on a pupil, having access to a staffed pastoral room – anything that allows children to seek reassurance from a trusted adult. Even just knowing that they could if they wanted to allows them to manage their stresses better in the classroom.

Sometimes it can all become a bit too much, though. Maybe there has been an incident, such as being pushed over in the playground, feeling embarrassed in class or an unexpected and significant change from the norm. Or perhaps low-level stressors have not been managed satisfactorily and have started to build up, at home or at school. Rather than feeling calm, safe and regulated – known as being in a *ventral vagal state* (where our heart rate is lowered slightly, we feel connected to those around us, our gut brain is focused on digestion and healing, and our immune system is functioning well) – we are now experiencing a very different state. As our stress levels increase, our amygdalae trigger the release of cortisol (a stress hormone) and adrenaline and the sympathetic nervous system takes over.[2] The vagal brake that was keeping our system calm is removed; our heart rate increases, adding to our awareness of anxiety; and our breathing rate and blood pressure increase too. With immature or traumatised frontal lobes unable to assess – and dismiss – the threat our subconscious brain has perceived, the downstairs brain effectively takes over and we lose access to all of our higher order processes. We are now at risk of going into a full-blown state of hyperarousal commonly known as fight, flight or freeze.

The *fight* response dictates that attack is the best form of defence. You might have a child who is physically or verbally aggressive to others, they may slam doors or throw things. These children can be very anxiety provoking to be around, and it can be difficult to intervene safely and effectively.

---

2   See Chapter 26 for more on the role of the amygdalae.

The *flight* response focuses on escape to keep the individual safe. These are your runners. They may also be your avoiders and procrastinators, if they manage to stay more regulated.

Then there is *freeze*. From an evolutionary perspective, we are keeping very still in the hope that the predator does not spot us. But we are still on high alert, and at the first opportunity we will run away or, if necessary, fight. In the classroom, these children sit very still but are wide-eyed and alert, and you can sense how highly strung they appear.

These sympathetic nervous system responses are largely effective when there is a real, sudden and short-lasting danger. However, in most day-to-day life, they can be disproportionate and can have negative consequences for the individual and the system around them. Remember, too, that you cannot choose your response. It happens automatically as soon as your downstairs brain registers that you may be under threat.

There is another response the nervous system can make. When the perceived risk is long-lasting or when the fight/flight/freeze strategies have proven ineffective, we can enter what is called a *dorsal vagal state*. This is one of low arousal, involving the gut brain rather than the heart or head brains. Now, the heart rate and blood pressure drop, maybe to below normal levels, causing us to feel faint. We may get digestive issues, such as stomach aches, diarrhoea or constipation, and, in the longer term, irritable bowel syndrome and perhaps chronic fatigue. Our immune system may be compromised – have you noticed that you catch more colds when you are feeling under a lot of stress? Our energy levels drop and we may feel immobilised. We may enter a state of dissociation, unable to fully process the world around us. It is a form of depression characterised by low mood and inactivity.

These children may not move much, they may be quite passive and hard to reach. They may seem to have given up and be hard to motivate. From an evolutionary point of view, they are entering a state of preparedness for death.

But all is not lost. All of these states serve a function, and we all experience them to a greater or lesser extent during a typical day. When we are feeling safe and socially connected, the sympathetic nervous system gives us energy, motivation and playfulness; the dorsal vagal pathway allows for rest, healing and intimacy.[3] Our daily emotional ups and downs are all perfectly normal. The difficulties come when we are too frequently triggered to be in fight/flight/freeze, or feel unsafe in our dorsal state, as this is not healthy and we can feel stuck in that dysregulated response.

A child in this state of dysregulation is one whose downstairs brain has perceived a significant threat and has taken over to try and protect the child. So, what should a teacher do next? This is where it might be helpful to imagine a simple traffic light

---

3   If you want to find out more on the dorsal vagal response, you could look at the work of Stephen Porges (https://www.stephenporges.com) or Deb Dana's work (https://www.rhythmofregulation.com) on polyvagal theory.

system where green is regulated and calm, red is dysregulated into fight/flight/freeze (with the downstairs brain fully in control) and amber means there are signs of agitation but there is still time to act.[4]

Remember, when a child goes red, they lose a lot of their upstairs brain function. If you ask them to 'make good choices' or 'stop and think about what you're doing', then you are asking them to use an underdeveloped part of the brain (their prefrontal cortex), which is just not available to them at this time. If you ask them to 'use your words' or 'tell me what has upset you so I can help', you are asking them to use the language centres in their brain, which also are not available to them. So, you are going to be ineffective in calming them down through no fault of theirs.

Just as challenging, when it has all blown over, and you talk to them about what has happened and explain that 'there have to be consequences' and ask them what they have learned for next time, you are asking them to recall the details of what happened. Yet, for the period they were dysregulated, their memory formation was impaired, so they genuinely can't remember what happened. They have learned nothing. They also won't have been able to track the passage of time, so you may feel aggrieved that you have lost most of a morning managing them, whereas for them it may have felt like fleeting moment.

In other words, when a child is in red, you are very limited in what you can do to help them regulate. They are being fuelled by adrenaline and cortisol and it takes time and movement in a safe environment for these levels to come down. At times, you just have to focus on keeping everyone safe. Any strategies you do try need to connect with the downstairs brain. So, we are looking at rhythmic movement, music, eating (particularly sweet, salty or crunchy food), calm lighting, reduced sensory input and, if they can tolerate it, company and physical contact. Remember how we feel safer when we aren't alone? A very dysregulated child may not be able to accept the presence of another person, especially if they are unfamiliar, but you need to constantly monitor this and, as soon as possible, they need to be with someone who can be calm and just present with them. That person is unlikely to be able to engage them in conversation, at least initially, as that is upstairs brain stuff. Just being calmly present is enough. When the child indicates they can accept some communication, then talk and listen, because it encourages them to increase upstairs activity which will aid regulation.

One other fact to be aware of is that even when a child has calmed and seems regulated again, their cortisol levels will stay elevated for quite a while. The downstairs brain was triggered by perceiving a threat to life, so it makes sense, from an evolutionary perspective, to stay on high alert for some time. This means that the child is more likely to continue to struggle throughout the day. If you have had a difficult morning with them, you may need to put extra support and breaks into the afternoon to help that child stay regulated.

---

4   These may differ from the zones of regulation that are sometimes used in schools.

If you have a child who seems stuck in a *dorsal immobile state* they will need a different approach. They may be sitting still at their desk, but they are not engaged in learning. Learning can't happen unless we feel safe in a ventral state. Our priority has to be helping them to move back into that socially engaged state. The most successful approach, in the moment, seems to be finding a way to gently encourage movement. I often pass someone a pencil, as they may instinctively reach out, or they may be able to start gently rocking. I might then encourage them to stand up and look out of the window. I am looking for a sign that they are ready to connect with me, maybe making eye contact. I use a gentle voice and make calming statements. I might reflect on what I think they are experiencing: 'I think you feel a bit overwhelmed at the moment – we were talking about some difficult things. Let's just take a moment to sit quietly ... When you feel you can, maybe we could stand together at the window and see what we can see.' Be aware that you might still need to manage fight or flight, so it might be useful to encourage movement towards their safe place and person in school.

Our conclusion has to be that it is better for everyone if we can support our children effectively, so they never or rarely go to red. Ideally, we are monitoring our children closely enough to be able to spot the warning signs that their nervous system is becoming dysregulated and intervene then – it really can't wait. Even better, we are working with the children so they can read their own nervous systems and learn self-regulation skills or know how to proactively seek help, so they can develop these important life skills.

If you have successfully spotted a child moving into amber, there are a range of options open to you to reduce the chance of it escalating, depending on your understanding of the trigger:

- If it is the work they are finding difficult, reducing the demand and increasing connection is likely to be helpful. Could you stand next to them and help them to work it out? Do they need to be redirected to their working partner so they don't feel alone with it?

- Are they showing signs of restless agitation and maybe need a movement break? If they have already released some cortisol, it's only movement that will really help to burn it off. Can you safely send them on a job? Has an occupational therapist provided some suggestions? Can the whole class stand up and have a wiggle?

- Have they been triggered by perceived rejection from a peer? If so, they will no longer feel connected. Listen to them and validate their feelings: 'It's not nice when that happens', 'It sounds like you're feeling a bit lonely right now', 'You seem quite cross that she said that.' Nothing promotes connection more than feeling understood and accepted by another. You don't have to agree with them, but you do have to accept that that is their perspective at that time. Maybe you can then think of a way they can have a positive peer experience.

■ Can you take a quiet moment and ask them how they are feeling? There is a phrase, 'Name it to tame it', which recognises that using the language centres on the left side of our brain releases neurochemicals that are calming to the emotion-focused right side. Talking about your feelings really does help, especially as it also emphasises how connected we are to the listener. Try to listen out for their feeling words and validate their experience: 'You feel stupid when you can't do the work? That's a really tough feeling. Let's see if I can explain it better', 'Nobody played with you at break? I'm guessing you felt left out and lonely. I'm sorry that happened to you.' We don't always have to have answers and 'fix it'. We just have to hear their feeling and be present.

■ Do they seem to be closing down, overwhelmed by a seemingly simple task? You will need to re-energise them (time for a class wiggle again?), before finding another way to present the task, whilst keeping your frustrations at bay. I am sure you face some demanding situations on a regular basis, but as soon as that child senses your disappointment or annoyance, connection is lost and so is their ability to regulate.

■ Remember the co-regulation that happens between parent and infant? The same thing happens between you and your class. I bet they are more challenging on the days you aren't feeling your best or have a lot on your mind. It's not just that it seems that way, they probably really are; you feed off each other, so it is important for you to engage in self-care as well.

Since being dysregulated is so distressing for all involved, the focus should be on pre-venting that situation arising. Ideally, aim for green with moments in amber to reflect the realities of life and build resilience. Remember, green is being in a ventral vagal state, which is having the resources available to meet any demands and feeling con-nected to others. So, when you know you are increasing the demands on a child, you should also increase your presence in a supportive way.[5]

The aim is to become skilled at recognising what state a child is in – are they feeling safe and connected? Are they becoming hyper- or hypo-aroused? Do you think you know why? Do you know what would be helpful to help them get back to a more regulated state (clue: it's about feeling connected interpersonally)? Are you and your staff ready to step in as and when needed, knowing that prevention is so much better than picking up the pieces afterwards?

Good luck.

---

5   This is where the PACE approach can help – see Chapter 34.

# Chapter 28

# THE SERIOUS BUSINESS OF PLAY

## Helen Dodd and Bo Stjerne Thomsen

> Studies from around the world show that free and guided play and their facilitation help children develop the breadth of skills they need. Not just ABCs and 123s, but also self-control, cooperation, and creativity.
>
> Dowd and Thomsen (2020: 3)

This is one of the conclusions of a recent report by the LEGO Foundation on the topic of play and its role in helping children who may otherwise be struggling at school to achieve. In particular, they highlight play's ability to 'tackle inequality and improve the outcomes of children from different socio-economic groups' (Dowd and Thomsen, 2020: 3). In a school system that is becoming increasingly rigid and where play is seen as an 'add-on', even with our youngest children, it is important that we understand what a serious solution play is when it comes to helping all children succeed. The science of how children learn through play illustrates that children who are curious, flexible and creative learners are naturally equipped to engage in complex challenges. As a matter of fact, learning through play represents the best long-term value for helping kids (Thomsen and Dowd, 2021), whether square pegs or not.

## Why children need time to play

For many children, school provides their only opportunity for active play with their peers, especially outdoors. Play – particularly child-led, social, unstructured play – brings with it myriad benefits for children. In fact, play is so vital to a healthy childhood that it is enshrined within the United Nations Convention on the Rights of the Child.[1] In the UK, approximately 20% of children's time at school is spent outside formal lesson time (Baines and Blatchford, 2019), and yet schools are given

---

1   See Article 31 at https://www.unicef.org.uk/what-we-do/un-convention-child-rights.

few resources and little guidance or training to ensure that the experience children have during this time is positive and of high quality. For many children, playtime can be a hugely rewarding experience, but for others, some of our square pegs among them, playtimes can be anxiety provoking, overly stimulating or even just plain boring. It doesn't need to be this way, though, and you are definitely missing a trick if that is the case in your school. With planning, imagination and creativity, schools can provide rich, diverse play experiences that benefit all children.

Put simply, play is what we do when no one is telling us what to do. It is something we do for the joy of it rather than for any specific purpose, but still children take it very seriously, and it's fundamental to their development and learning. In education, play features strongly in the early years foundation stage curriculum (but it is under pressure even here), yet all but vanishes from the curriculum from Key Stage 1 onwards. There is plenty of research which finds that opportunities for play beyond school have greatly diminished in recent years too (Baines and Blatchford, 2019; Dodd et al., 2021; Dodd and Lester, 2021). Strikingly, a report published by Hunt et al. (2016) cited that in 2015, 1.6 million UK children did not play in or visit a natural environment at any point. This is crucially important because exposure to nature improves mood and overall mental health, and it also stimulates movement and supports connection with nature (McCurdy et al., 2010; Collado and Evans, 2019).

In school, the picture is also one of play in decline. Data from a national survey in England showed that for children in Key Stage 1, playtimes reduced by an average of 45 minutes per week between 1995 and 2018 (Baines and Blatchford, 2019). The decline is even more striking in secondary schools, where the average decrease was 65 minutes per week. The same survey showed that schools cite the need for more formal learning time to cover the curriculum and issues around behaviour during lunchtimes as the drivers of these declines in time for play.

This all matters because we know that play confers a range of developmental benefits that support children's learning (Brooker et al., 2014; Hirsh-Pasek, 2019) and cognitive development (Barker et al., 2014) as well as stimulating creativity (Canning, 2013). When children play with others, they experience feelings of social joy (Panksepp, 2010) and gain vital opportunities to develop socio-emotional skills like turn-taking and negotiation (McElwain and Volling, 2005; Gray, 2011). Importantly, at a time when obesity and mental health problems are at an all-time high, play stimulates physical activity (Veitch et al., 2008; Ramstetter et al., 2010) and supports children's mental health (Dodd and Lester, 2021).

The benefits of play – and the necessity to engage in it in a meaningful way – do not stop in childhood either. While children have the mental flexibility to learn new skills, this function declines as we grow older (Gopnik, 2017). A significant part of sparking creativity has to do with challenging – and, in turn, being able to adjust – your mindset. Adults need to remain engaged in learning, play and creativity to thrive in life.

Specifically, curiosity, confidence and emotional regulation are critical for adults to succeed in careers and be flexible to new challenges (Yogman et al., 2018).

Those working in schools clearly have an opportunity here both to address the play deficit our children are experiencing nationally and also to improve the chances of all children succeeding inside and beyond school.

## Whatever happened to playtime?

Table 28.1 outlines what playtime currently looks like in a typical UK school (and we shouldn't just think it's younger children who need playtime). A number of these existing practices are not well matched to children's developmental needs or remove opportunities that might benefit children, especially our square pegs. For example, it is striking that approximately 60% of primary schools have policies that mean children can miss a full break or lunch playtime. In the Breaktime and Social Life in Schools survey, 80% of children stated that they had been forced to miss a playtime (Baines and Blatchford, 2019). Withholding playtime in this way is typically used as a means to manage behaviour or to ensure that children finish schoolwork. While it may be common practice, withholding playtime goes against what we know about child development, motivation and attention, as well as the evidence described above regarding the benefits of outdoor, unstructured physical activity and play.

If this is your school policy, then over the course of a term make a note of which children are most often missing playtime. Are there any patterns, familiar faces or recurring (mis)behaviours here? Research shows that when children, particularly those with a diagnosis of attention deficit hyperactivity disorder, are given playtime, they are less fidgety and more focused afterwards compared to when they are not given playtime (Jarrett et al., 1998). It is counterproductive therefore to punish a child who perhaps has had difficulty concentrating, sitting still and focusing by denying them playtime; the very experience they need to help them to concentrate, sit still and focus. Are the children most likely to miss playtime in your school the ones who would benefit from it most?

**Table 28.1. Playtime in a typical UK school**

|  | Typical UK school playtime | What playtime could look like |
|---|---|---|
| **Time for play** | On average schools in England provide 85 minutes of break time at Key Stage 1, decreasing to 63 minutes at Key Stage 4. The majority of primary and secondary schools provide a morning break but no afternoon break after Key Stage 1. Even at Key Stage 1, only 54% of schools in England provide an afternoon break (Baines and Blatchford, 2019). | Schools provide more time for play. For example, in Finland children have 15 minutes of playtime after every 45 minutes of lesson time even though the school day is shorter. Some schools outside Finland have successfully adopted this model, reinstated afternoon break or increased the length of playtime. |
| **Training of staff** | School playtimes are supervised by a range of staff including teachers, learning support assistants and lunchtime supervisors. Training for the supervision of play is most often informal. The provision of formal training has decreased in recent years (Baines and Blatchford, 2019). | Staff supervising children's play during school playtimes are given training in playwork principles to help them support children's play effectively. |
| **Attitudes to risk** | Playtime supervision takes a risk-averse approach where the focus of supervision is on minimising the potential for physical injury. | Schools adopt a risk-benefit approach where injury prevention is balanced against the potential benefits of allowing children to explore healthy, age-appropriate risks, including developing independent decision-making and evaluation of risk, exposure to uncertainty and opportunities to learn to cope independently. |

|  | **Typical UK school playtime** | **What playtime could look like** |
|---|---|---|
| **Space** | Driven by concerns about children getting muddy, play typically occurs on a hard-packed, asphalt area, even when green space is available. Children are not allowed to use the green space during playtimes. | Schools provide children with as much space as possible for play and allow children to play in green spaces, even if this means they might get muddy. |
| **Equipment and materials** | Play equipment varies from school to school, but most schools have some fixed play equipment available for children to use. Typically, only a limited number of children can use this equipment at any given time. Equipment of this nature (climbing frames, trim trails, etc.) are typically expensive and require significant investment. | Schools provide movable play equipment such as scooters or skateboards, as well as loose parts such as tyres, planks and other materials which provide creative open-ended play opportunities. Many of these materials can be sourced for free or for a relatively low cost. It also encourages the recycling and reuse of items that would otherwise be thrown out. |
| **Structured vs unstructured** | Some schools hire sports coaches to run activities during playtime and others fill playtime with structured activities and clubs. | Schools prioritise unstructured playtime which allows children to explore, create, imagine, negotiate, socialise, build relationships and solve problems. Unstructured play puts children in control of their own activities and gives them time during the school day when they are not being told what to do by an adult. A range of environments ensures that playtime is inclusive and beneficial for all children. |

| | Typical UK school playtime | What playtime could look like |
|---|---|---|
| **Wet play** | Across the UK, it is common practice to have 'wet play' when children stay indoors because it is raining. They may also stay indoors because of ice, snow or high temperatures. Only 11% of primary schools allowed children to go outside to play when it was raining (Baines and Blatchford, 2019). | Schools aim to allow children to play outside every day and work with parents and the school community to ensure all children have access to waterproof clothing and wellies. |
| **Withholding play** | 60% of primary schools have policies that mean children can miss a full break or lunch playtime, typically to manage behaviour or for children to catch up on schoolwork (Baines and Blatchford, 2019). | Playtime is protected to ensure that all children have the opportunity for active, outdoor play with their peers. Playtime is not withdrawn as a punishment or for catching up on schoolwork. |

As mentioned earlier, what if existing playtime practices are problematic for certain children? Imagine the girl who is anxious and finds social situations difficult. Imagine how it feels for her to walk out into a large open area with one or two pieces of play equipment, 100 or more other children, with 30 minutes before she can leave again. Imagine the boy who needs to move a lot, who is physically very capable and finds it hard to sit still, being told to wait in line for his turn on the equipment and then told not to climb too high or jump off the equipment in a certain way. Imagine a girl who is having a difficult time at home, who is feeling angry about things that aren't her fault, who is plain bored by the limited play opportunities during playtime. What might she decide to do when she spots a child who she perceives as weaker or isolated?

When playtimes are stimulating, diverse and fun, such children can feel calmer, more engaged and more emotionally balanced, with benefits that go back into the classroom with them.

There are many examples of proven play strategies for schools to turn to as they embrace fully the many benefits of play. One is the Taking Outdoor Play Seriously (TOPS) programme delivered in a range of schools across Northern Ireland.[2] It is an

---

2    See https://www.playboard.org/what-we-do/tops-taking-outdoor-play-seriously.

intensive programme that uses a range of approaches including staff training, play audits, participation work with pupils and engagement with parents/carers. As one school reported: 'Staff saw behaviours changing with pupils. Staff saw the children much more settled back in formal learning. They were happier and excited' (J. O'Laughlin, personal communication, 20 August 2021).

TOPS takes a similar whole-school approach as the Outdoor Play and Learning (OPAL) programme, a UK-based mentor-supported school improvement approach used by over 500 schools.[3] Visiting an OPAL school is a delight since children are happy and busy, engaging in a wide range of activities, from building ball runs from drainpipes to making bubbles, dancing to music or climbing up a fort made from old tyres. Staff support children's play, but the play is led by the children and they are given space to make decisions and judge risk for themselves. Indoor play due to bad weather is rare and avoided unless absolutely necessary, and children have access to all the space available including fields and trees. Schools that have successfully transformed their playtimes by working with OPAL report that they get more teaching time because the children return to the classroom happier and settle faster, that behaviour during playtime improves and that children enjoy playtime more (Lester et al., 2011). Similar benefits have been reported following other play-improvement programmes (McLachlan, 2014; Farmer et al., 2017).

Importantly, both TOPS and OPAL include provision of a range of play spaces, including areas for quieter play as well as areas for physical and sensory play. In doing so, they ensure that playtimes are accessible and enjoyable for all children, from those who need and benefit hugely from physical exertion to those who need some space and quiet time, from those who want to escape into an imaginary world to those who want to build a den or perform on stage.

What is striking in reading so much of the literature about play is the consistency of the benefits that schools report and the relative lack of adverse outcomes. There is an understandable fear that increasing playtime and reducing structure and rules might lead to more bullying or more injuries, but the evidence suggests that if we make playtimes engaging and diverse then, if anything, the opposite happens (Lester et al., 2011; McLachlan, 2014; Farmer et al., 2017).

## Play isn't just about playtime

Beginning in childhood, learning through play helps people to embrace uncertainty, instils a stronger sense of curiosity, provides new ways to approach challenges – to test and try things over again – and to innovate. Research shows that learning through

---

3   See https://outdoorplayandlearning.org.uk/the-opal-primary-programme.

play is core to a child's wellbeing and ability to thrive by helping them to develop the life skills (creative, social, physical, emotional and cognitive) that are critical drivers of success in adulthood (Zosh et al., 2017).

There are far wider benefits to play beyond timetabled playtime. More than 50% of children are passive and disengaged in school because we don't see 'class time' as an opportunity to integrate the benefits of learning through play (Hodges, 2018). We need to reframe teaching and the aims of education to prioritise a joy of learning inside as well as outside the classroom – a joy in exploring, being curious, testing and trying things out – because this enables the pedagogical practices, which have been proven to support both holistic skills and knowledge (Parker et al., 2022). Joy and curiosity also impact overall life satisfaction and are the main predictor of our capacity to grow, adapt and thrive throughout life (Gottfried et al., 2006). And we must start to appreciate the diversity of outcomes which will be needed by our children and young people in the future.

Just as playtime helps our square pegs, so an approach to pedagogy that focuses on a joy of learning and a playful mindset also reduces inequalities. Research shows that play facilitation in and out of the classroom helps teachers to improve their pedagogical approaches to better serve the diversity of pupil background and knowledge. Another LEGO Foundation report, *Play Facilitation: The Science Behind the Art of Engaging Young Children* (Jensen et al., 2019), shares policy examples and teacher practice from across the United States, Canada, Mexico, South Africa, Denmark, China and Finland, and shows that it can be done, in particular in the early years.

School leaders have the ability to bring forward alternative approaches, despite the system, by embedding a mindset of playfulness throughout school culture and focusing on that one critical measure of success and growth from childhood into adulthood – a genuine joy of learning. This is not only an effective equaliser for the square pegs, but prepares all pupils for a future in which creativity and adaptability will be critical life skills.

To close, let's revisit the findings of the LEGO report we mentioned at the beginning. Among the many benefits play confers on children, the report also highlights the following: 'Evidence suggests that play that enables children to make their own choices, that allows them actively to test out ideas, and that gives them enjoyment, is also what works best in closing achievement gaps' (Dowd and Thomsen, 2020: 3).

# References

Baines, E. and Blatchford, P. (2019) *School Break and Lunch Times and Young People's Social Lives: A Follow-Up National Study. Final Report.* Available at: https://www.nuffieldfoundation.org/wp-content/uploads/2019/05/Final-report-School-break-and-lunch-times-and-young-peoples-lives-A-follow-up-national-study.pdf.

Barker, J. E., Semenov, A. D., Michaelson, L., Provan, L. S., Snyder, H. R. and Munakata, Y. (2014) Less-Structured Time in Children's Daily Lives Predicts Self-Directed Executive Functioning, *Frontiers in Psychology*, 5, article 593. doi:10.3389/fpsyg.2014.00593

Brooker, E., Blaise, M. and Edwards, S. (eds) (2014) *The SAGE Handbook of Play and Learning in Early Childhood.* London: SAGE.

Canning, N. (2013) 'Where's the Bear? Over There!' Creative Thinking and Imagination in Den Making, *Early Child Development and Care*, 183(8): 1042–1053. doi:10.1080/03004430.2013.772989

Collado, S. and Evans, G. W. (2019) Outcome Expectancy: A Key Factor to Understanding Childhood Exposure to Nature and Children's Pro-Environmental Behavior, *Journal of Environmental Psychology*, 61: 30–36. doi:10.1016/j.jenvp.2018.12.001

Dodd, H. F., FitzGibbon, L., Watson, B. E. and Nesbit, R. J. (2021) Children's Play and Independent Mobility in 2020: Results from the British Children's Play Survey, *International Journal of Environmental Research and Public Health*, 18(8): 4334. doi:10.3390/ijerph18084334

Dodd, H. F. and Lester, K. J. (2021) Adventurous Play as a Mechanism for Reducing Risk for Childhood Anxiety: A Conceptual Model, *Clinical Child and Family Psychology Review*, 24(1): 164–181. doi:10.1007/s10567-020-00338-w

Dowd, A. J. and Thomsen, B. S. (2020) *Learning Through Play: Increasing Impact, Reducing Inequality. Summary Report.* Billund: LEGO Foundation. Available at: https://learningthroughplay.com/explore-the-research/increasing-impact-reducing-inequality.

Farmer, V. L., Fitzgerald, R. P., Williams, S. M., Mann, J. I., Schofield, G., McPhee, J. C. and Taylor, R. W. (2017) What Did Schools Experience from Participating in a Randomised Controlled Study (PLAY) That Prioritised Risk and Challenge in Active Play for Children While at School?, *Journal of Adventure Education and Outdoor Learning*, 17(3): 239–257. doi:10.1080/14729679.2017.1286993

Gopnik, A. (2017) Artificial Intelligence Helps in Learning How Children Learn, *Scientific American* (1 June). Available at: https://www.scientificamerican.com/article/gopnik-artificial-intelligence-helps-in-learning-how-children-learn.

Gottfried, A. W., Gottfried, A. E. and Guerin, D. W. (2006) The Fullerton Longitudinal Study: A Long-Term Investigation of Intellectual and Motivational Giftedness, *Journal for the Education of the Gifted*, 29(4): 430–450. Available at: https://files.eric.ed.gov/fulltext/EJ746291.pdf.

Gray, P. (2011) The Decline of Play and the Rise of Psychopathology in Children and Adolescents, *American Journal of Play*, 3(4): 443–463.

Hirsh-Pasek, K. (2019) *Play: How Play Motivates and Enhances Children's Cognitive and Social-Emotional Growth.* New York: Oxford University Press.

Hodges, T. (2018) School Engagement Is More Than Just Talk, *Gallup* (25 October). Available at: https://www.gallup.com/education/244022/school-engagement-talk.aspx.

Hunt, A., Stewart, D., Burt, J. and Dillon, J. (2016) *Monitor of Engagement with the Natural Environment: A Pilot to Develop an Indicator of Visits to the Natural Environment by Children. Results from Years 1 and 2 (March 2013 to February 2015).* Natural England Commissioned Report No. 208. Available at: https://assets.publishing.service.gov.uk/government/uploads/system/uploads/attachment_data/file/498944/mene-childrens-report-years-1-2.pdf.

Jarrett, O. S., Maxwell, D. M., Dickerson, C., Hoge, P., Davies, G. and Yetley, A. (1998) Impact of Recess on Classroom Behavior: Group Effects and Individual Differences, *Journal of Educational Research*, 92(2): 121–126. doi:10.1080/00220679809597584

Jensen, H., Pyle, A., Zosh, J. M., Ebrahim, H. B., Scherman, A. Z., Reunamo J. and Hamre, B. K. (2019) *Play Facilitation: The Science Behind the Art of Engaging Young Children. White Paper.* Billund: LEGO Foundation. Available at: https://learningthroughplay.com/explore-the-research/engaging-young-children-in-play.

Lester, S., Jones, O. and Russell, W. (2011) *Supporting School Improvement Through Play: An Evaluation of South Gloucestershire's Outdoor Play and Learning Programme.* London: National Children's Bureau.

McCurdy, L. E., Winterbottom, K. E., Mehta, S. S. and Roberts, J. R. (2010) Using Nature and Outdoor Activity to Improve Children's Health, *Current Problems in Pediatric and Adolescent Health Care*, 40(5): 102–117. doi:10.1016/j.cppeds.2010.02.003

McElwain, N. L. and Volling, B. L. (2005) Preschool Children's Interactions with Friends and Older Siblings: Relationship Specificity and Joint Contributions to Problem Behavior, *Journal of Family Psychology*, 19(4): 486–496. doi:10.1037/0893-3200.19.4.486

McLachlan, B. (2014) Project Play at Swanson School, *Play and Folklore*, 61(1): 4–8.

Panksepp, J. (2010) Affective Neuroscience of the Emotional Brain Mind: Evolutionary Perspectives and Implications for Understanding Depression, *Dialogues in Clinical Neuroscience*, 12: 533–545.

Parker, R., Thomsen, B. and Berry, A. (2022) Learning Through Play at School: A Framework for Policy and Practice, *Frontiers in Education*, 7: 751801. doi:10.3389/feduc.2022.751801

Prisk, C. and Cusworth, H. (2018) *From Muddy Hands and Dirty Faces … To Higher Grades and Happy Places: Outdoor Learning and Play at Schools Around the World.* Available at: https://outdoorclassroomday.com/wp-content/uploads/2018/10/Muddy-hands-report-full.pdf.

Ramstetter, C. L., Murray, R. and Garner, A. S. (2010) The Crucial Role of Recess in Schools, *Journal of School Health*, 80(11): 517–526. doi:10.1111/j.1746-1561.2010.00537.x

Thomsen, B. S. and Dowd, A. J. (2021) Learning Through Play Represents the Best Long-Term Value for Helping Kids, Regardless of Background, *World Economic Forum* (17 March). Available at: https://www.weforum.org/agenda/2021/03/learning-through-play-represents-the-best-long-term-value-for-helping-children-regardless-of-background.

Veitch, J., Salmon, J. and Ball, K. (2008) Children's Active Free Play in Local Neighborhoods: A Behavioral Mapping Study, *Health Education Research*, 23(5): 870–879. doi:10.1093/her/cym074

Yogman, M., Garner, A., Hutchinson, J., Hirsh-Pasek, K., Golinkoff, R. M., Committee on Psychosocial Aspects of Child and Family Health, and Council on Communications and Media (2018) The Power of Play: A Pediatric Role in Enhancing Development in Young Children, *Pediatrics*, 142(3): 1–17.

Zosh, J. M., Hopkins, E. J., Jensen, H., Liu, C., Neale, D., Hirsh-Pasek, K., Solis, S. L. and Whitebread, D. (2017) *Learning Through Play: A Review of the Evidence. White Paper.* Available at: https://learningthroughplay.com/explore-the-research/the-scientific-case-for-learning-through-play.

# Chapter 29

# TAUGHT HAPPY

## Adrian Bethune

It's easy to look at the world of square pegs through the lens of things that can be measured: lateness; behavioural incidents and consequences; assessment results, both internal and external; absences, both explained and unexplained; fixed-term exclusions; permanent exclusions; school moves, managed or otherwise; destinations beyond school, known or otherwise. Indeed, you can fit a square peg into quite a few boxes on a spreadsheet.

What if you created a happiness league table for the children in your care as well? How would your square pegs fare on that spreadsheet? And what might happen if you then made happiness a key performance indicator in your school? And put happiness ahead of league table positions, Ofsted and test results? What might happen then?

Well, despite how pie in the sky that might sound, research indicates that your school would improve across a number of indicators, including measurable ones like exam results (and staff retention) and immeasurable ones like the manner in which you transformed the lives of your most vulnerable children and young people for the better. That said, and before we look at the research, don't take my word for it; ask Aristotle. Some 2,500 years ago, he suggested that 'Happiness is the meaning and purpose of life, the whole aim and end of human existence' (Aristotle, 2009: 92).

In other words, we are happiness-seeking organisms, programmed to avoid pain and move towards pleasure. So, if making school a happy place (and no, I don't mean making it easy or being soft) becomes a key focus of its leadership and staff, we are tapping into the natural forces that will benefit us all, especially our square pegs.

## What is happiness?

Happiness expert Professor Paul Dolan (2014: 4) sums it up neatly when he says, 'Happiness is experiences of pleasure and purpose over time.' We are generally said to be 'flourishing' when we experience both high levels of positive emotion and are engaged in life with a strong sense of purpose. This definition not only includes those fleeting feelings of happiness we experience when, for example, we get our hands on a new gadget or item of clothing, but also those longer term feelings of satisfaction and contentment when we look back and appreciate that we are leading a good life (what psychologists often refer to as 'subjective' and 'psychological' wellbeing, respectively).

It used to be thought that our levels of happiness were fixed and there wasn't much we could do to change our baseline levels of wellbeing, but positive psychology (the scientific study of what makes life worth living) has proved this theory incorrect. Professor Sonja Lyubomirsky's studies of identical twins, separated at birth and raised in different homes, showed that genes play a significant role, but that a massive 40% of the participants' happiness was determined by the intentional choices and actions they took (Lyubomirsky et al., 2005).

In the UK, the *Good Childhood Report 2020* (Children's Society, 2020) shows that there has been a significant decrease in children's life satisfaction over the last decade and that children here are some of the unhappiest in the whole of Europe. It is abundantly clear that an increasing number of our children are struggling emotionally and more needs to be done.

Obviously, we all have a different starting point in life, but the research is clear: it doesn't have to be that way and we can all learn to be happier. So, as children, why not learn to be happy where we do so much other learning of important things – at school.

## Happier children learn better

If you are concerned that there is no place for such learning in your knowledge-rich curriculum, then remember firstly that teaching children about happiness, wellbeing and leading a good life *is* knowledge – and probably some of the most powerful knowledge they will encounter. Secondly, miserable children do not learn as effectively as happy children, regardless of how rich the knowledge is.

A report by Public Health England (2014) showed that schools which put in place programmes to boost students' social and emotional skills have, on average, an 11% gain in attainment as well as (square peg watchers take note) improvements in student behaviour and attendance. Moreover, in a large, randomised control trial carried out by Dr Alejandro Adler (2016), where students were taught a wellbeing curriculum over a period of 15 months, the students not only showed significant improvements in their levels of wellbeing compared to the controls but their exam scores increased by 20%. An ever-growing number of studies (e.g. Lindorff, 2020) are showing the clear link between children feeling good about themselves and their lives, and succeeding in school and beyond.

# Happier children, happier adults

A focus on happiness in schools is not just about boosting test scores, though. A longitudinal study led by Professor Richard Layard at the London School of Economics tracked people from childhood through to adulthood. The study sought to establish what were the strongest predictors in childhood of adult happiness. In *The Origins of Happiness* (Clark et al., 2018: 30), Layard and his colleagues observe: 'If we go back to childhood and ask about the best predictor of an enjoyable adult life, the best predictor is the child's emotional health, which … is significantly more important than all the qualifications a person ever obtains.' However, this was not all the study found. The researchers go on to say that 'Primary and secondary schools have major effects on the emotional well-being of their children' (Clark et al., 2018: 192).

So, there is solid evidence to show that not only do happier children do better at school and grow up to be happier adults, but that schools and teachers have a major impact on children's happiness whilst at school. If we do truly believe that the purpose of our lives is to be happy – and that all children have that right – then schools are well placed to contribute to this incredibly important goal.

# Promoting happiness and wellbeing in school – where to start?

We know so much more now about the factors that underpin a whole-school approach to mental health and wellbeing than ever before.[1] It is important, therefore, that we put this knowledge to good use, embed it in our school communities and make the happiness of students and staff a core focus of our schools. To help, here are five key ideas to get you started.

## 1. Make a commitment to wellbeing

A whole-school approach to wellbeing requires both bottom-up and top-down efforts. That said, without a firm commitment from senior leaders this – like so many other initiatives – will fail. Leaders must make it clear that the happiness and wellbeing of staff and students really matters. This might mean putting it on your school development plan with a long-term vision for how you wish to embed wellbeing across your school community. It could be that it's part of your vision and (lived) values for your school. It might also mean joining a movement like Well Schools[2] and working

---

1   See https://www.ncb.org.uk/what-we-do/improving-practice/wellbeing-mental-health/schools-wellbeing-partnership/whole-school.
2   See https://www.well-school.org.

alongside other schools across the UK that are putting wellbeing at the heart of what they do.

## 2. Model wellbeing

One of the most important things an adult can do to promote happiness and wellbeing in children is to show them that you take care of yourself. If you are overly stressed, irritable and low on morale a lot of the time, your children will see this and respond and react accordingly. As developmental psychologist Alison Gopnik (2016: 90) says, 'Children actually learn more from the unconscious details of what caregivers do than from any of the conscious manipulations.'

The same applies to our colleagues too – as school leaders, your staff will follow your lead, so make your own wellbeing a priority. Set clear boundaries for work and home. Take part in activities that nourish you – see friends, walk in nature, play sports, read, watch a good movie. Eat, sleep and drink well and fit in regular exercise (walking is fine – no need to sign up to triathlons!). A happy and healthy school leader is a better school leader.

## 3. Put wellbeing on the curriculum

As the Adler (2016) study shows us, there can be real value in dedicating space on the timetable to teaching students the skills of wellbeing. A good wellbeing curriculum will be evidence based, knowledge rich and include things like the importance of good nutrition, sleep hygiene and physical activity. It may introduce students to mindfulness – how to become aware of and at ease with our thoughts and emotions – so we can relate to them more skilfully. A wellbeing curriculum would certainly explore how young people can foster and maintain positive relationships in person and online, and how to resolve conflicts. Some great programmes already exist, such as the Healthy Minds curriculum for secondary schools,[3] and there is a wealth of rich resources provided by organisations like the Anna Freud Centre's Schools in Mind project,[4] Action for Happiness and their toolkit for schools[5] and Teachappy have some free resources too.[6]

## 4. Measure wellbeing

'You treasure what you measure' the adage goes, so if you truly value wellbeing then it makes sense to measure it. And yes, it can be measured.[7] Schools that measure

---

3   See https://bounceforward.com/healthy-minds-for-secondary.
4   See https://www.annafreud.org/schools-and-colleges.
5   See https://www.actionforhappiness.org/toolkit-for-schools.
6   See https://www.teachappy.co.uk/resources-and-downloads.
7   Which means that you can make your results into a banner and hang it outside your school instead of the you-know-what one.

wellbeing know their starting point and the unique issues facing their students and staff. Only then can interventions and whole-school policies be designed, chosen and tailored to suit their needs. Once wellbeing programmes and interventions are in place, schools then need to measure and monitor their impact and effectiveness over time.

Measuring wellbeing can also help schools to identify children and young people who might need specialist intervention; otherwise, they risk falling through the gaps. By measuring wellbeing you are showing students and staff that you care about what they have to say and value their insights. It also begins a conversation – and measuring wellbeing is just the start. It's important to share the results with staff and children and invite them to work on projects to improve things in school wherever possible. There are some great resources and guides to help you in this area, so do your research and start measuring your school's wellbeing.

## 5. Make your school humanity rich

Don't think that by placing happiness and wellbeing at the heart of your school that it means you have to be smiley and positive the whole time. There is such a thing as toxic positivity, and a relentless drive to always be upbeat can actually make us miserable. Psychologist Tal Ben-Shahar (2012) says a key to happiness is giving ourselves 'permission to be human', something that means allowing ourselves to experience the full range of human emotion. It's perfectly natural to feel angry, disappointed, frustrated and hopeless at times. By allowing yourself to feel what you are feeling and accepting that sometimes things feel a bit shit and that is okay, you also give permission to others to do the same. When a school community allows everyone to be their authentic and emotionally rich selves, you are well on the way to being a happy community.

And a happy community might just be one with far fewer square pegs struggling in its midst.

## References

Adler, A. (2016) Teaching Well-Being Increases Academic Performance: Evidence from Bhutan, Mexico, and Peru. Unpublished dissertation, University of Pennsylvania. Available at: https://repository.upenn.edu/edissertations/1572.

Aristotle (2009) *Nicomachean Ethics*, tr. W. D. Ross. New York: World Library Classics.

Ben-Shahar, T. (2012) Five Ways to Become Happier Today [video] (24 April). Available at: https://www.youtube.com/watch?v=fLhpyzVTc8A.

Dolan, P. (2014) *Happiness by Design: Finding Pleasure and Purpose in Everyday Life*. London: Penguin.

Children's Society (2020) *The Good Childhood Report 2020.* Available at: https://www.childrenssociety.org.uk/sites/default/files/2020-11/Good-Childhood-Report-2020.pdf.

Clark, A. E., Flèche, S., Layard, R., Powdthaveee, N. and Ward, G. (2018) *The Origins of Happiness: The Science of Well-Being Over the Life Course.* Princeton, NJ: Princeton University Press.

Gopnik, A. (2016) *The Gardener and the Carpenter: What the New Science of Child Development Tells Us About the Relationship Between Parents and Children.* London: Bodley Head.

Lindorff, A. (2020) *The Impact of Promoting Student Wellbeing on Student Academic and Non-Academic Outcomes: An Analysis of the Evidence.* Oxford: Oxford University Press. Available at: https://oxfordimpact.oup.com/home/wellbeing-impact-study.

Lyubomirsky, S., Sheldon, K. M. and Schkade, D. (2005) Pursuing Happiness: The Architecture of Sustainable Change, *Review of General Psychology,* 9(2): 111–131.

Public Health England (2014) *The Link Between Pupil Health and Wellbeing and Attainment: A Briefing for Head Teachers, Governors and Staff in Education Settings* (November). Available at: https://assets.publishing.service.gov.uk/government/uploads/system/uploads/attachment_data/file/370686/HT_briefing_layoutvFINALvii.pdf.

# Chapter 30

# THE DREAMS LIST

## Dave McPartlin

I don't remember a lot about the moment David Walliams pressed the Golden Buzzer. We were on stage at Manchester's Lowry theatre in our *Britain's Got Talent* audition and it was all a bit too much to take in, to be honest. How could our working-class school from up north, which entered with no expectations beyond simply showing our children that they should dare to dream, end up going straight through to the live finals of one of the biggest TV shows in the world in London?

Flakefleet Primary School, like so many these days, is based in an area of significant deprivation with high unemployment and 50% of the children eligible for free school meals. Square pegs? We have plenty. But this is not what defines us. Having worked in other schools serving similar areas, and fiercely proud of my working-class roots, I have always found that what a school lacks in advantage, it makes up for in heart, togetherness and sense of community. And our little part of the world has these in abundance.

I worked out early on in my time leading this school that first and foremost – before looking at SATs results, league tables and Ofsted – I needed to challenge the 'We can't, we're from Fleetwood' mentality that I saw, especially among some of our parents who had really tough lives and didn't believe in themselves as much they should. Just as others have highlighted in this book, it was so important for us to start focusing on successes, on achievements, on raising the bar of what was possible and, yes, even on dreams. I started to obsess about how we might go about changing this mindset and one lunchtime, in discussion with staff, the idea came to us – the Dreams List.

We decided to ask all our children what their biggest dreams were, and over the course of the next year we would try to make them happen, to a greater or lesser degree. All of them. It was interesting how hard it was for some children (not all – some had too many!), but eventually we had nearly 420 dreams listed on a chart in the staffroom. Now, all we needed to do was to work our way through them as we had promised.

We have always had a very positive relationship with social media. It's a great way to break down home–school barriers and show the world our real personality – warm, friendly and approachable, with a passion for making the world a better place as well as making people smile. We now found the large social media following we had built up came in very useful. There are so many kind people out there just waiting to do good deeds, and Facebook soon became the 'middleman', brokering kindness in so many ways.

For some of our families school conjures up bad memories, and their expectations of education and its professionals can be unfairly – but understandably – tainted by previous experiences. By proactively engaging with our parents and community online, we have found that this has a positive impact on engagement in the real world. We often go 'live' on Facebook to share happy stories or deliver important messages, and some of the parents who are unable to make it into school as frequently as they would like often comment that they feel like they already know us because of our online presence.

Over many months, we had many, many happy children ticking off their dream experiences. Children 'became' princesses, doctors, nurses, vets and even skydivers, and it was a wonderful time, full of possibility, joy and happiness. Some of the dreams were relatively easy to achieve; some required substantially more effort. 'Being a pop star' was one of the more extreme challenges, but not one we shied away from. We decided to have a crack at a Christmas number 1, as you do.[1]

If you are asking yourself (as I know many did) what on earth did we think we were playing at when there were SATs to pass and gaps to close, it is worth pointing out that a local GP commented on how there was a notable decrease in the number of Flakefleet children attending surgery at this time. Who knew that a focus on happiness, joy and possibility is good for what ails you?! Also, our attendance figures were noticeably up. Children wanted to come to school (and, yes, we made them do literacy, numeracy and everything else while they were there).

What is more, staff were enjoying themselves at work too. They loved the excuse to let their imaginations run wild, and when staff are in such a positive headspace, everyone wins.

Shortly after the number 1 quest, we took a step towards making another dream come true when we were offered an audition for *Britain's Got Talent*. However, after much planning and our first rehearsal, the production team rang to say that the standard of choirs that year was so high that they would no longer be progressing our application. Our *BGT* adventure had ended before it began.

If lesson number one is to have a dream, then lesson number two is not to let others stand in the way of that dream, especially if they are in admin. Within a few hours, we had knocked up a video with the kids doing all sorts of daft things and me embracing a bit of cross-dressing. I put my editing skills to the test and we sent off our new video

---

1  We ended up with a Vodafone top 40 hit and managed to be the third most downloaded single in the country over the festive period.

application. After a few days, just when we were beginning to assume it wasn't to be, we got *the* call. Our *BGT* journey was back on!

The children had experienced a real and bitter taste of rejection and disappointment, reality even (dreams are hard work and don't always come true), but they had tempered their frustration and sadness with perseverance and resilience. Little did we know how important these skills would become over the next few weeks.

We had said yes to the producers without really having an act. Another lesson. Over time, I have learned that having a 'dare to dream' attitude [2] and not living in fear of failure means we rarely regret saying yes to something. But we do often rue the opportunities we have missed by saying no.

We realised that we needed to increase the numbers in our choir from the normal 20 or so. Starting with reception, we asked anyone who wanted to be on *BGT* to stand up and show us their best dance moves. An hour later, we had auditioned the whole school and had a list of the liveliest and most diverse group of children you can imagine, none of whom had any idea what they had let themselves in for.

Inclusivity at its best, our new-look choir contained children who had been excluded from other places, children on the special needs register, children whose attendance left lots to be desired and many quiet children who wouldn't say boo to a goose, let alone Ant and Dec. Watching them grow in confidence and develop into their new roles was a joy to behold. We knew we would never be perfect, and there was something beautifully liberating in the permission we gave ourselves to just have fun. In schools, it's far too easy for us to put pressure on square pegs to conform, to crave uniformity and to seek only the highest polished standards. We just wanted our children to smile and enjoy the experience. After all, this is how children (and adults) truly flourish.

We quickly began to notice how some children enjoyed a sense of purpose they had never experienced before. Many had frequently struggled with the more academic side of school life, and you could see their self-esteem and confidence growing as they realised they were improving – and with it a burgeoning sense of pride. For me, *every* child is entitled to experience this, to feel *that moment* when they know they are enjoying real success in something. Surely, it's the responsibility of every school leader to make sure every child has that experience in their school too. It's the best part of the job, after all!

With the audition approaching, the children were encouraged to unleash their imagination and their costumes were left completely up to them. The community also stepped up, donating clothing, props and anything else we might need for the big day. Parents worked around the clock stitching and sewing and indulging us in all our madcap ideas. I could feel the community's sense of belonging to the school growing

2   Our school motto.

as they took every opportunity to get involved. My sense of responsibility was huge; the heady mixture of complete fear and extreme excitement was interesting to stomach on top of running a big, busy school.[3]

On the day itself, there was a real sense of occasion even though none of us knew what to expect. The older kids helped the younger ones to get ready, we slapped on the face paint, loaded up our eclectic range of props and set off. There was a real family feel to the bus journey, and I reflected that we really need to give our children more opportunities to mix across year groups and key stages, to give them the opportunity to nurture others and take on real responsibilities.

Manchester greeted us with a torrential downpour and gale-force winds. Face paints became smeared, our bedraggled hair made it look like we had been dragged through a hedge in both directions and our cardboard boxes were starting to wilt. Most of the children had never been to a city before and, yet, here we were, despite the odds and the weather. Fleetwood minnows ready to take on the world.

Throughout our adventures, there were so many moments when we didn't feel we belonged – not posh enough, out of place. We learned, however, with time and experience, that this feeling passes. We have the right to be wherever we choose to be, just as much as anyone else. This is social capital in action. Learning that sense of confidence, of being comfortable in any environment, is a real advantage for some social groups, one that you only realise you don't have when you really need it. It might not help, not directly anyway, with their SATs results, but we want our children to feel safe and secure in any environment, from theatres and restaurants to hotels and public buildings. And, yes, even backstage at the Lowry theatre.

With little advance warning, we were making our way to the stage ready to take a step into the unknown. Nerves, the smell of face paint, bright red, white and blue lights, children, cameras, more children, some of whom were fiddling with equipment they shouldn't have been fiddling with, the hum of an audience out there somewhere, the unnerving tightness of Lycra, the threat of Ant and Dec – it was a complete sensory overload for me, let alone the kids. When the act before us unexpectedly received the loud rejection buzzer we all jumped. One of our lead singers started to cry. My heartbeat was off the scale, most probably heading towards the 'medical concern' ballpark. We were proud of ourselves for seizing an opportunity and taking a risk – but what if it all went wrong?

It couldn't go wrong though. We were already winners and we hadn't even stepped onto stage …

I could tell you all sorts of stories about our kids and the lives they have had so far. For some, their lives will always be tougher than most. But, no matter what happens,

---

3  I worried that the sequinned Lycra I had insisted on wearing was one of those decisions that would reach the *Daily Mail*, but then decided, hey, in for a penny … Having 'BGT' stitched on my backside was an inspired decision though.

our little square pegs choir will forever be worthy of Golden Buzzers and they will always see life a little bit differently. In their darker moments, they will do what we all have done since (and many of you have done too, I know) – get on YouTube and watch our moment carved in digital history, edited beautifully for us all to watch again and again.[4] Bring hankies.

As a community, I have had many parents tell me that they have started taking driving lessons, signed up for courses and applied for jobs because we inspired them to raise their aspirations. We are all only limited by our imagination. Self-efficacy – the belief that we can achieve what we set out to if we work hard and believe in ourselves – is truly contagious. The more we can show this to be true, the better.

Our adventures are not for the faint-hearted. We don't expect to be everyone's cup of tea. What we do works for us because it is authentic. We are okay with making ourselves vulnerable and risking failure. Everyone has their own individual gifts and talents to offer the world. Identifying what they are, and giving ourselves and others permission and the freedom to pursue them, can lead to special things happening and the development of something so much more profound and meaningful than simply being a bit better than the school down the road at reading, writing or arithmetic. Our square pegs, especially, need us to think like this. The current system is loaded against them and we owe it to them to do things differently, wherever they are from.

---

4   See https://www.youtube.com/watch?v=itSbV3YiRkI.

Chapter 31

# THE SQUARE PEGS IN YOUR SANDWICH LAYER

## Natasha Devon

Mental health is a gigantic umbrella term. It can encompass anything from long-term, chronic mental illnesses, like bipolar disorder, to common or garden exam stress, and everything in-between. It's this in-between, middle-of-the-sandwich layer that most occupies me in my work with schools across the UK, and the one we need to explore in some detail when it comes to helping our square pegs.

First, the good news. Over the past decade or so, society has become much better at recognising the universal relevance of mental health. Rather than dismissing the topic with the endlessly repeated (and oft misquoted) 'one in four' statistic,[1] most people now acknowledge that four in four of us have a head with a brain in it and that there are basic ways in which we can look after that brain, in much the same way as we do our bodies. Prevention of mental illness and promotion of wellbeing are now firmly on the agenda, which is cause for celebration, even if it has been rather hijacked by influencers trying to sell us vegan candles on Instagram.

However, what is less recognised is the importance of the space that exists between prevention and diagnosable mental illness.[2] To draw a parallel with physical health, these are the middle-of-the-sandwich equivalents such as migraines, flus, tummy bugs, muscle sprains, hay fever and so on. They don't usually warrant a trip to the doctor, yet they can have a profound impact on your ability to focus, perform, connect and enjoy your life.

How prevalent such mental health issues are in our children and young people is a hard one to ascertain because of the way they are measured – through a mixture of self-reporting and formal diagnosis.[3] However, since these difficulties encompass issues such as body image insecurity, orthorexia (obsession with 'healthy' or 'clean'

---

1   It is actually: '1 in 4 people will experience a mental health problem of some kind each year in England,' and, over the course of a lifetime, experts estimate that it is around half of us who will personally encounter mental ill health. See https://www.mind.org.uk/information-support/types-of-mental-health-problems/statistics-and-facts-about-mental-health/how-common-are-mental-health-problems.
2   That is, requiring referral to child and adolescent mental health or other services.
3   Media reporting has an annoying habit of assuming that middle-class girls are peculiarly afflicted (e.g. Sanghani, 2017), not taking into account that young people from poorer backgrounds and boys are less likely to be able to access services and often endure higher levels of stigma. But that is a subject for another day.

eating), debilitating academic stress, social media addiction, bullying, toxic friendships, struggles with identity (race, gender, sexuality, class, religion) and low self-esteem, I think anyone working with young people could assume the percentage is high.

Of course, some argue that these issues are timeless and universal. Previous generations had the same battles and 'they were fine'. If that was your response to the above, consider the following:

- The idea that historical cohorts emerged unscathed from 'character-building' mental health struggles is a deeply flawed and rose-tinted narrative. We have only just begun to understand – and record – mild to moderate mental health issues. We have no data for how many of the baby-boomer generation (and before) were technically 'functioning' whilst having their life satisfaction and performance significantly hindered by anxiety, depression and addiction.

- Data suggests that generation Z (teenagers and people in their early twenties in the 2020s) are less likely to self-medicate; rates of alcohol, tobacco and drug use are decreasing (BBC News, 2017; Jones, 2021).

- Young people today exist in a culture with relatively low levels of mental health stigma (although, of course, it still exists). They are also more likely to have been taught about mental health at school, giving them a high level of emotional literacy, and they are able to articulate struggles for which their parents and grandparents didn't have names.

- Simultaneously, austerity measures first introduced in 2010 meant local authorities spent significantly less on mental health services (Meikle, 2015; Webb and Bywaters, 2018). Additionally, subjects with a proven therapeutic value, like sports, music and drama, have been deprioritised within the curriculum and systematically defunded by education policy-makers (Parr, 2020; Weale, 2021).

In summary, young people are in a position in which they are generally better able to express the symptoms and causes of their distress, but have fewer coping tools and lines of support to deal with them. Anyone proclaiming that young people are 'snowflakes' is effectively blaming them for being emotionally literate yet structurally disadvantaged. (Bear this in mind, too, when you hear people suggest that children choosing not to go to school simply need more discipline from their parents.)

For the purposes of this chapter, and given the vastness of the field we are discussing, I want to focus on two aspects of the sandwich that I feel are of particular relevance to those who are finding getting to school, and fitting in when they are there, problematic: resilience and anxiety.

# On resilience

Resilience has become a buzzword in education circles over the past decade, and, in my experience, it's often misused. 'Resilient' is not a personality type, resilience is not an attitude you can switch on or off at will and teaching it is not a magic wand when it comes to supporting your square pegs.

The standard definition of resilience is the capacity to recover quickly after something unpleasant has happened, such as shock, injury or adversity. Whilst not incorrect, I suggest that this definition places too much emphasis on the individual and not enough on their environment. Far more useful for our purpose in schools is the widely accepted definition of resilience amongst psychologists – that it is the number and quality of meaningful connections a person has in their life.

In other words, resilient people tend to have: (1) someone they can talk to about anything, (2) a means of creative expression and (3) an environment in which they feel a strong sense of belonging. Any school looking to build resilience needs to ensure that every child has access to these three vital cornerstones.

# On anxiety

My personal observation is that anxiety is one of the fastest-growing issues in the sandwich layer of mental health. Whilst it's difficult to provide concrete evidence for this (for the reasons mentioned above), my assertion is supported by the fact that Childline's annual reports consistently show a significant increase in the number of calls it receives for mental health-related issues, with words like 'overwhelmed' and 'anxious' emerging as key themes (Packham, 2017; NSPCC, 2021).[4]

Whilst anxiety is a universal and entirely normal human emotion, it can evolve into something completely debilitating. The distinction between anxiety and an anxiety disorder is something I am asked about by young people all the time. The official advice states that we should seek medical attention when our mental health issue prevents us from functioning/doing what we need to do, is constantly present, regardless of what might be happening to 'trigger' the distress, and has lasted for a period of two weeks or more.[5] However, with life becoming increasingly stressful for many young people, that line can often be a difficult one to draw definitively.

---

4   The number for Childline is 0800 1111 – please make sure that all children in your school are aware of this.
5   See https://www.nhs.uk/mental-health/conditions/generalised-anxiety-disorder/overview.

Stress and anxiety are part of life. Working with them, not avoiding them, is a vital lesson to learn.[6] But too much of either can close down our ability to be at our best.

My instinct is that we can be too quick to medicalise anxiety. In doing so, we also send the message that the problem lies in an individual's brain rather than in their environment. Even when a person does have a diagnosable anxiety disorder, adapting their lifestyle to allow them to manage their symptoms will likely be a key part of their recovery or management process.

Anxiety can also lead to body image issues, eating and exercise disorders, self-harm and even suicidal ideation and behaviours. Whilst we tend to associate these symptoms more with depression, being anxious and worrying obsessively is exhausting, and it is common to channel that energy into a dysfunctional behaviour – a belief that if you looked different, you would feel better – or to just feel overwhelmed and unable to cope.

Note, too, that anxiety is a tricky one to spot. I was a high-flying student (whose first panic attack at the age of 10 was put down to asthma), but my confidence when addressing large groups of people or berating politicians live on TV quickly disappears when taking public transport or engaging in small talk. Anxiety can manifest in any number of ways, from aggression, physical violence, defiance and obstinacy to compliance, disengagement and withdrawal – many of the behaviours you will observe in your square pegs. These behaviours are also stress and trauma responses (see Chapter 27).

## Solutions

I know there are schools that do not see addressing mental health issues as part of their remit. After all, government cuts and fallacious claims about increased spending have meant that schools have been left with so much more to deal with.[7] However, this objection makes the fundamental error of conflating therapeutic and educational psychology services (which are the remit of local authorities) with the ability to offer support to children and young people that will help their overall mental health and wellbeing.

I would suggest that things like role modelling, coaching, mentoring, peer support, early symptom spotting and provision of safe spaces are all within the remit of any

---

6   The best way I saw this balance described was in a headline which suggested that 'stress is to mental health what avocados are to dieting'.

7   Despite several announcements of 'extra funding', a 2015 investigation by then shadow mental health secretary Luciana Berger found that only half of local authorities increased their spending on mental health in real terms, and even then it was generally by a tiny percentage – see https://www.parallelparliament.co.uk/mp/luciana-berger/debate/Commons/2015-12-09/debates/15120945000001/MentalHealth. See also Montoya et al. (2016).

school. Initiatives like these not only help with the sandwich layer but also, given that mental illness gets worse the longer it goes undetected and untreated, they can help to prevent some pupils from developing chronic mental health issues further down the line. They also improve academic outcomes.[8]

None of the solutions listed below are a panacea, and how well they work will depend to a large extent on the wider culture of your school or college. However, they are very likely to open up a broader discussion about mental health and anxiety management amongst both staff and pupils, which will in turn help you to undertake an ongoing assessment of how well they are working and what needs to be tweaked.

## Mental health first aid training

Many organisations offer this type of training, with some of the best being provided by Mental Health First Aid England.[9] There are also branches in Scotland and Wales. The courses teach you how to spot symptoms of common mental health difficulties within the context of case studies, which you can tailor so they resemble the types of pupils you see day to day. You will also learn what to say (and what not to say) to someone who is experiencing mental health difficulties, possible coping strategies to suggest and appropriate recommendations for further support.

## Panic cards and chill-out zones

In some of the schools I visit, pupils are given panic cards to hold up in class to indicate that they are feeling overwhelmed and anxious. They can then spend 10 minutes or so in a designated safe space or chill-out zone, such as a quiet library or the school counsellor's office. The trick here, I have noticed, is to make the cards available to everyone, rather than singling out those pupils with high anxiety (who may then feel self-conscious about using them). You must also be aware that, for the same reason, some children will need a more subtle cue that they need time out.

## Guidance counsellors and warrior poses

Whilst young men are tearing up the rule book on traditional masculinity and the stiff upper lip expectations placed on their fathers, I still observe that girls are more likely to make use of school-based wellbeing resources than boys. Perhaps this is because girls are, generally speaking, less fearful of ridicule if seen to be struggling by their peers.

---

8  I elaborate on this much further in my book *Yes You Can: Ace Your Exams Without Losing Your Mind* (Devon, 2020).
9  See https://mhfaengland.org.

Some schools have circumnavigated this challenge by 'rebranding' their mental health resources so they appeal to boys too. For example, in one school I visited, break time yoga sessions became 'warrior pose' and school counsellors were introduced as 'guidance counsellors'. This meant that pupils could make an appointment to discuss a range of topics (careers advice, for example) without their classmates knowing the specifics.

## Peer support schemes

Some schools nominate peer supporters from older age groups, giving them special sweatshirts or lanyards so they are visible when 'on duty' at break or lunchtimes and can be approached for a chat. This can work incredibly well, especially for younger pupils who may just need someone who has been through it themselves to talk about a challenge they are facing. It also bridges the gap when pupils have been used to being closely monitored by staff in the playground at primary school and feel the absence of this at what is usually a much larger secondary school site.

Remember, though, that peer supporters need to be supported too. They should have training in active listening skills,[10] and, as it's recognised by mental health professionals that talking to people in distress can have an impact on them, they should have at least one designated member of staff they report to weekly to offload and share any safeguarding concerns. This member of staff should ideally be offered regular counselling sessions too, something known as 'supervision' (see Chapter 7).

## Exercise and creativity

Recent cuts in time and money for sports and the arts in the state sector have not helped when it comes to wellbeing either. Not only do these activities offer a form of self-expression to young people who may be struggling otherwise, but they are also the exact subjects that have a measurable benefit in improving mental health.[11]

Some schools have found innovative ways to compensate for this. For example, the Morning Mile involves the entire school doing a walk together every day before classes begin. If you can do this in a natural environment, such as a local park, then the evidence shows that the benefits of the exercise are magnified.[12]

There is an old Italian proverb which implores us to not let 'the perfect be the enemy of the good'. I believe many school leaders feel beleaguered by the perceived enormity of the task of tackling mental health because the issue is so vast and complex. But,

---

10  The Samaritans are one of the organisations that can provide this – see https://www.samaritans.org/how-we-can-help/workplace/workplace-staff-training.

11  See https://www.mind.org.uk/information-support/tips-for-everyday-living/physical-activity-and-your-mental-health/about-physical-activity. See also Slawson (2017), Jackie (2020) and Pascoe et al. (2020).

12  See https://www.instagram.com/p/CRiw1icodKD/?utm_medium=copy_link and WWF-UK and Mental Health Foundation (2021).

even small changes can make a huge difference, and every day is an opportunity to make a relatively minor intervention to the sandwich layer and help a struggling young person to find a different and more positive path.

# References

BBC News (2017) Why Young People Are Now Less Likely to Smoke (7 March). Available at: https://www.bbc.co.uk/news/health-39192635.

Webb, C. and Bywaters, P. (2018) Austerity, Rationing and Inequity: Trends in Children's and Young People's Services Expenditure in England Between 2010 and 2015, *Local Government Studies*, 44(1): 1–25.

Devon, N. (2020) *Yes You Can: Ace Your Exams Without Losing Your Mind*. London: Pan Macmillan.

Jackie, J. W. (2020) Sports and Art Suggested as Means to Promote Teens' Mental Health, *IDN-InDepthNews* (21 November). Available at: https://www.indepthnews.net/index.php/sustainability/health-well-being/4000-sports-and-art-suggested-as-means-to-promote-teens-mental-health.

Jones, D. (2021) Gen Z – The Generation of Sobriety?, *RDSi Research*. Available at: https://www.rdsiresearch.com/genz-the-generation-of-sobriety.

Meikle, J. (2015) Councils Spending Just 1% of Health Budgets on Mental Health, *The Guardian* (9 November). Available at: https://www.theguardian.com/society/2015/nov/09/councils-spending-just-1-of-health-budgets-on-mental-health.

Montoya, E., Henao, E., Hernández, D., Zapata, E. and Gómez, I. (2016) Availability and Effectiveness of Meaningful Relationships: Key Elements to Promote Resilience in Young People, *Index de Enfermeria*, 25: 22–26.

National Society for the Prevention of Cruelty to Children (NSPCC) (2021) Childline Raise Concerns About Mental Health as Counselling Sessions Delivered to Children Passes 50,000 [press release] (13 January). Available at: https://www.nspcc.org.uk/about-us/news-opinion/2021/childline-press-release.

Packham, A. (2017) Children Counselled for Anxiety by Childline at Highest Ever Levels, and They Don't Feel Like They're Being Heard, *Huffington Post* (8 December). Available at: https://www.huffingtonpost.co.uk/entry/children-anxiety-panic-attacks-increase_uk_5a293adce4b03ece03007220.

Parr, C. (2020) Tate Warning Over Decline in Arts Education, *SecEd* (15 January) 2020). Available at: https://www.sec-ed.co.uk/news/tate-warning-over-decline-in-arts-education.

Pascoe, M., Bailey, A. P., Craike, M., Carter, T., Patten, R., Stepto, N. and Parker, A. (2020) Physical Activity and Exercise in Youth Mental Health Promotion: A Scoping Review, *BMJ Open Sport and Exercise Medicine*, 6: e000677.

Sanghani, R. (2017) Why Are So Many of Britain's Teen Girls Struggling with Mental Health Problems?, *The Telegraph* (16 March).

Slawson, N. (2017) It's Time to Recognise the Contribution Arts Can Make to Health and Wellbeing, *The Guardian* (11 October). Available at: https://www.theguardian.com/healthcare-network/2017/oct/11/contribution-arts-make-health-wellbeing.

Weale, S. (2021) 'Creativity Crisis' Looms for English Schools Due to Arts Cuts, Says Labour, *The Guardian* (15 July). Available at: https://www.theguardian.com/education/2021/jul/15/creativity-crisis-looms-for-english-schools-due-to-arts-cuts-says-labour.

WWF-UK and Mental Health Foundation (2021) *Thriving with Nature: A Guide for Everyone*, 2nd edn. Available at: https://www.mentalhealth.org.uk/explore-mental-health/publications/thriving-nature.

# Chapter 32

# A TRAUMA-INFORMED CULTURE

## Wendy Coetzee

During my professional career of over 25 years as a clinical psychologist, I have had the privilege of specialising in supporting children, young people and families who have experienced trauma. During this time, research has increased our awareness of how trauma can impact children in their formative developmental years and beyond as they develop into young adults. Science has helped us to understand the impact of trauma on the architecture of the developing brain and subsequently on social, emotional, physiological and cognitive development.

If we want to understand and better support our square pegs, then understanding trauma is a hugely important starting point.

For the purposes of this chapter, we are referring to children and young people who may have experienced developmental and relational trauma. This kind of trauma can be induced by experiencing neglect, sexual/physical/emotional abuse, experiencing domestic violence, experiencing poor/disrupted attachments to parents/caregivers, having a parent(s) with mental health difficulties or being a young carer.[1] This can also include other traumatic experiences such as racism or others forms of oppression and discrimination, loss/bereavement, bullying or other school-based trauma, complex or undiagnosed chronic ill health or family breakdown. When we are referring to the impact of trauma, we are focusing especially on the impact of toxic stress on a child's developing brain and nervous system and on their fear of relationships/mistrust.

While this may seem daunting to teachers and leaders, it is worth remembering that at the heart of trauma-informed practice is one eminently human word – *relationships*. Put simply, traumatised children need relationships with secure and safe adults in order to thrive and learn. 'All children need relationships to thrive: traumatized children need relationships to heal' (Golding and Hughes, 2012: 224). The challenge for our teaching staff is enabling them to create a safe and nurturing learning environment by offering trusted relationships with safe adults.

---

1   These are examples of typical adverse childhood experiences or ACEs.

Children and young people who have experienced relational and/or developmental trauma develop relationship patterns based on their traumatic experiences. Their relational style and interactions with others can be complex and their difficulties in trusting others is often combined with a hypervigilant approach to relationships characterised by mistrust and shame-fuelled interactions. Added to which are the demands of the school environment, the demands of their peers to navigate social relationships and the demand to engage their upstairs/learning brains (see Chapter 27) in order to engage and learn can prove overwhelming.

For many pupils, the task of learning may have previously been traumatic, resulting in overwhelming levels of shame, concerns about underachievement or failure and a fear of relationships. The combination of these factors can make the school day extremely stressful, challenging and anxiety provoking for many children. In my experience, such pupils can include looked-after children, young people with social, emotional, mental health difficulties or who are neurodiverse, and children who have been traumatised in their relational experiences at home or with peers or teaching staff. These children may arrive in school with extraordinarily high levels of anxiety coupled with high levels of shame, a fear of failure, of not being *good enough*, and difficulties in trusting the very professionals whose job it is to support them. These difficulties can become significant barriers to being open to learning and engaging our thinking (upstairs) brains. They account for a large number of our square pegs.

It is vital to note that these learners may express their vulnerabilities through being disruptive, attention-seeking, rude, aggressive, defiant, disengaged or withdrawn.

In order to know where to begin in our relational support of our square pegs, it is worth noting that, as with all human beings, relationships start with the bonds of understanding, security and trust. This is where, for example, a PACE-informed approach and attitude can help (PACE was developed by Dan Hughes and stands for playfulness, acceptance, curiosity and empathy – see Chapter 34), along with the other strategies mentioned elsewhere in this book.

## Supportive staff need support too

Schools that want to embrace trauma-informed practice at a systemic level will recognise the importance of supporting their staff as well as their pupils. It can be challenging for professionals to remain emotionally anchored and calm; responding to traumatised children and young people can evoke powerful feelings and emotions, which can cause us to become reactive and even defensive. If our threat systems have been triggered, we are vulnerable to being drawn into re-enacting the child's previous insecure relational patterns and experiences.

Traumatised children and young people can often present with a range of 'challenging' behaviours, from acting out to shutting down. As a teacher supporting children with complex emotional needs, it can be challenging to deal with these behaviours as part of professional life, but it's important to remember that it's not personal. These behaviours are the child's survival responses to keep them (feeling) safe and in control, and to prevent others from seeing their vulnerability and fear. When we adopt the role of the 'safe adult', we become emotionally invested to succeed in creating connected relationships with our vulnerable pupils.

Supporting these vulnerable pupils is something that can be as challenging as it is rewarding, and staff who invest in these children need somewhere to make sense of this relationship experience, to reflect on how the work is impacting on them and to be curious about how the child is behaving/responding in relationship with them. Working with a child with intense feelings of anxiety and relational fear can be challenging and emotionally draining, and even the most resilient staff member can become weary and suffer from compassion fatigue (or 'blocked care'). In order to maintain connection and trust with traumatised children, teaching staff need to be supported to process their own responses to the child, to recognise when they are feeling threatened or triggered by their own nervous system responses, to have space and time to explore these interactions and the behaviour and reactions to it, and – as per the C in PACE – to be curious about what is happening. This relies on the safe adult being able to remain emotionally regulated and calm themselves.

Adopting PACE entails modelling the model – that is, embracing a systemic attitude of acceptance and empathy towards staff, which is essential with respect to validating their emotional responses to their pupils. Recent recognition of the need for teaching staff to have access to 'supervision' and reflective sessions to support them in their work has been gathering momentum (see Chapter 7). Ensuring that staff have protected time to reflect on their relationship with their pupils and resolve any ongoing challenges or obstacles to learning is vital. Supporting teacher–pupil relationships is key here.

## TAC – tick!

Regular therapeutic team around the child (TAC) meetings can bring together all staff working with a young person to consider their experiences, their progress and the perceived barriers to learning and engagement, which can help create a narrative to understand the child's behaviours, difficulties, successes and challenges.

This narrative/understanding of the pupil's behaviour can enable staff to adopt an attitude of acceptance and empathy (PACE again), and can support teaching staff as they consider their personal feelings and responses in the context of factors such as the child's attachment style or trauma history. An external facilitator in these meetings is vital, by the way, helping staff to explore the meaning behind the child's actions – the issues lurking in the waters beneath the behaviour tip of the iceberg.

An attitude of curiosity can help everyone to wonder and think about the child in the context of their story. In this way we move from 'What's wrong with you?' to 'What happened to you?' This encourages staff to see behaviours as a form of communication, encouraging them to ask, 'What is this pupil telling me about what is going on for him/her?' It also helps us to make sense of what is happening, something that paves the way for the development of acceptance and empathy in our PACE approach.

The TAC meeting model also means carers/parents can be part of these conversations, as well as the young person, who can be invited to reflect on what is happening for them and with them (rather than to them) and influence therapeutic safety and support plans. Where possible, a psychologist or pastoral support staff member should facilitate these meetings.

# Trauma-informed culture eats trauma-informed strategy for breakfast

Adopting a whole-school culture to a trauma-informed approach can be transformational. A trauma-informed school strives to embed and embody trauma-informed ideas into everyday practice. This will be evidenced in, for example, how behaviour policies are written, and procedures practised, team meetings, discipline, safety, recruitment procedures, the physical environment, staff training and support, supervision, mentoring, governance, language and more. It is a journey that needs to involve the whole school community.

The work of Sandra Bloom on the Sanctuary Model[2] and Dr Karen Treisman, who has received an MBE for her work on organisational trauma,[3] has enabled those working with traumatised and vulnerable children and families to recognise that we need to adopt a congruent, systemic and trauma-informed organisational approach and culture in our schools. After all, when organisations are working with trauma and anxiety, they are also at risk of themselves becoming traumatised at a systemic level through vicarious and secondary trauma.

---

2    See https://www.thesanctuaryinstitute.org.
3    See http://www.safehandsthinkingminds.co.uk.

# Traumatised systems

There are many examples of traumatised systems across the public sector where those responsible for supporting vulnerable and traumatised children and their families face higher demand with fewer resources. The services that are there to support traumatised families can themselves suffer from secondary and vicarious trauma, compassion fatigue and systemic trauma. The symptoms of this are many and varied:

- Staff feeling overwhelmed and powerless.
- A culture of shame and blame.
- A lack of accountability from the leadership team.
- An 'us and them' divide.
- Reactive, defensive and closed responses to crises.
- A culture of not feeling safe, valued or understood.
- Poorly written and implemented policies and procedures. This leads to staff feeling overlooked and undervalued, and a dysfunctional and fragmented team approach with poor communication and a greater risk of accidents. This in turn leaves staff feeling vulnerable and unsafe, with staff turnover and sickness becoming a significant problem.

Adopting a systemic, trauma-informed, relational and empathetic culture can help to address so much of this.

# Making the change

While many schools are now claiming to be trauma informed, it is important to distinguish what we mean when adopting this title and what needs to happen for a school to become truly trauma informed at a systemic level. It can seem a daunting task but, like all journeys, it's the many smaller steps that can support longer term growth.

Here are some examples of what schools can do as they start to make the change:

- Ensure that children and young people have a voice to tell you how they feel at school.
- Ensure families and carers can communicate how they are experiencing the school (and not just because Ofsted are visiting).

- Develop a culture of 'doing with' and not 'doing to', encouraging a collaborative approach where pupils, teachers and families come alongside each other and work together, and where all staff are valued, regardless of seniority.

- Ensure all staff can access regular attachment, trauma and relationship-based training to continue improving practice.

- View behaviour as communication and from a trauma and various other lens – and to be curious.

- Integrate knowledge of trauma, attachment, and brain development into all aspects including the curriculum, and key areas like transitions and endings.

- Ensure adequate reflective supervision, training, and support for staff, helping them to engage in self-care and recognising compassion fatigue and burnout.

- Dedicate time in staff meetings to discuss and address staff wellbeing.

- Ensure staff have time to debrief and are encouraged to seek support from other designated staff.

- Allocate a wellbeing room/space (where possible) for staff.

- Allocate a safe and quiet wellbeing room for pupils with appropriate sensory items and comfort materials.

- Integrate the principles of trauma-informed practice into the physical environment of the school including in the playground.

- Integrate regulating activities throughout the day.

- Develop policies and processes that demonstrate compassion, safe practice and a commitment to self-care.

- Develop behaviour and discipline policies that support a relationally informed ethos and approach.

- Build systems and processes and a school environment that supports staff to feel safe, valued and listened to in their work.

- Record and measure staff turnover, sickness, and retention.

- Train staff in developing emotional intelligence and focusing on the importance of connections and relationships.

- Create a culturally trauma-informed ethos, modelled by the head to the senior leadership team, the senior leadership team to all staff, and all staff to all pupils, with a growth mindset and an openness to reflection and learning and avoiding a shame/blame culture.

A trauma-informed school will, for example, demonstrate a PACE-informed (or similar) attitude across the school system. This will be in evidence in the senior management and leadership team, which will foster an environment that encourages self-care, compassion, reflection and permission to make and learn from mistakes. This learning culture asks itself questions such as, 'How could we do this differently?', 'What happened here?', 'Are we getting this right?', 'What could we improve?', 'If we did get it wrong, what can we learn from this?' This cultivates a culture of openness and accountability, recognising that when we work with trauma, we can expect to make mistakes. It will make sure there are 'safe spaces' and time allocated for staff to reflect, share and offload, as mentioned above. It will also ensure that all staff receive the necessary training in attachment and trauma, and emotional wellbeing.

In this way, everyone around the site – from support and administrative staff to teaching staff and the leadership team – all understand trauma and its impact on vulnerable pupils. Creating a collaborative 'we're in this together' approach within a staff team is vital, helping staff – no matter how senior they are – to model an attitude of kindness and compassion, supporting one another regardless of position.

As the school develops a trauma-informed culture that prioritises the development of emotional intelligence, staff will feel safe, emotionally anchored, contained and valued. This culture of valuing staff and prioritising their wellbeing should also improve staff retention and enable teachers to be more effective in their work as valued and valuable team members supporting vulnerable pupils. This culture will support staff to offer a relationally informed approach that prioritises safe, trusted, and connected relationships with their pupils, which are the foundation for learning.

## References

Bloom, S. L. (2013) *Creating Sanctuary: Toward the Evolution of Sane Societies*, revised edition. New York: Routledge.

Golding, K. and Hughes, D. A. (2012) *Creating Loving Attachments: Parenting with PACE to Nurture Confidence and Security in the Troubled Child*. London: Jessica Kingsley.

Hughes, D. A. (2006) *Building the Bonds of Attachment: Awakening Love in Deeply Troubled Children*. Northvale, NJ: Aronson.

Treisman, K. (2021) *A Treasure Box for Creating Trauma-Informed Organisations*. London: Jessica Kingsley.

# Chapter 33

# A TRAUMA-INFORMED JOURNEY

## Stuart Guest

As a parent of a birth child and adopted children, I have had the privilege of learning about trauma and the complex issues that can arise because of this. What I have also learned is that knowledge of these issues and the practice of specific approaches, plus a huge dollop of self-care, can support the journey for children to achieve well and be successful. And, as a primary head teacher of over 15 years, I have also seen the huge role that school has in supporting not only such children but also their families.

As you have read elsewhere in this book, just as is there is no one-size-fits-all approach to supporting our square pegs, there is no one-size-fits-all approach to becoming trauma aware in a school. But, based on my experience and in the interests of keeping things simple, here is a three-step plan that will help schools to get started.

The three broad steps are: principles; policies and procedures; and provision and practice.

## 1. Principles

What does the research have to say on the matter, and how can this best be shared across the whole school? There are a great many principles to learn, and it will take a while to get this into the school's collective psyche, so where to start? These questions will help:

- What generates healthy attachment?
- What is trauma (acute and complex)?
- What are adverse childhood experiences?
- What are the various stages of brain development, and what is the impact of trauma on them?
- What are the long-term consequences of trauma?

- What are zones/windows of tolerance?
- How does the fight/flight/freeze/flop/friend response manifest itself in the classroom?
- What is sensory processing and why is it relevant?
- What is the PACE (playfulness, acceptance, curiosity, empathy) approach and how can we use it? (For more on this see Chapter 34.)
- What do restorative approaches to discipline look like?
- What does self-care and blocked care look like in the classroom?
- What do we know, and do, about teachers' self-regulation?

Some overall whole-school training is vital to introduce staff to trauma and attachment with expert guidance. This is a very suitable use of pupil premium funding or any recovery money that might have wafted your way. There are several training providers out there you could contact.[1]

## 2. Policies and procedures

Once you 'get' the principles, you can begin to look at making changes to those policies and procedures that are not trauma friendly. Reflect on all your policy approaches and check that your systems provide truly equal opportunities for all children, but especially those who are disadvantaged due to their circumstances. Policies should provide enough opportunities to support and develop the child's chances rather than simply punish them for not fitting in. Again, where to start? Here is what I suggest:

- Behaviour policy.
- Rewards and sanctions.
- Homework.
- Attendance.
- Lates.
- Interventions.
- Access to support.

---

1 For example, Trauma Informed Education (https://traumainformededucation.org.uk) and/or Trauma Informed Schools UK (https://traumainformedschools.co.uk). The Solihull Approach (https://solihullapproachparenting.com) also offers various courses for professionals and has been adopted with great success across several public services, including education, in Scotland.

Of all of these, clearly it is the behaviour policy that will drive the rest. Indeed, it will drive the culture of the entire school. It needs to stand up well to questions like:

- Is there a clear acceptance that behaviour is communication and that it may indicate unmet needs?
- Is priority given to relationships?
- Is there a strategy for repair between children and children, and grown-ups and children, when things go wrong?
- Does the policy look at supporting long-term improvement and not just rely on short-term sanctions?

Some staff (and governments) have a need for consistency here, and this is often a key stumbling point. Surely, the idea that 'If X happens then Y is the consequence' must be applied consistently across the board for us to be a fair school. Sometimes that is true, but the consistency in the policy comes from *consistency in the approach* rather than *consistency in the sanction*. What do I mean by that? Let me give two examples:

- School 1 lateness policy: Any child who is late will receive a 20-minute detention.
- School 2 lateness policy: Any child who is late will be asked for a reason. Where concerns arise, the pastoral staff will discuss with the child the circumstances around the lateness and provide support where needed.

Fortunately, there is an increasing movement towards a more relationship-based approach to behaviour policies, and there are many good examples out there. The following statement can be found on the very first page of Colebourne Primary School's behaviour policy: 'Thinking of a child as behaving badly disposes you to think of punishment. Thinking of a child as struggling to handle something difficult encourages you to help them through their distress.'[2]


# 3. Provision and practice

This is where a school moves from understanding trauma and adversity and applying that new knowledge to its systems – to action. The hardest part of all!

It can be useful to consider this new approach to provision through the Birmingham Safeguarding Children's Partnership's Right Help, Right Time model where the types of provision are categorised into four sections:[3]

1   Universal – the standard level of provision for all children.

---

2   See https://www.hazwebs.co.uk/colebourne/?wpdmpro=behaviour-policy.
3   See https://www.lscpbirmingham.org.uk/delivering-effective-support.

2   Universal plus – for when a child and their family have needs that require support and interventions above and beyond normal universal services. These would usually be provided by staff in school.

3   Additional – when specialist or more intensive support is required; support that is often more expensive, but vital for those with increasingly complex or a variety of needs, and often requires involvement from more than one agency.

4   Complex and significant – when substantial extra provision and support is needed or there is reasonable cause to suspect the child is at risk of significant harm.

So, what sort of provision fits into these areas?

## Universal

Here are a few examples of universal provision that can be implemented in a trauma-responsive school at very little cost:

- Staff listen to children, are curious and empathetic, and have a desire to do what they can to help a child who is having a tough time.

- Trauma-responsive policies are applied consistently.

- There is no shouting from adults.

- The effective tracking of incidents helps to identify patterns and changes for support to be targeted.

- There are structures, routines and boundaries for all pupils with careful adaptations to meet individual needs.

- There is a predictability of people and situations.

- Any transitions and changes are planned with care.

- Staff consider the child, not the behaviour.

- The whole school community is reflective, looking at what the adult, the child and the system could have done differently, and then makes changes.

- Every member of staff knows what they can do on a day-to-day basis, from smiling and saying hello to children to recognising when a child is having a tough time.

## Universal plus

This is where schools need to start using existing funds or staff to provide additional support. The earlier schools can do this, the better chance there is of improved outcomes. Examples here include:

- Learning mentors.
- Family support workers.
- Pastoral or nurture rooms and sessions.
- Social and emotional groups.
- Learning intervention groups.
- Tuition.
- Outdoor learning sessions (e.g. forest school).
- Sensory equipment and tools.

## Additional

This is for those children with increasingly complex needs, and provision – at a cost – could include:

- One-to-one support.
- External specialists (e.g. psychologist, occupational therapist, music/drama/art therapist).
- Safe spaces such as nurture rooms that are available at any time should they be needed by the child.
- Higher levels of containment and/or structure for difficult times such as transitions.
- Key adults to 'meet and greet'.
- Adult support on hand at tricky times.
- Learning breaks.
- Alternative lessons and support when needed.

## Complex and significant

This is where significant support is needed for the child or family – potentially to avoid or reduce the risk of harm. This often requires support from child and adolescent mental health services or other statutory agencies.

In addition to the support they may receive under this area, the previous three areas remain critical for the day-to-day support required while the child is in school.

## Where to start?

It is important to have a plan to implement these three stages. A starting point could be:

- Add 'becoming trauma responsive' to your school improvement plan (as discussed under 'Making the change' in the previous chapter).

- Review your vision and values so they are aligned with your new thinking and approaches.

- Develop champions – teachers who are naturally nurturing or good with structure, and who build good relationships. In my experience, these will be the easiest to bring on board and the quickest to 'get it'.

- Engage with parents, especially those of the most vulnerable children and those with needs, and listen, listen, listen. Don't judge, don't become defensive, just listen. They will give you honest opinions – positive and negative – both of which can help you to move forward. (See Chapter 7 for more information on co-production.)

- Once you have made your mind up, remain open-minded to further change. As you learn, your approaches will develop.

All of this doesn't happen overnight or following a training day but develops over many years. It requires strong leadership and a plan – but it's worth it. How do I know? Since introducing this approach over many years, we have seen behaviour improve; there is less use of exclusions, higher levels of achievement and strong attendance figures. We have also seen high levels of satisfaction from parents. Oh, and the kids, including our square pegs, run into school smiling every morning (mostly!).

# Chapter 34

# SIX ESSENTIALS OF TRAUMA-INFORMED PRACTICE

## Mary Meredith

## Understand the neuroscience

The key message to take from the neuroscience, as we have heard in Chapter 27, is that children cannot learn, cannot develop in healthy ways and cannot fulfil their infinite potential if they do not feel psychologically safe.

The infant's brain develops from the bottom up – the downstairs brain maturing first (Perry and Szalavitz, 2017). These are the brain structures responsible for survival-related functions and our response to stress. The upper parts, which develop throughout childhood, are responsible for processes such as executive functioning, emotional regulation, reflection, memory, empathy and conscious learning.

The development of these upper regions depends on prior development of the lower regions. This means that when the stress response is repeatedly activated in the lower part of the brain – typically in the absence of safe, predictable and consistent relationships or through exposure to alarming experiences – then the sequence of brain maturity is disturbed. Neural connections are reduced or lost through a level of stress that has become damaging, and executive functioning in the upper cortical brain is compromised.

However, the developing brain is highly malleable and with the right stimulus – for example, immersion in a relational and nurturing school environment – children, young people and our square pegs can and do recover from what is properly called 'relational and developmental trauma', sometimes in rapid and seemingly miraculous ways.[1] What this means is that the stakes in relation to either acting on these lessons from neuroscience or neglecting their implications for practice could hardly be higher.

The relevance of this work in a pandemic era that has seen escalated hardship and adversity could not be clearer and any 'closing the gap' strategy or 'catch-up' campaign not underpinned by an understanding of the impact of childhood trauma is lacking a sound, biologically literate basis. Children cannot learn effectively in hypervigilant survival mode with access to the cortical brain constricted. The emotional regulation to counter this needs to be understood as the foundation of learning, and is the responsibility of all school staff.

## Relationships, relationships, relationships

As we have seen throughout this book, the antidote to trauma and the foundation for building a healthy adulthood is human connection. When we build an attuned relationship with a traumatised child, we help them to literally heal from trauma and strengthen their resilience.[2]

Of course, it is easy to argue that all teachers are engaged in relationships with their pupils on a daily basis, but for effective trauma-informed practice this must be done in a more strategic way. This means identifying – and then closing – relational gaps by providing those pupils who need it most with repeated positive relational experiences to help move them out of survival mode and allow stressors to be tolerated.

The behaviour of such pupils will often need the practitioner to be curious, not furious, and a useful tool for quantifying 'psychological belonging' – or the risky lack of this – is Carol Goodenow's (1993) sense of psychological belonging scale. Her research shows that 'school membership' weakens significantly after the transition from primary, which isn't really surprising. Without a relational strategy, adult–pupil relationships will inevitably be more superficial, transient and thus less psychologically safe than during the primary years, where one teacher and a limited number of teaching assistants are able to develop strong and protective bonds. Arguably, we see the impact of these looser connections through the differing exclusion and elective home education rates in England, as well as long-term absence and pupil mobility data, such as that provided in the deeply concerning 'Who's Left' report from FFT Education Data Lab (Nye and Thompson, 2018). The secondary-aged population is more mobile than the primary, multiple transitions correlating with both poorer academic and wellbeing outcomes (National College for School Leadership, 2011).

---

1   Note that trauma-informed practice has a wider reach than attachment theory, in that it acknowledges that the biological disturbance created by repeated activation of the stress response system can be rooted in a range of adverse experiences, not just disrupted attachment. See Cherry (2019).
2   Remember that, as we saw in Chapter 31, resilience isn't a personality type; it is all about connections and connecting.

Secondary school pastoral arrangements are vital, therefore, in that they can and must optimise the conditions for relationship-building. House systems which create a smaller community within the larger; tutors who remain with their forms all the way through to Year 11; mentoring and key adult schemes; access to a safe base or nurture room with a higher staff–pupil ratio; the wonderful coaching circles seen in schools such as Carr Manor where the mantra is, 'We know our pupils well' and XP where 'We are crew' (see Chapters 19 and 24). Pastoral structures such as these all allow consistent relationships to deepen over time.

# Set the PACE

Developmental dyadic practice (DDP), developed by Dan Hughes (Golding and Hughes, 2020), is a proven tool to support teachers – indeed, all school staff – as they develop their trauma-informed practice. At the heart of DDP is PACE – playfulness, acceptance, curiosity and empathy. For an example of how this can be used, see Brighton and Hove City Council's (2018) Attachment Aware Schools Toolkit which explores the use of PACE and emotion coaching in schools.

## Playfulness

Being playful around distressed and mistrustful children involves creating an atmosphere of lightness and interest when communicating with them. It means adopting a soft tone of voice, not an irritated or lecturing one. It's about being prepared to have fun and foster a sense of joy and playfulness.

Social bonds are strengthened by endorphin-releasing fun and laughter, and the strongest school communities make time for this, inside and outside the classroom. Cultural capital is one thing, but social capital has at least as much, and probably more, potential as a vehicle for social justice.[3]

## Acceptance

Unconditional acceptance is at the core of a child's sense of psychological safety. If we respond to dysregulated behaviour with a punitive, one-size-fits-all response, we quickly erode feelings of safety, thereby increasing vulnerability. Trauma-informed boundary-setting involves demonstrating, explicitly, that we accept the wishes, feelings, thoughts, urges, motives and perceptions that are underneath any unwanted

---

3   The saddest and most counterproductive behaviourist tactic in the traditional discipline rulebook is the barring of vulnerable pupils from fun, extra-curricular events under the label of 'consequences'. This denies them the very experiences they need to regulate and thrive, and serves to confirm their worst life lessons about the world of grown-ups, which is that they will let you down and cause pain. Consequences are important but they need to be productive, not vengeful.

outward behaviour, even as we unequivocally set limits on that behaviour. Pupils must learn to trust that whilst behaviour may be criticised and limited, this is not the same as criticising the self.

From your own practice, can you honestly say that fixed-term exclusions fix a child's behaviour on return? Anything that ostracises us is registered by our ancient brain as a threat to life, as Kip Williams' (2007) work on ostracism and social rejection confirms. Trauma-informed settings do not expect exclusion to improve behaviour, using it rarely.

## Curiosity

Curiosity without judgement is how we help children to become more aware of their inner life and able to reflect on the reasons for their behaviour. It asks us to consider the meaning behind the behaviour.

It means that when young Tyler is 'acting up', we ask (as we saw in Chapter 32) not 'What's wrong with you?' but 'What happened to you?' Whatever Tyler's response (or otherwise), he will have been soothed by these words because they communicate unconditional acceptance. More than that, they say to Tyler: here is an adult really trying to get me. Not condemning or judging me, but curious, interested and seeking to understand.

And once we have Tyler's emotional attention …

## Empathy

Tyler, it must be really scary to feel out of control and overwhelmed like that. Trust me, it'll get better and I'm always here to help you, but right now it's hard for you and I just want you to know that I'm really sorry about that.

With empathy, the teacher is demonstrating that they know how difficult an experience is for the pupil and that comfort and support is available. Empathy also opens children up to the possibility of learning:

Empathy builds secure attachment. The pupil feels more secure when inner experience is understood, accepted and empathized with. It is only with this experience of security that attachment systems can settle and the pupil's exploratory system can become active. Exploration is essential for learning. Empathy is central to helping pupils get into a state for learning. (Golding et al., 2021: 100)

If all staff understand something about PACE and attempt to relate to pupils in this way, then it is not difficult to imagine the positive impact on school climate. Small moments of kindness and connection provide the patterned, repetitive experiences which enable new connections to become hardwired. All staff, from lunchtime supervisor to head teacher, have an equally important contribution to make to a school's relational culture.

# The power of emotional regulation

We know that hypervigilant children are very easily triggered, and even seemingly inconsequential events can dysregulate highly sensitised children:

> Eye contact for too long may be perceived as a life-threatening signal. A friendly touch on the shoulder may remind one child of sexual abuse by a stepfather. A well-intentioned gentle tease to one may be a humiliating cut to another, similar to the endless sarcastic and degrading abuse he experiences at home. A request to solve a problem on the board may terrify the girl living in a home where she can never do well enough. A slightly raised voice may feel like a shout to the boy living in a violent home. (Perry and Szalavitz, 2017: 298)

Schools are challenging environments for a square peg with a sensory vulnerability or an autobiographical one (Mother's Day activities might be painful, for example). Reasonable adjustments should be carefully considered when a child is unable to cope with an excess of stimuli and anxiety-provoking unpredictability, such as during unstructured time.

However, even with everything in place, vulnerable children may well still dysregulate from time to time, and all staff need to be prepared and able to co-regulate them – to help them regulate themselves – when this is the case. Punishing children at this point will be hugely counterproductive in the long run, and it is far better to adopt Bruce Perry's three Rs of *regulate* (to bring the thinking brain back online), *relate* (to create psychological safety) and *reason* (to promote reflection and learning).[4]

Of course, what we really want is for children to learn to healthily regulate themselves, sometimes known as self-soothing. Introducing and practising such strategies needs to be done when children are calm and also shared with all pupils, not least so they are in the best possible position to support their struggling peers.

---

4   See https://beaconhouse.org.uk/wp-content/uploads/2019/09/The-Three-Rs.pdf.

The regulation toolkits for primary and secondary settings developed by Lincolnshire Behaviour Outreach Support Service (2020a and b) suggest a number of grounding and regulating strategies, from deep breathing exercises to muscle relaxation. Every child is different and will benefit from a different approach, so it is important to practise a range of approaches.

Thought should be given to the school day itself and whether it is biologically respectful. We are not designed to be still for long periods, after all. Stress-reducing classroom brain breaks are strongly supported by the evidence (Desautels, 2017) and can be utilised as 10-minute distractor breaks that enable spaced learning – another biologically respectful approach (Fields, 2005). The sensory circuits seen in many primary school corridors are proving effective here too.

Practising co-regulation and teaching self-regulation require the adult to be regulated. Because of the mirroring neurobiology of our brains, one of the best ways to help another person become calm and centred is simply to be present for them and to be calm and centred ourselves.[5] This is why staff wellbeing is such a priority in any school that priorities high-quality pastoral care.

# Harness the kindness of children

There is no more compelling truth in the whole of the trauma field than Alexander den Heijer's observation that when a flower fails to bloom, it is asking for more conducive conditions (2018: 22).

This is vividly illustrated in the final case study of *The Boy Who Was Raised as a Dog* (Perry and Szalavitz, 2017), about an adopted child who had endured extreme neglect in a Russian orphanage. Despite his loving home, Peter was struggling badly in school, much to the frustration and anger of his classmates and the distress of his adoptive parents. To help, Perry arranged to speak to the class about Peter's early experiences, the way that his 'amazing brain' had adapted and the issues that this was now creating for him.

The chapter is called 'The Kindness of Children' because, when that was harnessed, Peter's world changed utterly and school quickly became a place of growth and healing rather than re-traumatisation. Hostile attitudes were transformed to the extent that classmates became an enthusiastic and compassionate support team for Peter, revolutionising his experience of school.

Peter's classmates contributed substantially to his progress once they understood not just his history but his neuroscience. In the UK, there is now a plethora of excellent

---

5   Emotional contagion means that the reverse is also true, of course – dysregulated adults dysregulate children.

teaching materials that can be utilised as a key component of the statutory mental health curriculum. For example, the Anna Freud Centre offers lesson plans and animations on brain development and neuroscience,[6] whilst the *Compassionate and Connected Classroom Curricular Resource* is a comprehensive, downloadable personal, social, health and economic publication from Education Scotland (2021), aimed at Key Stages 2 and 3.

The hallmark of great resources in this area is that they have the potential to increase both compassionate understanding and self-acceptance. Too often, children and young people are filled with a sense of themselves as 'mad or bad' because of their maladaptive behaviours. Belonging to a supportive educational community has the potential to transform this self-defeating mindset into one of hope.

# Prioritise staff wellbeing

Trauma-informed staff must give of themselves. A lot. Empathy is hard emotional labour and compassion fatigue is real 'because in order to connect with you, I have to connect with something in myself that knows that feeling' (Brown, 2013). Because of this, staff wellbeing is always a priority in a trauma-informed setting with leaders consistently modelling the model.

Again, achieving this need not be that onerous. For example, a Coqual study found that the most powerful strategy was one that was both simple and light touch (Twaronite, 2017). Employees felt happiest when their colleagues simply checked in with them, both personally and professionally. This was true across genders and age groups. By reaching out and acknowledging their colleagues on a personal level, school leaders can significantly enhance the wellbeing of staff by making them feel valued and connected.

As mentioned elsewhere, supervision is important within a trauma-informed organisation, providing staff with a reflective 'safe space' to offload work that might be impacting them personally. Supervision should be long term, consistent, not a chore and not necessarily provided by line managers (unless trained in supervision). Group or individual models can be effective, and there is certainly no one-size-fits-all approach to this.

A training day does not a trauma-informed school make. At a time, in England especially, where the long-held traditions of discipline, authority and what constitutes 'standards' in the classroom are resurgent,[7] it can be hard to go against the grain amidst accusations of being 'soft' or 'progressive'. However, a grassroots movement of

---

6   See www.annafreud.org.
7   England is traditionally punitive: we were, after all, the last country in Western Europe to abolish the cane, in 1986, and in an atmosphere of moral panic.

trauma-informed practice is gathering momentum, and there are an increasing number of models of great practice demonstrating how we can transform the troubled lives of our square pegs. And with every such transformation there is a reason to hope.

# References

Balvin, N. and Banati, P. (2017) *The Adolescent Brain: A Second Window of Opportunity – A Compendium*. Florence: UNICEF Office of Research – Innocenti. Available at: https://www.unicef-irc.org/publications/933-the-adolescent-brain-a-second-window-of-opportunity-a-compendium.html.

Brighton and Hove City Council (2018) *Developing an Attachment Aware Behaviour Regulation Policy: Guidance for Brighton & Hove Schools* (September). Available at: https://www.brighton-hove.gov.uk/sites/default/files/migrated/article/inline/Behaviour%20Regulation%20Policy%20Guidance%20-%20Sep%2018_1.pdf.

Brown, B. (2013) The Power of Vulnerability [video] (15 August). Available at: https://www.youtube.com/watch?v=sXSjc-pbXk4.

Cherry, K. (2019) What is Attachment Theory? The Importance of Early Bonds, *Verywell Mind* (24 June). Available at: https://www.verywellmind.com/what-is-attachment-theory-2795337.

den Heijer, A. (2018) *Nothing You Don't Already Know: Remarkable Reminders About Meaning, Purpose, and Self-Realization*. N.p.: Alexander den Heijer.

Desautels, L. (2017) Quick Classroom Exercises to Combat Stress, *Edutopia* (23 October). Available at: https://www.edutopia.org/article/quick-classroom-exercises-combat-stress.

Education Scotland (2021) *The Compassionate and Connected Classroom Curricular Resource*. Available at: https://education.gov.scot/improvement/learning-resources/compassionate-and-connected-classroom.

Fields, R. D. (2005) Making Memories Stick, *Scientific American* (1 February). Available at: https://www.scientificamerican.com/article/making-memories-stick.

Golding, K. S. and Hughes, D. A. (2020) Dyadic Developmental Psychotherapy: Using Relationships to Heal Children Traumatised By Their Early Relationships, *Adoption Today* (February). Available at: https://ddpnetwork.org/backend/wp-content/uploads/2020/02/Dyadic-Developmental-Psychotherapy-DDP-Golding-and-Hughes-Adoption-UK-2020.pdf.

Golding, K. S., Phillips, S. and Bombèr, L. M. (2021) *Working with Relational Trauma in Schools: An Educator's Guide to Using Dyadic Developmental Practice*. London: Jessica Kingsley.

Goodenow, C. (1993) Classroom Belonging Among Early Adolescent Students: Relationships to Motivation and Achievement, *Journal of Early Adolescence*, 13(1): 21–43.

Lincolnshire Behaviour Outreach Support Service (2020a) *Toolkit for Regulation: Maintaining Positive Behaviour in the Classroom*. London: Family Action. Available at: https://www.family-action.org.uk/content/uploads/2022/04/Toolkit-for-Regulation-Primary-1.pdf.

Lincolnshire Behaviour Outreach Support Service (2020b) *Toolkit for Regulation: Secondary School. Maintaining Positive Behaviour in the Classroom*. London: Family Action. Available at: https://www.family-action.org.uk/content/uploads/2022/04/Toolkit-for-Regulation-Secondary-School-1.pdf.

National College for School Leadership (2011) *Managing Pupil Mobility to Maximise Learning: Full Report*. Available at: https://www.gov.uk/government/publications/managing-pupil-mobility-to-maximise-learning.

Nye, P. and Thompson, D. (2018) Who's Left 2018. Part One: The Findings, *FFT Education Datalab* (21 June). Available at: https://ffteducationdatalab.org.uk/2018/06/whos-left-2018-part-one-the-main-findings.

Perry, B. and Szalavitz, M. (2017) *The Boy Who Was Raised as a Dog: And Other Stories from a Child Psychiatrist's Notebook*. New York: Basic Books.

Twaronite, K. (2019) The Surprising Power of Asking Coworkers How They're Doing, *Harvard Business Review* (28 February). Available at: https://hbr.org/2019/02/the-surprising-power-of-simply-asking-coworkers-how-theyre-doing.

Williams, K. D. (2007) Ostracism, *Annual Review of Psychology*, 58: 425–445.

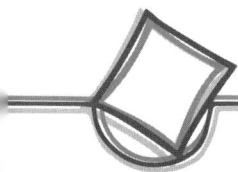

Part V

# BEYOND THE
# HERE AND NOW

# Introduction

So where does this leave us? There are many (including Square Peg, Not Fine in School and several of the contributors in this book) working to change the system – we believe this is necessary and will happen. But it will take Time with a capital T, and requires a complex shift in mindset from government through to the whole of society.

In the meantime, what can we learn from beyond the mainstream – from the progressive side of education (which is growing daily – a sure sign of the deficits in the mainstream), from youthwork, from business? Even paramedics attending a 999 call involving a child have learnings to share with us, as we saw in Chapter 8.

This broader learning should give us hope and inspire educators to find creative ways around the system constraints. It should fuel partnerships with those working outside the system for mutual benefit. It must persuade business to better prepare our young people for the working world they are about to encounter. And it needs to encourage everyone involved to network their socks off, bolstering the support they can offer, so we end up with fewer and fewer square pegs as our system slowly morphs and extends to accommodate the needs of the individual. And one day, hopefully, the mainstream system will be less volume sausage factory and more crafted artisan bakery, full of choice, individuality and joy.

# Chapter 35

# BEYOND THE CONVENTIONAL

## Ian Cunningham, Peter Gray, Martin Illingworth, Trevor Sutcliffe and Jo Symes

Darren can tell you the difference between a 'pet' and a 'breeder' if you are looking for a new ferret. He can tell you what gender a new-born ferret is and can instruct you on what the best feeds are and where to get them. He can estimate the weekly cost of keeping a ferret and can show you how to make a great living space for it. He can let you know how long it will be before the ferret is an adult and will lose its friendly nature. He is also good at showing you how to handle a ferret.

On the subject of ferrets, Darren speaks with knowledge, clarity and confidence.

His teachers may not think of his knowledge about ferrets in terms of being educated. What he knows, his expertise, is entirely separate from his schooling. Darren's knowledge and skill will go unrecorded and unremarked. What is noted is his ignorance about other things (the Weimar Republic, Banquo's ghost, the French for 'post office'). Unforgivably, he is likely to leave school carrying that ignorance with him.

Sammy doesn't like to talk much and has few real friends, but she can't half play the clarinet. She has reached Grade 7 in her music exams (one more to go) and has completed Grade 6 in her music theory. She is an intuitive player who is able to add a good sense of feel for the music alongside her technical ability to follow the score. She has also learned about classical music and has noticed its echoes in some modern music. She was not able to go on a recent school trip to see the Birmingham Symphony Orchestra because her scores in English and maths were not high enough.

No one knows she plays the clarinet, and her knowledge and skill will also go unrecorded and unremarked, unlike her ignorance (also unforgivably).

Darren and Sammy are square pegs.

Current assessment systems are not only flawed but inherently unfair. To start with, they are imposed on children. This seems to be an unacceptable impact on the freedom of the individual. Testing can be useful but needs to be chosen by the individual. For instance, people choose to take a driving test – or not. And they can learn to drive in any way they want – 1,000 hours with a motoring school or 20 hours learning from mum and dad. As a society, we don't care how the person learns to drive so long as they can prove their ability in the test in a real car on a real road. The driving test is the most important test in our society, and it's important that individuals are free not to take the test if they don't plan to drive and, if they do take the test, they are free to learn any way they want.

Choice works. For example, at SML College, near Brighton, students choose whatever tests and exams they take, when they take them and how they learn in preparation for them.[1] There is a long and rich history of self-directed learning in the UK, United States and elsewhere. It goes against the narrative that children are feral unless closely directed, and that some children's situations are too chaotic for them to be able to make the right choices about their lives and education. But time and time again, the evidence shows us that choice and consensual education works.

Take Sudbury Valley School in the United States, a self-directed, democratic school founded in 1968, with no formal timetable and no curriculum (unless requested by the students). Psychologist and researcher Dr Peter Gray's 10-year-old son attended this school. His son was happy, but Dr Gray had several concerns and questions which went on to inform his research (Gray, 2013):

- Might such a school be narrowing his son's future options?
- Would he be able to go on to college?
- Might certain career paths be cut off?

Despite reassurances from staff members and parents of former students, as a scientist and conscientious parent he was not fully satisfied. To address his concerns, he conducted a systematic study of the school's graduates with fellow researcher David Chanoff. The results, published in the *American Journal of Education* in 1986, found that:

- 75% of graduates went on to higher education.
- Those who pursued higher education reported no difficulty getting into colleges of their choice.
- Graduates were remarkably successful in finding employment that personally interested them.
- The students had gone on to a wide range of careers that are valued by society (Gray and Chanoff, 1986; see also Greenberg and Sadofsky, 1992; Greenberg et al., 2005).

---

1   See https://smlcollege.org.uk.

Subsequent detailed studies have shown that Sudbury Valley graduates can be found working as entrepreneurs, artists, musicians, scientists, social workers, skilled craftsmen, nurses, doctors and more. Importantly, they report that they are happy with their lives.

As we have seen elsewhere in this book, there is a misconception that being kind means being soft. Equally, it is a fallacy to believe that progressive alternatives underperform in terms of academic achievement, no matter how counterintuitive this might seem to those of us raised, albeit apparently successfully, in a conventional system of command and control.

Let's look at a UK example now – Summerhill, founded in 1921 by Alexander Sutherland Neill in Suffolk.[2] Following Ofsted's inspection in 1999 it was threatened with closure. One complaint concerned assessment. The school's view is that formal assessment and testing should only be carried out with the student's permission. Ofsted's complaint alleged that this approach inhibited student progress.

In response to the Ofsted report, a team of education experts carried out its own independent inquiry into Summerhill School (Cunningham, 2000), and found substantial evidence of students succeeding academically where they had previously been failing in the state system.

The independent report also demonstrated how results from progressive alternatives can't always be compared like for like with those from the state sector. Students at Summerhill (like many independent schools) can stagger their GCSEs. Therefore, comparing Summerhill results from examinations taken at 16 with those from state schools won't show the true picture, as this would exclude results from the bright, keen students who take their exams early, as well as those from the majority who, given the freedom to work at their own pace, take them at 17. When compared fairly, the independent inquiry found that Summerhill's results were actually above the national average, with the school pointing out that, over the previous five years, 82% of students have received a pass or higher in their GCSEs.

In 2000, the school won a historic legal battle against the Department for Education and Employment when it defended the rights and voices of its children at an independent schools tribunal (see Wells, 2000). Summerhill is now the most legally protected school in the country with a unique inspection process that is the first to include the voices of children.[3]

Teacher training rarely touches on the principles of self-directed learning, but there are some important lessons that all school leaders need to know. You may not have the agency to remove your school from the mainstream, especially when it comes to

---

2   See https://www.summerhillschool.co.uk.
3   A CBBC drama, *Summerhill* (2008) was made out of the story - see https://www.youtube.com/watch?v=xFf49hALm58. The report of the independent inquiry into Summerhill can be found at http://summerhill.paed.com/summ/sml.htm.

assessments, but you have a responsibility to be aware of what lies beyond, to challenge where the mainstream ethos compromises your own beliefs about education and to support those families whose square pegs are failing in the mainstream.

In essence, self-directed education is about creating an environment designed to optimise young people's abilities to educate themselves. In summary, the primary elements are as follows:

- **The social expectation in school is that their education is the children's responsibility.** Children come into the world with the intuitive understanding that they are in charge of their own education, but they can be disabused of such notions through coercive schooling practices, where they have little autonomy and are told repeatedly that, to become educated, they must do what they are told. With self-directed learning, staff do not attempt to direct children's education and do not undermine children's understanding that education is their responsibility.

- **Unlimited time to play, explore and pursue their own interests.** To educate themselves well, children need great amounts of free time – to make friends, explore, play, daydream, get bored, overcome boredom, make mistakes and learn from mistakes. They need time for fleeting interests and to immerse themselves deeply in activities that engage their passions. This is how children learn about themselves and discover what is meaningful and satisfying to them. Such discovery is the foundation for education.

- **Opportunity to play with the tools of the culture.** Much of anyone's education has to do with learning to use the relevant tools of the culture in which we live. Some of these tools are relevant to nearly everyone growing up today in a developed country, such as the written word, the number system and computers. Research shows that children growing up in a literate, numerate and digital environment will learn to read, calculate and use computers effectively simply through living (Pattinson, 2016). To what extent is your school such an environment? To what extent, as you will find in self-directed schools, do children have free access to other tools, such as a fully equipped kitchen, a shop for tinkering, sporting equipment and a variety of other tools bought or donated to serve the expressed needs or interests of enrolled students? To play with the tools is to do your own thing with them, to use them creatively, not just follow someone else's directions.[4]

- **Free association among school members of all ages.** Children are designed by nature to learn from other children, and they learn most when they are interacting with others over a broad range of ages. One of the detrimental aspects

---

4  Of course, with some tools the children need to show that they know the potential dangers and can use them safely before they are allowed to do their own thing with them. Just as it is with adults.

of our coercive schooling system is the segregation of children by age. But it doesn't have to be that way. Maybe your school has experimented with vertical tutor groups, for example. Research at Sudbury Valley, where students typically range from age 4 to late teens, has revealed many ways in which younger children learn from older ones and older children learn from younger ones (Gray and Feldman, 2004; Gray, 2011). For example, children who can't yet read or can't yet add (or subtract or multiply or divide) numbers, commonly learn such skills through playing games or engaging in other activities involving these skills with older children who can do them. In turn, older children learn to nurture and lead through interactions with younger ones and are often inspired by the younger children's energy and creativity.

- **Access to a variety of adults who are helpers, not judges.** Adult staff members at most self-directed schools don't call themselves 'teachers' because they don't think they do any more teaching than anyone else at the school. Yet, the adult staff are crucial. They manage most of the business of the school. They provide the upper end of the age-mixed social environment. They provide models of what it is to be an adult. And, when asked, they provide help, advice and wisdom. Nor do they judge. After all, judgement from anyone other than the learner, unless the learner has solicited that judgement, is meaningless. Everyone is on a different track and there is no rationale for comparing one student with another. If a student asks a staff member for feedback on an essay she has written, most staff members will gladly comply, but they would never impose such judgement.

- **Immersion in a stable, moral and caring community.** Children are designed to develop best when they grow up in a community of people who care about one another, care about the community they are part of, and experience – through the community – a set of values and norms that enable people to get along peaceably with one another. It's no surprise then that democratic principles underpin so many unconventional schools. Traditional schools may teach lessons about democracy and responsibility (in an autocratic way), but in schools such as Sudbury Valley and Summerhill these lessons are learned through living them.

Alternative schools, such as those described here – without required courses, tests, grades or passing or failing – also bypass another pernicious element of the traditional exam system – the discrimination against summer-born children (see Chapter 18).

With an exam system focused on the summer and where cohorts of children are formed from those born between 1 September and 31 August, many studies show us that summer-born children are hugely discriminated against (Department for Education, 2010; Cunningham, 2021). For instance, the Department for Education's own research shows that at least 10,000 summer-born children have significantly worse results at GCSE than autumn-born children just because of their birth date. They found that 18.8% of August-born young people enter university at 18 compared with 21.3% for September-born young people. Figures also show that by the age of 7,

August-born children are nearly 90% more likely to be identified as special educational needs than September-born children, experiencing a range of challenges including learning, speech and language difficulties (Department for Education, 2010).

The COVID-19 pandemic showed us something important: that you can switch off the button marked 'exams' across the world and life still goes on. This should give heart to all of us in education who know how much the exam dog wags the education tail. And let's not forget the catastrophic pressure that exams put not just on our square pegs but on all children. Just look at Ditch the Label's 2020 Annual Bullying Survey (of over 13,000 children and young people) and you will find that the top two contributors to negative mental health were not bullying but school and exam pressures.[5]

While school ministers (and for-profit exam boards) try to get the toothpaste back in the tube, it is worth considering what we can do to ensure children like Darren and Sammy leave school with their knowledge and skill highlighted, not simply their ignorance. That they enter adulthood with the same life chances as Dr Peter Gray's son and other alumni of successful unconventional schools. You might not be able to defeat the system, no matter how flawed you know it to be,[6] but as we have seen throughout this book, there is still so much you can do.

Step one, again a common theme, is to consider how you can make your school an environment which is less coercive and more consensual, where you can build in choice and flexibility, and demonstrate to your students that this is their school as much as it is yours. This requires you to know your children – square pegs included – inside out. Everyone deserves to be celebrated for something. You might need to dig deep, but so be it. Great tutors can help here, as can non-academic mentors and coaches.

Step two is to ensure you offer the widest possible range of opportunities for children and young people to experience, both academic and non-academic, exam-based and otherwise. Be creative with time, people, places and budgets. Resist that pressure to make every moment in school about grades. Remember to fight the academic snobbery that exists, especially with parents and staff.

Step three is to make sure you communicate your intentions fully with all parents and carers, and especially with the families of your square pegs who may have already switched off – or been switched off – from education. Always talk in terms of hope, possibilities, multiple pathways and opportunities. Highlight positives; again, dig deep where you have to.

---

5   See https://www.ditchthelabel.org/research-papers/the-annual-bullying-survey-2020.
6   And don't get us started on the English Baccalaureate.

In a world where employment rates can be as low as 6% for our disabled and special educational needs children (Silvester, 2020), this 'can do' attitude is essential. So, while schools continue to endure the examination-led system of assessment, senior leadership teams must plan for the successes of all pupils.

For example, some families have no tradition or experience of going to university. This limits the likelihood that university is an option for children from these families (just as Will Carter experienced in Chapter 5). Schools should make all children and their families aware of the route to higher education and the links the school has established with university admissions officers, university open days and university budgeting and bursary planning. To limit access to this kind of provision would limit the potential for a child to choose this pathway.

Similarly, university (and debt) is not the only way to leave school with your head held high and your name on a plaque somewhere. We must support all students in understanding the full range of options available to them.

Perhaps, though, before we consider any of these steps, we need to agree on what we mean by 'education'. Perhaps, we need to identify a definition that helps us to move away from one that can be measured in or defined by tests passed, courses completed or grades obtained. 'Success' in education can be many things and should never be focused on qualifications. How about: *education is everything a person learns that enables that person to live a satisfying, meaningful and moral life*?

Isn't this what we want for our own children? Isn't this what governments should want for their citizens? Isn't it clear that our schooling system fails to educate by this definition? How many people have university degrees but still fail to live satisfying, meaningful or moral lives?

Education, real education, is different for every person. We aren't all on the same life path. What is satisfying and meaningful to one person will be quite different from what is satisfying and meaningful to another. That is wonderful. That is what makes life interesting and makes an economy hum. We need people with different goals, tastes, insights and knowledge.

Our schools try to squeeze everyone through the same round hole. It's not just a few square pegs who don't fit; nobody fits. Everyone gets distorted (Olson, 2009). Real education requires freedom, not coercion, and freedom includes the freedom to choose your own path. Coercion freezes the mind. It creates anger and anxiety. It inhibits enquiry, critical thinking and curiosity. Children learning what they want to learn shine; children learning from coercion, just to pass a test, can often look quite dull.

# References

Cunningham, I. (2000) *An Independent Inquiry into Summerhill School*. Brighton: Centre for Self Managed Learning.

Cunningham, I. (2021) *Self Managed Learning and the New Educational Paradigm*. Abingdon and New York: Routledge.

Department for Education (2010) *Month of Birth and Education*. Research Report DFE-RR017. Available at: https://www.gov.uk/government/publications/month-of-birth-and-education-schools-analysis-and-research-division.

Gray, P. (2011) The Special Value of Children's Age-Mixed Play, *American Journal of Play*, 3, 500–522.

Gray, P. (2013) *Free to Learn: Why Unleashing the Instinct to Play Will Make Our Children Happier, More Self-Reliant, and Better Students for Life*. New York: Basic Books.

Gray, P. and Chanoff, D. (1986) Democratic Schooling: What Happens to Young People Who Have Charge of Their Own Education?, *American Journal of Education*, 94(2): 182–213.

Gray, P. and Feldman, J. (2004) Playing in the Zone of Proximal Development: Qualities of Self-Directed Age Mixing Between Adolescents and Young Children at a Democratic School, *American Journal of Education*, 110(2): 108–145.

Greenberg, D. and Sadofsky, M. (1992) *Legacy of Trust: Life After the Sudbury Valley School Experience*. Framingham, MA: Sudbury Valley School Press.

Greenberg, D., Sadofsky, M. and Lempka, J. (2005) *The Pursuit of Happiness: The Lives of Sudbury Valley Alumni*. Framingham, MA: Sudbury Valley School Press.

Ofsted (1999) Summerhill School: Standard Inspection (1–5 March). Available at: https://files.ofsted.gov.uk/v1/file/758971.

Olson, K. (2009) *Wounded by School: Recapturing the Joy in Learning and Standing Up to Old School Culture*. New York: Teachers College Press.

Pattinson, H. (2016) *Rethinking Learning to Read*. Shrewsbury: Education Heretics Press.

Silvester, P. (2020) Pathways to Employment for SEND Pupils, *SSAT Journal*, 17(spring/summer). Available at: https://www.ssatuk.co.uk/blog/pathways-to-employment-for-send-pupils.

Wells, M. (2000) Summerhill Survives After Ofsted Mauling, *The Guardian* (23 March). Available at: https://www.theguardian.com/education/2000/mar/23/schools.mattwells.

# Chapter 36

# 14 LESSONS FROM YOUTHWORK

## Simon Edwards, Richard Evea, Gina McCabe and Alasdair McCarrick

## Lesson 1

Richard: As a whole-staff team, we had asked the Year 11 students to break with tradition and not throw eggs on their final day at school. Almost to a student they accepted our request, but one student threw an egg in my direction and ran off. I saw him a couple of days later when he came in to sit an exam. I asked him to sit down with me so that I might understand why he had disobeyed.

He was slightly apologetic, since he said that he understood my request, but then he surprised me. He explained that he expected that I would say something to the effect that I had earned not just his respect but also his gratitude for all I had done for him and others as head of school.

However, he pointed out that he owed me nothing. I should, he said, take comfort in my own reward. I had done everything I had because I was doing what I regarded as a 'good job'. I did it for myself and not for him. My sense of fulfilment was all the reward I deserved. If I had genuinely cared about him, then where was I when he and his dad were hungry? Where was I when a long list of things had gone wrong? Where was I when he needed me? I was not there for him. I was doing a job based on my understanding of the needs of the majority.

He was correct. Harsh, but still correct. The challenge is daunting. He challenged me to find a way in which I could increasingly focus on individual needs, whilst at the same time working for the good of the whole school community.

This insight and many others served to help me become a better leader. They were serendipitous, unplanned and random. There must be ways in which school leaders can capture feedback on the impact their work has on all their young people. For me, the insights gained from youthwork and the insights of youth workers constituted an obvious starting point.

Youth workers have a quite different relationship with young people from the one most teachers have; it is less formal, less bound by rules. They can engineer, or at least wait for, opportunities for informal discussion of highly personal topics in a safe environment: gender identity, relationship issues, who I am becoming and so much more. General pictures will emerge of community and sub-community issues that can be shared, and alerts raised for individuals that a mentor or coach would find invaluable.

But youth and community work is not a single entity. It appears to me to be a collective noun that encompasses a broad range of youth- and community-centred activities which have a familial relationship. They appear to belong to the same family but, in fact, are quite different.

If there is a set of core objectives that accurately reflect the drivers of youthwork, it would be instructive to lay these alongside those for teaching and social work, and see the opportunities for cooperation and collaboration, and creating space to listen to the voices and lived experiences of young people in our care. More than that, it could also provide an opportunity to identify areas of apparent conflict in understandings.

## Lesson 2

Simon: It seems a bit odd, perhaps, to suggest revisiting the ethos and practices of youthwork as a way forward, particularly as much of what might be considered as youthwork in England today is associated with an eclectic mix of uniformed and religious groups, community organisations and some statutory projects that seemingly have different aims and objectives and ways of working with young people.

A significant proportion of youthwork also receives targeted funding and meets a brief embedded in the underlying ethos of the organisation, one that can be very different from that of other organisations that may also be working with the same young people.

For example, some organisations focus on diverting young people away from crime through sport, whilst others support them via mentoring programmes. Some devise a curriculum of activities to create pathways for young people into membership of the organisation's adult communities and social norms, whilst others support young people as they transition more generally through adolescence to become adult citizens in wider society.

This may seem like a confusing mix of different ways of working with young people, but they can be brought together under the umbrella of four overarching models. Furlong (2013: 245–246) identifies these as:

1 **Social control.** Youth organisations view the young people they support as a threat to social order. The work focuses on monitoring and controlling young people's behaviour.[1]

2 **Socialising.** This model focuses on developing young people's values in line with social expectations. Its focus is on empowerment to seize new opportunities but in reality takes a deficit view of young people.[2]

3 **Informal education.** Drawing on the work of Freire (1972) and liberation education, this approach places young people – seen as an oppressed and subordinate group – at the heart of decision-making processes in order to take responsibility for their own development and human flourishing.[3]

4 **Citizenship.** This model places emphasis on supporting young people's access to support services and focuses on their social integration in order to become active participants in society.[4]

Generally, each model of youthwork falls, according to Banks (1994; cited in Furlong 2013: 244), within the remit of either personal and social development, preventative work, leisure-based work or youth social work.

Perhaps, then, youthwork can still offer viable principles and practices that can support school leaders in addressing issues around education disadvantage and inequity.

# Lesson 3

Simon: The approach to youthwork that Richard and I applied in the schools where we both worked emerged from my own experiences of working with young people whilst living on council housing estates for 18 years. These experiences framed my understanding of the interrelationship between young people, family and community members, and the need to develop youthwork *with* young people rather that do youthwork *to* them, in order to affect personal and social change.

---

1 For example, in the early 1960s, the social control model was primarily endorsed by youth services in response to moral panics related to the activities of the Mods and Rockers.
2 Socialising approaches coincided with growing employment and leisure opportunities provided by the consumer boom of the late 1960s.
3 A focus towards informal education and its inherent process-led, rather than target-led, approaches emerged in the 1970s to coincide with the economic crash and growing political unrest, particularly among young people. This model remained central to youthwork in statutory services until the late 1990s.
4 This model was central to much statutory youthwork when the New Labour government introduced the Transforming Youth Work agenda which refocused youthwork on meeting police targets. This model later developed into the National Citizen Service (NCS). However, as the NCS was underpinned by police targets, this might be seen as a passive social control model.

One particular experience informs this mindset. The estate on which my wife and I lived with our two young children in our one-bedroomed flat experienced a spate of arson attacks, damage to properties (including our flat) and growing unrest among young people, which resulted in a number of assaults. At this time, my wife and I were asked by friends on the estate (who seemed to like, confide in and respect us – one was also our babysitter) to support their children in their social development and also their schoolwork.

This led to us setting up our first youth club, in our flat, with the support of a forward-thinking church youth worker who offered guidance (but no financial or practical support). We ran small groups or video evenings with about six young people in our flat with the consent and knowledge of their parents. This youthwork culminated in the young people and their parents working together to hire a local community centre and a band for a benefit event for the community. Over 50 young people attended, and many of these young people and those attending our small youth group went on to access and attend a larger church youth provision which supported their developmental and personal learning needs.

It was this ethos, with its mindset of education as a relationally inspired and community-led – not top-down organisation-led – process of personal and social transformation which underpinned the youthwork that I and a team of seven part-time youth workers later delivered.

We focused on the processes involved in establishing relationships with young people, rather than on specific targeted outcomes, which meant we could concentrate on young person-led activities that supported their social, educational and personal development to flourish, rather than focusing on meeting the outcome-led targets of the statutory youth service and formal school Ofsted frameworks at the time.

Moreover, this model was adopted in the local school where Richard was the head teacher. He authorised the extension of some of the school's alternative curriculum provision to the youth centre.

This school/youthwork partnership was not just a paper exercise. It required the youth centre and its youthwork provision and principles of practice to be accepted and reserved as a safe relational space in which the school's leadership team could meet and discuss issues the young people faced in their schooling openly and candidly, but always with a view to exploring new ways forward without the threat of punishment, coercion or retribution.

In particular, the young people wanted a social space on the school site that was free from the oversight of teachers, but where their academic learning could be supported holistically alongside their social and personal development. The collaboration between the school and the youth centre's team of youth workers then created this space in a democratic way.

Specifically, the school leaders did not impose school-based behaviour expectations or rules within that social space, and voluntary participation was essential for all activities carried out by any school-based staff wishing to use the centre. Neither was withdrawal of freedom to attend the youth centre site or its activities used as a threat in the light of perceived poor behaviour in classes.

Rather, the senior leadership team (SLT) focused on this site as a place of social restoration and positive relationship-building. This was not to overlook poor behaviour, but behaviour was not the focus of the youthwork being carried out. Instead, the youthwork programme worked on a strengths-based approach which sought to identify and develop young people's innate abilities and recognise their true worth, regardless of accredited outcomes or school expectations.

# Lesson 4

Simon: In practice, the approach outlined above put young people in the driving seat of their own development and future goals, but within a highly supportive relational framework. The site was one of nurturing their 'being' and also their 'becoming' by creating a central space and context of social relationships in which they also felt they belonged.

They were affirmed and loved (yes, I use this word deliberately) unconditionally. Moreover, this trust developed with young people resulted in appointing 22 junior youth leaders from among them whom we supported to develop the curriculum, manage and raise funds, appoint staff members, lead youth sessions, arrange offsite trips and residential breaks, and liaise with the local MP, councillors, police chief inspector and the SLT at the school on issues that affected their lives. They each had job descriptions and specific responsibilities in the centre and also collectively developed their own behaviour rules and boundaries, which were agreed by the other 200 young people who attended the centre each week. This process was adopted by the SLT with their own student council who developed the behaviour system across the whole school accordingly.

These processes formed a trust-based relational platform, which enabled the SLT to develop and introduce an alternative curriculum course that was supported by teachers and enabled excluded students to remain on the school site and sit their GCSEs. This extended to the SLT authorising payment for a cafe to be built in the youth centre, which was designed by the young people attending the alternative curriculum course. They gained accreditation for this design and also for later designing the menus and staffing models applied there.

These same young people served in the cafe with their peers and developed their confidence to host local events with their MP and community groups. Of course, this was not a place just for our square pegs but for all young people attending the school. Indeed, over 50 students subsequently gained food hygiene and first aid certificates alongside their Duke of Edinburgh's Awards. Moreover, many of the junior leaders were highly academic but had little self-confidence or opportunity to flourish socially elsewhere.

## Lesson 5

Simon: Despite what it may look like, approaches taken from youthwork, which are designed to support the personal and social development of young people, such as those outlined above, don't reject structure. Their apparent informality is based around the fluid nature of young people's relationships as *subjects* within school and wider local communities, rather than *objects* to be acted on as a means to an end. It is within these relationships and social networks that informal education, in the form of personal and social skills development alongside values transference, begins and emerges. Here, voluntary participation embedded in social and community practices is key.

Furthermore, if SLTs are to draw on this model of youthwork as a guide to developing more holistic approaches to working with young people in their care, they need to recognise that successful holistic development is largely by nature a democratic process. Hence, the transformational processes of relationships developed between young people, teachers and senior leaders must be driven and guided by a genuine concern for meeting their holistic needs – in particular, for those who are vulnerable and disadvantaged.

Essentially, education, teaching and working with young people should be seen as a social justice issue, a perspective that ought to form the focus for any intervention or education practices, be they formal or informal. Youthwork thrives within the conditions of risk and uncertainty – conditions we find ourselves in today post-COVID-19. However, effective youthwork requires collaboration, voluntary participation and democratic and dialogic relationships. It is, essentially, democracy in practice.

## Lesson 6

I had no idea these kids were doing this!

Head teacher at a youth club annual award ceremony

Gina: It was a dark wintery night in a West Cumbrian coastal town. Not a night for being out on the streets, if you could avoid it. Young people, staff and volunteers at the bustling town centre youth club nervously readied themselves for the annual open evening. Presentations cued. The tea urn was boiling. Biscuits were plentiful. The first guests began to arrive. Family members, parents, community members and more came in from the chill and took a seat to join us in celebrating this snapshot of young people's achievements.

And there he was – the head of one of the large local secondary schools.

As director of the youth club, I was nervous that he wouldn't make it. Connections with secondary schools were becoming increasingly hard, even with the fully grant-funded activities we were often able to offer. The team were all the more delighted when this particular head accepted our invitation. New to the area, he wanted to get to know the community in which the students lived – music to our ears, especially as that evening we would be presenting awards for Duke of Edinburgh's achievements to some of his students.

So, I was a little taken aback when he enquired, 'What are *those* boys doing here?'

'They're here to receive their Duke of Edinburgh's Award,' I replied.

The ensuing conversation revealed that, based on their behaviour and reputation in school, these were not the kind of boys you would expect to be receiving (or even doing) a Duke of Edinburgh's Award. Yes, admittedly, they were among the 'liveliest' group we had ever had the pleasure of working with, and some colourful memories are etched in our minds about camping expedition antics, but that is where our knowledge of the boys stopped. We had no idea of their standing in school.

In the coming weeks, anecdotal reports from both students and head teacher highlighted the positive change in relationships on the school corridors and in classrooms that had resulted from that offsite connection to another part of community life. These boys were now more than troublemakers at school; they were the boys who had done their Bronze Duke of Edinburgh's Award.

That is why they were there.

## Lesson 7

Gina: The extent to which schools and youthwork provision collaborates varies greatly, from long-established relationships to no connection at all. In my experience, where there is a connection, it's by way of an intervention to 'fix' a challenge with a particular cohort or individual, as opposed to an ongoing strength-based approach for all young people. Access to funding, capacity to communicate, and foster connections and perceptions of value all have a role to play in supporting or impeding partnerships.

Set against this knowledge, Place Schools Trust, a school still in the embryonic planning stages[5] worked with the Innovation Unit to create a learning ecosystem framework which was both robust and credible. Design principles focused on creating a school that would be deeply connected with its local and wider community and where the metaphorical and physical boundaries of school as a venue for learning are blurred and positively challenged.[6] This was seen as a pathway to authentic connections and collaborations:

> Learning ecosystems comprise diverse combinations of providers (schools, businesses, community organizations as well as government agencies) creating new learning opportunities and pathways to success. They are usually supported by an innovative credentialing system or technology platforms that replace or augment the traditional linear system of examinations and graduation. They need not, however, be confined to their geographic location in terms of resources overall. They may exploit the technologies now available to choreograph global learning resources. (Hanon et al., 2019: 7)

Much of the literature points to learning ecosystems as being more than partnerships and networks, and there is a call for shared governance, diverse resources and models that are learner driven with learner agency at their heart.

## Lesson 8

Gina: One aspect of our approach involves emulating some of the principles of youth-work through an Equalities Literacy framework (EQL) (Stuart et al., 2019). The EQL framework provides a practical response to the complex challenges associated with a socially unequal society. It has a particular application in education settings, as this is where the framework was first researched and developed, with a focus on understanding learner perspectives of marginalisation and exclusion from mainstream education.

Being equalities literate means being aware of the complex range of factors that can impact the path any person might follow in life. Developing this literacy requires an ability to be open to considering the situation a person is born into, their lived experiences, how they view themselves and how they are viewed by others. For EQL to be impactful it requires, firstly, awareness and, secondly, the skills to transfer that awareness into practice. Being aware of the impact of beliefs, language, labelling, stereotyping and unconscious bias are all important parts of becoming more equalities literate.

---

5   See https://www.placeschoolstrust.org.
6   See https://9862d728-dfb1-442a-b9d6-ce37c53e2a70.filesusr.com/
    ugd/443a57_145ab75bf3074aa6911fd90ba96b34f9.pdf.

An equalities literate practitioner therefore will be:

■ Reflective and reflexive about their assumptions of the world.

■ Able to develop a deeper understanding of inequality and to recognise the sometimes hidden ability for our actions to compound that inequality.

■ Able to create a culture of practice-based research that can inform future methods, theory and practice.

Implementing an EQL framework in schools is new ground, and Place Schools Trust looks forward to contributing towards learning in this area. Written into the school design is the belief that 'wellbeing, resilience and the ability to think with clarity in any circumstance are vital to a successful learning environment, and to happy, caring and fulfilling lives for students, staff, and communities'. This design principle is intended to create the foundation for the school population, including our square pegs, to realise their innate potential in this area, developing their own understanding of themselves and others, and examining their own beliefs and judgements. This is fundamental to the success of the EQL framework in the Place Schools setting.

# Lesson 9

Gina: Wider collaboration and partnership with youthwork provision, together with a commitment to better understanding the contexts and lives of learners, undoubtedly play a beneficial role in making schools more inclusive and equal. Implementing change is challenging and thinking in small 'chunks' is critical. With this in mind, the following four changes may help schools to better meet the needs of more children more of the time:

1   Consider school as a hub or base camp that can facilitate existing and new connections with the wider community.

2   Connect where students are already connected or where they could be connected. Be part of the scaffolding that fosters and celebrates those connections.

3   Learn about and promote the value of non-academic achievement and ensure these are not just school based, but also accomplishments that young people are driving in their own lives.

4   Provide opportunities for staff and students to become reflective and reflexive about their assumptions of the world, leading to a deeper understanding of lived experiences and changes to practice that makes school more equal and inclusive.

# Lesson 10

Gina: Youth clubs didn't officially start until 6pm, so I was surprised when two of our older members turned up just before 4pm. I knew one of the girls still lived locally and one had been away at university, so it was great to see that they had reunited in the holidays.

They were completing their Gold Duke of Edinburgh's Award together and wanted some support filling out their expedition reflections and to use a youth club computer. So, the kettle went on and they settled in to reminisce about why the tent had fallen down, who was supposed to bring the pasta and how long the post-expedition blisters had taken to heal. All fairly typical stuff.

But what was not typical was the unlikeliness of the friendship.

From strikingly different backgrounds and with extremes of lived experience, these two young people had found common ground at the youth club, learned from and about each other, and fostered a friendship that continues today. It was a moment of awakening for me, an important reminder of how our own belief systems can consider a duo unlikely, incompatible even, and how we should take care when seeing barriers and stereotypes in young people. Instead, we should focus on creating the conditions where young people can view the world through fresh eyes, creating kinder futures for themselves for the benefit of all.

# Lesson 11

Alasdair: In 2009, and as a fairly new youth worker, I attended an interview for a post with my local authority's care leavers team. The role involved offering one-to-one support for young people who had grown up in local authority care and learning about their individual social, education, financial and practical needs, so their transition to independence had the best chance of success.

In the interview, the senior member of the panel asked me two questions on how I had previously advocated for young people to ensure their needs and rights were being genuinely considered. I provided what I thought were good anecdotes about building meaningful relationships with young people, listening to their hopes and fears, and working constructively with colleagues in other services to achieve a positive outcome for these young people.

I was then pressed to explain how I might stand up for a young person whose rights were being overlooked or minimised by a social work colleague because of other constraints associated with their role – time, money, remit and the like. The diplomatic response I provided – I explained about pressures on other agencies, maintaining positive professional relationships and how, well, we are all often hamstrung by the policy decisions of central government – was instantly shot down. I was told in no uncertain terms that I had a duty to challenge colleagues who might otherwise do a disservice to young people whose personal experiences have made them among the most vulnerable in society.

I didn't get the job.

# Lesson 12

Alasdair: Jay came to my attention because he was struggling with mainstream education and the social demands that secondary school expected of him. He had been diagnosed with autism, along with his older and younger brothers (the older brother also having extreme episodes related to his additional diagnosis of obsessive-compulsive disorder), which meant that life at home could be challenging at times.

Jay was a square peg.

He was already learning at a level lower than his Year 8 peers, which meant he was placed in lower-ability and more disruptive classes. He was easily manipulated by his peers into making poor behavioural choices which resulted in him getting into trouble and falling further behind. One of the major difficulties that Jay faced was his belief that his classroom outbursts, encouraged by his so-called friends, would make him more popular with his peers.

In previous multi-agency meetings in which Jay had been present and suggestions made about how to improve his situation and avoid further trouble at school, I noted how Jay had invariably agreed to all the proposals and plans that had been made. I was also aware, following conversations with him, of his disguised compliance and his desire to avoid additional scrutiny and leave the meetings as soon as possible.

This invariably led to agreements being reached in which Jay was not emotionally invested, which in turn led to additional meetings to discuss what had gone wrong and why Jay had refused to uphold his end of the agreements. In one such meeting, and with Jay facing the prospect of a managed move to another secondary school, I felt it was right to get Jay to open up more about why he so often agreed to the suggestions that were made in these meetings.

We needed to learn more about what was needed for him to genuinely buy into the support offered at school and curb his more negative behaviours and attitude towards teachers. And time was running out.

The school had agreed that Jay would get to school early each day to see a member of staff based in the school's learning centre. Here, he would receive his daily report card and have a 'friendly chat' with the teacher. Although the school's plan sounded positive in theory, involving a genuine attempt to help Jay manage and monitor his behaviour and provide the space and time to talk to staff, in reality this proposal failed to recognise the social stigma associated with one-to-one support to which Jay was acutely sensitive.

Arriving at school early to go to the learning support base for a chat with a teacher was not only 'uncool' but also a cause of ridicule, as it turned out. Embracing the support offered would make Jay more of a target with his 'friends'. It was an approach that could do more harm than good and was doomed to fail.

In the meeting, I not only verbalised his reality but also supported him to express in his own words how he felt. Only then did it dawn on my colleagues – especially those representing Jay's school – that their well-intentioned proposals and systems of support were not going to be successful and could actually make things worse. By ensuring everyone considered Jay's lived experience – and also reflected on their own school experiences and the complex social pressures to which they were exposed – it became clear that more creative thinking and a greater level of empathy was required to understand Jay's personal circumstances. Opportunities needed to be created that would allow Jay to express himself in more meaningful ways.

## Lesson 13

Alasdair: Whilst working with a local authority edge of care team, I was supporting a family whose 10-year-old daughter, Lucy-Jane, was at risk of being accommodated due to the relational breakdown with her mother. She was becoming increasingly neglected and experiencing a profound sense of rejection. This had been compounded by a further breakdown in her relationship with her father and his new girlfriend with whom she had a fractious relationship. Ultimately, neither biological parent demonstrated much desire to meet Lucy-Jane's basic needs or to celebrate her achievements at school, which could be described as the one area of Lucy-Jane's life where she benefited from consistency, routine, positive friendships and a sense of achievement.

Lucy-Jane was a square peg.

My work with the family started near the end of the summer term at a time when Year 6 pupils were applying for secondary school places and hoping desperately to attend the same school as their friends. This was making Lucy-Jane very anxious, and she told me that if she didn't get into her first choice with her friends, then she would refuse to attend school altogether.

I was aware of Lucy-Jane's experiences of bullying because of her home life and the stress-related eczema that she suffered visibly around her hairline and neck. Getting into the right school where she would have a familiar friendship group wasn't just a matter of promoting her attainment, it was also a health issue for Lucy-Jane. The problem was that, when it came to choosing her school place, both her mother and father had expected the other to complete the relevant forms and neither had done so.

The deadline had passed, and Lucy-Jane had missed out on her preferred choice. She was allocated to a school that none of her friends would be attending. The problem was not just an educational and social one, it was a medical one too, so I needed to do whatever I could to help.

I helped Lucy-Jane's mother draft a written statement as part of the appeal process and was delighted when we were offered a hearing before the panel at the city council chambers. I also supported Lucy-Jane to visit the school to which she had been allocated, partly to assess her emotional state but also to try and encourage her to consider the school as an alternative were the appeal to be unsuccessful.

With the date of the appeal set, both parents then informed me they were unable to attend. It was down to me now. I called ahead to enquire whether the panel would be prepared to have a representative speak on behalf of the family and, given my prior work with Lucy-Jane and my knowledge of her personal circumstances, this was agreed.

Long story short: Lucy-Jane was granted a place at her preferred school. The feedback I received validated my belief, born out of experience, in the powerful role that a passionate and informed practitioner can play in shaping a child's life in profoundly positive ways, changing some of the negative narratives that can dominate if left unchallenged.

## Lesson 14

The most forward looking head teachers recognise the value of helping their pupils to develop their soft skills. Similarly, the most forward looking youth workers use their unique skillset to work with schools and deliver high quality programmes that relate to measurable outcomes. (National Youth Agency, 2013: 5)

# References

Banks, S. (1994) Contemporary Issues in Youthwork: Editorial Introduction, *Youth and Policy*, 46 (autumn): 1–5.

Freire, P. (1972) *Pedagogy of the Oppressed*. New York: Continuum.

Furlong, A. (2013) *Youth Studies: An Introduction*. Abingdon and New York: Routledge.

Hanon, V., Thomas, L., Ward, S. and Beresford, T. (2019) *Local Learning Ecosystems: Emerging Models*. Doha: Qatar Foundation/World Innovation Summit for Education and Innovation Unit. Available at: https://stage.innovationunit.org/thoughts/local-learning-ecosystems-emerging-models.

National Youth Agency (2013) *Commission into the Role of Youth Work in Formal Education*. Leicester: NYA.

Stuart, K., Bunting, M., Boyd, P., Cammack, P., Frostholm, P., Gravesen, D. et al. (2019) *Developing An Equality Literacy for Practitioners Working with Children, Young People and Families Through Action Research*. Available at: https://www.tandfonline.com/doi/full/10.1080/09650792.2019.1593870?scroll=top&needAccess=true.

# Chapter 37

# TECH-MATE

## Nina Jackson

I don't like the term SEND (special educational needs and disabilities). It implies that there is something wrong. That if a child isn't 'normal',[1] then that child needs 'fixing' so they fit in. That they are the ones with the difficulties, so they must do something about it. I much prefer thinking about the 'learning and living differences' we all have. How we are all square pegs to a lesser or greater extent.

So, how do we educate a bunch of square pegs who are not one homogenous whole within a one-size-fits-all system? Technology can provide the means to support a raft of differences, to ensure we measure progress appropriately for each child, to assist staff in the mountain of admin required of them, and to make learning engaging, relevant and fun. And it's one of the most underused resources in the education system.

Think about gaming and how engaging it is for some children – perhaps those who struggle in a particular subject or see no relevance in the whole concept of school. Can you use initiatives from the gaming industry to connect with them, and maybe even open their eyes to a future in the industry?[2] Think of mobile phones as a relevant and familiar tech asset in the classroom rather than a distraction to be locked up for eight hours and handed back at the end of the day. Explore the myriad of free and inexpensive apps available to alleviate a child's anxiety or use video to encourage a learner's confidence in public speaking. Upskill your staff to deliver effective online content and utilise the added advantage that remote provision can offer. It's entirely possible to offer children social interaction with their peers and one-to-one support whilst still maintaining the personal safety of everyone involved.

All of this and much, much more is possible, but it requires school leaders to prioritise technology and ensure that someone is tasked with staying abreast of relevant developments, investigating what would best help a particular student or cohort and liaising with providers to ensure value for money. A school's job is not to make everyone the same but to help all children find their special 'stamp' – the thing that makes them shine. A talent, a spark, a gift. Whether this lies inside or outside the traditional curriculum, technology can help, especially when the usual routes of discovery,

---

1 There is a good Welsh term for what I think of that word – *ych-a-fi*!
2 See Digital Schoolhouse, a gaming industry initiative backed by Nintendo, at https://www.digitalschoolhouse. org.uk. At the time of writing it is free to schools.

communication and expression are problematic. It's not about whether or not children use their phones in lessons or access YouTube at school. It's bigger than that. It's about using the amazing technologies that are available to help all children and young people flourish, and for those who are struggling in the system as it is, to bring hope.

So, let me introduce two very special and uniquely magical square pegs – Leo and Ffion.

## All about Leo

Leo is a quiet child. He is 12 and three-quarters. The three-quarters is very important when you are nearly 13. Leo finds school difficult and challenging at times as he is a boy of very few words. In fact, just a handful of words are in his limited vocabulary due to a lack of interaction with others, often being alone and lonely, with no circle of friends, low self-esteem, high levels of anxiety about accessing learning and the not-so-small issue of being what some would describe as 'non-verbal' due to his autism.

Leo doesn't like people very much but he has found a friend in the digital world. His new 'tech-mate' (a digital learning device such as an iPad, laptop or 'handtop'[3]) has helped him to share his voice with others and allowed him to discover learning through a different path. He has discovered a way of producing sounds and words through the use of various applications, and he can mimic words and mouth shapes in particular through Lingraphica TalkPath Therapy.[4]

Since using these tools, Leo has also been able to use text to speech as well as slowly practising some word pronunciations with speech to text, to enable him to see and hear his words pronounced through artificial intelligence (AI). Now, not only can Leo develop his speech but he can also share his amazing thoughts with others. Thoughts that had been buried deep inside his thinking brain with no way to communicate them to the world. Leo is now a much happier student in school, and the integration of his tech-mate in class and around school has helped him to socialise properly and develop a sense of purpose. Think of it as a mobility aid for his thoughts.

Leo is progressing well with all aspects of school: learning, socialising, communicating and leading the way in helping others to see the enormous value of a tech-mate for learning and living.

---

3   My term for a smartphone. If you cut out the 'phone' bit, you see the device for what it really can be. After all, take the SIM card out of a smartphone and it can still be used as a digital device, as long as it can connect to Wi-Fi.

4   See https://apps.apple.com/us/app/lingraphica-talkpath-therapy/id887481664.

# All about Ffion

Ffion is a vibrant, vocal and excitable learner. She is 14. She loves to call out, shout out and gets very excited when learning happens in the classroom. Ffion has much to say about lots of things and finds it a challenge to be quiet, sit down and stay still. Writing in her books is also a challenge as she would rather be moving, jumping, standing, wiggling and jiggling. Ffion has both attention deficit hyperactivity disorder and dysgraphia.

If you peer inside her amazing brain, you would observe one of the most curious, awe-inspiring, creative individuals ever. As her teacher, though, she keeps you on your toes and is so active and vocal that you can feel quite drained. Will she ever stop, or at least slow down?!

Ffion experiences episodes of depression. This is when she does slow down. She gets very upset when she's had an episodic outburst in class, especially when she can't remember it. And she feels even worse when the teacher (or, on many occasions, the head teacher, threatening her with yet another exclusion for disruptive behaviour) explains that her actions and choices were not compatible with the school's behaviour policy. She simply doesn't recognise the person they are describing. And that is hard.

Ffion hates writing and doesn't understand why others can't read what she writes. One evening at home, she watches her mother using an iPad. She doesn't just use the keyboard to write but something that resembles a pencil. Sneaking behind her, she sees that the 'pencil' turns her handwriting into text. Mouth agape, Ffion asks her mother if she can have a go and Mum lets her try.

Before she writes, Mum tells her that she has the 'Scribble' function turned on, which means that anything she writes in any random way on the iPad, even at a slant or with huge spaces between the letters, intuitively turns into text. She holds the pencil and off she goes.

Four hours later and Ffion is still writing! She can't believe how this magic pencil can take her illegible handwriting and turn it into text. She has discovered an amazing tech-mate to support her with so many things in school and for her future life. Think of it like a mobility aid for her words.

Ffion is now progressing well with all aspects of school. She can focus more and communicate much better when she is allowed to use the device to help with her writing. She has persuaded her school (and her mum) to let her use the iPad in class, and now the school has ordered a few more to help others in the same situation.

# What we know about assistive technology

The (true) stories above are examples of the power of using what are called assistive technologies. Don't let the name put you off. If you are reading this on a device and have changed the background colour or tweaked the font to read it better, that is assistive technology in action. Even if you are reading this through a pair of spectacles, you are using assistive technology.

In the classroom, assistive technology can be used to support challenges in areas including communication, mobility and learning. When the correct assistive technology is available and implemented, students with particular learning and living differences are able to perform and complete tasks that may previously have been too difficult for them to finish. It also supports independence, self-esteem and self-confidence, and our square pegs can then be empowered to complete tasks with greater success and efficiency.

Assistive technology includes services that can be offered to students as well as devices they can use. This may include tools such as graphic organisers, highlighters, personal timers, text to speech and word prediction facilities, often incorporated within technology such as tablets, computers or mobile digital devices. Then there are the amazing possibilities of virtual reality, augmented reality and AI to support learners. Most people are now aware of our AI helpers Siri and Alexa. Did you know, though, that you can personalise many digital devices to accept your own voice-activated instruction? This is known as 'VoiceOver' and is how a totally visually impaired person can use a digital device to navigate the world by giving it instructional cues on what they would like to do or where they need assistance.

Equipping our teachers and learners with an understanding of the accessible features on different devices and the many assistive apps available can make a massive difference to struggling learners, so let's look at what is freely (as in widely and for free) available for everyone.

# Reading

iPhones and iPads can read text aloud for you. In 'Spoken Content', under 'Settings' and 'Accessibility', you have the option to activate 'Speak Selection', which allows a 'Speak' button to appear when you select text.

You can also choose to activate the 'Speak Screen' function. When you swipe down with two fingers you can hear the content of your screen spoken aloud. There are additional tools such as 'Speech Controller', 'Highlight Content' and 'Typing Feedback' as well as different spoken voices in over 27 languages.[5] The fabulous 'Speaking Rate' option allows you to slow down or speed up any spoken text. There is also a 'Pronunciations' option, which enables you to dictate how certain phrases are expressed. This is particularly helpful for speech, language and communication difficulties, as well as people like me who pronounce 'earrings' in a Welsh accent. All in all, the accessibility functions just in 'Spoken Content' are invaluable, if you know they are there and how to use them. Training and a play-and-practise mindset are key here.

Other functions in the 'Accessibility' feature on iPhones and iPads include a 'Zoom' function to make text larger, a 'Magnifier' which you could use in the classroom to enhance written text, an option to increase 'Display and Text Size', 'Motion' to stop the back of the screen moving and 'Audio Descriptions'.

Android devices have a 'Select to Speak' feature, as does Google, which is called 'Google Speech'. And, of course, there are the 'Learning Tools' in Microsoft Office.

## Writing

You have the option on all mobile digital devices as well as desktops and laptops (PC and Mac) to speak aloud rather than type or write. The word prediction option is also there to help with sequencing sentences for those who may have cognitive processing issues. As we saw with Ffion, using a smart stylus, such as an Apple Pencil, to write can be life-changing, especially when activated with the 'Scribble' feature.

## Physical and motor accessibility

Within the 'Physical and Motor' section of iPad and iPhone 'Accessibility' functions you have choices within 'Assistive Touch' if you are having difficulty with touching the screen or if an adaptive accessory is needed. There are other options too such as 'Haptic Touch', where you can press on the display for differing lengths of time to reveal content previews, actions and contextual menus.

---

5   I know they are currently working on Welsh. About time too.

# Hearing

An excellent added feature to many digital devices in recent years is the ability to connect 'made for phone' hearing devices to a phone or tablet, so they can connect to the function for hearing aids and processors.[6] The 'Hearing Aid Compatibility' function also improves audio quality within some hearing aids to support learners.

# Emotional self-regulation

As we have seen elsewhere in this book, emotional self-regulation can be difficult for some learners. Cognitive overload, anxiety, inability to focus for extended periods, listening skill issues and the organisation (or otherwise) of thought processes can all take their toll. The following emotional self-regulation applications can help with emotions as well as the management of issues around anger, anxiety and even exam revision:

- Sensory Sound Box[7]
- Fluid 2[8]
- fluidity HD[9]
- Tayasui Sketches Pro[10]

# Time management and personal organisation

Productivity, time management and daily organisation can be a real challenge for many of our square pegs. From notifications and system management applications to the effective use of the camera to track and organise activities, the following apps can help:

- Google Tasks for Android and iOS[11]
- Google Chrome desktop extension[12]

---

6   You might see it as 'MFI' or 'Made for iPhone'.
7   See https://apps.apple.com/gb/app/sensory-sound-box/id548622567.
8   See https://apps.apple.com/gb/app/fluid-2/id317959717.
9   See https://apps.apple.com/gb/app/fluidity-hd/id399403909.
10  See https://apps.apple.com/gb/app/tayasui-sketches-pro/id671867510.
11  See https://play.google.com/store/apps/details?id=com.google.android.apps.tasks&hl=en_GB&gl=US and https://apps.apple.com/us/app/google-tasks-get-things-done/id1353634006.
12  See https://chrome.google.com/webstore/detail/desktop-app-for-google-ta/lpofefdiokgmcdnnaigddelnfamkkghi?hl=en.

- Notes for iOS [13]
- Word Salad for iOS [14]
- Microsoft Lens (PDF Scanner) for Android and iOS[15]

# Building a tech-mate toolkit for school, home learning and parental support

Tapping into the ever-growing variety of assistive and accessible hardware and software will empower struggling learners at school, at home and in any blended approach of the two.[16] From video and photo management to visual learning boards and interactive mind maps, when building a toolkit of applications that works for each individual learner, be prepared to be amazed by the innovative tools on offer. For example:

- Seeing AI[17]
- Popplet[18]
- Book Creator[19]
- Haiku Deck[20]

As you start using assistive technologies for those children struggling in your classrooms, it is worth asking yourself a few questions:

- What specific living and learning differences does the learner have?
- Does that learner need both digital and analogue support to access the curriculum and learning both in class and at home?
- Does the learner have different needs, which warrants the purchase of a digital learning device, when compared with the majority of their peers in the class?
- As a teacher, where can I access specialist digital support if I am not sure about the best tools to use?

---

13  See https://apps.apple.com/us/app/notes/id1110145109.
14  See https://apps.apple.com/us/app/wordsalad-smart-word-clouds/id545164778.
15  See https://play.google.com/store/apps/details?id=com.microsoft.office.officelens&hl=en_GB&gl=US and https://apps.apple.com/gb/app/microsoft-office-lens-pdf-scan/id975925059.
16  The COVID-19 pandemic showed us how, overnight, teachers had to grasp, produce and create online lessons using technology they may have never used before. Creating schoolwork for home is part of this blended approach, and we would do well to remember the hard-earned lessons here. A recent Organisation for Economic Co-operation and Development (2021) article on the subject is worth a read, as is Shenoy et al. (2020).
17  See https://www.microsoft.com/en-us/ai/seeing-ai.
18  See https://www.popplet.com.
19  See https://bookcreator.com.
20  See https://www.haikudeck.com.

■ How will I monitor the effective use of the technology and the impact on learning?

This topic is vast – a fact that can be overwhelming for some – and I have only touched on the simplest, cheapest, easiest and most common tools. That said, accessing just one simple tool was life-changing for Leo and Ffion, and it can be just as life-changing for the square pegs in your own classrooms. Remember that it's not a question of technology: it's about equity, fairness and hope. So, yes, there is an app or two for that.

## References

Organisation for Economic Co-operation (2021) OECD Policy Responses to Coronavirus (COVID-19): How Will COVID-19 Reshape Science, Technology and Innovation? (23 June). Available at: https://www.oecd.org/coronavirus/policy-responses/how-will-covid-19-reshape-science-technology-and-innovation-2332334d.

Shenoy, V., Mahendher, S. and Vijay, N. (2020) COVID 19 Lockdown Technology Adaption, Teaching, Learning, Students Engagement and Faculty Experience, *Mukt Shabd Journal*, 9(4): 698–702. Available at: https://www.researchgate.net/profile/Veena-Shenoy-2/publication/340609688_COVID_19_Lockdown_Technology_Adaption_Teaching_Learning_Students_Engagement_and_Faculty_Experience/links/5e94b438299bf13079978159/COVID-19-Lockdown-Technology-Adaption-Teaching-Learning-Students-Engagement-and-Faculty-Experience.pdf.

# Chapter 38

# THE BUSINESS OF EDUCATION

## Nick Shackleton-Jones, Andrew 'Bernie' Bernard and Jo Symes

## A pandemic-driven economy

At the time of writing, no one is really sure what the long-term economic impact of the global COVID-19 pandemic will be. There are as many predictions as there are organisations making predictions. We do know that we have witnessed the 'deepest recession since World War Two' (UN, 2020). A report by the World Bank Group (2020: xv), underlining this uncertainty, suggested that 'global coordination and coop-eration will be critical' to recovery and that we are not out of the woods yet, medically or economically.

The effects of the UK's departure from the European Union are also beginning to be felt across a number of industries. The final demise of the fishing industry looks likely, regardless of how the fish might feel about it (Guardian, 2021), a reduction of £5.6 billion (40.7%) in exports to the EU in January 2021 compared to 12 months before (ONS, 2021) and the financial exodus from the City of London could all have a long-term impact on UK jobs and career opportunities. And then there is the collapse of British manufacturing, not to mention the death knell of the high street being sounded every time an Amazon delivery driver rings a doorbell.

It's against this gloomy backdrop that we note how 69% of employers surveyed by the British Chambers of Commerce (2015) believed that schools are 'not very effective' or 'not effective at all' at preparing young people for work, with 52% simultaneously admitting that they don't work with schools to offer work experience placements.

All of which means, with our creative thinking hats on, it could be a good time to be a square peg.

# Businesses love diversity

There are examples of companies that go out of their way to do the right thing and have an ethos of support for individuals who have been marginalised or who made mistakes earlier in life, such as Timpson, the shoe repairer and key-cutting retail shops. The company's website states: 'Everyone deserves a second chance. Timpson is a proud supporter of work rehabilitation and the employment of ex-offenders. We believe that as long as you have the right attitude, you can be an asset to our team.'[1]

Companies like Apple, Google and Netflix don't look for degrees any more, according to the business news website, Business Insider (Akhtar, 2019). In the same article, Apple CEO Tim Cook is reported as saying that 'many colleges do not teach the skills business leaders need most in their workforce'.

If we shift our focus from degrees to skills, we will enable a bigger workforce that represents the diversity of our populations, and we will help close the all too familiar opportunity and employment gaps. This will mean transitioning to always-on skills-based education and employment infrastructure that embraces not just credentials and certification but fitness-for-job and employment as outcomes (Kumar S. and George, 2020).

Similarly, Sir Richard Branson announced at the Made By Dyslexia Global Summit in 2019 that the Virgin Group – which employs over 70,000 people in businesses ranging from gyms to space tourism – 'will not ask anyone for their exam results ever again'. He added that exams designed to test reading, memory abilities and time management skills might become 'irrelevant': 'It's not just employers that will be forced to change, but schools too. If nobody asked for exam results, I think schools would be different places.'[2]

In a huge multinational management consultancy such as Deloitte, it matters not a bit that you have a 2.1 in art history because it says next to nothing about your aptitudes or interests. But it does suggest that if you are set a deadline to hand in a piece of paper, you will have been conditioned to feel anxious about meeting that deadline, whether or not the purpose of the act is something you really care about.

Is this, then, the real cost of our current education system? Billions of people leading purposeless lives? Afraid of learning? Children may be bored – a common claim – but we compound that by frightening them, and even drugging them, to sit still when the threats don't work. And then we express our disappointment should they fail. Soon they are obsessing over test scores and pass marks, and then they are fit for employment, where they will fret over whatever deadline they are set and their next performance review. Sometime in their mid-life they may realise that they have led a

---

1   See https://www.timpson.co.uk/how-to-recruit-great-people-from-prision.
2   See https://www.youtube.com/watch?v=ZPPS8ZuoM_A.

purposeless existence – never really having paused to wonder what it is that really matters to them – and perhaps then it will be too late.

What can we learn from the square pegs who are refusing to play this game? Schools may not want them, but industry does.

It is true, of course, that on average graduates earn more than non-graduates (Britton et al., 2020). But this is only by virtue of the artificial monopoly we have created to sustain the education system (much as the trade in indulgences sustained the Church in medieval times).

A reputable business such as Deloitte may set out to hire 'the best of the best' – graduates with first-class qualifications from the finest schools. They will interview graduates with a degree in chemistry or English literature who, if successful, will be asked to lead meetings, respond to emails and develop PowerPoint slides.

Some businesses also like to hire school prefects. They love infantilised employees who are so anxious about what their parent/teacher/boss might think that they work through the night to meet their deadlines. They hire the 'good' boys and girls because they conform neatly to a parent–child organisational model. They hire people like them. Lacking in diversity of thought, bound by policy and process, and sapped of entrepreneurial spirit, these are brittle, ponderous places to work. They manufacture the hollowed souls and middle-aged misery that you soak in on the morning commute. These are organisations that will have to acquire or hire some lively start-up in order to persist. These are vampire organisations.

Businesses need their staff to read and write, interact passably well with others and learn (and not just out of fear or because it is 'in the test'). Most children can do this by the age of 12. What if, from an employment perspective, they were also taught how to develop a saleable idea, take the lead in a meeting, manage an inbox, present to clients or run a project, not to mention how to manage their emotional life and well-being in the process, as well as connect and communicate with others?

Dr Grace Lordan, a behavioural scientist, economist and associate professor at the London School of Economics, says that economists have known for a number of years that such soft skills, focused on character and health, leave a long arm on adult outcomes (including traditional labour force outcomes), income and educational attainment:

I study the fourth industrial revolution. I am interested in the type of skills that are going to still be needed in a decade's time, given what is coming on stream from patents and from big firms. And these skills, character skills, are absolutely what is going to be needed by children. Soft skills are increasingly in demand in the labour market given that these skills are not readily substituted with technology.[3]

What is more, business leaders are also calling for an increased focus on creativity. According to an IBM (2010) survey of more than 1,500 chief executives from 60 countries and 33 industries worldwide, creativity is the skill most needed for facing 21st century business challenges. Creativity ranked above rigor, management discipline, integrity and vision. LinkedIn also carries out employer analysis. In 2018, it used exclusive LinkedIn data to determine the skills companies would need most in the year ahead. In accord with the findings from IBM, they confirmed that creativity topped the list of desired attributes (Petrone, 2018).

In a much-viewed TED Talk (no, not that one), 'The Failure of Success', Dr George Land (2011) gives a brief history of human innovation and stresses the importance of creativity. Land is an author, speaker, consultant and general systems scientist with a background in communications, business, education and government.

He tells his audience how NASA briefed him to develop a test that would enable them to measure the creative potential of NASA's rocket scientists and engineers. The test proved very successful, and the scientists subsequently gave it to 1,600 children between the ages of 4 and 15.

The study looked at the ability to come up with new, different and innovative ideas to problems. It measured the percentage of the sample whose imagination was found to be at 'genius' level. They found the following results:

- Genius level at 5 years – 98%.
- Genius level at 10 years – 30%.
- Genius level at 15 years – 12%.
- Genius level of adults – 2%.

At 5 years of age, the majority of children are genius innovators, but by the time we reach adulthood, following years of schooling, only 2% of us are at genius level. This study has been replicated many times with the same results.

Think about your square pegs. To what extent do the very traits and characteristics that make fitting in such a struggle for them ironically help them to succeed beyond education's narrow confines? How can you help them not only to achieve at school but also to ensure they are best placed to exploit what they have to offer the world of work?

---

3   See https://www.youtube.com/watch?v=HvQDrjXybnM.

There are companies that are invested in the true sense of equity of opportunity. There are also a number of charities that support the development of opportunity for people from all areas of society. However, when it comes to your square pegs, there may not be that many willing to take a chance – unless, that is, they get to know you and your students first.

The following ideas will help you to make those connections, bring the concept of innovation and enterprise to your school, and inspire engagement from students and business alike.

## Start at the beginning

Be brave. You know those students who need to be given responsibility and who need to be treated more like adults. They are ready for a day in a workshop, a day of making or a day of helping to serve customers.

You also know that there are some students who, although they need responsibility, will be difficult to engage and challenging to manage. You know that there will be very few companies that want to be bothered with trying to help you with your complex students. Or do you? Have you asked?

Have you ever worked out exactly what it is you want from businesses in support of your students? What might a placement look like? What skills do you want your students to understand and develop?

## Big picture strategy

What is your strategy? Let's call it an employer engagement strategy or EES. Without it, any activities will be piecemeal and less effective.

Nominate someone as an outreach coordinator or employer network manager to coordinate activities across the school, someone whose role it is to activate and manage the EES.

Your strategy could link into a framework such as the Gatsby benchmarks, which is a measurement tool for careers education.[4] Although it's well structured, it does leave out some key elements of future thinking such as entrepreneurship. (With 5.6 million businesses in the UK having fewer than nine employees (Hutton and Ward, 2021: 12), this seems like a major omission.) Maybe your square pegs have untapped,

---

4   See https://www.gatsby.org.uk/education/focus-areas/good-career-guidance.

unnoticed entrepreneurial flair? Make sure that enterprise and self-employment opportunities are explored as potential work experience and careers offerings.[5]

The seven survival skills for the future devised by Tony Wagner (2009) in *The Global Achievement Gap* is another framework that can support not only your strategy but also the way you help your students to consider their skills. To what extent are you offering opportunities to promote, develop and celebrate the following important skills?

1 Curiosity and imagination.

2 Accessing and analysing information.

3 Agility and adaptability.

4 Creativity and entrepreneurship.

5 Collaboration and leading by influence.

6 Good oral and written communication.

7 Critical thinking and problem-solving.

Develop the EES at senior leadership team level and – whether you use the seven survival skills above or another self-developed structure that fits your own setting – agree how you are going to use that strategy to drive, record and assess the success of your students and the opportunities they are offered.

Governor involvement is key too. You need a nominated outreach governor who can use their influence and links to mobilise the rest of the governance team to support your EES, including their contacts and network of friends in business and industry who would be willing to support your students.

## Calendar

Develop a calendar of activities for your students, interwoven into their regular academic timetable, which regularly interject work-related activities from the EES. Use events like National Careers Week, National Apprenticeship Week, British Science Week, Debt Awareness Week and the like to theme the activities, learning and visits, and to provide a reason to get people from external organisations involved.[6]

Be unapologetically ambitious and don't set things up so businesses can say no. If a local business can't come to your planned careers fair during National Apprenticeship Week, be more flexible: 'Why not sign up to help at our virtual interview skills

---

5   See Martin Illingworth's (2020) challenging book *Forget School* for more on how young people are increasingly doing it for themselves, regardless of what happened at school for them.

6   There is a full calendar of awareness events at https://www.awarenessdays.com.

afternoon next month? I'm sure you can spare an hour or so to help our students then, can't you?'

# Approaching businesses and outside agencies to help your students

Once you know what you are looking to offer your students and what you want the students to develop from the offer, it's time to start asking people within organisations for their help and support. Ordinarily, young people attend companies for work experience, and therefore can see, feel, hear and get involved with the reality of a workplace (pandemics notwithstanding). There are a number of different ways that businesses and outside organisations can help you with your EES, so we will summarise some national schemes and make some suggestions for ideas that you can discuss with your local business contacts.

## National schemes

National schemes are often good sources of free content and resources to back up your in-house offering. Some will provide local business volunteers to support what you are looking to achieve. Some will help you to invite people in. Most are free.

National Careers Week provides resources and a video channel with free access for the whole year, not just during the week itself (which is the first full week of March each year). The website includes a number of presentations, guides, printable booklets and flexible tools to support the development of skills and activities to embed them.[7]

## Local contacts

Wherever you are based, there will be local businesses in all sectors and industries who need staff. Just as we saw in Chapter 21, consider local authorities and councils too, which also need and want to provide employment for local people.

Some firms will be keen to support local schools and colleges, and some won't. Some might be keen but won't know where to start. They may be concerned about red tape and safeguarding issues, for example, so be prepared to reassure them that the requirement for Disclosure and Barring Service (DBS) certificates to work with your students is ameliorated by the fact that they will be chaperoned at all times, or perhaps offer to support their staff to secure DBS clearance as part of the payback they receive from supporting your students.

---

7   See https://ncwresources.com.

It is also the case, sadly, that there are businesses that have reached out to schools only to be ignored or not have their calls returned. In some cases, businesses have spoken to someone at the school or college who doesn't recognise what they can gain from a business relationship. It helps to be ready with the mutual benefits.

Linking with local further education colleges can be a conduit to working with employers, many of which will be sponsoring apprenticeship programmes and benefitting from the support the college gives them. The college will also be open to discussing opportunities with secondary schools, which could mean students finding the right path to local further education support. Get to know the recruitment and business development team at the local college; the conversations you have could help both organisations as well as providing links to business and industry.

Contact your local Chamber of Commerce, Rotary club and/or local economic partnership because they are all likely to have a number of schemes and options which will support your students. These sometimes include volunteer visits and activities.

## What to ask?

Never be stuck for things to talk about with potential business supporters again with this handy list of obvious and not-so-obvious questions:

- How could your organisation support our school?
- Can you help to make our students' career education experience better than yours was?
- Could your organisation use some corporate social responsibility time or funds to help our students with their futures?
- Do you run any initiatives to promote your business skills and industry in the local community?
- What are the key skills your industry is looking for in the next five to 10 years?
- What will happen in your industry in the next decade?
- Does your company struggle to find people with the right skills? If so, what skills do you most want to see in the people you recruit?
- Do you expect young people to be work-ready? If so, how do you define this and how could you help our students to gain these skills?
- Is there anyone in your organisation who would like to come and inspire us in one of our assemblies (face to face or virtually)?

- Do you have any young staff/apprentices who could come and speak to our students?

- Could any of your team help with mock interviews (face to face or virtual)?

- Could you help with developing skills for the future – for example, time management, interview skills, making a good impression?

- Could we come and visit your workplace? Are there any walk-through videos we could see?

- Do you ever sponsor or fund activities? Would your organisation consider supporting the funding of our online careers package for students?

- Do you have any team-building exercises we could use with our students?

- Could your organisation design a challenge which could engage our students and help them to gain an understanding of your business and industry?

- Do you have a real project that could be used in some way as a challenge for our students using maths, languages, science, art, design and so on? (Perhaps you could come and support us with running it – face to face or virtually?)

- How could you help our students to learn about running their own business?

- What charity events do you get involved with that our school could get involved with too?

By first developing an ambitious and imaginative employer engagement strategy, and then sharing it widely amongst your stakeholders – crucially including your students – you can then start to open the communication channels to the various support offerings there may be nationally as well as closer to you that also want the best for young people.

Remember, everyone in a position of responsibility has a past in which they were supported, helped, advised and given chances. As we saw with the example of Timpson earlier, many will also have been square pegs too. They know what it's like and what it means when someone gives them the opportunity they need.

# References

Akhtar, A. (2019) Apple, Google, and Netflix Don't Require Employees to Have 4-Year Degrees, and This Could Soon Become An Industry Norm, *Business Insider* (10 April). Available at: https://www.businessinsider.in/strategy/apple-google-and-netflix-dont-require-employees-to-have-4-year-degrees-and-this-could-soon-become-an-industry-norm/articleshow/68819464.cms.

British Chambers of Commerce (2015) Businesses and Schools 'Still Worlds Apart' on Readiness for Work [press release] (11 November). Available at: https://www.britishchambers.org.uk/news/2015/11/bcc-businesses-and-schools-still-worlds-apart-on-readiness-for-work.

Britton, L. D., van der Erve, L. and Waltmann, B. (2020) The Impact of Undergraduate Degrees on Lifetime Earnings. Research Report (29 February). Available at: https://ifs.org.uk/publications/14729.

Guardian, The (2021) Jacob Rees-Mogg Says Fish Are British and 'Happier' Because of Brexit [video] (14 January). Available at: https://www.theguardian.com/politics/video/2021/jan/14/jacob-rees-mogg-fish-british-happier-because-brexit-video.

Hutton, G. and Ward, M. (2021) *Business Statistics. Research Briefing* (21 December). Available at: https://researchbriefings.files.parliament.uk/documents/SN06152/SN06152.pdf.

IBM (2010) *Capitalizing on Complexity: Insights from the Global Chief Executive Officer Study.* Available at: https://www.ibm.com/downloads/cas/1VZV5X8J.

Illingworth, M. (2020) *Forget School: Why Young People Are Succeeding On Their Own Terms and What Schools Can Do To Avoid Being Left Behind.* Carmarthen: Independent Thinking Press.

Kumar S., R. and George, S. (2020) Why Skills – Not Degrees – Will Shape the Future of Work, *World Economic Forum* (21 September). Available at: https://www.weforum.org/agenda/2020/09/reckoning-for-skills.

Land, L. ( 2011) The Failure of Success [TEDx talk] [video] (16 February). Available at: https://www.youtube.com/watch?app=desktop&v=ZfKMq-rYtnc.

Petrone, P. (2018) The Skills Companies Need Most in 2019 – And How to Learn Them, *LinkedIn Learning Blog* (31 December). Available at: https://www.linkedin.com/business/learning/blog/top-skills-and-courses/the-skills-companies-need-most-in-2019-and-how-to-learn-them?.

Office for National Statistics (ONS) (2021) *UK Trade: January 2021. Statistical Bulletin.* Available at: https://www.ons.gov.uk/economy/nationalaccounts/balanceofpayments/bulletins/uktrade/january2021/pdf.

United Nations (UN) (2020) Coronavirus: World Bank Confirms Deepest Recession Since World War Two, *UN News* (8 June). Available at: https://news.un.org/en/story/2020/06/1065902.

Wagner, T. (2009) *The Global Achievement Gap: Why Even Our Best Schools Don't Teach the New Survival Skills Our Children Need – and What We Can Do About It.* New York: Basic Books.

World Bank Group (2020) *Global Economic Prospects* (June). Available at: https://openknowledge.worldbank.org/bitstream/handle/10986/33748/9781464815539.pdf.

Epilogue:
# COURAGE

My daughter is a square peg.

She is now 23 with a degree in criminology. I asked her if she would write this epilogue but she said she couldn't.

She told me she didn't remember much about the six or so years when she was unable to go to school (a sure sign of trauma), and that I would be unable to print what she might want to say (too many expletives).

If she could, I think she would probably tell you that she didn't know – and still doesn't – why she couldn't 'do' school. That she had to block out the constant questioning from adults since it was both exhausting and scary. That she would have loved to cope like many of her friends. That no one 'got' her or deserved her trust. That she tried really hard to fit the system but it got the better of her. That we teach young people the importance of consent when it comes to relationships, yet in the context of education there is none, with a default that 'You do as I tell you because I'm the adult and you're the child.' That you must have been out of your tiny mind if you thought that telling her we would go to prison if she didn't go to school was going to help with anything. That she, and the rest of us, were put in an unbearable position for something that was not her fault and that she will never forgive the injustice of it all. That she is proud of me for doing this, but also that it shouldn't be necessary.

She is bright, funny, kind and perceptive (my words), and I am thankful that we finally became complicit[1] and acknowledged that she simply couldn't do it. I just wish we had reached that point sooner and had the confidence to stand up to the stream of professionals who came and went like buses. We were not the criminals in all of this; the system was. I would be happy to see it in court, where my daughter's degree might come in handy.

I am also eternally grateful for those educators and professionals within the system who went that extra mile, who exerted effort to try and 'get' my daughter, despite being repeatedly pushed back by the impenetrable walls she had built around herself to stay safe. It shows me even now (when, arguably, the system is more rigid, academic and budget-stretched than ever) that every individual within the system has the agency to make a difference.

---

1   An interesting word, complicit. I was complicit to the extent that I eventually refused to be browbeaten by so-called professionals into forcing her to try and do something she couldn't. And that is a criminal offence, as the word implies, which is criminal in itself.

So, as I sign off here, I have one plea to all school leaders: be brave, have courage. Follow a path that allows you to work within the system, but still be a champion for all your square pegs and their families. And one day may there be none.

# ABOUT THE AUTHORS

## About Square Peg

Square Peg started as the seed of an idea in 2018, following Fran's experiences with her own daughter, with the goal of effecting change in the education system for those children, like her own daughter, who struggled to attend. It was propelled by a meeting with Fran's local MP, Peter Kyle, in December that year. Peter submitted questions via the House of Commons, requested information about attendance data from the House of Commons library and wrote to the education secretary (then Damien Hinds) raising the issue of forced attendance and the consequences that result.

Square Peg started to build a multi-disciplinary network of contacts that spanned education, academia, law, voluntary groups, and the media, appearing on *Channel 4 News* and *BBC Breakfast*, with articles in the press as the name became known amongst journalists covering this topic. As part of this networking process, Fran met Ian Gilbert of Independent Thinking Press, who suggested this book (much smaller in scale at the outset, but we kept finding amazing contributors!).

In April 2020, Square Peg became a community interest company (CIC) with the addition of two directors – Ellie Costello and Simon Kay. The goal is, and always will be, to effect change, because without change children and families will continue to be failed by an education system which increasingly forces a one-size-fits-all approach. To build the evidence it needs, and to ensure it can represent the voices of the parents and educators fighting for change, the organisation works closely with Not Fine In School (www.notfineinschool.co.uk), a Facebook-based voluntary organisation for parents and educators which predominantly offers support and information on the barriers to attendance. When Square Peg began in 2018, NFIS had a few hundred members – mainly parents whose child was unable to attend. When we became a CIC in 2020 there were 11,800 members. As I write this in October 2022 there are 32,200.

Fran retired from Square Peg in April 2022 and Ellie took over running the organisation. Since then, Ellie has secured a huge number of media opportunities, including articles in the national papers, and numerous radio and TV interviews. Of particular note is the *Panorama* programme which aired on 30 September 2022 and explored why so many children are struggling to attend school. Square Peg continues to give evidence to all relevant inquiries and consultations and is currently lobbying parliamentarians as new school attendance management and enforcement legislation makes its way through the House of Lords. A '3 Asks' campaign focuses on ending the truancy laws, introducing an attendance code of practice and creating a mental health and wellbeing authorised absence code for school registers. We do all of this with a very small team of volunteers and precious little funding.

Our network is one of our key strengths, and we are honoured that so many stepped up to contribute to this book. If you would like to make contact, please email ellie@teamsquarepeg.org. You can also visit our website at www.teamsquarepeg.org and follow us on Twitter @teamsquarepeg.

Thank you.

## Fran Morgan

As a parent with lived experience, Fran previously set up a parent support group and was co-chair of Family Voice Surrey. She founded Square Peg (www.teamsquarepeg.org), initially as a social enterprise in 2019 and then as a CIC in 2020.

## Ellie Costello

Ellie is the director of Square Peg, working across policy, lobbying, campaigns and research. She engages as an expert by experience with her local authority, clinical commissioning groups and integrated care services in Warwickshire and co-facilitates SEND Crisis Warwickshire. She is parent carer to her two incredible and courageous children.